EMOTION IN M

New Directions in Tourism Analysis

Series Editor: Dimitri Ioannides, E-TOUR, Mid Sweden University, Sweden

Although tourism is becoming increasingly popular as both a taught subject and an area for empirical investigation, the theoretical underpinnings of many approaches have tended to be eclectic and somewhat underdeveloped. However, recent developments indicate that the field of tourism studies is beginning to develop in a more theoretically informed manner, but this has not yet been matched by current publications.

The aim of this series is to fill this gap with high quality monographs or edited collections that seek to develop tourism analysis at both theoretical and substantive levels using approaches which are broadly derived from allied social science disciplines such as Sociology, Social Anthropology, Human and Social Geography, and Cultural Studies. As tourism studies covers a wide range of activities and sub fields, certain areas such as Hospitality Management and Business, which are already well provided for, would be excluded. The series will therefore fill a gap in the current overall pattern of publication.

Suggested themes to be covered by the series, either singly or in combination, include – consumption; cultural change; development; gender; globalisation; political economy; social theory; sustainability.

Also in the series

Social Media in Travel, Tourism and Hospitality
Theory, Practice and Cases
Edited by Marianna Sigala, Evangelos Christou and Ulrike Gretzel
ISBN 978–1–4094–2091–0

Tourists, Signs and the City
The Semiotics of Culture in an Urban Landscape
Michelle M. Metro-Roland
ISBN 978–0–7546–7809–0

Stories of Practice: Tourism Policy and Planning
Edited by Dianne Dredge and John Jenkins
ISBN 978–0–7546–7982–0

Sports Event Management
The Caribbean Experience
Edited by Leslie-Ann Jordan, Ben Tyson, Carolyn Hayle and David Truly
ISBN 978–1–4094–1855–9

Emotion in Motion
Tourism, Affect and Transformation

Edited by

DAVID PICARD
CRIA-New University of Lisbon, Portugal

MIKE ROBINSON
University of Birmingham, UK

Routledge
Taylor & Francis Group

LONDON AND NEW YORK

First published 2012 by Ashgate Publishing

Published 2016 by Routledge
2 Park Square, Milton Park, Abingdon, Oxfordshire OX14 4RN
711 Third Avenue, New York, NY 10017, USA

First issued in paperback 2016

Routledge is an imprint of the Taylor & Francis Group, an informa business

British Library Cataloguing in Publication Data
Emotion in motion : tourism, affect and transformation. –
    (New directions in tourism analysis)
    1. Tourists – Psychology. 2. Tourism – Psychological
    aspects. 3. Travel – Psychological aspects. 4. Culture and
    tourism.
    I. Series II. Picard, David. III. Robinson, Mike, 1960–
    306.4'819–dc23

Library of Congress Cataloging-in-Publication Data
Emotion in motion : tourism, affect and transformation / edited by David Picard and Mike Robinson.
    p. cm. -- (New directions in tourism analysis)
    Includes bibliographical references and index.
    ISBN 978-1-4094-2133-7 (hardback)
    1. Tourism. 2. Tourism--Social aspects. 3. Emotions. I. Picard,
David. II. Robinson, Mike, 1960-
    G155.A1E4287 2012
    306.4'819--dc23

                                                                    2012004584

ISBN 13: 978-1-138-26114-3 (pbk)
ISBN 13: 978-1-4094-2133-7 (hbk)

Contents

List of Figures *vii*

List of Contributors *ix*

INTRODUCTION

1   Tourism, Awe and Inner Journeys   1
David Picard

2   The Emotional Tourist   21
Mike Robinson

PART I: EMOTIONS AND INNER JOURNEYS

3   The Dark is on the Inside: The *honne* of Japanese Exploratory
Tourists   49
Nelson Graburn

4   Seeking the Existential Moment   73
Elvi Whittaker

5   Affect and Moral Transformations in Young Volunteer Tourists   85
Émilie Crossley

6   Overwhelmed by Divinity in Jerusalem   99
Eliezer Witztum and Moshe Kalian

7   Passionate Movements: Emotional and Social Dynamics of Padre
Pio Pilgrims   117
Michael A. Di Giovine

PART II: THE EMOTIONS OF ATTRACTIONS

8   Religious Devotion and Sublime Experience during the Procession
of the Romería in El Rocío, Spain   139
Eddy Plasquy

9   Emotional Memory Formation at Former Nazi Concentration
         Camp Sites   161
         Jessica Rapson

10   World War II Tourism in France   179
         Bertram M. Gordon

11   Tourist Attractions as Sites of Suicide: The Case of Beachy Head,
         England   199
         Angelina Karpovich

12   The Affective Life of the Spa   211
         Jill Steward

PART III: INSTITUTIONALIZING EMOTIONS IN TOURISM

13   'I'm sorry I got emotional': 'Real' Work and 'Real' Men at the
         Canadian Cottage   231
         Julia Harrison

14   Romancing the Colonial on Ilha de Mozambique   247
         Pamila Gupta

15   Dancing Tourists: Tourism, Party and Seduction in Cuba   267
         Valerio Simoni

16   On Edge in an Impossible Paradise   283
         Kenneth Little

Index   *297*

List of Figures

8.1	Surging the tempest © Eddy Plasquy, 2009	147
8.2	Praising the Virgin Mary © Eddy Plasquy, 2009	148
8.3	Bringing children close © Eddy Plasquy, 2009	149
8.4	Tension around the stretcher © Eddy Plasquy, 2009	150
10.1	Pointe du Hoc, France © Bertram Gordon, 2009	182
10.2	Musée du Débarquement, France © Bertram Gordon, 2009	184
10.3	Mont Valerien (inaugurated 1960), France © Bertram Gordon, 2009	188
10.4	Le Mémorial des Martyrs de la Déportation, Ile de la Cité, Paris (inaugurated 1962), France © Bertram Gordon, 2009	192
10.5	Birthplace of Marshall Petain, Cauchy-à-la-Tour, Pas-de-Calais, France © Bertram Gordon, 2009	193
12.1	Postcard c. 1905. Herculesbad/Herculesfürdo in Transylvania. Collection of author	211
12.2	Postcard. Romantic emotions (the Kneipp cure). Collection of author	219
14.1	Statues. Ilha de Mozambique © Pamela Gupta	248
14.2	Street lamp, Ilha de Mozambique © Pamela Gupta	250
14.3	Hospital de Mozambique, Ilha de Mozambique © Pamela Gupta	255
14.4	Municipal office, Ilha de Mozambique © Pamela Gupta	264
16.1	'Peter Pete at work' © Kenneth Little, 2009	285
16.2	'Bob's tourist dream world in ruins' © Ken Little, 2009	290
16.3	'The Tree of Wisdom' © Ken Little, 2009	294

List of Contributors

Émilie Crossley, School of Social Sciences, Cardiff University, Cardiff, Wales.

Michael A. Di Giovine, Anthropology Department, University of Chicago, Chicago, USA.

Bertram M. Gordon, History Department, Mills College, Oakland, California, USA.

Nelson Graburn, Department of Anthropology, University of California, Berkeley, USA.

Pamila Gupta, WISER, University of the Witwatersrand, Johannesburg, South Africa.

Julia Harrison, Frost Centre for Canadian Studies and Indigenous Studies, Trent University, Peterborough, Ontario, Canada.

Moshe Kalian, District Psychiatrist Office, Ministry of Health, Jerusalem, Israel.

Angelina Karpovich, School of Engineering and Design, Brunel University, Uxbridge, United Kingdom.

Kenneth Little, Anthropology Department, York University, Toronto, Canada.

David Picard, Centre for Research in Anthropology, New University of Lisbon (CRIA-FCSH/UNL), Portugal.

Eddy Plasquy, Anthropology Department, University of Leuven, Belgium.

Jessica Rapson, English and Comparative Literature, Goldsmiths College, University of London, United Kingdom.

Mike Robinson, Ironbridge Institute, University of Birmingham, United Kingdom

Valerio Simoni, Centre for Research in Anthropology, Lisbon University Institute (CRIA-ISCTE), Portugal.

Jill Steward, School of Historical Studies, Newcastle University, Newcastle upon Tyne, United Kingdom.

Elvi Whittaker, Anthropology Department, University of British Columbia, Vancouver, Canada.

Eliezer Witztum, Mental Health Center, Be'er Sheva, Division of Psychiatry, Ben-Gurion University of the Negev, Israel.

Chapter 1

Tourism, Awe and Inner Journeys

David Picard[1]

Tears ran down Eberhard's cheeks. His face was red and sweaty. Interrupted by heavy breathing, he screamed out fragments of sentences, 'all this beauty', 'we would have all come back', 'we should have done like the Romanians did' and, later, 'we should have killed them all'. Eberhard was standing on a view point above the wide empty plain of the volcanic caldera. He seemed far away with too many things happening too quickly in his mind. The other tourists, initially unaware of his state, taking photos and exchanging smiles and kisses, became silent. They looked away. A woman, a work colleague of Eberhard's, approached him. It was his idea to do this trip together, to escape the 'sadness' and 'stress of work life' as he later explained. She gently touched his arm. Eberhard shook his head, and then looked at her. 'How is it possible that someone had the right to prohibit someone else to see all this beauty?', he asked. In the evening, having a beer before dinner, Eberhard started to talk about his emotions at the volcano. He told me that he was from East Germany and, while under the ruling Socialist regime, travel outside the (former) German Democratic Republic (GDR) had been strictly regulated. 'Let us out!' was one of the refrains shouted during the Monday demonstrations in East Germany that preceded the eventual fall of the Berlin Wall in November 1989. Travel especially beyond the Iron Curtain, and by extension the experience of faraway exotic locales in Cuba, East Africa or South America had become a tool to gratify citizens for their work and submission to the political rule of the Socialist party. On the other hand, the non-granting of tourist visas had become a tool to punish those with whom the regime felt uncomfortable. Following the opening of the borders Eberhard, along with millions of other people from East Germany, travelled for the first time to countries in Western Europe, the Caribbean and the USA.

I met Eberhard in 1998 in the Indian Ocean island of La Réunion, on his first trip to what he described as an 'exotic island destination'. As a PhD student at the Anthropology Department of the University of La Réunion, I was studying social transformations brought about by the development of European mass tourism (Picard 2011). I was particularly interested in the role of tourist experience and the representations of tropical island space through which this experience was framed both before and after the actual trip. To observe actual tourist practice from an

1   The work invested into the editing of this book is partly financed through national funds provided by the Portuguese Foundation for Science and Technology project « PTDC/CS-ANT/114825/2009 ».

inductive perspective I had found employment as a tour guide and driver for a local tour agency. Within the two years of this employment, from 1998 to 2000, I had the chance to observe a great number of tourists, mainly Germans, who travelled on a 3-day round trip itinerary through the island. Through open interviews in the evenings after the trip and during visits I later made at their homes, I deepened, in dialogical fashion, my understanding of what appears to stimulate emotions in the tourists and the different modalities of their unfolding. Among the tourists observed in my study, it was not uncommon that they spontaneously started to cry, laugh, smile or felt faint when surrounded by something they found beautiful or captivating, or deceiving. In this sense, Eberhard's oddly 'extreme' reaction provides clues to what other tourists may have lived through in a milder way. It was quite common that certain spaces, such as the volcano, left them speechless for a moment. Seemingly unable to find words for what happened in their mind, many were left with their eyes and mouth wide open, inhaling air and shaking their heads. While some tourists appeared overwhelmed by the encounter of certain landscapes, others showed similar reactions when looking at art works, listening to music, inhaling the atmospheres of a crowded market, etc. It happened that tourists felt they needed to sit down 'to keep their balance' or shake their heads to 'come back to reality' (in their words). In most cases, the initial emotion induced by the encounter of a particular touristic realm triggered further emotions unrelated to the actual encounter. In Eberhard's case, it is unlikely that his anger was a direct emotional reaction to the 'beauty' of the site. It is more plausible that the aesthetic emotion induced by the encounter with the site fed an inner dialogue that only partly surfaced and that, in turn, generated his anger. This dialogue was about an apparently still unresolved trauma related to the injustices committed by the former Socialist regime of the GDR. Referring to the strict travel regulations under Socialist rule, he questioned how 'some people could prohibit others to see such beauty'. 'We would have all come back', he affirmed. Referring to the execution of the former Socialist dictator of Romania, Nicolae Ceauşescu, by a revolutionary military court, he claimed, 'we should have killed them all'.

Exploring Emotions in Tourism and Travel

Tourism is one of those fields of social practice in which the relation between the physical motion of the body and the emotions subjectively experienced by a person becomes most obvious. It thus offers itself as a field *par excellence* for the study of the articulation between personal subjective experience of the world and collective emotional and cognitive cultures through which this experience is framed, learnt, and put into meaningful words, images and categories. Tourism moves tourists out of their quotidian environment and changes the daily rhythms of life. Tourists are in some cases confronted with previously unfamiliar places, stories and people. In other cases, they almost ceremonially return to sites they are familiar with, to visit friends and relatives, to indulge in their passions for artworks or religious shrines, to revitalize memories of earlier travels and childhood places, or to simply find the comfort and security of familiar holiday environments. What is common to these different cases is that tourism generates an emotionally heightened social realm that both distances tourists from their daily routines and challenges them to create order in the changed environment. The distance from home weakens social norms and thus allows them to test the boundaries and foundations of their being in the world. It allows and actively challenges them to experiment with new identities, engage in new social practices, and renew relationships (Lanfant et al. 1995). The destinations and peoples visited often function as a mirror in which tourists discover facets of themselves (Chabloz and Raout 2009). Tourists frequently recognize here a link between their own person and the locale visited. The physical and moral boundaries that *a priori* separate destination from home become – at least temporarily – blurred. In many cases tourists experience sensations of transhumance, or deep connections to nature or the divine. At the same time they frequently feel physically aroused by certain sites, – often without being offered, by their own culture, any meaningful explanation or story for such arousal. It usually leaves them perplex and often makes them search for a form of rationalisation. Nancy Frey (1998), for instance, relates the case of a female pilgrim who, at the sight of a particular landscape on the way to Santiago in Spain, experienced spontaneous orgasms. Similarly, Elvi Whitaker, in Chapter 3 of this book, observes the speechless awe that accompanies the peak experiences of nature tourists in Canada. Such touristic emotions are usually amplified where they are subjected to intense pre-travel anticipations. Hannah Wadle, in a personal communication, relates the case of a German woman, the child of post-World War II Polish refugees to Germany, who, after years of anticipating the trip to her 'homeland', Poland, spontaneously soils herself once she sets foot on Polish ground. These cases indicate that the experience of emotions in tourism and travel relate to forms of embodied 'emotional knowledge' (Lakoff and Johnson 1999) which evolves at the interface between personal experiences of the world and collectively held moral orders of specific tourist attractions (MacCannell 1976). Tourism disturbs and destabilizes such moral order. It challenges tourists to reflect about their desires and ideas of belonging, also about their fears of loneliness, time, mortality and the (hopefully not too) soon-to-come event of death. As a result of their exposure to alterity, tourists often realize the fact or at least the potential that what they hold as true about the world is bound to cultural norms.

While emotions are experienced at the individual level they are collectively framed, both in terms of the actual experience and the way this experience is articulated and communicated to others.[2] Both, the experience and the expression of emotions are subjected to cultural conventions, normalization and processes of

---

2 Edward Bruner (1986) emphasizes the differences between reality (which he considers a factual reality), the experience of reality (which is subjective, yet subjected to collective perceptive modes learnt in society) and expressions of experience (which are negotiated and normalized in society).

learning. Emotion and emotional culture can thus be studied as an anthropological object within specific social and historical contexts. One aspect of this study developed in the first and second part of this book, focuses on the social processes of forming, maintaining and reproducing such emotional cultures within specific society contexts. The chapters of this first part of this book in particular will explore how personally experienced emotions relate to wider normative frameworks prescribing and, to a certain extent, disciplining how certain emotions shall be felt and how these feelings shall be expressed. The chapters of the second part then explore processes of producing and maintaining emotional cultures formed around specific tourist sites. The chapters of the third part of the book subsequently investigate the consequences of such touristic emotional cultures at a wider political and sociological scale. If destinations have a mirror function in tourism, then this mirror is not a blank surface reflecting a lifelike image of the tourists' self. What this 'mirror' reflects has been produced and remains usually stage-managed. It thus anticipates an image to be thrown back onto tourists prior to the latter's entry into the performance. In this sense, destinations can be seen as large theatrical grounds that, by means of their décor, the roles played by locals and the scripted temporality of touristic activity programmes, lead tourists through a tourism specific play and liturgy. From that point of analysis, it makes sense to approach destinations within the enlarged social sphere of what has been called 'world society' (Burton 1972). Such an approach implies important questions about the identities, social roles and political order this highly ceremonialized tourist play fashions at the global scale.

Emotions of Awe and Inner Journeys

Emotions are generated by what psychologists call stimulus. Stimulus can be external, for example, related to the encounter of specific sites that spontaneously induce emotions of surprise, anxiety, awe, thrill, and even love. In the context of tourism, in such situations, tourists often remain initially speechless, in search of references. Certain types of natural sites, architectural monuments, art works, religious shrines or local people seem able to induce deeply felt emotions of affect and even wonder.[3] Often, tourists feel that such sites exert power over them and destabilize their identity. Many describe sensations of mystic encounters with 'forces' and 'spirits', but also uncanny[4] sentiments, such as when they

---

3   Stephen Greenblatt (1991) argues that the experience of the 'marvellous' among the early European discoverers and colonisers of the New World was not necessarily, or uniquely, an agent of empire, but made manifest a form of genuine wonder induced by the recognition of cultural difference.

4   For Freud (2003), uncanny defines the class of frightening things that leads us back to what is known and familiar, at the same time a revelation of what is private and concealed, of what is hidden – not only from others, but also from the self.

spontaneously recognize 'hidden' facets of their selves in the visited other. Since the romanticist revolutions of the 18th and 19th centuries in Western Europe and North America, the emotions related to the experience of 'fearful beauty' or 'sublime magic' of certain places have been called 'awe' (Spode 2003). Awe and tourism are historically interconnected. For the romantics, experiencing awe in face of specific natural sites, e.g. 'wild' mountains and sea fronts, was considered a liberating process. The painting, *Der Wanderer über dem Nebelmeer* (*The Wanderer Above the Sea of Fog*) by Caspar David Friedrich, is a good example for an expression of such awe. The image is composed of a man standing on top of a rock, under a colourful sky, apparently gazing over a 'sea of clouds'. For John Gaddis (2004), the image epitomises the ideological underpinning of the romanticist movement, in particular the idea of a profound contradiction of the human condition, on the one hand working to tame nature, and, on the other, being aware of their insignificance within the wider cosmos of space and time. For the 18th- and 19th-century Romantics the experience of awe was considered a means to reveal this contradiction. It was considered a form of moral learning. It is remarkable that this painting continues to supply one of the most reproduced visual tropes in contemporary nature tourism advertisement. It may seem that the experience of awe as a tourism related emotion never disappeared. The surrealists of the early 20th century – artists, writers, ethnographers – claimed that the experience of awe in the face of alterity was able to reveal latent desires e.g. related to sexuality, death or violence whose satisfaction has been regulated or prohibited by public morals. Travel and the immersion in exotic cultures, found both in faraway places and in local immigrant groups and working classes, became a means to make such experience happen (Clifford 1988).

Emotions can also be induced by forms of inner stimulus. While the encounter with certain touristic sites has the ability to generate emotions, the cognition of these emotions – the memories these bring alive, the images and associations they evoke – can, in turn, become a stimulus for further emotions. In this sense, the cognitive processes dealing with these emotions may, in turn, evoke and 'bring to life' other personal memories, unrelated to the actual site, that had long been 'buried', such as childhood memories, previous holidays, memories of youth and first love, etc. (Lerner and Keltner 2000). The mental work accompanying the touristic journey thus entails an ongoing inner dialogue where emotions become stimulus for new emotions and where the outer experience of sites is progressively interiorized and articulated with a mental 'inner journey'.[5] In many cases, tourists chose a particular destination to find answers or at least some form of stimulus to specific personal hobbies and pre-occupations (Hennig 1997).

---

5   Following Nancy Frey (1998). The term was taken up later by Nelson Graburn (2002, p. 30) who, quoting the earlier works on pilgrimage by Frey and also by Myerhoof (1993) emphasized the importance to study how 'inner' and 'outer' journeys parallel the inner world of consciousness and the outer world of experience.

Travel Syndromes

Cases, such as that of Eberhard recalled at the beginning of this chapter, are extreme but they demonstrate what most tourists experience in a much milder way, i.e. how emotions are experienced and articulated. His case is neither unique nor particularly astonishing. The literature produced by travellers of various époques, but also the more recent scientific literature by psychiatrists working in hospitals near major tourist sites, describe numerous similar occurrences of what has come to be called 'travel syndrome'. One of the most famous cases is that of French 19th-century author Stendhal (1990) – real name Marie-Henri Beyle – who relates the symptoms of increased heartbeat and sensations of vertigo he experienced when facing the sublime art displayed in the city of Florence, Italy in 1817. Apparently similar cases are related by Berta Spafford-Vester, a late-19th-century American emigrant to Israel (cf. Witztum and Kalian, Chapter 6). In her memories, she describes various characters encountered in Jerusalem who, seemingly overwhelmed by spirituality, temporarily lost their references and identity thinking they were saints on a holy mission. In a more contemporary context, various authors relate cases of Japanese tourists who suffer from what is now called the 'Paris syndrome' (Viala et al. 2004; Graburn, Chapter 3). Similar to what had been observed in Florence and Jerusalem, this syndrome is characterized by psychiatric symptoms such as acute delusional states, hallucinations, feelings of persecution, depersonalization, and anxiety, and also by psychosomatic manifestations such as dizziness, tachycardia and sweating. The first systematic study of this extreme form of touristic awe was produced during the 1980s by Graziella Magherini (1989), a medical doctor in the psychiatric ward of a hospital in Florence. Magherini notes that the spontaneous 'attacks' to which certain foreigners were subjected when facing Renaissance art and culture in Florence can usually be related to previously existing repressed trauma. According to Magherini, the combination of anticipation, stress, culture shock and the deep veneration of the artworks in question pulled such trauma to the surface. Similarly, for the Japanese tourists in Paris, the syndrome appears to be triggered by the combination of disappointments related to the intercultural context (e.g. different language and modes of interpersonal communication), idealized images of Paris and travel stress. In their reaction to an earlier publication on the so-called Jerusalem syndrome,[6] Witztum and Kalian (cf. Chapter 6 of this book) equally claim that all patients treated in Jerusalem hospitals had previous psychiatric conditions.

Contrary to a widespread popular belief (also among many academics), it is unlikely, based on available evidence, that specific sites, landscapes or objects have an inherent power to trigger travel syndromes in people with no previous health

---

6   Bar El et al. (2000) suggest that Jerusalem as a place had a capacity to create emotions in people with no previous pathological conditions yet could not provide evidence to actually substantiate the argument.

or spiritual conditions[7] – unless their culture has strong expectations that they will. Before venturing into the slippery realms of what could be termed 'esoteric anthropology' (presuming that certain sites or objects actually are imbued with specific forms of 'energy' or 'power'), it seems prudent to explore the emotional reactions of tourists initially in terms of a socially framed subjective experience. From this point of view, claims to the universality of specific aesthetic or spiritual qualities associated with particular religious, artistic or historic sites[8] must be considered within the wider political and social contexts within which such claims emerge. Critically examined, they will most likely reveal themselves as a rhetorical means making manifest a specific moral order and world-view. Subsequently, from this epistemic perspective, there is no landscape or other aesthetic form out there with universal appeal.[9] If landscape constitutes a desirable, frightening or otherwise awe-inspiring realm in certain tourism contexts, then this realm is bound to specific social contexts and aesthetic cultures and histories. For instance, as I have proposed elsewhere, the ascription of magical powers to specific mountains, waters, seashores, or cities observed in much of the contemporary Western tourism practice (Picard 2011) can be historically related to a romantic nature image instituted by the post-Enlightenment movement, if not earlier. The very personal awe individuals experience when facing specific attractions such as waterfalls or religious shrines thus seems to be a socially normalized one, articulating collective moral frameworks and emotional cultures through interiorised embodied moral practices and emotions experienced at the individual level (Zigon 2009).

Emotional Cultures in/of Tourism

Extreme cases of emotional affect (such as that expressed by Eberhard or the travellers to Jerusalem, Florence and Paris) provide useful pointers toward the wider emotional cultures of specific tourist populations and the processes that maintain or

---

7 The idea of the Stendhal syndrome was picked up by Hollywood movie-makers and increasingly also appears in neo-pagan and new-age movements build around a mystic engagement with 'powers' believed inherent in particular objects, spirits, people or places.

8 A prominent example is UNESCO's world heritage programme whose claim to universality is based on ideas of common humankind whose 'story' is being materialized in particular sites of 'outstanding beauty', etc. It builds a linear world history marked by cycles of progress (empires, high cultures, wars). More recently, a shift in UNESCO's approach could be observed. Since the mid-1990s, new types of sites have been classified on the World Heritage list stressing no longer only the historical achievements and masterworks of human culture, but also the very process of humans living together (materialized in sites of creolization, culture contact, and cultural creativity).

9 Reader Nelson Graburn suggests that there are certain landscapes that produce strong emotions in all cultures though different from one to the next, e.g. caves, waterfalls – often water-related phenomena, cliffs, waves, big trees. Reader Felix Girke notes that some evolutionary anthropologists claim that humans have a particular affect for Savannahs.

transform such cultures in time. Social phenomenologists since Immanual Kant and most psychologists agree that there is an important cultural dimension to the way reality is experienced and mediated through the perceptive apparatus of the body, and also to the way such experience is articulated and communicated (Mesquita 2007). A majority of anthropologists and psychologists agree on the existence of basic emotions shared by all humans, and of others that are dependent on specific society contexts.[10] In this sense, while all humans appear to have a talent to experience various emotions, the largely unconscious moral norms guiding social practices in society can prescribe an active cultivation of some emotions and repress others (Eid and Diener 2001). As a consequence, the actively encouraged learning of certain emotions is likely to lead to increased abilities at the personal level to experience such emotions. For instance, in specific social contexts, people actively cultivate the experience of emotions of nostalgia (through poetry, music, etc.). As a result of the repetitions that accompany such a cultivation, subjects who grow up in such specific contexts are likely to develop a greater ability to experience emotions of nostalgia than subjects who grow up in societies where emotions of nostalgia are not part of public or private culture. The differentiated valuation of specific emotions in different societies thus is likely to generate differentiated abilities to experience specific emotions at personal level. Anthropologists can study such differences between emotional cultures in different groups or societies. For example, Goody (1993) shows how it has become 'normal' in some societies to find flowers beautiful and to be able – as if it were natural – to be emotionally moved by them and to express such emotion through specific affective displays. Affect for flowers is ascribed with moral value where people who like flowers are, in such contexts, considered as 'good' people, whereas those who destroy flowers are considered 'bad' or 'insensitive' people. Such moral ascriptions and valuations are normally not negotiated; they are done as if they stemmed from a positive moral order, as a form of bourdieusian habitus whose ideological structure remains in most cases hidden to individual consciousness.[11] Most of the tourists observed in my study in La Réunion were middle class Germans. Most experienced emotions

---

10 Psychologists have classified emotions according to various schemes (e.g. cognitive versus non-cognitive emotions; ephemeral versus lasting emotions; basic versus complex emotions.). The early anthropological works on emotion by Margaret Mead and Gregory Bateson contested such categories, suggesting instead that emotions are culturally determined. In current psychology and anthropology, it is widely acknowledged that some 'basic' emotions (such as anger, happiness, disgust, fear, sadness, etc.) are predominantly biological while differently expressed and embodied according to the cultural norms of a specific society (Lakoff and Johnson 1999).

11 Zigon (2009) alternatively describes how in situations of ambiguity different moral systems can meet, enter in competition or dialogue, and sometimes clash. Such situations of 'moral breakdown' often induce reflections and debate about the ethics of moral values. Situations of social friction and culture contact (such as those observed in tourism) therefore represent moments of cultural creativity, where normative orders are challenged, broken down, reassessed and possibly transformed.

of awe when encountering specific natural sites such as mountain-scapes, waterfalls or rocky cliffs. Similar to the example of flowers, this specific form of 'awe' of nature experienced by these German tourists is not a universal emotion, but seems to result from a historical process of institutionalization where 'nature' is elevated as a symbolic good and a key metaphor to make sense of time and being in the world, in Germany and elsewhere.[12] The ceremonially repeated valuation of such specific ideas of nature in German public culture since the 18th century (through education, music, the arts, poesy, hiking and leisure practice, botany, gardening, etc.) may well explain the formation of an individual embodied ability among the tourists observed here (who have all grown up within this culture) to be affected by, and experience awe when facing, such specific natural sites.

Displaying Emotions

Some societies actively value what is referred to as 'showing one's emotions' or to be 'sincere about one's emotions'. In such societies, 'bad mood' or 'good mood' may be acceptable emotional states, and be publicly communicated. Yet, even 'being sincere about emotions' is subjected to a codified language. The same types of emotion – bad mood, good mood, or being angry or happy – are expressed through different codes in different societies. Societal processes of normalization of specific emotions therefore also concern the way in which individuals articulate their experience of emotions, usually by means of words, sounds, movements, performances, signs, or specific facial expressions. For example, one of the leading values in many Western societies is that individuals shall experience happiness and communicate this experience of happiness by means of smiling. A smiling – and thus apparently happy – person is here often morally equalized to a good, or even a beautiful person. In the tourism context, airline and hotel front office staff are expected to smile to their customers, as a means to display their happiness to welcome the *a priori* strangers and offer their hospitality (Hochschild 1982). Yet, many front office staff may deeply dislike their customers, while charmingly smiling at them. In this professionalized context, the display of specific emotions thus becomes a social performance in itself, disconnected from actual experienced emotion, yet able to communicate conformity with the leading moral standards and values of a society – and mostly achieving its effect. The tourists feel welcomed and happy. Badly, or inaccurately performed signs of happiness, to the contrary, regularly lead to situations of ambiguity and often to suspicions by the tourists of being cheated by a 'fake smile'. While tourists do indeed face in many cases service staffs who dissimulate their unhappiness through fake smiles, the ambiguity of contact may in other cases stem from cultural differences in the way in which emotions are displayed. In contrast to the Western public culture of smiling, many societies value

---

12   Reader Hasso Spode suggests that similar institutionalization processes have taken place in England and in the USA.

the absence of publicly shown emotions. Individuals may be expected here not to show any visual signs of emotion however they feel. In the tourism context, this often leads to misunderstandings, for instance where tourists complain about their 'coldness' or 'indifference' of front-office staff (who are not smiling).

Emotions and Attractions in Tourism

The first influential theoretical studies of tourism stressed the ability of tourist attractions to add meaning to the tourists' everyday life. For many of these early academic works, the widespread historic 'success'[13] of tourism as an institution of social life stemmed from the structural frameworks of modern social life. Within the influential field of leisure studies (Veblen 1934; Dumezedier 1967), tourism was considered a particular form of leisure time, whose 'function' was both to reward workers for the constraints suffered in labour life and to physically re-create the work force. During the 1970s, tourism was approached in terms of a modern pilgrimage, an emotionally heightened time-space of social life in which the fundamental dreams, myths and symbols of modern life were invoked and brought to life (MacCannell 1976; Graburn 1977; Selänniemi 2003). Dean MacCannell, in his still influential book, *The Tourist* (1976), suggests that modern tourist attractions can be analysed as signs, and as such reveal a wider underlying moral order of modern life in general. In this sense, tourist experiences become socially and morally meaningful through the specific semiospheres[14] configured by itineraries of tourist sites. MacCannell observes, for instance, that the guided visit tours addressed to American middle class tourists usually imply a similar pattern of attractions, e.g. a public garden, a museum, a law court, a university, a factory, etc. He concludes that the significance of such a pattern is not directly related to the actual place visited, but to a set of moral institutions governing social life in the tourists' home context. Adopting Irving Goffman's theatrical approach to the nature of everyday life,[15] MacCannell claims that tourist destinations are purposefully produced as stages or scenes evoking familiar tropes, allegories and mythical images; as modern ritual grounds allowing tourists to invoke and eventually reproduce the mythical universes governing modern social life.[16] In our view, MacCannell's approach today

---

13   Success referring to the ability of the practice to maintain itself and even spread in new social realms.

14   A concept only later developed by Lotman (1990) which seems able to summarizes MacCannell's approach. The latter does not explicitly refer to it.

15   Goffman (1973) suggests that social life evolves in a highly theatrical way, with individuals enacting roles and stage themselves as persons in the public sphere.

16   In this sense, the attraction of a museum lay in its allegorical power to evoke and legitimate the modern quest to understand the world, that of a park to evoke modern naturalist, artistic and scientific engagements with nature, that of a factory to invoke the principle of industrial production, capitalism, and modern divisions of labour, that of a

continues to provide a good framework to study the structural semiotics of tourist attractions.[17] However it is less pertinent to explore the emotional engagement – the 'embodied moral' (Zigon 2009) of awe, wonder and affect – that tourists experience at certain sites. The study of such emotional engagement needs a shift of perspective – away from the distanced structuralist scope, adopting instead the subjective perspective of social actors as suggested by phenomenology. This does not go without methodological problems. Tourists move quickly through space and their emotional states and 'inner worlds' are not directly accessible to observation. To address this problem, Edward Bruner (1986) suggests an approach of experience in terms of hermeneutic cycles. He distinguishes here between experience and expression, where 'experience' relates to the actual lived experience by tourists and 'expression' to the more concrete way in which this experience is articulated and communicated. This distinction is similar to that between emotional culture and cultures of expressing emotions, as suggested in the section above. Bruner proposes that expressions are texts that, enacted and mobilized, have the ability to re-generate (lived) experience and thus generate a hermeneutic cycle. He seems to imply a model for cognitive development where an image or expression informs experience, and experience, in turn, informs an image or expression.

What Bruner does not address is the important dimension of affect, and the process of learning affect that accompanies experience. One could talk about a parallel hermeneutics of affect where one experience generates ability for new experiences, which in turn becomes relevant when an individual once again is confronted with a situation similar to that in which the affect was initially generated.[18] For example, tourists are frequently affected by cats they see in the street while on tour, not because cats are part of any particular text or gaze

---

university to invoke the rightfulness of scientific thinking, that of a law court to evoke the institution of the modern justice systems, etc.

17   In particular, destination image analysis. I suggest my students to start their research with a MacCannell – like type of approach to attractions, to set the scene, to understand the ontological order within tourism practices occur, by which they are informed, and which in terms they form. A good (and economical) way of doing this is to focus on travel catalogues from a particular 'resource market' (or 'outbound' market) and analyse the images and key texts associated to a particular destination. I usually suggest my students to focus on adjectives and from there to construct semantic fields that regroup these adjectives. The discussion about these semantic fields lead to interpretations about what these denote. Put in relation with the context of observation within which such catalogues are read (e.g. the urban centres of modern life in which the university is located), this classroom exercise allows a fairly good demonstration on how to explore the socially contextualized moral order of particular destinations. Annette Pritchard and Nigel Morgan (2000) propose a similar method, based on more semantic refinement.

18   For Shouse, paraphrasing Massumi's comments on the translation of Deleuze and Guattari's *Thousand Plateaux* (1987) 'Affect is the body's way of preparing itself for action in a given circumstance by adding a quantitative dimension of intensity to the quality of an experience'. In this sense, affect is outside of consciousness, yet as a device according

about tourist experience (except for some Greek islands), but because they have developed a more general ability to be affected by cats (or cars, kids, girls, art, waterfalls, architecture, etc.). Until recently, psychologists have thought about affect and cognition as being situated at different levels of mental experience (a distinction today widely contested in the psychological literature). Affect used to refer here to an unconscious disposition to experience an emotion, whereas cognition to the more abstract interpretation and objectivation of experience. Robert Zajonc, suggestes accordingly that affective reactions to a stimulus occur without extensive perceptual and cognitive encoding, and can be made sooner and with greater confidence than cognitive judgements (Zajonc 1980). Other psychologists stress that affect is post-cognitive, that it only emerges as a result of various cognitive processes. Richard Lazarus (1982) proposes a cognitive theory of emotion where the latter occurs only as a result of a previous cognitive appraisal (e.g. the recognition of a particular situation, the judgement of this situation: dangerous, beautiful, etc.) and a bodily reaction to this appraisal (e.g. excitement, increased heartbeat, production of adrenalin, fever).

In their complementarity, Zajonc's and Lazarus' theories seem able to provide a good model to describe the mental processes that occurred more or less systematically among the tourists observed in my own study in La Réunion. In the first instances of an encounter, most remained silent or made unarticulated noises such as 'ah' or 'oh' or 'wow'. Many seemed to show light symptoms of shock (e.g. agitation, feelings of nausea and anxiety, sweating, light-headedness, shallow breathing). The tourists then usually articulated their visual and sensual experience by words associating values with the experience of the encounter. 'Amazing', 'awesome', 'beautiful', 'awful', 'magical', 'disgusting' were words often pronounced with no further sentence structure. In most cases a more structured cognitive process of encoding followed when they searched for meaningful analogies. This phase was typically articulated through the terminology of 'it is like…' – like on the moon (the volcano), like in Colorado (a valley), like at home (flowers), like life in the past (a rural farm), like debates about the holocaust in Germany or debates about slavery in La Réunion. The recognition of this analogy, and thus of the link between the site and the tourists' personal life worlds often created a new stimulus which in turn, was evaluated (e.g. 'but the valley is much wider', 'but the flowers are much bigger', etc.). Each new recognition induced a new stimulus, progressively generating chains of associations that guided the tourists away from reflections about the actual experience of the site, towards reflections about that what preoccupied them in their life back home, their partners, parents, children, projects, etc. The experience of emotions thus eventually led them to reflect events of their life and rework their life stories. In this sense, the active challenge to recreate meaningful orders of social life thus seems to represent a fundamental element of tourism practice.

---

different degrees of importance to different experiences, is culturally formed. Affect allows certain experiences to happen, other are filtered out.

The Semantic Trap of the Hermeneutic Approach to Experience

Within the framework of my study in La Réunion sites did not work as attractions in the way Dean MacCannell suggests. Tourists did experience emotions that could be related to a moral structure of attractions (that could be studied through semiotic analysis). Yet the reproduction of such attractions – according to MacCannell a fundamental function of tourism – happened in an oddly different way. In the post-tourist experience context – in the evening at the hotel and eventually back home – the tourists talked about their emotional experiences. It is here that they reiterated, in a largely reflexive manner, a terminology of public culture. A good example is the mobilization of the term 'magic' which appears both in pre-tourism public discourse about many destinations (e.g. claiming to be 'magical countries'), but also during these post-touristic reflections. 'It was truly magical,' tourists frequently said, referring to their personal experience of a site. Yet, the pre-tourism 'magic' – a public representation or at best a 'promise' of future experience – is different from that used in the post-experience context. Tourists (and everyone for that matter) usually search for terms, images or metaphors that 'best' describe a personal emotion or experience. Coincidentally, tourists usually use here precisely those words or images that are used in public and commercial culture to promise or anticipate the same experience. They did not do this in a drive to conform to public discourse, but simply because they seemed unable to find other or 'better' words to describe and communicate their experience. Looking at the phenomenon superficially (e.g. by interviewing tourists before and after a trip) will give the impression that tourists experience exactly what was promised by advertisement (e.g. the 'magic' of a site) and thus idiosyncratically reproduce a public discourse of social life. Yet, the same words have different meanings. Tourists observed here were often unhappy about this ambiguity, well aware that what they expressed verbally sounded very much like a clichéd public discourse about destinations. 'You cannot describe such a feeling, you have to experience these sites yourself', was a frequent observation made. The ambiguity seemed to grow even stronger when they returned back home. Months after their holiday, when I revisited them at their homes, most of them had attractive and rehearsed souvenir stories of their trip which largely sounded like public culture tourism advertising discourse. They often added, at the end of their explanations, 'you were there too, you know what I mean'.

In this sense the limitation and poverty of language to talk about experiences, both as a public discourse of anticipation and as a personal post-tourist expression of experiences made, has a disciplining effect and operates a form of normalization at the semantic level. The impression is given that personal experiences and public imaginaries of a specific site are articulated in a hermeneutic cycle, leading to the reproduction of a moral order inherent to tourist attractions. Individual tourists can claim that they had a 'real' experience. Yet, as long as they reproduce the public language of attractions to make sense of their individual experiences, they reproduce the institutional framework of the attractions, maintain their underlying moral order and the public culture of anticipation associated with, and seducing tourists to, specific sites.

The political implications of this observation are important. The public semantics of (anticipated) experience in tourism has a normalizing effect in that it prescribes where to go and what to do in order to have a particular experience. The public and commercial imaginaries lead to a particular experience, and offer words to talk about experience, but they are not the experience itself. In a society in which individuals agree on shared codes of communication, e.g. the use of language, they will eternally be trapped by the semantics of these codes, tempting to convey a sense of personal experience to others, while necessarily using a collectively meaning framework of communication.

Emotions in an Intercultural Context

As explained above, different historical and societal contexts have the potential to bring about socially differentiated emotional cultures and forms of articulating personal emotions. Where people with different emotional cultures meet, certain emotional abilities by individuals may be subjected to moral judgement and be mobilised as markers to delineate Other from Self. In the Western world, associations are often made between specific forms of emotional culture and specific social categories, e.g. age, gender, origine, ethnicity. For instance, in many contexts the dominant model of maleness ascribes to be 'less emotional' or at least not to show 'emotions'. Similarly, childhood often implies that children are 'more emotional' than adults. Another recurrent stereotype demands, for instance, that Mediterranean peoples are 'more emotional' than 'cold' northern Europeans. The historical institutionalization of such stereotypes may well lead to the formation and reproduction of socially differentiated emotional cultures among and within different societies. The dominant models of personhood may value here, in each respective context, certain emotional abilities in certain people, while devaluing the same abilities in others. Where a particular emotion is not valued and trained, people may well develop little ability to experience it. Thus differences in emotional culture can reinforce themselves in situations of social contact where they become signs to define and delineate specific social identities.

Tourism constitutes an intercultural field *par excellence*. It generates in most cases 'contact zones' (Pratt 1992) or 'borderzones' (Bruner 1996) where people with different emotional cultures meet. Much of the eroticism tourists and hosts ascribe to relationships with the respective Other stems from effectively different moral and emotional cultures, but also from expectations of such difference. Cultural difference, or the representation of such a difference across categories of gender or ethnicity, often becomes here an attraction itself. In some cases, specific emotional cultures are actively claimed and cultivated as a tourist asset by some host societies. Valerio Simoni's (Chapter 14) work on cultures of informality in Cuba explores, among others, processes of appropriation among Cubans of outside conceptions about what it means to be Cuban. For instance, in recognizing that one of these outside attributions is that Cubans are 'more emotional', many Cubans in turn start to claim, and actively perform, such an attribute as an ethnic and national marker. Similarly, my own work on the aesthetic transfigurations of Creoleness in La Réunion, Indian Ocean (Picard 2010) shows how a local claim to Creoleness defined as 'magical' and 'more emotional' only emerges once Creoleness becomes a publicly valorized theme in the French mainland. In these cases, the public performance of particular forms of emotion, or of 'being emotional', become tourist assets produced and made available for tourists, while initially not carrying deeper significance for most hosts. A consequence of the institutionalization of stereotypes in the contact zones of tourism is a global re-mapping of the world in terms of emotional categories and stereotypes. Anthropologists have a share of responsibility in this process, especially for having long focused their attention to the presumably 'more emotional' cultures of 'pre-industrial' societies. Within Europe, the attributes today associated with different destinations often recreate a topographic map with a clear distinction between 'Latin' and 'Northern' cultures. The North is often represented here as emotionally introverted and hard working in counterpoint to a more open, expressive party-going South. In his novel *Platform*, French writer Michel Houellebecq (2002) telescopes the social systematic of such a North–South map at the global scale; with a hard working, yet sexually frustrated North finding emotional comfort, beautiful bodies and sex in the South.

Outline of the Book

As a second part of our Introduction, in Chapter 2 Mike Robinson develops and extends a number of the themes identified here and exemplified in my fieldwork. He positions the emotions as being central, and yet often by-passed, in our understandings of tourism and explores them as an intentional strategy for dealing with transformations brought about through *being* a tourist. A central point made is that the emotions and their expressions are culturally framed and beyond any simple 'cause and effect' principle; rather they are intimately bound to ways in which the world is imagined, mediated and communicated and to the ways in which we perform, record and recall our place in the world.

The strength of anthropology to explore emotions in tourism, as compared to clinical psychology which has largely monopolized this field, is that reality is observed as it unfolds normally and naturally. Ethnographers can follow tourists throughout their journey and within their own rhythm. This focus on quotidian tourist practices and the means by which emotions are manifested and talked about presents us with the potential to observe patterns, processual principles and, also the limits of such emotional cultures. Combined with historical analysis and philosophical rigour this approach can explain how the individual's perceptive and cognitive apparatus is formed and transformed as a result of socialization and institutionalization processes. Importantly, and what is touched upon in a number of chapters, are the processes which lead to the formation of social differences in emotional culture among different societies or groups within a society. As Robinson, in the following chapter clarifies, social actors (tourists) who learn the contexts for certain emotions are able to develop a sense of experiencing such emotions. In this sense differences in the emotional culture between subjects emerge from processes of delineation and normative practices of socialization and learning. Such processes and their social and bodily consequences deserve more attention. At the same time the study of the social frame of individual experience cannot replace the study of individual experience itself. Emotions may be learnt, they may even be contagious, yet whatever their historical or situational context, they are experienced at the personal level, by the personal body and cannot be detached from character and wider experience.

The book is divided into three parts. These are of course divided by somewhat artificial and permeable boundaries but effectively they seek to locate three 'domains' of tourist emotions. The first explores 'inside' the tourist's mind while on a journey – in motion if you will – and the realizations and transformations of self, in relation to the other and the world. The chapters of this first part include studies on the inner journeys of Japanese tourists (Nelson Graburn), on peak experiences among nature tourists in North America (Elvi Whittaker), the moral transformations of European volunteer tourists in Kenya (Émilie Crossley), 'mad' travellers in Jerusalem (Eliezer Witztum and Moshe Kalian), and religious tourists in Italian pilgrimage sites (Michael A. Di Giovine). Variously drawing upon anthropological, socio-psychological and psychiatric approaches, these chapters investigate the emotional processes and transformative powers of travel and tourism.

The second part of the book focuses upon the ways in which attractions and sights become associated with, and are seen to be imbued with various emotions, entailing a form of transmission of emotion to those who visit. Through case studies on the veneration of a Virgin figure in a Spanish popular-religious ceremony (Eddy Plasquy), the emotional memory construction at former Nazi concentration camp sites (Jessica Rapson), French World War II tourism sites (Bertram M. Gordon), tourist locations that are 'popular' sites to commit suicide (Angelina Karpovich) and the affective allure of spas (Jill Steward), it investigates some of the most commonly recurring semantic fields describing emotions experienced at tourist sites. The authors re-discover the presence of deeply romantic themes – 'forces of nature', 'sublime beauty', 'desire of death' – in contemporary tourism attractions and tourist practices.

The third part of the book deals with the ways that certain emotions become embedded in the behaviours of tourists and the representations and imaginaries of places and peoples. The chapters of this part include studies on the historical formation of emotions (many) Canadian men associate with their work at the cottage (Julia Harrison), processes of romantic enchantment of the colonial heritage in the island of Mozambique (Pamila Gupta), the cultivation of erotic awe among Cubans to seduce Western tourists in Havana (Valerio Simoni) and the ambivalent forms of affect generated by running stories about a tourist in Belize (Kenneth Little).

References

Bar-el, Y., Durst, R., Katz, G., Zislin, J., Strauss, Z., and Knobler, H.Y. (2000) 'Jerusalem syndrome', *British Journal of Psychiatry*, 176, pp. 86–90.

Bruner, E.M. (1986) 'Experience and its expression', in V.W. Turner, E.M. Bruner and C. Geertz (eds), *The Anthropology of Experience*, Urbana: University of Illinois Press, pp. 3–32.

Bruner, E.M. (1996) 'Tourism in the Balinese borderzone', in S. Lavie and T. Swedenburg (eds), *Displacement, Diaspora, and Geographies of Identity*, Durham, NC and London: Duke University Press, pp. 157–179.

Burton, J.W. (1972) *World Society*, Cambridge: University Press.

Chabloz, N. and Raout, J. (eds) (2009) Tourismes: La quête de soi par la pratique des autres. Special Issue of *Cahiers d'études africaines* XLIX (1–2/193–194).

Clifford, J. (1988) *The Predicament of Culture: Twentieth-Century Ethnography, Literature, and Art*, Cambridge, MA: Harvard University Press.

Cohen, E. (1988) 'Authenticity and commoditization in tourism', *Annals of Tourism Research*, 15(3), pp. 371–386.

Dumazedier, J. (1967) *Toward a Society of Leisure*, New York: Free Press.

Eid, M. and Diener, E. (2001) 'Norms for experiencing emotions in different cultures: inter- and intranational differences', *Journal of Personality and Social Psychology*, 81(5), pp. 869–85.

Freud, S. (2003) *The Uncanny*, London: Penguin Books.

Frey, N.L. (1998) *Pilgrim Stories – On and Off the Road to Santiago*, Berkeley: University of California Press.

Gaddis, J.L. (2002) *The Landscape of History: How Historians Map the Past*, Oxford: Oxford University Press.

Goffman, E. and Accordo, A. (1973) *La mise en scène de la vie quotidienne,* Paris: Minuit.

Goody, J. (1993) *The Culture of Flowers*, Cambridge and New York: Cambridge University Press.

Graburn, N. (2002) 'The ethnographic tourist', in Dann, G. (ed.), *The Tourist as a Metaphor of the Social World*, Wallingford, Oxon: CABI Pub.

Greenblatt, S. (1991). *Marvellous Possessions: The Wonder of the New World.* Chicago: University of Chicago Press.

Hennig, C. (1997) *Reiselust: Touristen, Tourismus und Urlaubskultur*. Frankfurt: Insel.

Hochschild, A.R. (1983) *The managed heart: Commercialization of human feeling.* Berkeley: University of California Press.

Houellebecq, M. (2002) *Platform*, London: Heinemann.

Lakoff, G. and Johnson, M. (1999) *Philosophy in the Flesh: The Embodied Mind and Its Challenge to Western Thought*, New York: Basic Books.

Lanfant, M.-F., Allcock, J.B. and Bruner, E.M. (1995) *International Tourism: Identity and Change*, London: Sage Publications.

Lazarus, R.S. (1982) 'Thoughts on the relations between emotion and cognition', *American Psychologist*, 37(9), pp. 1019–1024

Lerner, J.S. and Keltner, D. (2000) 'Beyond valence: toward a model of emotion-specific influences on judgement and choice', *Cognition and Emotion*, 14, pp. 473–494.

Lotman, I.U.M. (1990) *Universe of the Mind: A Semiotic Theory of Culture*, Bloomington: Indiana University Press.

MacCannell, D. (1976). *The Tourist: a New Theory of the Leisure Class*. New York: Schocken Books.

Magherini, G. (1989) *Le syndrome de Stendhal*, transl. by Françoise Liffran, Florence: Uster.

Massumi, B. (1987) 'Notes on the translation and acknowledgements', in Gilles Deleuze and Felix Guattari, *A Thousand Plateaus*, Minneapolis: University of Minnesota Press.

Mesquita, B. (2007) 'Emotions are culturally situated', *Social Science Information*, 46(3), pp. 410–415.

Myerhoff, B. (1993) 'Pilgrimage to Meron: Inner and outer peregrinations', in S. Lavie, K. Narayan and R. Rosaldo (eds), *Creativity/Anthropology*, New York: Cornell University Press, pp. 211–222.

Picard, D. (2010) 'Being a model for the world': Performing Creoleness in La Réunion', *Social Anthropology*, 18, pp. 302–315.

Picard, D. (2011) *Tourism, Magic and Modernity: Cultivating the Human Garden*, Oxford: Berghahn.

Pratt, M.L. (1992) *Imperial Eyes: Travel Writing And Transculturation*, London: Routledge.

Pritchard, A. and Morgan, N. (2000) 'Constructing tourism landscapes – gender, sexuality and space', *Tourism Geographies,* 2(2), pp. 115–139.

Selänniemi, T. (2003) 'On holiday in the liminal playground: Place, time and self in tourism', in Bauer, T.G., and McKercher, B. (eds), *Sex and Tourism: Journeys of Romance, Love, and Lust*, New York: Haworth Hospitality Press, pp. 19–34.

Shouse, E. (2005) 'Feeling, emotion, affect', *M/C Journal*, 8(6) (Retrieved 04 Mar. 2011 from http://journal.media-culture.org.au/0512/03-shouse.php).

Spafford-Vester, B. (1950) *Our Jerusalem. An American Family in the Holy City. The American Colony*, Lebanon: Middle East Export Press.

Spode, H. (2003) *Wie die Deutschen "Reiseweltmeister" wurden*, Erfurt: Landeszentrale für politische Bildung Thüringen.

Stendhal (1990) *Roma, Napoli e Firenze: Viaggio in Italia da Milano a Reggio Calabria*, Roma: Laterza.

Veblen, T. (1934), *The Theory of the Leisure Class: An Economic Study of Institutions*, New York: Modern library.

Viala, A., Ota, H., Vacheron, M.N., Marti, P. and Caroli, F. (2004) 'Les Japonais en voyage pathologique à Paris: un modèle original de prise en charge transculturelle', *Nervure* (supplement), 17(5), pp. 31–34.

Zajonc, R.B. (1980) 'Feeling and thinking: preferences need no inferences', *American Psychologist*, 35(2), pp. 151–175.

Zigon, J. (2009) 'Within a Range of Possibilities: Morality and Ethics in Social Life', *Ethnos*, 74(2), pp. 251–276.

Chapter 2

The Emotional Tourist

Mike Robinson

Introduction

In the novel 'The Outsider' or 'The Stranger' (*L'Etranger*) by Albert Camus (1999), the central character Meursault pursues a life as if he is effectively detached from the world and what is generally considered to be meaningful.[1] Meursault is portrayed as a person without feeling and without empathy. He is indifferent to the world and to the acts of violence that he perpetrates. Indeed, he appears to exemplify complete emotional detachment from the events that pattern his life and eventually led him to face the death sentence. In 'The Outsider', as in other novels which explore existentialist themes of disconnection and meaninglessness, the central character is set apart from the world, wilfully disengaging from it and being unresponsive to it. Meursault, in the course of the novel is a person emotionally immune from his environment and fellow human beings and, as the exception, he highlights the behaviours of others who do display their emotions and have to deal with them accordingly.

I use this example of Camus's classic exploration of 'The Outsider' to make the point that the central character is the exception and that the novel itself is exemplary of a genre which does *not* play upon the emotional experiences of its key figure. However, on reading the novel, whereas Meursault is prepared to accept 'the gentle indifference of the world' (p. 139) the reader is not, or at least I was not. Rather, the reading of the novel had the effect of arousing my own emotions. It also cemented a sense that any absence of emotional engagement is largely imaginary existing within the confines of fiction, or at least is restricted to a pathological extreme confined within the minorities of incarcerated criminals.

This opening seems far, far removed from any consideration of tourism and the realities of the world of leisure. However, for me it is the very exceptional imaginings of Camus which provides a salutary reminder that for most of the time, any engagement with the world and its peoples is an *emotional* engagement, in the sense that we neither read, experience, or recall the world and our place within it, solely as fact and without sensation, judgment, consideration of value and the

---

1   Albert Camus's novel is indicative of a modernist genre which is essentially moral exploring as it does notions of absurdity and indifference in changing society. Similar themes are explored in Robert Musil's novel 'The Man without Qualities' which problematizes the ability to 'feel', or at least feel in any empathetic sense within periods and situations of anxiety.

processes of evaluation. Indeed, picking up on David Picard's observations from the field (Chapter 1), I shall argue in this chapter, that the emotions are necessary, and in many ways inevitable, for engaging with the world. The tourist is part of the world not detached from it, and is engaged in processes of ordering knowledge of the world but also, in what Chloe Chard (2002, p. 188) terms the 'adventure of the self'.[2] The word adventure is important, for even the most ordinary act in the context of a different place and culture can be readily accelerated as a form of exploration, testing the boundaries of our own identities. The celebrated gaze of the tourist is not objective but rather imbued with subjective intimacies which surface during, and as part of, the experience of moving through the world. As the tourist moves through landscapes of otherness, guided (or not) by the grooved narratives of previous tourists and the mixed-up meta-narratives of what Chris Rojek and John Urry (1997) refer to as 'travel cultures', he or she experiences sensations, feelings, and emotions (what Elvi Whittaker in Chapter 4, drawing from Maslow, terms 'peak' experiences). These states of mind and body are constitutive of the overall tourist experience and are in some way linked not only to the ways in which we apprehend, or are apprehended by, the material world, but also to the ways in which we process and imagine the world. In the act, in the imagining of being elsewhere and in the physical processes of travelling, we are, to varying degrees, outside of our normative environment and arguably more exposed to an increased number of emotional states and triggers.

By way of introduction we can position the study of tourism as representative of a wider legacy in western thought which has struggled with the role of the emotions. In short, what we look upon as a persistent tension in metaphysics relates to what constitutes the world (and indeed the universe). Broadly speaking we look to make sense of the world by accounting for the vast variety of objects and actions in it, and in the knowledge that things constantly change. While we can recognize difference, we can also recognize sameness and continuity. While we can recognize that the world is constituted by many actions and objects, we also recognize that there is unity and stability. And while we may search for ways in which we can simplify the world, we consistently reveal its complexities. In the context of tourism studies, scholars have made significant in-roads to revealing, mapping and even predicting, the flows, processes and structures of international tourism. In the traditions of post enlightenment thought, social science approaches to the study of tourism as a modernist project have tended to focus upon rather discrete analyses of processes and moments which constitute tourism; specific transactions, particular behaviours, discourses, narratives etc. The case study is a particularly well used vehicle for uncovering what happens in tourism. It is certainly the case that we understand,

---

2   Chard is referring to 'romantic travel' of the eighteenth century and refers to a form of travel which is 'holding out possibilities of self-realization and self-discovery, but also placing the self at risk ...' (p. 188). Whilst the environments, encounters and experiences may have altered, this would nonetheless seem to demonstrate the essence of continuity with present day tourism.

better than ever, the ways in which tourism works. We are ever more aware of its environmental, economic and social impacts. The fact that we enjoy this level of understanding arguably relates to the rationalist, empirical model of the social sciences within which much of tourism studies has been situated for the past forty years or so.[3]

However, while we need an understanding of 'tourism' as a shorthand term for the enabling and inter-connected systems and structures, processes and activities which (some) people engage with, we also need an understanding of tourists as persons and how they encounter, receive, respond and react to the effective change in conditions which tourism ultimately entails. This is where things become complex. Tourism is but one of a long list of complex human activities which work within and with, the objective and largely rational, material world. But the key point is that it is predicated on our 'human-ness' and our capacities to imagine, play, pretend and subjectively experience the world (Salazar 2010). Tourists move between the real and the imagined world with educated ease, and the power of the imagination cuts through the material to the extent that we can neither rely on the merely observable, nor the discrete. In the context of tourism studies, and in line with the trajectory of the rational social sciences, much emphasis has been given to the *tourist* as a somehow separate and disconnected category. Certainly within the extant literature which deals with the relations between tourists and emotions (largely with reference to the role of marketing in tourism) there is a tendency to deal with emotions as if they are particular to the tourist moment or tourist place (see for instance: Goosens 1997; Gnoth 2007; Farber and Hall 2010; Hosany 2011). In reality it is problematic to separate the 'being-ness' of a tourist to the being-ness of everyday life. There is inevitable overlap between our normative experience of social life and our experience as a tourist providing not only a methodological challenge but also an ontological critique regarding where the *being* a tourist and the *doing* of tourism begins and ends.

At one level it makes little sense to even conceive of understanding tourist behaviour/motivation/experience without the appreciation that the emotions are woven into every dimension of the complex category of mobility we call tourism. The 'being' of a tourist, for those economically and socially able, and culturally attuned to this modern condition, is also an extension of the human condition, replete as it is with the diverse interior worlds of the emotions. At another level we must ask the questions: What is it about the doing of tourism and the being a tourist which appears to heighten our emotional engagement with the world? Is our emotional state of being a tourist contingent upon our experience of difference – of new places and cultures – on *what* we apprehend, rather than *how* we

---

3   The understanding of tourism as a located in the social sciences and its directions is discussed by, among others, John Tribe in 'The Truth about Tourism', *Annals of Tourism Research* (2006). The tension between humanistic approaches and more positivistic studies is generally well documented though there has been a general lack of research regarding the emotions and tourism from either a philosophical or psychological perspective.

apprehend? To what extent does the process of being mobile alter the way in which we psychologically and physiologically respond to the world? What emotions are played out in tourism? Does it make sense to speak of 'emotional destinations' – places which induce emotional reactions? Can we be a dispassionate tourist? Given that tourism deals with the crossing of cultures as well as spaces, also pertinent is the question of whether emotions are socially constructed and shaped by their wider cultural setting or, rather universal in being characteristic of all humans? Such questions, and more, are both intellectually and methodologically challenging but given the need to ever deepen our understanding of the tourist condition, and in the allied spirit of qualitative and conceptual inquiry, we should at least address them.

Making Sense of the Emotions

It is beyond the scope of this chapter to fully engage with a discussion of emotions and the attempts made to understand them over the years from both a philosophical perspective and, more latterly, from a psychological point of view. The debates surrounding what constitutes an emotion, how the emotions work and their role in wider social life are ever active and touch upon many dimensions. Robert Solomon (2008) provides a very useful overview of the ways in which the emotions have been discussed in philosophy and draws out a historical position still prevalent in common discourse and our understanding of the emotions. Solomon identifies the tension which persistently locates emotion as being the inferior, if not the antithesis, of reason. This tension he tracks back to Aristotle and the concern shown in his 'Rhetoric' (1984) that the emotions cloud judgement and take a direction away from reason.[4] Aristotle in his 'Nicomachean Ethics' (2004) saw rationality as both the telos of human beings and the very mark of our uniqueness. Similarly the Stoics took the emotions to be misguided judgements about our relations with the world and, much later, Spinoza identified the majority of emotions as rather passive reactions to 'our unwarranted expectations of the world'. Solomon also points to both Hume and Kant, who each in various measure, gave influential pre-eminence to 'reason' as the essential pathway to knowledge, understanding and virtue. Further prominent intellectual schools of thought such

---

4   Aristotle described various emotions (fourteen 'passions') in the Rhetoric and discussed their influence upon human judgement. He saw the emotions as integral to the human condition and characterizes, compares them and importantly locates them in a broader ethical context. This is taken to be the first attempt to systematically analyse the role of emotions. For further reading see D.M. Gross (2006) *The Secret History of Emotion: From Aristotle's Rhetoric to Modern Brain Science*, Chicago: Chicago University Press. Aristotle's concerns for the emotions appear at odds with his appeal for reason but his acknowledgement of them and of dealing with them in a cause and effect way is a means of reaching a rational judgement.

as utilitarianism and logical positivism have also projected rationality as the driving force behind development, while at the same time largely rejecting any influence of the emotions as either positive (particularly in the realm of ethics) or meaningful. Moreover, modernity, in which we can situate both the structural and behavioural phenomena of tourism, is itself a complicated product of what Weber (2001) termed instrumental rationality; the progressive extension of goal oriented capitalism.[5]

In a sense, consideration of the emotions and how they impact / are shaped by, and in, touristic contexts, could be said to have suffered neglect as a function of the study of tourism's position within a largely social science framework which has itself evolved from a fundamentally rationalist philosophical position. The emotions have long been portrayed as a dimension of human development; vestigial of the early stages of social organization, aligned with the basic instincts and to be moved *away* from. In counter-point, reason and rationality were taken to be the drivers of modernity, the underpinning of scientific enquiry and a more sophisticated goal of humanity rooted not in old cosmologies, but in new, ordered structures of thought. Over the centuries this tension has revealed itself in various oppositions as between Galileo's 'divorce' of religious faith and scientific reason,[6] between the European Enlightenment and the Romantic reaction it provoked, between evolutionists and creationists and, between ideas of culture as posited by Matthew Arnold and culture as explored by the likes of Franz Boas, Levi-Strauss and Clifford Geertz. However, and with a measured dose of hindsight, it is apparent that in many readings where the emotions and their discordant subjectivities are seen to be rejected, there is an undercurrent of recognition of the power of the emotions. Solomon (2008) points to the ways in which even the most celebrated upholders of reason often struggled to reconcile the power of the passions and matters of feeling. With remarkable continuity to Aristotle's position, the emotions have seldom been denied but rather their need to be tamed recognized. Furthermore and apposite to this discussion, is a more recent resurgence of a more liberational understanding of the emotions as a counterpoint to reasoned action and espoused in a rather poetic way by Nietzsche who extolled the virtues of the passions and the power of instinct. While not explicitly theorizing about the emotions, Nietzsche presciently pointed to a role for the emotions in the social world which was to be taken up by psychologists in their attempts to make sense of the emotions not as 'add-ons' to life but rather as an essential part of the human condition and as a way of dealing with the absurd

---

5 Weber identified four types of rationality one of which was instrumental and progressive (Zwerkrational), the others being 'traditional' and 'Wertrational' (based on value judgement). He also identified 'affectual rationality' which was taken to be determined by emotion or feeling. This was seen to be spontaneous and not as 'efficient' as the goal oriented Zwerkrational.

6 The relationship between religion and the emotions is close. As Robert Emmons (2005) puts it: 'Religion likely influences the generation of emotion and regulation of emotional responses.' (p. 237).

and making the world meaningful. Solomon (1993, p. 50) cites Heidegger who, in the mould of Nietzsche, elevated the emotions (Heidegger used the term 'moods') as something meaningful, always in the background, and a way of 'being tuned into the world'.

Work by psychologists has firmly situated the emotions as being not opposed to rationality but rather a part of it (Izard 1977, 1991; Frijda 1986, 1988; Oatley 1992; Damasio 1994). Damasio (1994) for instance, working with patients whose frontal lobes of the brain had been damaged, highlighted that a fully rational approach to life is not possible (partly through never having access to all the knowledge needed to make decisions and partly because our lives are frequently shaped by others, so that life goals can collide), and thus emotions are a way of making up the deficiencies of reason, acting in a way to provide some structure to social life, bridging what gaps may remain in our knowledge and helping to stimulate motivation and action, particularly with regard to relations with others. This now widely accepted psychological view merges with the phenomenologically attuned thought of Jean-Paul Sartre (2002) who in his 'Sketch for a Theory of Emotions' posits that 'the emotion is a specific manner of apprehending the world' (p. 35). This echoes Heidegger's notion of 'being-in-the-world'; a way of making sense of the world and our place within it, in almost a magical way. Though using the term 'magical' Sartre effectively saw the emotions as having a *strategic* role in assisting us to deal with difficult situations which arise.[7] They are used intentionally, functionally, almost in a performative sense, to direct our actions, shape motivations and transform ('magically') our experiences.

The importance and new found understanding of the emotions clearly makes them a vital target for researchers wishing to understand social relations in a general sense, but it also raises several points for further reflection with regard to more specific considerations concerning the tourist. Given the understanding that emotions are intentional and part of the structures we employ in daily life, how does this impact upon what we frequently seem to experience in tourism as an emotional encounter? Do the notions of intention and structure negate the idea of spontaneous reaction to external stimuli as apprehended, for instance, outside of the normal 'home' environment? It seems clear that tourists when encountering certain landscapes, natural features, buildings, events and peoples can 'have' an 'emotional' experience.

The oft cited Stendhal 'syndrome',[8] the quasi mythical effect upon the body produced through the sensory experience (primarily discussed relating to the

---

7   For Sartre, consciousness is 'directed' toward changing our relationship with the world not by acting on the world itself but by 'magically' attributing new qualities to the world.

8   The Stendhal syndrome, and related conditions referred to as the Paris syndrome and the Jerusalem syndrome, refers to a psychological breakdown with related physiological symptoms as a response to a physical encounter with the rarified objects of the material world. The Italian psychologist Gazelle Maharani coined the term Stendhal Syndrome

sense of sight) of an aspect of the material world, which is taken to generate certain physiological changes, has long been linked to the capacity of the object to 'produce' an impact. In the account of Stendhal's visit to Florence (1960) in 1817 he writes (p. 302): 'As I emerged from the porch of Santa Croce, I was seized with a fierce palpitation of the heart (the same symptom which, in Berlin, is referred to as an *attack of the nerves*); the well-spring of life was dried up within me, and I walked in constant fear of falling to the ground.' Romantic as this reads this may have had more to do with the ill health that Stendhal suffered from throughout his life. Nevertheless, we can witness tourists perform embodied acts in an apparently spontaneous way. As Witztum and Kalian (Chapter 6), along with Di Giovine (Chapter 7) both discuss in their cases, this spontaneity manifests itself an almost 'spiritual' way. The more secular pursuits say, of sailing in the mists of the Niagara Falls, standing on the glass platform which now overhangs the edge of Grand Canyon,[9] or indeed, gazing at the art collections of the Uffizi in Florence, nevertheless are frequently described using the allusion of the immediacy and force of religious-like intervention. Such encounters may well provoke certain reflex reactions but the nature of such reactions will vary from person to person and will also vary across time.

Peter Goldie (2009, p. 12) refers to an emotion as being typically 'complex, episodic, dynamic and structured'. The idea that emotions are processes does beg the question as to how they are stimulated, structured and sequenced but, though there are variations discussed in the literature, a common conception is that an emotion is made up of 'episodes' (Lazarus 1991; Ellsworth 1994). Dissecting an emotion into episodes and applying it to some a tourist encounter with an aspect of the world produces an initial episode of evaluation where he, or she, assesses the relevance of the experience (of, for instance, how important it is to us to see a view or experience an event). This is followed by an episode of wider appraisal, in which further contextual evaluation takes place regarding what actions are possible and what are not; relating such an appraisal to, for instance, notions of time, social mores and appropriateness. Then follows what is normally taken to be the core element of an emotion, the act of readiness. This refers to the processing of the evaluated information and involves the prioritization of, and planning for, possible actions. It is at this stage where changes in the body (facial expressions, dry throat, sweating etc.) can be identified as the possibilities are contemplated and their meaningfulness assessed. The duration and intensity of these episodes,

---

for her 1989 book which described cases among tourists in Florence who experienced tachycardia, confusion and hallucinations when shown masterpieces of renaissance art. Such psychosomatic reactions were named after the French author 'Stendhal' who provided a detailed account of the symptoms he experienced during his visit to Florence.

9   The Grand Canyon Sky Walk was constructed as a 'tourist attraction' to accentuate the experience of gazing below on a vertical drop of up to 240 metres. It induces fear from some tourists who will not walk on it, apprehension from others who also walk upon it and a pride or triumph from those who do not show any fear.

or affective states, varies from being quite rapid to more cumulative. An emotional state would seem to last longer than what Frijda (1993) terms 'moods' which refer more to a short term state and somewhat disconnected from a particular object of attention (Goldie 2009). Somewhat strangely, this process account of various episodes of an emotion appears as rather mechanical and counter-intuitive to the idea of spontaneous reaction.

Emotions as intentional and variable would seem to challenge any notion of the intrinsic power of an object to stimulate. This is also emphasized by considering the cultural positioning of the tourist. Notions of awe, wonder and the discourses which surround these would appear to be culturally located and closely connected to aesthetic sensibilities and general life experience. The emotional state of a tourist who normally lives in the heart of a busy city and travels to the unpopulated mountains may be expected to differ to one who lives with or close to the mountains. The so-called 'wow' factor of a tourist setting sight on Mount Everest for the first time may not be the same for the Sherpa who lives and works nearby. Similarly, the Sherpa travelling to a large city may have an emotional experience though different to the city dweller. Tourism constantly plays with such oppositions and dislocations but this does not mean that the city or the mountains are somehow imbued with the power to *produce* an emotional state in the tourist.

Front line sensory reactions – sight or otherwise – to a different location would not appear to be a sufficient stimulus for an emotional reaction. Rather, there is a 'reading' process which accompanies any visit in which the tourist processes and interprets the landscape in a particular, culturally and socially informed, way. As Judith Adler (1989) and others (MacCannell 1976 and Urry 2002) have argued, 'sight-seeing' and the 'tourist gaze' is learned and tied to longer histories and wider and changing socio-cultural conventions. Aesthetic frameworks change over time and hierarchies are produced in, and shared by, some societies as to what has the power to *move* the tourist. Heritage, which has been inscribed by UNESCO as being 'World Heritage' by virtue of 'outstanding universal value',[10] would seem, for instance, to have a greater capacity to impress and to 'move' tourists than heritage without such official international standing. Despite its 'world' claim, the category of 'World Heritage' works mainly within a largely Eurocentric, neo-Kantian framework of universal value and aesthetics. While not denigrating the value of such sites, their emotional resonance with visitors coming from outside of such value systems may not be as strong. This is largely conjecture as there appears to be little in the way of any empirical work on emotional engagement with World Heritage on the part of both local and visitor and much in the way of assumption regarding how tourists respond or should respond emotionally to what, for some, is a privileged category of human design.

Stephen Bochner (2003), following Kalervo Oberg (1960), uses the term 'culture shock' to refer to the reactions induced not only by contact with the material

---

10   UNESCO use the term 'Outstanding Universal Value' as the key criteria for deciding whether a cultural (or natural) site is worthy for inscription on the World Heritage List.

world, but also with the different peoples which inhabit it. Interestingly, Bochner and others (Furnham and Bochner 1982; Irwin 2007) writing of 'culture shock', seldom interrogate the emotions as such and work more with the notion of feeling or affect in a much more passive and non-intentional way. I mention this by way of a reminder that in the context of trying to understand the emotional universe of the tourist, it is useful to bear in mind that we need to take into account the interplay not only between tourists and objects / nature, but also between tourists and the cultures and societies they temporarily inhabit. As Graburn (Chapter 3) discusses in relation to Japanese tourists, the format and experiences of travel are imprinted with the patterns of individual and social behaviour played out 'at home'.

Learning, Language and Narrative

Recalling the Stendhal syndrome usefully points to the idea that the power for emotional engagement may not lie in the object itself but in the drama and romance of the *story* of encounter with the object. Whether Henri-Marie Beyle (to give Stendhal his real name) really did almost faint at the art on display in Florence is largely beside the point, but the story has persisted and has succeeded in permeating our ostensibly European collective consciousness. The myth that something exists within the world which is the embodiment of all known beauty or purity is a persuasive (and arguably, universal) idea akin to the stories surrounding the Golden Fleece of Greek mythology or the Holy Grail in Christian culture. The motif that objects, events, places and peoples are present in the world which can produce significant and visceral reactions which both confirm and transcend our own humanity is powerful and persistent. Though straddling the age-old transformatory plot lines of 'the quest' and 're-birth' (Booker 2005), investing objects or natural features with the power to draw out the passions of man became embedded in European romanticism in the eighteenth and nineteenth centuries and paradoxically continue to influence tourism as a modernist project. It is difficult not to over-estimate the ways in which the development of the romantic trope continues to frame contemporary touristic experiences of, and encounters with, both nature and culture. I use the term development to avoid thinking of romanticism as somehow stranded as a discrete period of the late eighteenth century but rather as an on-going, reproductive process whereby societies and individuals continue to frame and order the world in a way which plays to the imagination and prioritizes certain aesthetic forms.

From the position of middle class, ostensibly white, Northern European tourists, how we 'read' a landscape, a painting or a building is effectively a learned process heavily cultivated from the repeated, collective and almost sub-conscious inscriptions of romanticism which not only provides us with direction as to how we should value certain elements of the world, but also how we should react to them. The well-trodden pathways to the Alpine views 'discovered' by Schiller, or the 'scenes' of life in the Istanbul Bazaar are ceremoniously walked and ritually photographed by tourists still. When *first* encountered, the scenes of the world may well have elicited emotions in the most visceral of ways amongst travelers who had little in terms of context or prior experience to appraise. Such emotions may well have been all the more dramatic in their intensity and duration precisely because of the immediacy of encounter (Plasquy in Chapter 8 intimates that this immediacy also translates to physical proximity which can make the difference between a fearful experience and a sublime one). However, in the context of contemporary tourism, rather than as first contact travelers and explorers, we already 'know' the world, consciously, deliberately but also passively and fleetingly. An unending circulation of images and texts of places and peoples greet us every day, whether we wish them to or not. Seeing places and doing things for the *first time* generates the strongest emotions. But we all too rarely see things in a state of innocence and are rather shaped by the texts and narratives that engulf us. As Paul Ricouer (1995) has noted, the vast majority of texts are referential and bring the world to us, not in any positivistic sense but through the imagination. The implications of this for tourists – as a sub-set of modern society – is that it seems as if we are destined to be trapped within a vortex of imaginaries, which carry us along to destinations which we have, in effect, already visited. As Edward Bruner (1984, p. 6) noted as tourists: 'Cultural narratives become personal narratives.' The site/sight of difference for the tourist is the product of an *accumulated* and *cumulative* layering of part thoughts and visions, partly processed, partly mediated, partly remembered and partly forgotten – and all *derived*. Furthermore, it seems impossible to un-imagine the world once presented to us.

Does this mean that our emotions are similarly derived? The fact that tourists seem to mobilize remarkably similar vocabulary when confronted with some instance of drama or beauty would tend to indicate that the emotions are rehearsed. If I am faced with the red glow of sunrise on Uluru – along with the hundreds of other tourists – then I almost know that I should be experiencing a sense of awe. Indeed, that is why I am there. Moreover, I 'know' what words to use to convey what I seem to 'feel' – 'wow', 'incredible', 'beautiful' etc. These are the words I may use at the moment of experience and in future recollections, but these are the words I have also already learned and am choosing to apply them to reflect a certain experience. Ian Ousby (1990) comments on the way that the identification of the sublime in the eighteenth century began a process of developing a highly stylized vocabulary which could then be used not only to describe the objects of nature, but which could also help express reactions to these. Such a process of correspondence between encounter and denotation and the subsequent 'feedback' between language and our emotional states shifts with cultures, sub-cultures and generations (Stearns and Stearns 1988).

The position of language with regard to the emotions is central and largely beyond the scope of present discussion. Micheal Bamberg (1987, 1997a, 1997b) among others (Heelas 1986; Lutz and White 1986; Wierzbicka 1994), have made the distinction between language as something which is a way of *performing* emotions, in the sense that being emotional produces a particular form of communication (this would also relate to various bodily reactions and facial expressions) and, language as something which reflects and refers to emotions, enabling us to talk *about* them. This latter view does not admit to the precise reality of emotions but rather is a way of us making sense of them. In the context of trying to understand the emotions of the tourist it is useful to consider the ways in which touristic discourse generates, maintains and reproduces its own lexicon of words and phrases that not only describe the world emotionally but prescribe the world to be apprehended in an emotional way.

Any emotion that I do experience when gazing upon Uluru is identified in large part by the language I use, but it does not necessarily follow that I had any emotional experience at all. How many times as tourists do we look upon destinations or landscapes and *without* any feeling at all? Such an occasion may well be contingent upon many other variables such as age, experience, cultural background, social relationships and the like. Whilst we may seek an aesthetic experience, our actual experience may be an anaesthetic one – we feel nothing at all.[11] This is distinct from the idea of 'disinterestedness' which implies a reflexive, objective position; rather, this is about taking no position at all. In forms of tourism marked by a compression of experiences and repetitive engagement, the anaesthetic may increasingly be the norm. Arguably, had Stendhal been immersed with the artistic outputs of more European cities for longer he may have experienced a yawn of indifference rather than a gasp of excitement. There is no universal at work here; no automatic process of emotional engagement despite any collective re-working of how we may frame the world. My 'seeing' of Uluru and any emotions I may experience are anchored in my own personal, messy and hyper-complex learning process and the wider, similarly messy and hyper-complex learning process broadly allied to the culture and society I have dwelled within. It is invariably a different experience to that of the Australian Aboriginals and is expressed differently (Tuan 1995).[12]

A cursory glance at the myriad of travel blogs and on-line accounts of holiday experiences reveals an emotional language which mirrors that used by the tourism sector. Destinations are 'loved'. People are 'passionate' about places and about peoples. Such words are directly linked to particular experiences and moments and seldom are places described in any value-neutral way. Only occasionally do we come across serious expressions of 'hate' linked to a place. Fear, when expressed, is frequently dressed as a positive and passing emotion regarding excitement and challenge. Surprise, when used, is also positioned as a fleeting feeling. In the

---

11   A point to consider is the extent to which routine and mechanistic viewings of the world are subsequently recalled / re-imagined in a more poetic fashion as if to compensate for the numbness of a first impression.

12   Yi-Fu Tuan considers the aesthetic world of Australian Aboriginal culture and contrasts it against Chinese culture and the cultures of Medieval Europe and links the understandings and meanings of nature and culture to the emotions felt by their respective populations.

context of what is sometimes referred explicitly to as 'emotional marketing',[13] organizations responsible for branding and promoting destinations attempt to appeal to potential tourists on an emotional level; in reality seeking to connect with positive emotions only, or at least the removal of negative emotions. Hence, the Cyprus Tourism Agency's recent promotional campaign which headlines with 'In Your Heart'. This is similar to a long standing campaign in Taiwan which reads as 'Touch Your Heart.' Both are very direct instances of suggesting that the destination will invoke an emotional response and yet, as labels only, both are incapable of stimulating anything other than mild curiosity. A number of studies focusing upon the texts produced by the tourism sector highlight the usage of such emotionally charged vocabulary (see for instance: Hallett 2010; Park 2010; Thurlow and Jaworski 2011). This in itself is nothing unusual or sinister but rather to be expected given the workings of international tourism. Indeed, appealing to the emotions is an age old narrative device.

Attempting to gauge the emotions of *tourists* through discourse reveals much about the emotion / language interface and the difficulties of researching this aspect of tourism. At the outset tourists provide *recollections* of their emotions which are thus already mediated through further experience and reflection. Further, we can detect a marked degree of semantic elasticity in way that particular descriptors are used to the point of banality. To say that one 'loves' every place visited tells us very little about the emotion of love, nor does it provide much detail or specificity from which to make meaningful judgements about what may have been experienced. This is not criticism but merely a wider reflection on the imprecision relating to how language is being used. Clearly there is room for further loss of meaning when moving between languages. As Jenefer Robinson (2005, p. 90) puts it: 'Different languages have different words for carving up the emotion landscape corresponding to the different values, interests, and goals characteristic of different cultures.' Matsumoto (1994) for instance, points to the fact that some African languages refer to the emotions of anger and sadness by the use of a single word. Robinson (2005) also makes the point that the labelling of emotions relates to the learning process in which the differences in labelling reflects the differences in emotional states.[14] While there would seem to be a clear distinction between the emotion of fear and the emotion of happiness, distinctions may be more blurred between say the emotions of sadness, sorrow, self-pity, regret and remorse. This confusion can be seen almost as a 'language game' in that we use one word as a 'short cut' to meaning, or we use an inappropriate word, but as Freud recognized (1935), and what we frequently experience, emotions are felt in a rather opaque

---

13   Emotional marketing is frequently characterized as a means of provoking an emotional response from an audience or 'transferring' emotions between groups. It correlates closely with 'relationship marketing'.

14   Robinson notes that there are emotional states which have yet to be labelled, relating to the wider point that our understanding of the emotions is still emerging.

way with effects that we sometimes do not understand, and it is only through reflecting upon them, or talking about them, that their meanings become clear.

The linking of language to the emotions underlines the learning aspect implicit in them. The emotions can be educated, in the sense that we acknowledge that there are things are in the world which are capable of generating an emotional response and that we can learn what response is appropriate and proportionate. Such learning is in part driven by experience and memory and partly by the complex processes of learning inherent in socialization. Our reactions to the world as tourists draw upon what we understand a tourist to be, and how 'they' have reacted previously. The term 'they' is, of course, non-specific and 'their' reactions part imagined, but we nonetheless draw upon the precedents of the collective as a way of informing and legitimizing our individual responses. This indicates that rather than our emotions being a category of psychological states that are disruptive rather, they are a way of confirming planned actions and of revealing existing personal dispositions. But Robert Solomon (1993, p. 100) makes the point that there is no either/or conception of an emotion as either an episode or a disposition and comments: 'My emotion is a structure of my world, which may at times manifest itself in certain specific displays of feeling or behaviour. But my emotion *is* neither such displays nor the disposition to display.' In such a way, the emotions are structured ways in which we constitute our own subjective world and make it meaningful. Such structures do not just come into existence but are learned and are socially and culturally informed. They relate to what we value as individuals and collectively and, also they can reveal those values through the emotions which we do display.

Tourist Emotions

While allowing for numerous grey areas in attempting to categorize and name emotions, a number of psychologists have sought to identify a smaller number of 'basic' or more primitive emotions (Fridja 1986; Shaver et al. 1987; Ortony and Turner 1990). Paul Ekman (1994) for instance names anger, fear, surprise, disgust, joy and sadness as basic emotions. Parrott (2001) highlights a similar list of what he calls primary emotions as being; love, joy, surprise, anger, sadness and fear. Such basic emotions, it is argued, are the building blocks of more complex emotions so that anger for instance, is expressed as either irritation or rage. The list of more complex emotions is long, and as long as an ever-creative vocabulary will allow. Thus, with the basic root of fear, we can express it (in the English language anyway) as, alarm, shock, fright, horror, terror, panic, or hysteria. The basic emotions are commonly taken to be natural, universal, or at least capable of being experienced across different cultures, and are taken to be more or less independent from higher cognitive processes. What seems to happen is that folk taxonomies of emotions and the semantic confusion which still dominates the psychological literature (Izard 2007), prevents any meaningful discussion of any sense of universalism appertaining to the basic emotions, whether it exists or not. While accepting that the expression of these basic emotions will vary and that issues of character, personal, and self-knowledge will differ, and that value systems, aesthetic frameworks and learning processes will also reflect cultural diversity, it is does appear that at least we can detect some degree of hierarchy amongst the emotions; that is some appear to be more important and relevant to how we function as humans than others. Teasing this idea out can we identify certain emotions more relevant to the tourist condition than others?

An initial reflection is upon the idea of tourism as a practice and activity which has been chiefly designed to bring *joy* to those who are able to engage with the world as tourists. The term joy is not commonly used as a description in relation to being a tourist[15] but in the very time framed experience of *doing* tourism one would expect various degrees of amusement, enjoyment, happiness, satisfaction, and delight. Such feelings, or group of feelings, may be better understood as a 'mood', expressing both a general emotional state as well as specific instances of more intense identification.[16] The problems of attempting to move between a general sense and a specific instance of the emotional condition of the tourist relates to the varying levels of intensity of particular activities and provides a reflection on the relevance, or not, of any particular object or stimuli. The 'doing nothing' of lying next to the hotel swimming pool is as much, if not more, about the condition of joy as seeing the Mona Lisa for the first time. Coded in much of the work done in trying to ascertain and even 'measure' the motivations for embarking on a holiday, is an intended search for a period of time wherein positive emotions can be engaged. Whilst I am not suggesting that as tourists we can pre-determine emotions to be felt, nor even that we deliberately or consciously dwell upon any aspect of our emotions, it would seem likely that in our expectations and imaginings of how we will be feeling in the time frame outside of daily routine, we implicitly seek positive emotional states. To put it another way, we do not go on holiday with the desire nor expectation to experience anger or sadness.

Dean MacCannell (2011) suggests that tourists are being driven by a 'new' social commandment to 'enjoy', an imperative of pleasure which is embedded in

---

15   Indeed, the term joy has suffered through the usage as part of the 'Strength through Joy' (Kraft durch Freude) programme operated to promote the advantages of National Socialism in 1930s Germany. The use of tourism to promote Nazi ideology is explored by Shelley Baranowski (2004). Baranowski's work points to the way that the emotions, or at least the promise they offer, are capable of being mobilized for wider social and political ends.

16   The distinction between the term mood and emotion is not clear in the literature of psychology. For a useful discussion of the issues see C.J. Beedie, P.C. Terry and A.M. Lane (2005) 'Distinctions between emotion and mood', *Cognition and Emotion*, 19, pp. 847–878. The term 'affect' is also used. Massumi (1987) in the Introduction to Deleuze and Guattari's 'A Thousand Plateaus' makes the distinction between feelings as being personal and essential biographical; emotions as being 'social' and affects as being prepersonal – an ability to affect and be affected.

wider social life. The consequence of this additional socially endorsed pressure to gain pleasure is that it raises the stakes with regard to both tourist and provider in meeting expectations. Using the term pleasure takes us directly to a myriad of destinations, attractions and entertainments which have been constructed for that very purpose. Steward in Chapter 12, for instance, notes the shift in the use of spas from places of treatment and therapy to places of pleasure. Notwithstanding the semantic fuzziness surrounding notions of enjoyment, pleasure, happiness and the like, the normative emotional landscape while *on holiday*, could be said to one of 'joy', in part defined by time or duration as much as a place or sight. Thus, as the liminal time comes to an end and the tourist is forced to contemplate the return home, he or she may experience a state of sadness elevated by the very contrast of what has been together with the prospect of 'normality'. Somewhat ironically, the experience of sadness may feel all the more intense against a backdrop of the general expectation to 'enjoy' and is directed outwardly toward an opaque sense of the inevitability of the modern condition.

Love would seem to be connected to the emotion of joy in some way, almost as a pinnacle of pleasure, and yet its position as a basic emotion is highly contested. Rather than thinking of love as a singular state, which like other emotional states 'comes and goes', love is frequently characterized as a 'complex of emotions' (Rorty 1980; Badhwar 2003) which is implicitly directed toward another, is (generally) relational and does not 'come and go'. Love is a focal point for a wide range of feelings (desire, lust, passion, infatuation, adoration, caring, longing, jealousy etc.) as well as interfacing at times with the emotions of sadness and fear as well as joy. The holiday may provide an opportunity for certain expressions of love, and while we may conventionally think of this as active between people, love is also directed toward the material world and expressed through memory and nostalgia. Gupta (Chapter 14) for instance, writes of a sort of love, or at least affection, expressed for the colonial past by the tourists in Mozambique, with all of its abilities to obscure and silence. A similar, though less destructive nostalgia, this time for a romanticized idyll is also explored by Harrison (Chapter 13) in her work on Canadian men escaping to their rural cottages in Ontario.

Paul Fussell (1980) writes of the 'romance' of travel as almost a euphemism for lust and sex. In his words (p. 113): 'Making love in novel environments, free from the censorship and inhibitions of the familiar, is one of the headiest experiences travel promises.' The holiday romance, holiday infatuation, and holiday casual sex are of course dimensions to any consideration of love within a tourism context and an often undisclosed part of the *a priori* motivation to travel. As Simoni in Chapter 15 explores, in his ethnography of dancing in Cuba, this is where 'seduction' comes into play as the mechanism which playfully offers promise of sensation and satisfaction. Both Simoni, and Little (Chapter 16), discuss the complexities of seduction and emotional sensations and the power that bodily encounters and 'out of place' feelings come together in a place or moment for the tourist.

While tourists may not wish to experience sadness within a general framework of joy, they nonetheless encounter, and indeed can court, objects and occasions which can induce the emotion of 'sadness'. Again, there is panoply of associated feelings attached to the emotion of sadness ranging from those associated with suffering, to acute and lasting states of depression and despair, to more fleeting notions of disappointment. Feeling disappointed is a common accompaniment to the doing of tourism as the realities of experience fail to match up both to the idealizations of the promotional literature and to one's own imaginations drawn from more innate desires. Disappointment is 'felt' instantaneously and indicated through phrases such as 'my heart sank' or 'it's not how it looked in the brochure' and points to the role of character and experience in the processing of the emotions. The immediacy of feeling correlates to being able to reference such feeling to others, accumulated and remembered from previous experience, as well as to a benchmark of expectation.

While a tourist to the UK for the first time may well feel disappointed with the food, several trips later the feeling of disappointment is capable of being *managed* in a strategic way. Feelings of disappointment may blur with feelings of irritation, frustration and resentment which are related to the emotion of anger. Anger is normally a direct and explicit projection of one's values and expectations of, and on, the world (Solomon 1993), and is rather explicitly a judgement directed toward an object. Though it would seem that anger is far removed from the normative experiences of the tourist, the heightened positive holiday mood along with the economic and emotional investment placed by the tourist can accentuate a sense of anger directed toward anyone who, for whatever reason, disturbs the frame of expectation. In recent years, reported incidents of angry tourists appears to have increased (though this may have something to do with the ubiquity of recording devices, the 'spectacle' of argument and the rise of the litigious society) and there are frequent media reports of 'angry' tourists annoyed at delayed or cancelled flights,[17] 'angry' tourists who have been refused entry to attractions,[18] and even 'angry' tourists who have attacked tour guides.[19]

A feeling of disappointment can also refer to the whole of a holiday where the overall expectation of joy is challenged by a *series* of disappointments. The pleasure of being on holiday is confronted by incidents outside of control of the tourist such as the intervention of bad weather or, the unexpected closure of a

---

17   For instance, the *Hong Kong Standard* carried a story in February 2011 about seventy angry Chinese Mainland tourists holding an overnight protest in Hong Kong International Airport because of a five hour delay back to Beijing. See: http://www.thestandard.com.hk/news_detail.asp?pp_cat=11&art_id=107887&sid=31220889&con_type=3 – accessed March 2011.

18   According to the Peru daily newspaper, El Comercio, hundreds of tourists were 'visibly' angry at having been denied access to Machu Picchu. See: 'Angry Tourists not allowed into Machu Picchu' by David Schneider, http://www.inside-peru.com/angry-tourists-not-allowed-into-machu-picchu.html – accessed May 2011.

19   According to the *Global Times*, 11 February 2011, Chinese mainland tourists attacked their Hong Kong guide after complaints of deception and price hiking. See: http://opinion.globaltimes.cn/chinese-press/2011-04/621689.html – accessed April 2011.

monument. In retrospect holidays are evaluated[20] and the process of reflection makes use of an emotional calculus which in essence tries to make sense of the variation in the scope and intensity of the emotions experienced over the holiday period. The strongest emotions are those which tend to be remembered, not just as an event but in terms of a recollection of the feeling induced by that event.[21] There are some tourist attractions / destinations which are inscribed with a sadness more in terms of grief, sorrow, hurt and remorse. Sites and markers of death, disaster and varying degrees of atrocity, would be expected to generate an emotional response of sadness beyond the more passive affect of being 'disappointed'. Pichel (2011, p. 206) refers, for instance, to the idea of an 'emotional landscape', relating this to the First World War battlefield sites of Verdun in France. This notion of a constructed or 'scaped' geography identifiable with conflict and acts of sadness is intriguing and powerful, though it requires a narrative to convey emotion to those that pass through such spaces, though as noted by Gordon in Chapter 10 with respect to the Second World War sites of France, this narrative is not always officially sanctioned or welcomed.

There is an extensive literature on the construction of what Seaton (2009) terms 'thanotourism' and less precisely what Lennon and Foley (2000) term 'dark tourism'. While such literature does allude to the motivation of tourists to such sites, essentially as a form of romanticized pilgrimage, in the main it side steps the nature and extent of the emotions generated at such sites. It would seem to be common sense to assume *some* emotional impact on the part of the 'visitor' (the tourist not having any monopoly on such sites), but this is not widely understood and marks out an opportunity for further research. A key point which relates to the spectrum of places denoted as sites of death and disaster is that they are heavily mediated and in some cases, designed to elicit an emotional response. In turn the tourist is fully aware of the mediation, indeed, the over-arching formalities of commodification which transforms a building or a landscape into a place of active commemoration. Again it is often the narrative which can be seen to stimulate the emotional response. Thomas Thurnell-Read (2009) in an analysis of young tourists visiting Auschwitz points to a sense of moral obligation to visit the site to learn and understand. He suggests (p. 48) that 'individuals readily speak of their engagement with the site yet do so in the somewhat standardized manner of the meta-narrative of holocaust remembering.' As tourists we arrive at many such sites with our own frame of emotional expectation derived from a collective consciousness and yet we still are effectively left to experience a site personally, which may, or may not, coincide with the collective view. But as Rapson (Chapter 9) discusses in her work on former Nazi concentration camp sites, even with the

---

20   Akin to what Edward Bruner terms 'post-trip narratives'. See E.M. Bruner (1984) *Culture on Tour*, Chicago: University of Chicago Press.

21   The literature on so-called 'adventure tourism' is extensive. For a broad introduction, see for instance, R. Buckley (2009) *Adventure Tourism Management*, London: Butterworth-Heinemann.

accompaniment of a narrative, comprehending the emotional experience may be difficult if not impossible. In counterpoint to the interpreted and sanctioned sites which focus on death, Karpovich (Chapter 11) brings our attention to extant tourist sights which are layered with the tragedy of suicide and as a result draw in the curious visitor by virtue of their association and allow for a more spontaneous emotional attachment.

Whatever its 'scientific' reality, the apparent extreme emotional reaction referred to in the Stendhal syndrome has generated a fascination in tourism studies as a shorthand way of responding to the impact of both the beautiful and the sublime, be it occurring in nature or the world of art. Frequently used in Anglophone tourist discourse to describe beauty in a neoclassical and a romantic sense is the word 'stunning', revealing not only a sense of drama and amazement, but also the idea of shock and bewilderment referring to the surprise of the moment. Surprise represents the difference between expectations and reality, the gap between our assumptions and expectations about worldly events and the way that those events actually turn out. Surprise is a fleeting emotion which, in the tourist context, is frequent and is generally associated with positive feelings. Surprise is implicated in the feelings of disappointment which can lead to anger (for instance, genuine initial surprise that a room in a quality hotel is not clean), but in the main the tourist experience as a whole is premised on the expectation/anticipation of pleasurable difference, indeed novelty and 'sensation seeking' (Lepp and Gibson 2003, 2008; Zuckerman 2007). There is a growing literature on the tourist as searching for novelty in everything from food to entertainment and being physically tested[22] and this would seem to point to the idea of some tourists liking the idea of being 'surprised' when encountering the 'unknown', but within an overall framework of security and against a background of pleasure. Surprise in this sense is structured and heavily mediated.

On cursory inspection the emotion of fear would generally not be associated with tourism. However, again we are confronted with the semantic elasticity associated with the emotions. Fear is generally taken to cover a spectrum of feelings from terror and fright on the one hand, to apprehension and worry on the other. Our understandings of genuine fear are clouded by the *laissez faire* way we use the term and the playful and frequent convention of exaggeration for dramatic effect. In daily discourse we may declare ourselves to be 'horrified' at something we witness but this does not mean that we, ourselves are in a state of fear.

The threat, or promise, of being terrified is a common device actively sought by many tourists almost as a means to test one's own parameters of emotion. In 2011, a new ride was opened at the Fuji-Q Highland amusement park in Japan.[23]

---

22   Surprisingly few researchers in this field go into any detail regarding the emotions of tourists in the context of adventure.

23   See: 'First Look at World's Steepest Roller Coaster' http://www.theaustralian. com.au/travel/news/first-look-at-worlds-steepest-rollercoaster-the-takabisha/story-e6frg8ro-1226092258655 – accessed July 2011.

The so called 'Takabisha' is the world's steepest roller coaster and it plays upon the fact that it will induce fear within those undertaking the 112 second ride. Already the cache of being the steepest roller coaster in the world is attracting tourists, all apparently seeking to be terrified. Technology has facilitated the existence of such a device but Takabisha demonstrates a continuity to be found in the earliest forms of tourism regarding the capacity to frighten. Visits to the great cemeteries and catacombs of Paris and London in the nineteenth century, the freak shows of early fairs and circuses, to the Jack the Ripper guided tours of contemporary London and the phenomenon of 'Dracula tourism' (Light 2007) resonate with constitutive notions of the romantic and the sublime and an apparent innate desire to undergo an embodied experience of fear. Such a desire is clearly not particular to the sphere of tourism but relates to wider social practices such as watching horror movies. Several reflections emerge. First, the power of the promise of fear would seem to represent a point of convergence between what John Caughey (1984) termed the 'real' and the 'imagined' worlds, producing moments of *sensed imagination*. Second, in such cases fear, and the feeling of being afraid, is *a priori* understood to be part of the wider narrative of encounter with the world and 'proven' to be secure and managed; a 'protective frame' to which a person accords to (Apter 1992). The sounds produced by people undertaking a roller coaster rides oscillate between almost indistinguishable shouts and screams of terror and delight. Third, the apparent sense of fear on the part of the tourist is swiftly negated by that of joy.[24]

Explaining the attraction of fear continues to exercise psychologists. On the one hand it is argued that the person is not really in a state of fear but rather is excited by the fear and can exhibit physiological traits similar to those experiencing genuine terror. This implies that the feeling of fear is more imagined than real or, at least that we struggle to differentiate between the two, experientially and also linguistically. On the other hand it is argued that we do indeed experience fear but are willing to undergo the emotion in order to gain satisfaction from the relief when a fearful episode ends. Work by Eduardo Andrade and Joel Cohen (2007) points rather to the ability to experience both positive and negative emotions at the same time. As Andrade and Cohen state (p. 286) 'the most pleasant moments of a particular event may also be the most fearful.' This points to the complexity and fluidity of the emotions and in the context of tourism challenges the idea that we can equate tourists with a simple search for 'pleasure', or a state of joy.

What we may term orchestrated, or staged, 'fear' which can be both produced and performed in tourism is distinct from genuine fears that may be felt within the doing of tourism. These differ in their extent, intensity and modes of expression and are again best conceptualized along a horizon. At one end is the very fear of travel itself. Fear of travelling, or *hodophobia*, is largely taken to be an intense fear of travel conceived of as various distances from outside of the home. Notably, this phobia, as with others, is frequently referred to in the literature as an 'irrational'

---

24 This is observable in the way that tourists recount their experiences often taking particular relish and animation in recalling these moments of fear.

or pathological fear, echoing the positioning of the emotions as somehow *against* reason. While it is the case that such states are not a majority condition, as most psychologists recognize, phobias are, in their own terms a rational response to some form of life trauma, a way of coping with past experience and managing the unknown. Hodophobia covers various fears relating either to a mode of travel or transport (fear of roads, cars, trains and commonly, fear of flying), with varying degrees of physical expression by way of such symptoms as shortness of breath, shaking, excessive sweating, nausea and an inability to articulate words. Extreme hodophobia results in stasis. Being worried about safety while on an aeroplane is not the same as not being prepared to fly at all. Further phobias which if experienced in their most extreme form would effectively prevent travel would be claustrophobia (as the fear of enclosed spaces), agoraphobia (as a fear of open spaces) and acrophobia (as the fear of heights).

At the other end of the emotional scale of fear are a set of feelings which I would suggest are a defining attribute of the tourist condition. These include feelings of anxiety, nervousness, uneasiness and apprehension. While accepting a common sense premise that some people are more at ease with being out of their home environment than others, it would also be fair to assume that a majority of people *work* at being a tourist, in terms of having to cope with the various bodily and mental stresses and strains brought about by encounters with difference. Temporarily living within a different physical and cultural environment generates a series of worries directed not only to the immediacy of the holiday but also to what has been temporarily left behind (loved ones, specific comforts, the security of the home) and what there is to return to (life and work problems). The detailed narrative of a holiday is littered with moments of angst and unease: Can I cope with the language? Will I have enough foreign currency? How much do I tip? Am I on the right train? What if I become ill? Am I being over-charged? Will this food make me ill? Will my baggage be overweight? Etc. Etc. Each moment of worry is countered by a feeling of achievement, a sense of momentary belonging as we negotiate our tourist identity and our normative notion of self. While accepting that there are 'types' of tourism which, through various processes of mediation (guides, couriers, hotel staff, phrase books, iPhones and the like) and standardization (what Jacobsen 2003 terms 'complicated abstract systems'), which seek to reduce tourist angst, even within the so-called tourist 'bubble' (Smith 1977) or 'enclave of familiarity' (Farrall 1979), feelings of apprehension and worry remain.

Concluding Thoughts

Implicit in the above account of the interface between the emotions and the 'being a tourist' is the recognition of the permeable (and often imperceptible) boundaries which do/do not separate tourism from everyday life. Tim Edensor (2009) reminds us that habits and routines of normative daily life, while challenged, contingent and negotiated, are not left behind when we become tourists. And neither are our emotions nor the components of 'character' and life histories which constitute the self we carry with us on holiday. As markers of our own humanity with its inherent frailties, our emotions travel with us. At the same time the act of travel, and the ways in which it exposes our relations with the world and all of its 'others', tests our physical and psychological make-up and, in line with Sartre's conception, our emotions drive us to act, to open up to the world and to transform it and ourselves. This is a far more complex and dynamic understanding of the emotions than that which is implied within Stendhal's account of his own reactions to a particular cultural form. While it is no doubt the case that the sights, sounds, tastes, smells and touch of the world can stimulate our emotions what we feel, how we feel it and importantly, how we comprehend and express what we feel, is far more complex. As tourists we have moments of joy, moments of sadness, anger and fear (and much angst), often fleeting, often within close proximity of each other; emotions we would not have experienced had we not travelled. But we also bring our emotions to bear upon the world; our own histories and understandings of encounter.

As I made note of at the outset of this chapter, if we seek to better understand the tourist we need to allow for the role that the emotions play in the processes of becoming, being, doing, performing and recalling. However, focusing in on the way that emotions are implicated in the tourist world would seem to be methodologically challenging and there would seem to be a need for more psychologists to direct their empirical attention toward the tourist condition. Yet even with psychology, there are significant problems relating to semantic imprecision, measurement and assessment. This is understandable, for as I have tried to demonstrate, any consideration of the emotions brings into play an expanse of hyper-complex and slippery variables relating to environment, culture, language, learning and memory. This said it is nevertheless rewarding to consider the emotional dimensions of tourism conceptually at the very least.

The tourism sector, now as a sophisticated, globally inter-connected series of sites, routes and entertainments, has learned the language of emotions as a way of motivating, connecting with, and managing tourists. In recognition of the fear of flying, airlines go through a series of rituals (safety drill, the playing of music and various entertaining distractions) to allay fear and to counter the irrational. Emotionally charged narratives weave and in out of the promotional texts for destinations and attractions promising some degree of emotional connection, the attainment of 'positive' emotional states and escape from 'negative' states. Even the negative states are projected as positive experiences, desires are directed and opportunities offered to empathize. The scripts of guides and guide books are no longer neutral descriptive texts of historical facts and visible features but rather they appeal to the emotional lives of others. Events are dramatized through the eyes of a person – factual or fictional – in order to invoke the feelings that may have been *felt*, and such feelings are conveyed to a tourist audience increasingly attuned to an emotional world and armed with the reflexive ability to move between the real and the imaginary.

Narrative theory is somewhat helpful here in understanding the ways in which the tourism sector 'plays' a sort of emotional game with tourists. Just as in reading literary fiction, characters are portrayed, their emotions revealed and concealed by the writer and appraised and re-appraised by the reader to induce a reaction and maintain interest in the text. The emotions on display in a novel resonate with our own to the extent that we can get angry or sad merely by the text while still knowing that we are only consuming the imagination of the writer. But the tourist also seems to engage in emotional game playing too. Post-trip narratives are littered with our re-inventions of our emotions. In retrospect we almost joyously describe our fear or disgust directed to a situation. We struggle for descriptive precision, we conflate different feelings, elongate the moments in which we felt angry or sad, and exaggerate the intensity of affect.

All of this points to importance of the emotions, the folly of a wholly rational approach to the world and indeed the inevitability of some degree of emotional engagement, which as Sartre tells us, is 'magical' in the sense that emotion allows us intentionally apprehend the world and transform it. 'Emotion' he writes (p. 61), 'is not an accident, it is a mode of our conscious existence, one of the ways in which consciousness understands its Being-in-the-World.' And being a tourist (at least in the context of the modern developed world) is an important way of understanding and validating our being in the world.

References

Adler, J. (1989) 'Origins of Sightseeing', *Annals of Tourism Research*, 16(1), pp. 7–29.

Andrade, E.B. and Cohen, J.B. (2007) 'On the Consumption of Negative Feelings', *Journal of Consumer Research*, 34 (October), pp. 283–300.

Apter, Michael J. (1992) *The Dangerous Edge: The Psychology of Excitement*, New York: Free Press.

Aristotle (1984) *The Rhetoric and Poetics of Aristotle*, New York: McGraw-Hill.

Aristotle (2004) *The Nichomachean Ethics*, trans. J.A.K. Thomson. London: Penguin Classics.

Badhwar, N.K. (2003) '*Love*', in LaFollette', H. (ed.) *Practical Ethics*, Oxford: Oxford University Press, pp. 42–69.

Bamberg, M. (1987) *The Acquisition of Narratives*, Berlin: Mouton de Gruyter.

Bamberg, M. (1997a) 'Emotion Talk(s). The Role of Perspective in the Construction of Emotions', in S. Niemeier and R. Dirven (eds), *The Language of Emotions*, Amsterdam: John Benjamins, pp. 209–225.

Bamberg, M. (1997b) 'Language, Concepts and Emotions: The Role of Language in the Construction of Emotions', *Language Sciences*, 19, pp. 309–340.

Baranowski, S. (2004) *Strength Through Joy. Consumerism and Mass Tourism in the Third Reich*, Cambridge: Cambridge University Press.

Beedie, C.J., Terry, P.C. and Lane, A.M. (2005) 'Distinctions Between Emotion and Mood', *Cognition and Emotion*, 19, pp. 847–878.

Bochner, Stephen (2003) 'Culture Shock Due to Contact with Unfamiliar Cultures'. *Online Readings in Psychology and Culture, Unit 8*. Retrieved from *http://scholarworks.gvsu.edu/orpc/vol8/iss1/7*

Booker, C. (2005) *The Seven Basic Plots: Why We Tell Stories*, London: Continuum.

Bruner, E.M. (2005) *Culture on Tour*, Chicago: University of Chicago Press.

Bruner, E.M. (1984) 'Introduction: The Opening Up of Anthropology', in Bruner, E.M., *Text, Play and Story: The Construction and Reconstruction of Self and Society*, Prospect Heights, IL: Waveland Press Inc., pp. 1–16.

Buckley, R. (2009) *Adventure Tourism Management*, London: Butterworth-Heinemann.

Camus, A. (1999) *The Stranger*, trans. Robert Ward, New York: Alfred A. Knopf.

Caughey, J.L. (1984) *Imaginary Social Worlds: A Cultural Approach*, Lincoln: University of Nebraska Press.

Chard, C. (2002) 'Lassitude and Revival in the Warm South: Relaxing and Exciting Travel', 1750–1830, in R. Wrigley and G. Revill, G. (eds), *Pathologies of Travel*, Amsterdam: Rodopi, pp. 179–205.

Damasio, A. (1994) *Descartes' Error: Emotion, Reason, and the Human Brain*, New York: Putnam.

Edensor, T. (2009) 'Tourism and Performance', in T. Jamal and M. Robinson (eds), *The SAGE Handbook of Tourism Studies*, London: Sage, pp. 543–557.

Ekman, P. (1994) *The Nature of Emotion: Fundamental Questions*, New York: Oxford University Press.

Ellsworth, P.C. (1994) 'Levels of Thought and Light Levels of Emotion', in P. Ekman and R. Davidson (eds), *The Nature of Emotion*, New York: Oxford University Press, pp. 192–196.

Emmons, R. (2005) 'Emotion and Religion', in R.F. Paloutzian and C.L. Park, *Handbook of the Psychology of Religion and Spirituality*, New York: Guilford Press, pp. 235–252.

Farber, M.E. and Hall, T.E. (2007) 'Emotion and Environment: Visitors' Extraordinary Experiences Along the Dalton Highway in Alaska', *Journal of Leisure Research*, 39(2), pp. 248–270.

Farrell, B.H. (1979) 'Tourism's Human Conflicts', *Annals of Tourism Research*, 6, pp. 122–136.

Freud, S. (1935) *A General Introduction to Psychoanalysis*, New York: Simon and Schuster.

Frijda, N.H. (1986) *The Emotions*, Cambridge: Cambridge University Press.

Frijda, N.H. (1993) 'The Place of Appraisal in Emotion', *Cognition and Emotion*, 7, pp. 357–387.

Frijda, N.H. (1988) 'The Laws of Emotion', *American Psychologist*, 43, pp. 349–358.

Furnham, A. and Bochner, S. (1982) 'Social Difficulty in a Foreign Culture: An Empirical Analysis of Culture Shock', in S. Bochner (ed.), *Culture in Contact*, New York: Pergamon, pp. 161–198.

Fussell, P. (1980) *Abroad: British Literary Travelling Between the Wars*, Oxford: Oxford University Press.

Gnoth, J. (1997) 'Tourism Motivation and Expectation Formation', *Annals of Tourism Research*, 24(2), pp. 283–304.

Goldie, P. (2009) *The Emotions: A Philosophical Exploration*, Oxford: Oxford University Press.

Goossens, C. (2000) 'Tourism Information and Pleasure Motivation'. *Annals of Tourism Research*, 27(2), pp. 301–321.

Gross, D.M. (2006) *The Secret History of Emotion: From Aristotle's Rhetoric to Modern Brain Science*, Chicago: Chicago University Press.

Hallett, R.W. and Kaplan-Weinger, J. (2010) *Official Tourism Websites: A Discourse Analysis Perspective*, Clevedon: Channel View Publications.

Heelas, P. (1986) 'Emotion Talk Across Cultures', in R. Harré (ed.), *The Social Construction of Emotions*, Oxford: Basil Blackwell, pp. 234–266.

Hosany, S. (2011) 'Appraisal Determinants of Tourist Emotional Responses', *Journal of Travel Research*, XX(X), pp. 1–12.

Irwin, R. (2007) 'Culture Shock: Negotiating Feelings in the Field', *Anthropology Matters*, 9(1). Accessed at http://www.nomadit.net/ojs/index. php?journal=anth_matters&page=article&op=viewArticle&path%5B%5D=6 4&path%5B%5D=123 – November 2010.

Izard, C.E. (1977) *Human Emotions*, New York: Plenum Press.

Izard, C.E. (2007) 'Basic Emotions, Natural Kinds, Emotion Schemas, and a New Paradigm', *Perspective on Psychological Science*, 2, pp. 260–280.

Izard, C.E. (1991) *The Psychology of Emotions*, New York: Plenum Press.

Jacobsen J. (2003) 'The Tourist Bubble and the Europeanisation of Holiday Travel', *Journal of Tourism and Cultural Change*, 1(1), pp. 71–87.

Lazarus R.S. (1991) *Emotion and Adaptation*, New York: Oxford University Press.

Lennon, J. and Foley, M. (2000) *Dark Tourism*, London: Continuum.

Lepp, A. and Gibson, H. (2003) 'Tourist Roles, Perceived Risk and International Tourism', *Annals of Tourism Research*, 30, pp. 606–624.

Lepp, A. and Gibson, H. (2008) 'Sensation Seeking and Tourism: Tourist Role, Perception of Risk and Destination Choice', *Tourism Management*, 29(4), pp. 740–750.

Light, D. (2007) 'Dracula Tourism in Romania. Cultural Identity and the State', *Annals of Tourism Research*, 34(3), pp. 746–765.

Lutz, C. and White, G.M. (1986) 'The Anthropology of Emotions', *Annual Review of Anthropology*, 15, pp. 405–436.

MacCannell, D. (1976) *The Tourist: A New Theory of the Leisure Class*, New York: Schocken.

MacCannell, D. (2011) *The Ethics of Sight-Seeing*, Berkeley: University of California Press.

Magherini, G. (1989) *La Sindrome di Stendhal*, Firenze: Ponte Alle Grazie.

Massumi, B. (1987) 'Introduction – Notes on Translation', in G. Deleuze and F. Guattari, *A Thousand Plateaus*, Minneapolis: University of Minnesota Press.

Matsumoto, D. (1994) *People. Psychology from a Cultural Perspective.* Pacific Grove, CA: Brooks/Cole Publishing.

Musil, R. (1997) *The Man without Qualities,* trans. Sophie Wilkins. London: Picador.

Oatley, K. (1992) *Best Laid Schemes: The Psychology of the Emotions,* New York: Cambridge University Press.

Oberg, K. (1960) 'Culture Shock: Adjustment to New Cultural Environments', *Practical Anthropology,* 7, pp. 177–182.

Ortony, A., and Turner, T.J. (1990) 'What's Basic About Basic Emotions?' *Psychological Review,* 97, pp. 315–331.

Ousby, I. (1990) *The Englishman's England: Taste, Travel and the Rise of Tourism,* Cambridge: Cambridge University Press.

Park, H.Y. (2010) 'Heritage Tourism: Emotional Journeys into Nationhood', *Annals of Tourism Research,* 37(1), pp. 116–135.

Parrott, W. (2001) *Emotions in Social Psychology,* Philadelphia, PA: Psychology Press.

Pichel, B. (2011) 'Making Sense of Verdun: Photography and Emotions During the First World War in France', in B. Hogue and A. Sugiyama (eds), *Making Sense of Suffering: Theory, Practice, Representation,* Oxford: Inter-Disciplinary Press, pp. 203–213.

Ricoeur, P. (1995) *Figuring the Sacred: Religion, Narrative and Imagination,* trans. David Pellauer, Minneapolis: Augsburg Fortress.

Robinson, J. (2005) *Deeper than Reason: Emotion and its Role in Literature, Music and Art,* Oxford: Oxford University Press.

Rojek, C. and Urry, J. (1997) *Touring Cultures: Trans-formations of Travel and Theory,* London: Routledge.

Rorty, A.O. (1980) 'Introduction', in A.O. Rorty (ed.), *Explaining Emotions,* Berkeley: University of California Press, pp. 1–8.

Salazar, N. (2010) *Envisioning Eden: Mobilizing Imaginaries in Tourism and Beyond,* New York: Berghahn.

Sartre, J.P. (2002) *Sketch for a Theory of Emotions,* London: Routledge.

Seaton, A. (2009) 'Thanatourism and its Discontents: An Appraisal of a Decade's Work With Some Future Issues and Directions', in T. Jamal and M. Robinson, M. (eds), *The SAGE Handbook of Tourism Studies,* London: Sage, pp. 521–542.

Shaver, P., Schwartz, J., Kirson, D. and O'Connor, C. (1987) 'Emotion Knowledge: Further Exploration of a Prototype Approach', *Journal of Personality and Social Psychology,* 52(6), pp. 1061–1086.

Smith, V.L. (1977) 'Introduction', in V.L. Smith (ed.), *Hosts and Guests: The Anthropology of Tourism,* Philadelphia: University of Pennsylvania Press, pp. 1–14.

Solomon, R.C. (1993) *The Passions: Emotions and the Meaning of Life,* Indianapolis/Cambridge: Hackett Publishing Company.

Solomon, R.C. (2008) 'The Philosophy of Emotions', in M. Lewis, J.M. Haviland-Jones and L.F. Barrett (eds), *Handbook of Emotions* (3rd edn), New York: Guilford Press, pp. 3–16.

Stearns, C.Z. and Stearns, P.N. (1988) *Emotion and Social Change*, New York: Holmes and Meier.

Stendhal (1960) *Rome, Naples, and Florence*, trans. Richard N. Coe, London: John Calder.

Thurlow, C. and Jaworski, A. (2011) 'Tourism Discourse: Languages and Banal Globalization', in L. Wei (ed.), *Applied Linguistics Review*, Berlin: Walter de Groyter, pp. 285–312.

Thurnell-Read, T. (2009) 'Engaging Auschwitz: An Analysis of Young Traveler's Experiences of Holocaust Tourism', *Journal of Tourism Consumption and Practice*, 1(1), pp. 26–52.

Tribe, J. (2006) 'The Truth About Tourism', *Annals of Tourism Research*, 33(2), pp. 360–381.

Tuan, Y. (1993) *Passing Strange and Wonderful: Aesthetics, Nature and Culture*, New York: Kodansha International.

Urry, J. (2002) *The Tourist Gaze* (2nd edn), London: Sage.

Weber, M. (2001) *The Protestant Work Ethic and the Spirit of Capitalism*, London: Routledge.

Wierzbicka, A. (1994) 'Emotion, Language, and Cultural Scripts', in S. Kitayama and H.R. Markus (eds), *Emotion and Culture*, Washington, DC: American Psychological Association, pp. 133–196.

Zuckerman, M. (2007) *Sensation Seeking and Risky Behavior*, American Psychological Association.

PART I
Emotions and Inner Journeys

Chapter 3

The Dark is on the Inside: The *honne* of Japanese Exploratory Tourists

Nelson Graburn[1]

Dark Tourism is the act of travel to sites of death, disaster and the seemingly macabre ... Learn more about the 'darker side of tourism' by visiting The Dark Tourism Forum at www.dark-tourism.org.uk

Philip Stone (26 Feb, 2007)

'Many travelers are Dark Tourists drawn to sites of devastation and destruction, suffering and trauma: Ground Zero, Kennedy's assassination site, battlefields, concentration camps, and places associated with atrocities, and the like. Such "thanatourism" has a long history ...' Jonathan Skinner and Carl Thompson, Call for Papers for 'Travel and Trauma: Suffering and the Journey – An Interdisciplinary Colloquium.'

(11–12 April, 2008, St. John's College, Oxford)

Introduction: Souls and Journeys

The idea that humans have a self, a human spirit that is separable from the human body has been around as long as we know of human culture. It is a central tenet of all animistic (spirit-bearing) views of the world, as well as world religions such as Buddhism, Islam and Christianity. The long-term fate of the spiritual self – which

---

1   An earlier version of this chapter was presented at the Interdisciplinary Colloquium 'Travel and Trauma: Suffering and the Journey', organized by the Nottingham Trent Centre for Travel Writing Studies, Nottingham Trent Univ. and the Centre for Research on Nationalism, Ethnicity and Multiculturalism (CRONEM) University of Surrey, held at St John's College, Oxford, 11–12 April, 2008. A revised version was presented at the conference 'Emotion in Motion: The Passions of Tourism, Travel and Movement', Leeds Metropolitan University, 4–7 July 2009. I extend my thanks to Maki Tanaka, Dr Yuko Okubo and Dr Kensuke Sumii, all of University of California, Berkeley, for assisting in the search for and interpretation of these data. I also wish to thank Mio Kitayama (University of California, Berkeley) and Dr Valerio and Hisako Simoni (Lisbon University Institute, Portugal) for their helpful critical reading of a later draft of this chapter.

we may call the *'soul' 'seele' 'l'*âme*' 'alma' 'inua' 'línghún'* 靈魂, *'tamashii'* 魂, *'anima'* [i.e. the animated, live, moving one] – is not identical in different cosmologies. It is said, for instance, that in Homeric times, the Greeks believed that the self died and was buried with the body and the individual but *personless soul*, left for ever; but by Platonic times the opposite was expressed, that one could kill and bury a body, but never capture a soul, because it was a 'free spirit' that could choose to remain near earth (and the body) or move away.

The earliest anthropology drew upon these beliefs. Edmund Tylor (1871) proposed an evolution of religion in which the earliest religion, he called animism, was the belief that all beings, including many of what we would call inanimate objects, had souls and were sentient, and often able to communicate with other beings of different species. Tylor used the widespread evidence of belief in dreams, when the soul leaves the sleeping body and travels and encounters its own experiences which are expressed as dreams. Thus the idea that the self has a separate existence from the body is almost universal. And bodies travel through life as on a journey, undergoing growth and changes according to hormones and external influences. At the same time the self, the spirit also has a life, which is marked by changes in status, often expressed as rites of passage (Van Gennep 1909), but the trajectory of that life is neither material nor does it end in the same fate as the physical body.

In early accounts travel, in Japan as in the West, we find that the animate self accompanies the body, but is capable of having its own ideas and feelings which may not necessarily be expressed at the time, and it is also capable of travelling in time away from the place of travel, as, for instance, when a travelling experience takes one back to one's youth or childhood, or forces one to face the 'unknown future'. Thus in life, as in ritual and in touristic travel, we have come to use the expressions 'the inner journey' of the self and the 'outer' or geographical physical journey of the body.

Inner and Outer Journeys in Tourism

Nancy Frey's book *Pilgrim Stories* (1998) about the religious and secular experiences of travellers along the Camino de Santiago, has best examined the relation of the two kinds of journey, following on the original formulation by Myerhoff (1974). Frey talked intimately with these Caministas in the days and the evenings, on the road and in the hostels, or even in Santiago itself and again after their return to their home countries (Frey 2004). She was able to discern their often vivid inner lives as they related the challenges of long distance walking with the struggles in their lives, and the relation of the landscape to their inner thoughtscape. In a very rich set of analytic descriptions, she shows us that even today's secular travellers may have spiritual lives as active as the supposedly religious pilgrims of the past.

Moore and Myerhoff (1977), like Frey, have taken seriously the concept of 'secular ritual'. They took the same stance that I suggested in my original essay on 'Tourism: the Sacred Journey' (1977). I was not trying to state that tourism is sacred in any orthodox religious sense, but I was suggesting that the kind of embodied feelings, attachments and identities that used to apply to religious beliefs, persons and objects, can now be found directed towards other phenomena such as 'nature', certain animals (whales, mountain lions) and 'noble savages', historical places and relics. According to Judith Adler (2006) there may be a direct historical connection between spiritual pilgrimages and the emergence of the wilderness ('nature') as the object of sacred travel, which started in the Holy Lands in the 2nd and 3rd centuries AD.

Japanese Travel Experiences

My chapter is an initial attempt to see if one can explore Japanese tourists' inner journeys for implicit or explicit comparison. Japanese culture is said (e.g. Benedict 1946) to foreground a surface of culturally and situationally appropriate expressions, *tatemae*, but to securely conceal the *honne*, that is personal and hence selfish experiences and desires, thus the challenge. I hypothesize that Japanese people might find it easier to express their inner feelings while away on a journey, far from the gaze and strictures of their home group or frame (Nakane 1971); indeed there is a saying that '*tabi no haji wa kakisute*' – 'when away on a trip [one's] shame is wiped away'. The only other situation where inner thoughts and desires may be expressed without shame is when drunk (Moeran 1986), another 'altered state of consciousness' or, in slang, a 'trip'. As one of the Japanese travellers discussed in this chapter said: 'During the trip … I met myself who did things I wouldn't dream of otherwise' (Oga 1974).

The data are preliminary. I have tried to avoid Japanese commentary by 'experts' though I have elsewhere made a study of Japanese 'theories of travel' (Graburn 2006). Much of the data come from travelogue and blogs, and anecdotes of my own experiences and those of acquaintances in Japan.

Two Kinds of Travel

Essayist Kenji Muro (1974) comments that there are two main types of Japanese travel:

> It seems that in Japan there is social group travel and there is travel (*tabi*) for feeling lonely (*sabishii*) (it would be a mistake to say that it is only Japan). If 'travel for feeling lonely' is not appropriate, then travel to seek a way/a road (道を求める旅), travel in search of truth (*kyūdō no tabi* 求道の旅), *haiku*-style travel, travel where you see the shadow projected by the outer scenery onto your

inner self, life-seeking travel. It is usually an individual travel (*hitori tabi*) or with a small group (*shōninzū no ryokō*).[2]

Muro recalls the name of the prototypical Japanese poet-traveller Bashō Matsuo, whose 'Narrow roads to the Interior' *Oku no Hoshomichi* (1670) is mostly about travelling to the interior (*naimen* 内面 = inner surface) where the reality is projected; rather than travelling into the geographical interior, or into the real world. It is a solitary journey (*tabi*), regardless of the number of people one is travelling with.Muro contrasts this well-known kind of travel, to another style of 'Japanese travel' and says: If the former travel (*tabi*) contains echoes of a kind of sadness, then this [other] travel is a group travel (*dantai ryokō*), *enkai* [party]-style, with boisterous merrymaking. Company trips and the current group tours by Japanese all over the world belong to this type. Yanagita Kunio traces this kind of travel to pilgrimage (1931) – as I have (Graburn 1983). Muro continues:

> These days, package tours overseas of this kind have brought issues of behaviours ignoring or harming the local life. The Japanese newspapers are reporting on them and easily employing the word *hansei* (reflection). However, if such a style of travelling (*ryokō*) did not emerge all of a sudden but has a long history in our culture, then it will not be more than temporary comfort to talk about reflection.

Initially we could take these two styles of travel as paralleling John Urry's (1989) famous categorization of tourism into: first, the Romantic where the traveller revels in being away from the home context, enjoying alterity, vs. the Collective where the self is submerged in the common social group as at home.

On contemporary travel, Muro comments:

> Every day, many Japanese leave for a foreign country for business and sightseeing. However, sometimes I seriously think that Japanese can never travel (*ryokō*) outside of this 'unbroken descent line' of their island country ... i.e. that they are 'in Japan' wherever they happen to travel.

Thus it is on the lonely, reflective, creative or spiritually purposeful kind of travel that we will concentrate, as it is here that we can reveal the inner self, the *naimen*, the inner surface, which we may oppose to the more 'socially conventional' *tatemae*, the outer surface of conformity.

---

2   Readers Valerio and Hisako Simoni commented (personal communication, 2009) that though seeking travel is usually alone, not all single travellers are 'seeking'. They suggest that, following Wang (1999), such travellers may be seeking intra- or inter-personal authenticity.

Discoveries of the Inner Journey

Accounts by men and women, travelling – usually overseas – in the past few decades, reveal two overwhelming reflexive concerns. Again quoting Muro (1974): 'Also, in [the poet] Bashō's travel, death looms prominently. No, not only in his case, but "Japanese travel" and death have a profound connection. The words and images of travel and death are intensely tied together in the Japanese language.' He cites Bashō with a quotation from *Oku no Hosomichi.*

> Our culture did not have methods to migrate from one place, one country to another; perhaps sometimes there was an emergence of such a culture, but was soon snipped off. For us, travel and movement did not indicate a bright and strong image, a constructive image, but a poetic one coupled with "death". Boldly put, this may be because of anxiety that "I may die in a place other than where I was born", and if so, there will be no "place for the soul to go back to" after death, making the soul drift somewhere.

As an aside I note here that in those days the concern was how the soul would find its way home. For contemporary travellers the anxiety is how to get the body home!

A blogger who called herself Nomura Tsuma [wife] (2003) wrote:

> It is often said that in Japan 'death is set apart from life (*seikatsu*),' and I must agree. I may not feel the shadow of death in everyday life particularly because I was born and raised in Tokyo. When young and thinking about marriage and having kids as I am now, it is natural to live day to day thinking that death has nothing to do with us. Every time death suddenly befalls someone close, I get terrified and I have a hard time regaining peace of mind, or it seems long before I find myself in control again.

She came to this statement after describing her visit to Oaxaca on the Day of the Dead and how it brought her mind back to an equally death-associated experience in Varanasi, India. And this in turn, reminded her of a visit to Auschwitz. She went on:

> I thought 'why didn't I think about war? I haven't had education about war'.[3] Now I feel 'I haven't had education regarding death'. It's not that I am blaming the Japanese education, but I think we hadn't sufficiently thought about death. Since I was a student, Kübler-Ross's book *The Moment of Death* has been popular, and Ross recently has had her autobiography published, perhaps there are more people willing to think about death these days. Whatever advancement

---

3   Many Japanese and foreigners complain that Japan fails to teach its children about World War II for reasons of shame and dissonance (Ashworth and Hartman 2005).

science and technology makes, the reason for human death is obscure, and the pain caused by someone's death is enormous, and we are all going to die. In Europe, there are places where 'death education' is incorporated in children's education; I think something like that is necessary. I would like to have more information not only about how to live, but about how to die. If only Tokyo had something where one can feel 'death' in festivals every year like Oaxaca.[4] I think we could maintain our mental/spiritual balance (*kokoro no baransu*).

Another frequent traveller, a woman who had her baby on a beach in India, said:

> I sit next to my daughter. You are called death. Since I began nurturing you, you became stronger, and you came to show your figure clearly. Your becoming rich is the richness of my life. Please light me up by your legitimate light. I wish, on the day when I am released beyond the graffiti-ed stars together [in death], we will be received by the gentle hands we remember from long time ago.

Travel blogger, Ogura (2004) brought this theme of death together with the other major theme of inner journeys, the discovery of the nature of 'self' via alterity, often with negative consequences for Japanese overseas. Ogura, after describing the shock of being seen 'as Japanese':

> When did I first notice that Korean poems often talked about me?

> It was probably when I was travelling Kangwon Do. It was a trip (*tabi*) of disappointment ... It comes from the fact that I am 'Japanese' ... 'Japanese + male'. This is nothing but a negative sign of 'absolute evil'. There was no way to run away from this simplified equation.

He went on to describe a murderous fantasy:

> I went mountain climbing – trekking. I saw a father and a daughter walking in front of me. The daughter was about ten years old. She held her father's hand, talking to him cheerfully, and hiking energetically. One picture depicting happiness of ordinary Korean people on a Sunday. It was at that moment that I got obsessed with an idea. Somehow I came in between the father and the daughter, and pulled apart their hands that held each other.
> I was a being that deranged and destroyed these people's peace and happiness. A being that bore the 'guilt' fully. It was as if I had lost my mind in the obsession.

---

4   Reader Mio Kitayama (personal communication, 2009) pointed out: 'Japan has Obon, which I understood to be something like the Day of the Dead in Mexico. It's a week during August when the spirits of dead ancestors come back, so we celebrate with dances and food ... I guess this person from Tokyo didn't participate in this Japanese tradition? Such traditions tend to be more intact in rural areas.'

I defined myself precisely as a 'disturbing subject'. I had to but live the imperial nature of the very existence of 'myself'. The imperialism named 'I' desired to destroy 'Korea'. 'I' was an evil desire.

The author Murakami Haruki also gets fixated on a past military adventure of Japan in Asia, on the Nomonhan War (the 'Second Russian-Japanese War', summer 1939). Since childhood he fantasized about the battle, and eventually visited the old site in Mongolia.

> I came to understand, albeit vaguely, something like the reason for my intense attraction to this war. That is, the history of this war may have been, in some ways, 'too Japan-like and too Japanese-like'. ... The most important thing is that in Nomonhan or in New Guinea, most soldiers died an insignificant death. They were killed extremely inefficiently as nameless and expendable supplies within a tightly sealed organization called Japan. And this 'inefficiency' or irrationality may be called Asianness.

He described his travels by air, train and automobile. He saw the remnants of fortresses of the Japanese and Russian sides. He mentions the shocking site of shrapnel, bullets and cans still scattered in the field. He picks up some of them as mementos of the scene. Then his Mongolian guides find a wolf on the way back, and shoot it – as if it was their instinct.

Afterwards:

> The hotel I stayed in Choibalsan, Mongolia, was better than many a worthless hotel that I stayed all over the world. But I could not fall asleep. When I woke up in the middle of the night, *it* was shaking the world vigorously. The whole room was vibrating up and down as if forcefully shaken in a shaker. In the complete darkness where I could not even see my hand, every single thing was wobbling and rattling. I had no idea what had happened, what was happening, but I tried to jump out of bed and turned on the light. I could not even stand on the floor because of the tremor. I couldn't remember where the light switch was in the first place. I staggered and fell, and got up by holding onto the bed frame. It must be an enormous earthquake, I thought. It was an earthquake vigorous enough to tear the world apart. Anyhow, I should leave this place – I did not know how long it took. I reached the door frantically, and felt for the light switch. The tremor stopped that moment. When the light was turned on and darkness was gone, the room all of a sudden fell silent. Unbelievably, there was not a sound. Nothing was shaking. The clock was indicating it was 2:30 in the morning. I could not make out what it was all about.
>
> Then it struck me. What was shaking was not the room, not the world, but myself. When I realized it, my body got cold to the bones. I stood there without the senses of my limbs ... The wolf, shrapnel, and the war museum in the

blackout, and everything else were in the end just part of myself, weren't they? Perhaps they were just waiting there for me to discover them.

This realization that the journey and the reality resides within oneself, whether good or evil, is a theme among many of these accounts: We have already noted how Muro wrote 'about travelling the interior (*naimen* 内面) where the reality is projected' for those engaged in solitary, purposive or '*haiku*' travel. Oga is very concerned with travel as means of revealing her bare self, her basic humanity:

> If I talk about 'I', I am only talking about the eye that sees the mind that experiences various conditions. That eye easily gets bored by the continuing state of the mind, and becomes the desire for knowing the unknown. ... As I turn more inwardly, it becomes harder to believe individual originality. 'I' surely belong to the humankind, but am not male or female. I have no idea where that energy would take me, but I'd like to know the destination.
>
> That I actually went on a trip, left Japan, was probably prompted by my impatience with myself at the time. I ... Although it was stifling me without my knowledge. Almost recklessly, instinctively, I chose the way for 'I' to survive. By placing myself in an unknown location, unknown people, I attempted to awaken 'I' that was dull. Essentially, even in the same location, surrounded by the same people, as long as there is time, every moment is necessarily a journey (*tabi*).
>
> The place names, locations, and other details of my journey are forgotten quickly. In the end, what remains is a solid feeling of experience that settled in my body unconsciously. That, perhaps, may explain what I am now ... I think travel (*tabi*) is about expanding the mind by actual feelings through placing oneself in various environments and situations. If 'I' is the energy geared towards the unknown world, then I will be travelling. Necessarily, through actual travel, it is in the end the travel of consciousness. Also, I have doubts over consciousness that was developed without repeated realization that the whole life exists within a journey (*tabi*). It is not an ideal, so only experience can expand one's mind. Changing one's consciousness, knowing oneself, is very enjoyable ... As long as I continue this journey, I will be able to go forward at some point. I would like to be able to grasp not the 'I' in myself but I that is around 'I'.

And after his nightmare episode in Mongolia, Murakami concludes:

> That – the tremor, darkness, fear and sign – did not suddenly come from outside, but had existed inside of me. *Something* grabbed an opportunity and pried it open. Just as one old photo of the Nomonhan War that I saw in a book in primary school had captivated me without obvious reasons and guided me to the hinterland of the Mongolian plain thirty something years later. It took me to a very far place. However, although I cannot explain very well, however

far I travelled, or farther I venture, what we discover there is only going to be ourselves.

Taka, travelling in Thailand in 2006, reminisced about how travel loosened the self from time:

As I look at a map of the world, various memories crop up. It is very different from how I look at maps usually. As the plane goes forward, my thoughts go backward. When I arrived in Thailand, I almost thought that I reached myself of a year and a half ago. Many things happened since then, and my mental state had ups and downs. I never thought that I would have these feelings just by flying. Returning to Thailand, to Japan is, perhaps not consciously, very significant. Poignant (*setsunai*) and lonesome (*sabishii*), I realize how much time I have spent in travelling (*idō*).

And we have already seen how Nomura Tsuma (2004) found that one travelling experience of 'death' took her back to another, and then in turn further into the past, to Auschwitz.

A well-known 'institutionalized' version of this anxiety is known as the 'Paris-Syndrome' (Viala et al. 2004), described by French psychiatrists as a kind of culture shock, with physical symptoms such as hyperventilation, rapid heartbeat and even fainting. It is reported to be more prevalent among Japanese than other international tourists; it can be brought on by stresses such as misunderstanding a foreign culture, language or menus and food, or faced with an excess of awe in the face of art and architecture or even natural beauty.[5] It can be cured by rest and going home. In this it is remarkably similar to the original 17th-century meaning of nostalgia as homesickness as experienced as a spatial displacement by soldiers, sailors, mercenaries, traders and missionaries, before it became associated with temporal displacement (Graburn 2000). A similar pathology was called *Mahora* for 10–11th-century Japanese warriors sent out from Nara or Kyoto to unify the provinces of Japan.

Anxiety and Self

From the preceding material we may agree that there are two existential types of Japanese tourism experience. The more common, and commonly known, is 'group tourism', which stems from a long history of pilgrimage going back to the advent of Buddhism in the 7–8th century (Graburn 1983). Group tourism is a form in which the members of a social group having important characteristics in common, e.g. religion, age, gender, sect, occupation, residence, make a tour which, these

---

5   It has been compared with Stendhal's syndrome which he experienced when confronted with the magnificent arts of Florence (Magherini 1989).

days, can be either domestic *kokunai kanko* or overseas (literally in the case of island Japanese) *kokusai kanko*.

The overwhelming nature of this tourism is the interaction between the members of the social group, rather than between the tourists and the people encountered; tour leaders may be professional outsiders, following the original leadership of experienced priests (*sendatsu*) or they may be members of the group themselves. Intergroup behaviour is likely to be conventional and spontaneous, and devoid of anxiety. The proper social 'face' is said to be *tatemae*, which is what is expected and does not threaten the group with individualism. The mood often arises to the effervescent feeling of *communitas* (Turner 1969) especially within the egalitarian group, even when the members' status outside of the tour situation might be more hierarchical. Barriers between individuals fall away and communication may be very free and boisterous, maintaining the typical Japanese pleasure of being firmly an accepted member of the group. Although under the circumstances of drinking or being away from home, more personal and other humorous or critical remarks may be uttered than in the 'structured' home situation, offence is not taken and slights are not remembered; indeed they may serve as a catharsis and be forgiven. We might say that this group tourist behaviour perfects or exaggerates Japanese group behaviour.

As Muro suggests, these commonly seen happy groups of Japanese 'are never abroad' even when overseas. Little or nothing, certainly nothing unplanned, upsets the social group (Beer 1993) which carefully manages its contacts with alterity.

The other form of tourism is almost the opposite. Called 'travel with a purpose', 'travel to find a way', 'lonely travel' or even '*haiku* travel', the traveller is effectively alone, risking direct contact with alterity, but they often search inside themselves for a self-alterity, while ignoring other humans. In this form of travel, the self is shorn of the protective circle of 'society' or the group, bereft of the safety of *tatemae*, expected social relations, the 'frame' of belonging (Nakane 1970) within which Japanese are alleged to feel at home, or even the ability to remake one's identity to conform to the expectations of others (Kondo 1990).

In the examples recounted above, the 'bare self' the exposed ego, encounters anxiety, fear and danger often in the form of nightmares or reminiscences. Even the encounters with dangerous alterity are reframed to be part of the self, to be carried within the self. This version of self, which is normally unconscious except in abnormal states, such as dreaming, travelling out of one's society, resembles Freud's concept of the *Id*, the irrational, selfish, repressed 'lower' part of the tripartite self (Freud 1927). It also parallels the Japanese concept of *honne*, the real, original, selfish interior true thoughts and feelings that, because they are individually selfish, are supposed to be repressed and never expressed except to one's most intimate friends, if then. Yet, this interior self (*naimen*) when discovered on lonely journeys is indeed frightening, difficult to control, and best left repressed!

Whereas the *tatemae*, the self as adjusted to conform to the group, resembles the internalized norms of society-as-judge, Freud's *Superego*. We have to ask then, when is the independent self, (Freud's) *Ego* experienced, a self that can act independently from the group or frame, the self which is distinguished from and can be opposed to others, to alterity? We do not find it directly in this analysis. Rather like Kondo's expression of the chameleon of self-in-society, perhaps the Ego-self is distributed across both the self-in-society (the safe, conformist *tatemae*) and the individual dangerous and should be repressed self (the always present but must not be let loose *honne*). However, this assertion comes dangerously close to the old fashioned claims of the lack of individualism among the homogenous group-oriented Japanese, harking back to Benedict (1946) and the origins of *nihonjinron* (Befu 2001).

A second problematic outcome of this analysis is the apparent lack of engagement with alterity and, conversely, the inner-directed emphasis on self-discovery which occupies the traveller when outside of their home reference group. Indeed Takito (1997) shows that the ultimate goal of Japanese extreme long distance backpacker-type travellers was to get as far away from Japan to a place as different as possible, not to engage with local native people but to be completely alone, undisturbed by oneself. This could be contrasted with the common Western claim of interaction with alterity experienced by lone travellers such as trekkers and backpackers. I would first assert that the Japanese experience is not outside the range of Western experiences under such circumstances. First, one could note that Western experiences of 'the other' have often been thinly disguised projections of aspects of self, most often the more negative parts of self that one might want to recognize as important characteristics of self, perhaps, indeed aspects of the *Id*, especially when directed towards radically different others as in travel experiences in the Third World. However, a long series of reports about Western youth long term travellers (from Teas 1988 [1974] to Cohen 2004) have suggested that such people are rather uninvolved with local cultures, except for the acquisition of superficial symbols of contacts, such as clothing and folk arts and, perhaps, sharing drugs; the converse, that is the intense concern of youth travellers with their peers and with the culture of their gathering places, is paramount, even for those studying or working abroad (Mathers 2003).

Further Considerations of Searching for Self

It is my intention to further contextualize the lonely travel and the analysis of the travel within the recent sociocultural history of Japan to emphasize that the phenomenon of individual exploratory *sagashi* travel has probably had its heyday. It was somewhat popular but never dominant, even in the 1970s–80s (Takito 1997) among those who had grown up during the fast and successful post-World War II revival of the Japanese economy and society. But it has tapered off recently among those coming of age after the 'bubble' collapsed in 1989–91, in favour of shorter travels to safer places (Yamashita Shinji, personal communication, 2008).

A more recent examination of hundreds of statements on the site *Tabi-kei zatsusudan-ban* [The travel gossip board] a question and answer website about anything related to travel, brings to light a mixed set of attitudes about *Jibun no*

Sagashi Kanko [Searching for oneself travel]. These are not narrative descriptions of travel performed but assertions of belief about the worth of 'seeking trips', sometimes illustrated by events; many are affirmative, showing little anxiety about 'finding oneself':

P1: I will soon have to look for a job. But I have no idea what I want to do with my life. I have no strong will or sense that I would like to do one or another thing. So I wonder – who am I? What's the *true me*? I don't know if I can figure it out while travelling, but it's better than doing nothing. I will go this summer.

P2: I think, travelling is just one more way of *jibun sagashi*. I think it's a great thing. Experience makes a person grow [spiritually].

P3: I don't think that one can find oneself or the meaning of life in such trips. But I also don't think that we can lump together in one group all the young people who go abroad for *jibun sagashi*. And I also think that, while young, it's not a bad thing to contemplate the issues of one's own being.

P4: In my case, the thing called 'self' (*jiko*) became visible through a trip. Leading busy days as a *sararīman* in Japan, there is not much time to think. I think it is good to go on a trip and think about one's life (*jinsei*).

Some felt themselves strengthened:

P5: After travelling abroad [alone], I quit my company.

P5: When I was young, travelling for me was like an ascetic practice. I didn't travel to cure myself or get rid of stress, but, to put it simply, search for myself (自分探し). That is, I went to discover something new [about myself] and to grow as a person …

P6: When I was young and travelled around alone, I didn't know the world (世間知らずのひとり), through the travels at young age, my outlook on life widened and I gained self-confidence …

A few waxed quite poetic about the experience and wrote *haiku*:

A1: A poem: 'When travelling alone, I hear the blues'. (一人旅ならブルースが聞こえる)

A2: A *haiku* about going for a two-day trip alone: 'Don't be afraid/ Get to like/ yourself more.' When you return home, after stopping for a night somewhere [during a trip alone], you will probably like yourself more!

Some of the questions are hopeful but express some scepticism:

> Q1: People who have travelled abroad alone – I want to hear your memories. When and where you went … what you felt, what you learnt (感動したこと), were you afraid … the things that changed in you (自分の中での変化)?

Some of these blogs point to sources of anxiety, such as loneliness:

> L1: [.] Felt that Edinburgh is a 'town of stone' (石の街) that gives one a feeling of history. Being there one feels kind of dark and *lonely*.

> L2: Made a decision to go to Nikko alone. 'Tension' rises while on the train to Nikko. While in the hotel, sit in *rotenburo* [open air bath in a hot spring resort], look at the sky and *loneliness* (*sabishiisa*) wells upon me.

> L3: From the moment one goes abroad, he/she has to think of 'survival' – what to eat, where to sleep, how to avoid dangers, etc.

And yet, others point out the positive side of this anxiety:

> L4: Of course, it would be lie to say that one doesn't feel loneliness (寂しさ) at all when travelling at all, but it is a loneliness that is hard to express. It somehow brings about the whole atmosphere. … One can deeply feel the climate and culture of the particular place – that's the uniqueness of travelling alone. One is embraced by a fresh new world, and there are times when one has no time to feel lonely.

> L5: It doesn't mean that there won't be lonely moments on the trip, but one must treat the lonesome thoughts as essential elements of the travel.

> L6: Feeling satisfaction inside oneself (自分の中では満足) when travelling with a certain goal in mind. 'Walking in a park, going to a famous sight, having a cup of tea in a cafe – if one is travelling alone, there is a certain drama (一人旅だとなんらかしらのドラマ) in it.' One's own responsibility.

> L7: Meeting people whom one wouldn't meet otherwise, and talking to them makes one forget one's [ultimate] *loneliness* (寂しさ).

Another source of anxiety or nostalgia is language:

> K1: I went alone to Australia, expected there to meet some Japanese people there, but there were only other foreigners in the local tour. I, who doesn't speak English, felt extremely disheartened (私は非常に心細かった).

K2: Travelling alone, the *lonely* thing was that, even having a meal, there was nobody with whom to share the impressions (一人なので感動しあえない淋しさがありました).

K3: In a taxi in the UK, I heard a radio announcer ask the question, what was the second city to be hit by the atom bomb after Hiroshima? Of course I knew the answer but I was profoundly moved.

Yet the majority of the opinions on 'self-seeking tourism' were negative or even scathing, rather than especially fearful, when commenting on *jibun sagashi* questions:

N1: The self is always self … why to look for it?

N2: Those who emphasize *jibun sagashi*, actually don't want to find their selves. Because finding the real self, the tiny self, the powerless and miserable self is unpleasant. Therefore the 'search' always continues.

N3: A hopeless person (*mudana yatsu*) is a person, wherever he goes and wherever he flies, is still hopeless. Such a person can search his self, but there is no content (*nakami*) to be found [in him].

N4: One's life usually revolves around family, so one has to travel alone. Let's find time to relax first, and start *jibun sagashi* from there …

N5: There are people who have gone abroad to look for themselves, but have lost themselves at the end.

N6: Somebody has stated: 'It is said that one goes on self-search trips (*jibun sagashi no tabi*)'. But one somehow cannot find himself. It is just that one can have time to gaze at himself.

N7: 'Before searching for ourselves, let's think if there is a self-worth looking for?' (*Jibun wo sagasu mae ni, sagasu hodo no jibun ga aru ka kangaeyõ.*)

N8: Search for oneself (*jibun sagashi*) is a strange phrase. I've always thought so. Whether going to the other side of the world or travelling in the space, it's only the self (*jibun*) who is [goes] there.

And perhaps most sadly:

N9: When I was on the trip, I thought everything had changed. When I returned home, I realized that nothing had changed. I think that is the sorrow of many backpackers.

These latter comments do not entirely do away with the possibility that there is not (much of) a real self, reinforcing the *Superego* [the self-in-society] and *Id* [the hidden inner self] dichotomy, but perhaps it is fruitful to examine some other aspects of recent changing Japanese society to further understand the relation between self and (geographical) travel.

The Stress of the Western Discovery and the Emergence of Individualism

In this section we examine the emergence of other modes of and reactions to aloneness and individualism in Japan. Since the gun-toting Western opening of Japan 150 years ago, the Japanese have been forced to face the West and worry about confident individualism.

Physical Strengthening

At first, the shock of facing up to physically superior and individually tougher Westerners led to a nationwide revolution of imposed physical education[6] *taiso*, centralized education, the formation of a peoples' army rather than elitist *samurai* (who were defeated when they turned against the new government) and the adoption of many technological and organizational Western practices, e.g. eating meat!. The Japanese maintained a civilization goal of 'Western technology and Asian spirit' which was a compound of traditional spirit and imperial nationalism. At the individual level, this inner strength was *seishin* – related to the Samurai-spirit of self-denial and loyalty *bushido,* something admired by all but felt lacking by most ordinary people *heimin* – something for instance, exhibited in the 20th century by soldiers who refused to surrender after WWII and lived on in jungles for years (Moeran 1984).

The Literary Self: Shishosetsu the 'I Novel'

At the literary level, there arose an unprecedented form: the experimental 'I-Novel' (literally: *Watakushi shishosetsu,* or *Shishosetsu* for short) early in the 20th century. This genre describes a new form of 'fiction' which is a thinly disguised writing about oneself, comparable to Western techniques of the essay, diary, confession or autobiography. The genre was founded based on the Japanese reception of the Western idea of Naturalism during the Taisho period (Fowler 1988; Hijiya-Kirschnereit 1996; Suzuki 1996). It was a method of writing which reflected greater individuality and freedom of expression, in opposition to the then

---

6 So threatening was the Japanese self-perception of physical weakness that the new leaders wrote to Sir Herbert Spencer and asked if Japanese women should be interbred with European men in order to improve the breed – he replied, after reflection – no, he did not believe in the mixing of the races.

conventional forms. There are several general rules for the creation of an 'I-Novel'. The story must remain in a natural realm and must be completely realistic. The idea was to prove that language is not transparent and that a real experience can be completely portrayed with language. The formula of the protagonist must be author = protagonist = hero; therefore the author must be the protagonist of the story. The story should also express a great knowledge of literature and reference as many works as possible in relation to a character's feelings (Delacour 2007).

The writers separated themselves from Japanese intelligentsia and from city life, often living alone or forming a loose group called *bundan*. They had few readers at first and were thought to be scandalous for making public their innermost *shishi*, their heart/mind's[7] temperament or nature. The first *shishosetsu* are believed to have been *Hakai* (Broken Commandment), written in 1906 by Shimazaki Toson, and *Futon* (Quilt) written by Tayama Katai in 1907. In *Hakai*, Shimazaki described a man who was born a member of a discriminated segment of the population (*burakumin*), and how he decided to violate his father's commandment not to reveal his community of birth.[8] In *Futon*, Tayama confessed his affection for a female pupil. From the start, the 'I-Novel' was a genre that exposed the dark side of society or the dark side of the author's life (cf. *honne* above). However, it was linked to Western novels and as these became accepted, e.g., Hemingway, *shishosetsu* gained mainstream respect. It is sometimes said that the work of contemporary novelist Murakami Haruki, very popular in the West, (see the story of the Nomonhan War, above) is a descendent of the I-novel (McVeigh-Schultz 2007).

McVeigh-Schultz (2007) was researching interpersonal behaviours, especially *nikki*, a kind of blog-diary, in the Japanese social media *mixi*. He notes that blogging is very similar to *shishosetsu* writing, in that both involve the 'intimate stranger', letting an unknown audience into one's inner life and one's *kokoro*. And this is turn reminds us of the Japanese saying (above) that 'there is no shame in travel', which is a version of the Western phenomenon of intimate conversations with a 'stranger on the train' who one will probably never see again.

Contemporary Youth and the Family

After the unprecedented defeat of WWII, Japanese strove mightily to recover their self-respect through industrial and commercial competition, with mass migration to urban industrial centres, enormous hard work with the men working long hours and women responsible for the home, the budget and the raising and education of the 3–4 children of the nuclear family. Children were brought up under pressures to (a) succeed in education getting to the right schools and universities, (b) to get

---

7 *Shin* or *kokoro*, an important Japanese concept related to inner feelings, sincerity or spirit.

8 In his novel *Shinsei* Toson wrote about a true affair with his niece, hoping for literary fame and recognition.

a good job with a respected companies and lifetime employment, in exchange for loyalty and long hours and (c) to marry respectably and reproduce the urban nuclear family.

This migration and restructuring of the family often led to isolation of the nuclear family from the extended family, left behind in the countryside, and hence the neglect of grandparents and the graves of ancestors at rural graveyards *haka*, the frequent separation of husbands transferred or going away for work while the wife had to stay home unaided and/or the relatively absence of the husbands on weekday evenings working or drinking and in the weekends sleeping it off rather than involving themselves with the children, or even their posting abroad for months or years.

As the economy plateaued and Japanese gained a sense of self-confidence with the growth of mass group travel and some individual travel abroad, the birth-rate dropped and the pressures in families grew. Many women did not want to marry Japanese men, and many men had problems in finding wives to be their loyal, hardworking partners. The divorce rate sky-rocketed. The sibling groups which produced the first wave of 'seeking travellers' discussed above, shrank to one child at home – leading to loneliness and the lack of experience or inability to find safety in the embrace of 'the group' (Hamada 1997).

The essential support of *amae* – the ability to lean on and trust others[9] became hyper-focused on the mothers – and there were even mass rumours of mother-son incest in these homes where men were absent and mothers and sons were left to battle for educational success. In the absence or weakness of patriarchal discipline and sibling group and take, many children felt they didn't fit in well or at school and found themselves being bullied – bullying being a common source of 'discipline' and self- regulation of peer groups at school. This led to a number of perhaps pathological phenomena, having to do with psychological loneliness and self-doubt:

School Refusal: *Futoko* – where those bullied or otherwise lacking self-confidence refused to go to school, and the parents (or mothers) allowed this refusal to conform, a selfishness that led to other refusals to conform to society's goals. Such children were labelled *shinjinrui*, a 'new kind of human being' by the older generation and the newspapers, for being inexplicably non-conforming to society's goals and shaming one's family by not living up to *tatemae* – the expected social conformity. But the strains in the family were manifested in many other ways. A genre of literature once more mocking the standards of the intellectual and literati flourish. Prime among them were the novels of Yamamoto Banana, a young women whose crazy imaginative novels of unconventional lives, loves and fictional families were devoured by the young, and appalled the establishment. The frequent protagonists of these novels were lonely youth who saw their parents' and

---

9   Japanese psychologist Doi (1973) asserted that the concept of *amae*, total emotional reliance on another, prototypically children on their mother, is the key to satisfactory relations of kinship and amity.

elders' foibles and created unconventional social worlds and relationships, some even semi-incestuous, for themselves and their search for a more meaningful life.

Young women more than young men have seen one solution to their predicaments by going abroad, not only searching for themselves, but search for loves and *amae* with foreign men and foreign family systems. For instance, Shinji Yamashita has found well over 400 women in Bali who have married into Balinese extended families, happily having children and yet remaining Japanese (Yamashita 2008). Within Japan there has been a rise on mixed/international/ inter-ethnic marriages (Graburn 2008) to more than 10 per cent in Tokyo, and these marriages have 2.5 times as many children as all-Japanese marriages, so that the next generation of elementary school children – already born – will be at least 25 per cent mixed/half foreign.

Others, including men, look for the ideal *gemeinschaft* community, the fabled rural *furusato* abroad (Rea 2000) as tourists, for instance 'Anne of Green Gables' countryside in Prince Edward Island, Canada, or Beatrix Potter's house and farmland in the Lake District, places where they reminisce, feel nostalgic for a past they never knew, and kiss the ground, plan to get married, have themselves photographed, and buy souvenirs of an imaginary happiness.

Another somewhat more alienated youth trend is known as *Otaku*, originally a polite term for someone else's home or that other honourable person. But the word has now devolved into a lifestyle and a type of young men who while not rejecting school and adult learning, like Yamamoto Banana's characters, refuses to participate conventionally in adult social life. While doing well at school or even in conventional middle class employment, these people bury their social life into the computer world. They seek out and create web-sites for the lonely, telling stories to each other, and creating dream worlds of social-constructed relationships, many of them becoming quite sexual without being personal. Many of them buy or create or photograph female dolls which may be semi-naked, have their clothes removed in a series of photos or subject to other sexual manipulations which they photograph and send out. This has become a huge 'socio-mental' world in Japan, a world originally tinged with weirdness or even fear as some tragic crimes of murder and rape were attributed to such loners, but now treated with greater respect as these millions of young men are seen as amongst the brightest and most creative if unconventional members of the next generation, having an enormous economic impact and living a more positive life than some alternatives.

In these and other ways, including youth suicide and even-internet arranged suicide pacts, there is a general refusal to 'grow up' and take on the proper role of *shakaijin*, an adult of 'person of society'. This is shown in many other ways, such as dressing more babyish than one's age, employing child-like handwriting, emphasizing everything and everyone *kawaii*, i.e. 'cute' i.e. harmless, pathetic and cuddlesome – from dolls, to clothing, to speech to images to accoutrements and furnishings – and a corresponding sexualization of the infantile by and for men who are afraid of the rejection that they are likely to meet from adult women or, as some have suggested, the conflation of the female adult with the very close mother-figure and those temptations.

While the ever smaller next generation grows up (or fails to grow up), or some would say 'regresses from adulthood', the birth rate diminished, the supply of respectable adult jobs and life time employment decreased, the Japanese economy never regained its pre-1989 vigour and the new generation also is accused of lacking vitality and energy by the older generations. The economic downturn and the changed psychosocial climate has produced new generational accusations, such as *parasite singles* – those whole live with and off their parents without ever getting married, *freeters*, who refuse to develop a career but engage in a series of short term, dead end jobs (we might say 'McJobs') to finance their hobbies and so on.

At the far end of this spectrum are the *Hikikomori* (lit. 'pulling away, being confined', i.e. 'acute social withdrawal'). This is a Japanese term to refer to the phenomenon of reclusive individuals (80 per cent are male) who have chosen to withdraw completely from social life, often seeking extreme degrees of isolation and confinement due to various personal and social factors in their lives. The term *hikikomori* refers to both the sociological phenomenon in general as well as to individuals belonging to this societal group. They live in their bedrooms and refuse to 'grow up' for fear of (1) failing their exams for entrance into good high schools or colleges, (2) failing to finesse their education by getting a respectable life time career job, and/or (3) failure to meet or attract girls in the social competition for adult relationships.[10] Because of the shame that *hikikomori* causes to parents and society and the lack of definition as to whether it is a sickness or a social pathology, the Japanese don't know exactly how to measure it or how to cure it (Zeilenziger 2005). According to psychologist Tamaki Saito, who first coined the phrase, there may be *one million hikikomori* in Japan, 20 per cent of all male adolescents and young men in Japan, or nearly one per cent of the total Japanese population. They live in their bedrooms at home, threaten their parents and even beat them up if refused food or threatened with expulsion, and they may stay closeted for ten years or more. What a disaster for a country with a plummeting population of young people and the world's highest proportion of old people!

In one sense these *hikikomori* are a mirror-image or a successor to the earlier *sagashi* tourists. Both have turned their backs on Japanese society, refusing to integrate themselves as ordinary members of their '*uchi*' their social peer group, and both have to face a striking loneliness. Whereas the seeking-tourists may be creative, face their anxieties and eventually assuage them by returning 'home' the *hikikomori,* suffer the whole outside world as their lonely fantasy terror and seek refuge in their often pathological loneliness to avoid that return to 'real world'.

---

10 I have met some ex-*hikikomori* who explained that their self-isolation was part of a battle of will with their parents over some life choices.

Conclusion

Tentatively we may conclude by suggesting that the first post-war generation of 'seeking tourists' in the 1960s–80s were partly descendants of the older Japanese tradition of individual seekers, *haiku* travellers, and partially experimental individualists as Japanese facing the West, like the *shishosetsu* writers had been in the early 20th century. They led temporarily experimental lives which exposed them to the dangers of NOT merging as mutually supportive and mutually surveilling members of their social frame (Nakane 1971), or not leaning on the *amae* of others and lending their own *amae* support to their peers. The lack of the ability to *amaeru* has caused, in my experience, many Japanese seeking travellers, to join up with other Japanese or even with Chinese and other East Asian trekkers during their extended trips, to feel mutual support and companionship and share their experiences.

Hikikomori youth also fear adult society with both its responsibilities and its obligations of mutual support. Their growing up experiences and perhaps their view of their parents' lives shows them that the adulthood proffered is not reliable any longer, its threats are greater than its rewards, and the young people, mainly young men, embark on a long inner and outer journey to their mental and social interiors, a trap-like journey with rare relief or way out, further distancing themselves from and causing mental and physical harm to their parents as members of society. They squander their lives refusing to encounter alterity in any form, just as Takito (1997) suggested Japanese long distance seeking travellers sought and encountered only themselves even when removed to other continents and cultures in the heyday of *sagashi* tourism. I hope this chapter has not left the reader with the impression Japan is unique or inscrutable. I think that many of the processes found in Japan have their parallels elsewhere, though sometimes in less noticeable fashion. Perhaps the Japanese are more aware of some of their own social processes than those of us elsewhere. And I hope that this examination of 'the other' may generate ideas which are productive and understandable for all.

Bibliography

Adler, J. (2006) 'Cultivating wilderness: environmentalism and legacies of early Christian asceticism', *Comparative Study of Society and History*, 6, pp. 4–37.

Ashworth, G. and Hartmann R. (eds) (2005) *Horror and Human Tragedy Revisited: The Management of Sites of Atrocities for Tourism*, Elmsford, NY: Cognizant Communication Corporation.

Bashō, M. (1933) *Oku no hosomichi* [A narrow road to the interior], Tokyo: Sankakusha [originally ca. 1670].

Beer, J. (1993) 'Packaged experiences: Japanese tours to Southeast Asia', Berkeley: Unpublished doctoral dissertation in Anthropology.

Befu, H. (2001) *The Hegemony of Homogeneity: An Anthropological Analysis of 'Nihonjinron'*, Melbourne: Trans Pacific Press.

Benedict, R. (1946) *Chrysanthemum and the Sword*, Boston: Houghton Mifflin.

Cohen, E. (2004) 'Backpacking: Diversity and change', in G. Richards and J. Wilson (eds), *The Global Nomad. Backpacker Travel in Theory and Practice*, Clevedon: Channel View, pp. 43–59.

Delacour, J. (2007) 'Shishosetsu and the myth of sincerity', in *The Heart of Things* [Originally 22 April 2003] weblog.delacour.net/shishosetsu_and_the_myth_ of_sincerity.php (Retrieved 24 November 2010).

Doi, T. (1973) *Anatomy of Dependence*, trans. John Bester, Tokyo: Kodansha.

Fowler, E. (1988) *The Rhetoric of Confession – Shishosetsu in Early Twentieth-Century Japanese Fiction*, Berkeley: University of California Press.

Freud, S. (1927) *The Ego and the Id*, London: Hogarth Press and Institute of Psycho-analysis.

Frey, N. (1998) *Pilgrim Stories: On and Off the Road to Santiago: Journeys along a Way in Modern Spain*, Berkeley: University of California Press.

Frey, N. (2004) 'Stories of the return: Pilgrimage and its aftermaths', in E. Badone and S.R. Roseman (eds), *Intersecting Journeys: The Anthropology of Pilgrimage and Tourism*, Chicago: University of Illinois Press, pp. 89–109.

Graburn, N. (1977) 'Tourism: The sacred journey', in V. Smith (ed.), *Hosts and Guests: The Anthropology of Tourism*, Philadelphia: University of Pennsylvania Press, pp. 17–32.

Graburn, N. (1983) *To Pray, Pay and Play: The Cultural Structure of Japanese Domestic Tourism*, Aix-en-Provence: Centre des Hautes Etudes Touristiques (Les Cahiers du Tourisme) Serie B, Numéro 26.

Graburn, N. (2000) 'Nostalgia', in J. Jafari (ed.) *Encyclopedia of Tourism*, London: Routledge, pp. 415–416.

Graburn, N. (2006) 'Hegemonic paradigms: East meets West', ISA, RC50 Conference Paper Durban, South Africa, 24–29 July.

Graburn, N. and Ertl, J. (2008) 'Introduction', in N. Graburn, J. Ertl and R.K. Tierney (eds), *Multiculturalism in the New Japan*, London and NY: Berghahn, pp. 1–33.

Guichard-Anguis, S. and Moon, O.P. (eds) (2007) *Japanese Tourism and Travel Culture*, London: Routledge.

Hamada, T. (1997) *Absent Fathers Feminized Sons, Selfish Mothers and Disobedient Daughters*, Rice University: Japan Policy Research Institute.

Hijiya-Kirschnereit, I. (1996) *Rituals of Self-Revelation: Shishosetsu as Literary Genre and Socio-Cultural Phenomenon*, Cambridge: Harvard University Press.

Kelsky, K. (2001) *Women on the Verge: Japanese Women, Western Dreams*, Durham NC: Duke University Press.

Kiel, C. (2005) 'Sightseeing in the Mansions of the Dead', *Social and Cultural Geography*, 6(4), pp. 474–494.

Kondo, D. (1990) *Crafting Selves: Power, Gender and Discourses of Identity in a Japanese Workplace*, Chicago University Press.

Kunio, Y. (1931) *Meiji Taisho Shi—Sesō Hen* [Meiji and Taisho History: Strange Social Conditions], Tokyo: Heibonsha.

Magherini, G. (1989) *La Sindrome di Stendhal*, Florence: Ponte Alle Grazie.

Mathers, C.F. (2003) 'American travelers and the South African looking glass: Learning to belong in America', Berkeley: Unpublished doctoral dissertation in Anthropology.

Matsumoto, D.R. (1996) *Unmasking Japan: Myths and Realities about the Emotions of the Japanese*, Stanford, CA: Stanford University Press.

McVeigh-Schultz, J.R. (2007) 'Uncanny collisions: Context clash in Japanese social media', Berkeley: MA Thesis in Asian Studies.

Moeran, B. (1984) 'Individual, group and *seishin*', *Man*, 19, pp. 252–266.

Moeran, B. (1986) 'One over seven: Sake drinking in a Japanese pottery community', in J. Hendry and J. Webber (eds) *Interpreting Japanese Society*, Oxford: JASO, pp. 226–242.

Moore, S.F. and Myerhoff B.G. (eds) (1977) *Secular Ritual*, Assen: Van Gorcum.

Murakami, H. (1998) '*Nomonhan no Tetsu no Hakaba* (Iron Graveyard in Nomonhan)', in *Henkyō/Kinkyō (Remote region/Close region)*, Tokyo: Shinchōsha, pp. 135–191.

Muro, K. (1974) '*Ryoko no Shikata* [The way to travel]', *Shiso no Kagaku*, 33, Jul., pp. 2–12.

Myerhoff, B. (1974) *Peyote Hunt: the Sacred Journey of the Huichol Indians*, Ithaca NY: Cornell University Press.

Nakane, C. (1971) *Japanese Society* [*Tateshakai no ningen kankei/a vertical society of human relations*], Berkeley: University of California Press.

'Nomura Tsuma (Nomura wife)', female, 30+ years old, travelled with her husband between April 5, 2003 and June 16, 2004. http://homepage.mac.com/khaosai/top/top.html (retrieved on March 11, 2007).

Oga, N. (1974) 'Tabi ni Mukau Mono (That which guides towards travelling)', *Shiso no Kagaku*, No. 40, Dec. 1974, pp. 33–40.

Ogura, K. (2004) 'Watashi to Iu Teikoku Shugi (Imperialism called 'Me')', *Gekkan Shinika*, 15 (1), Jan. 2004, pp. 94–99.

Rea, M. (2000) 'A furusato away from home', *Annals of Tourism Research*, 27(3), pp. 638–660

Stone, P.R. (2006) 'A dark tourism spectrum: Towards a typology of death and macabre related tourist sites, attractions and exhibitions', *Tourism: An Interdisciplinary International Journal*, 52(2), pp. 145–160. [Available via www.dark-tourism.org.uk or visit http://www.iztzg.hr/turizam/last.htm].

Suzuki, T. (1996) *Narrating the Self – Fictions of Japanese Modernity*, Stanford: Stanford University Press.

'Taka', (male, born in 1973) travelling the world since November 9, 2004. http://www.sekai-purapura.com/diary/01asia1/thai05.htm (retrieved on March 11, 2007).

Takito, H. (1997) 'The Japanese Long Distance Traveler', Paper delivered at the Workshop 'Travelling Cultures in Asia' organized by Prof. Eyal Ben-Ari, Hebrew University and Prof. Brian Moeran, University of Hong Kong, 7–9 April.

Teas, J. (1988 [1974]) 'I'm studying monkeys-what do you do? Youth travelers in Nepal', *Kroeber Anthropology Society Papers*, 67–68, pp. 35–41.

Thompson, C. (2007) *The Suffering Traveller and the Romantic Imagination*, Oxford: Clarendon.

Turner, V. (1969) *The Ritual Process: Structure and Anti-Structure*, Chicago: Aldine.

Tylor, E.B. Sir (1871) *Primitive Culture: Researches into the development of mythology, philosophy, religion, art and custom*, London: J. Murray.

Urry, J. (1990) *The Tourist Gaze*, London: Sage

Van Gennep, A. (1960 [1909]) *Rites of Passage*, Chicago: University of Chicago Press.

Viala A., Ota, H., Vacheron, M.N., Martin, P. and Caroli, F. (2004) 'Les Japonais en voyage pathologique à Paris: un modèle original de prise en charge transculturelle' [The Japanese in Paris on a pathological trip: an original model of culture shock], [Revue – Supplément à] *Nervure: Journal de Psychiatrie*, 17(5), pp. 31–53.

Wang, N. (1998) 'Rethinking authenticity in tourist experience', *Annals of Tourism Research*, 26(2), pp. 349–370.

Yamashita, S. (2008) 'Transnational migration of women: Changing boundaries of contemporary Japan', in N. Graburn, J. Ertl and R. Tierney (eds) *Multiculturalism in the New Japan*, London and NY: Berghahn Press, pp. 101–166.

Yanagita, K. (1993 [1931]) *Meiji Taisho Shi—Sesō Hen* [Meiji and Taisho History—Strange Lifeways], Tokyo: Chūō Bijutsusha, Shōwa 3.

Zielenziger, M. (2005) *Shutting out the Sun: How Japan Produced its own Lost Generation*, New York: Vintage.

Chapter 4

Seeking the Existential Moment

Elvi Whittaker

A few years ago I browsed through a small pile of postcards in an antique store in Portland Oregon. They had been dumped into a large bowl on the front counter ostensibly to separate them, as rubbishy and ephemeral, from the classy up-market antiques for which the store wished to be known. The proprietor was busily dusting a Lalique vase, handling it very carefully. Suddenly my attention was riveted on one card. Into my head flowed a multitude of thoughts, 'my intellectual life flashed before my eyes': the winds of existentialism and phenomenology that blew across North American campuses when I was a graduate student in anthropology at Berkeley in the 1970s, my current interests in tourism, my early adulation of Hannah Arendt and *The Human Condition*, my perusal of humanistic psychology, the ongoing theoretical puzzle that was the analysis of experience and the cultural scripts that braced up what I saw. I had had a minor epiphany, the 'ah-ah' experience. It seemed so right.

I then became aware that the proprietor had been regarding me in silence.

> 'Why do you look at the backs of those cards? Everyone else looks at the picture on the front.'

> 'I'm an academic.'

> 'That explains it.'

On the back of the card that caught my attention was written:

> As I stood on the edge of that huge abyss, the silence rushed up to meet me, I was so shaken with the enormity of it that I almost stopped breathing. Then I broke out in goose flesh.

On the front of the card was a stereotypic view of the Grand Canyon. The writer was, I assumed, a tourist perhaps viewing this site for the first time.

More mundanely I was aware that it fitted perfectly into a data collection I had been gathering for some years. This collection was inspired originally by an experience reported by a student in a senior sociology of knowledge class I taught. He described his experience in the following way:

It was midnight and I lay on the bottom of a boat on Shuswap Lake looking up
at the stars. Quite suddenly I felt one with the universe, the skies, the stars. My
whole self seemed to disappear and I was completely at peace and in some other
world.

The collection includes a rich array of imaginative, yet also very real occurrences
gathered from interviews and writings in various sources. These accounts bear
witness to an emotional culture. These experiences perhaps not as uncommon in
tourism, not infrequently encountered, not widely acknowledged yet expected
by the traveller and fostered by the industry. The remarks of the anonymous
tourist captured magnificently this exceptional personal feeling. Accounts of this
experience have a remarkable similarity. Not only tourists, but also others in a
wide variety of pursuits, recognize the occurrence and give it a similar description.
They report strong emotions, an unprecedented intensity – a sense of spirituality,
mysticism, ecstasy, elation, epiphany, mystery, awe, fantasy and drama. Their
sense of existence is also heightened by an extraordinary awareness. Clear focus.
Tremendous concentration. Timelessness. Otherworldliness. Sacredness. Solitude.
Magic. Exhilaration. God-likeness. The sublime. Dreamlike. Transpersonal.
Reality shifting. Supernatural. Lacking in motivation. Peace. Transcendence.
Added to these emotions are reported sensations of loss of selfhood, humility, deep
transformation, unity with the universe, a soaring soul, serenity, heightened sense
of reality, new sense of power, arrival at a new dimension. Suspension between
the earth and the sky. It feels right. Life is worthwhile. The tourist setting appears
to drop away, human interaction and all companions seem to disappear and one
stands in solitary isolation from the world and yet very much with the world.

How to understand this phenomenon? Abraham Maslow has called these
sensations 'peak-experiences'. It is little wonder that he finds them in religion
(1964). In tourism, peak-experiences can be desired or avidly sought like the
Holy Grail of human well-being. Or, alternately, they can come upon the person
quite unexpectedly, as a staggering event. Surely they are the side-products of
expectation. To have them arrive, are the preceding expectations too high or not
high enough? Is there a narrowness of prevision thus creating the surprise that
always seems present in the actual experience? Or a largeness of prevision, of
expectation, thus setting the ground that makes the vision possible? In all cases
when they do appear they seem to be mind-altering, cataclysmic, unexpected.
There is nothing logical, even-handed, calm or everyday about them. Ordinary
tourist emotions, whether lived through the window of a bus or the porthole of
a liner, or sought through the authority of the tourist guidebook are anticipated,
predictable, and come as a preordained happening part of the tourist package.

Yet many travel encounters seem planned with the hope of encountering peak-
experiences. It is believed that it is actually possible to arrange planned pilgrimages
and risk-seeking activities in the hope of producing these mind-altering highs.
Adventure tourism clearly seems one such undertaking, where it is believed that
inevitable triggers are present. Opportunities suggest themselves for courting

danger and a 'high' in nature and wilderness. Mountaineering, parachuting, bungee jumping, hang gliding, swimming with sharks, mountain biking, rappelling, Grand Prix racing, running of the bulls, space travel are sought in the name of living on the dangerous edge. The 'trick' of adventure tourism involves exposing oneself to enough danger to trigger excitement, yet remain within a protective frame, carefully chosen as something the individual can handle, even if just barely (Apter 1992, p. 33).

The other side of peak-experiencing can be fear, whether overt or tacit. Pain and pleasure are curiously intermingled. 'One buys excitement with fear, and the greater the cost, the better the product' (Apter 1992, p. 39). Overall brinkmanship, yearning and hankering to reach a place where no one has been, that one oneself has not entirely imagined, though afraid of the journey, seems to sum up the experience. Michael Apter who has studied the dangerous edge and risk taking has noted the utter pointlessness of so much of human behaviour and has asked himself again and again,

> Why ... are people freely engaging in such strange activities – activities that are uncomfortable, unnecessary, and even unsafe? Why would people exert energy when they don't have to; or set up goals for themselves that lead nowhere beyond themselves...? (1992, pp. xi–xii)

Earlier Edgar Allan Poe observed on the same subject: 'We stand upon the brink of the precipice. We peer into the abyss – we grow sick and dizzy. Our first impulse is to shrink from the danger. Unaccountably we remain.' These reports seem to capture part of the mystery. Defying nature, sporting with it, mastering it is part of the game for some, while for others it is a worshipful stance towards wilderness. John Muir wrote in his journals 'forests, mountains and desert canyons are holier than our churches' (Muir 1979, p. 51; Scheese 1996, p. 317). What seems to distinguish these moments of surprise, wonder, and even fear is that what is beheld is more powerful by far than the beholder, more intimidating than the imagination had predicted. They come with an equally powerful solitude. Thus wilderness and solitude have become a powerful dual enticement, as seen in an advertisement with the invitation to visit Canada's latest territory Nunavut in the far north.

Canada's Arctic

Untamed. Unspoiled. Undiscovered
.... Away from cities and crowds and machines,
On a sea of tranquility, closer than you ever imagined,
You come to understand exactly why,
People come to, and fall in love with, Nunavut.
Enjoy! (Nunavut Tourism 2009, p. 55)

The advertisers have suggested, not entirely tacitly, the ever-present possibility of encountering a peak-experience. Uniqueness. The promised escape from the boredom of the everyday. The stunning silence as the noises of life drop away.

There is, however, a dark side to the tourist experience. Perhaps a peak-experience of another sort. There is a type of tourist encounter often given the name of cities that appear, more than others, to encourage these dark negative reactions. The Jerusalem syndrome, the Paris syndrome and the Florence syndrome are the most familiar among them.[1] Psychiatrists have noted that some tourists suffer a 'psychotic decomposition' upon encountering the realities of these famous cities about which they have a significant and burdensome number of expectations. In Jerusalem some tourists, who later become patients, manifest identification with religious characters from the Old and New Testaments. Others identify with a mission like a need to replace Islamic holy places with Jewish ones, or claim magical connections to holy sites or famed burial places. Yet others hope to bring about the resurrection of the dead. Or, perhaps more reasonably, others are disturbed by the differences between the present Jerusalem and the Jerusalem of their imagination (Bar El et al. 2000). Paris syndrome has been associated with Japanese tourists who come to the city they know as the cultural centre of the world (Viala et al. 2004) and consequently are gravely disappointed with the 'actual' Paris. Likewise, Florence syndrome and Stendahl syndrome are used to describe art lovers voicing disappointment on viewing the artistic treasures of that city, reacting like Stendhal who experienced in Florence a disenchanting *deja vu*. Some psychiatric colleagues have noted that clearly such patients come to these cities with pre-established psychiatric problems that are exacerbated at the location. Their hopes for some kind of peak-experience are unfulfilled and expectations are frustrated by the perceived realities of the actual site. These psychiatric findings support Maslow's proposition that only those with a high level of emotional health, which he calls 'self-actualization' and 'self-transcendence', are able to have peak-experiences (Maslow 1954).[2]

Obviously peak-experiences are associated not only with tourism, but also with the more recognizable 'highs' of religion, romance, sex and drugs. After all, these are also part of the human condition as we know it. Studies of these 'issues'

---

1   David Picard first drew my attention to the Jerusalem syndrome when I began to think about this chapter.

2   While Maslow's Pyramid of the Hierarchy of Needs, with its self-actualization and self-transcendence as the epitome of successful living, seems to provide a theoretical link to the peak-experiences of tourists. At least, Western tourists. An anthropologist should add a proviso. Maslow theorized in one of the cultures most known for its individualism, North America. In addition he based his research on subjects often deemed perhaps the most enthusiastic seekers for individualistic success, healthy college students, who also are believed to be gifted with innate curiosity. A tempting puzzle presents itself. What are peak-experiences in the cultures most remote from those known to Maslow? How do they manifest themselves?

are multitudinous, yet the analysis of the 'highs' they produce, the psychological and social nature of this euphoric reaction, is somehow compartmentalized and relegated to some nebulous category assumed beyond meaningful social interest or inquiry. Such highs seem largely unexplored in the religious context.

Besides the work of Maslow and those of his students, there are a few contemporary humanist psychologists, some psychiatrists, and a sprinkling of others writing articles on the peak-experiences of artists, students and skydivers. The most prominent scholar dealing with many of the issues raised by Maslow is Csikszentmihalyi (1990, 1996, 1997). He attempts to deal with the bases of happiness, engagement, enjoyment and creativity. In attending to these issues he has created the notion of 'flow'. There are similarities to the discourses of Maslow in his attention to the harnessing of emotion, the focusing of motivation, the continued curiosity and persistence, the near absence of self-centredness and the experience of rapture and joy in doing an activity.[3] Also relevant is the work of Ian Marshall (2003) who makes direct use of Maslow's peak-experiences and self-actualization in a volume addressing eco-psychology using the writings of Thoreau, Whitman, Homer, John Muir and his own walking of the Bald Eagle Ridge.[4] All told, however, there is seemingly little work addressed directly to these spiritual and transformative sensations. They remain mysterious.

So what are these experiences? This is a very seductive question for academics, who tend to see it as part of their mission in life to clarify mysteries or, in other words, to normalize such enigmas. Where do they come from? What do they mean? What causes them? In short, we are obsessed by the notion of providing the definitive explanation. Our usual stance is to translate and transpose the problem into the warm arms of our favourite master narrative, the one which makes the world turn for us. Then we will presumably know and can then explain 'what it is really about'. That too is the human condition. How can we resist doing it? Isn't the rush to interpretation the academic game after all?

There is one common dimension to the problem of peak-experiences that is somehow integrated, whether centrally or peripherally, into every master narrative evoked to deal with the phenomenon. This dimension has been addressed by psychologists and poets, neurologists and anthropologists, and it has become an explanatory staple, the *lingua franca*. I refer to what has been called the greatest discovery of all time – the idea of the *unconscious* (Tallis 2002; Shear 1990). The unconscious is a psychic *terra incognita*, often called one of the world's greatest and most radical of discourses, the ultimate mythology, the deepest imponderable.

---

3   Undoubtedly there are interesting comparisons to be made between the work of Maslow and that of Csikszenthihalyi. the latter's writings emphasize most directly the contribution to learning, the attainment of optimum performance and personal growth, while Maslow is less obviously committed to these pragmatic educational outcomes. Some work exists in this area, see Privette and Bundrick (1991).

4   So committed is Marshall to Maslow's contributions that he named a mountain, for which there appeared to be no previous name, Mount Maslow (2003, p. 6).

If visiting the unconscious were actually possible, one would be able to view all those elusive elements that have long been relegated to this collect-all storage bin: imagination, memory, knowledge – all parts of the fathomless human psyche. Merely the tip of a strange iceberg, the unconscious holds unknown secrets. Commonly associated with Freud, it has a history that goes beyond his work, into the past and into many terrains that may have been foreign to him. Among its early proponents are such diverse figures as St. Augustine, John Locke, Mesmer, Leibniz, Coleridge, Nietzsche and even Shakespeare, as well as ancient Hindu and Classic texts. There has been a pause of some decades. Time taken up ostensibly with recovering from the mythic creations of Freud that coloured a good part of the 20th century. The archaeology of human consciousness has made a comeback and has become academically popular again. Its rejuvenation is encouraged by considerations far from the psychoanalysis that once promoted it. It has become of interest to neuroscientists, evolutionary theorists, experimental psychologists, researchers into artificial intelligence – all those who are forced to admit that numerous extremely important functions are performed outside of, or below, the level of awareness (Tallis 2002, p. xi). There can be little doubt that the unconscious holds the key to those imaginings that make up the mystery of peak experience, as well as the mysteries of everyday life (Adams 2001). What was it then that peaked? The concept of experience itself, despite the efforts of phenomenology, philosophy and cognitive psychology, continues to hold onto its secrets. Yet to understand peak-experiences surely the unconscious must be involved?

Take the tantalizing findings of neuroscience about the content of the unconscious. After years of looking on the unconscious as a figment of antiquated psychoanalysis, they have returned to it as a hot topic of research. Not being content to glaze over how knowledge becomes integrated into the mind – whether by culture, human interaction, or some other means – neuroscientists have experimented on how much knowledge the central nervous system can actually process at any given time. Despite the supposed enormity of our abilities, they claim, we are actually quite limited in being able to manage, at the very most, only seven bits of information (sounds, visual stimuli, emotional nuances etc.) at the one time. For example they show that the shortest time it takes to discriminate between bits of information is $1/8$ second. They claim that 'it is possible to process at most 126 bits of information per second, or 7560 per minute, or almost half a million per hour'. Over a lifetime of seventy years, they calculate this amount to be about 185 billion bits of information. It is out of this total that everything in our life must come – every thought, memory, feeling, or action. To understand what another person is saying we must process 40 bits of information each second. It follows that to understand what three people are saying simultaneously is theoretically possible, but only by managing to keep out of consciousness every other thought or sensation (Csikszentmihaly 1990, p. 29). In other words, beyond the level of awareness are people's facial expressions, guesses about their motivation, their relationships to each other, their clothing, and anyone else who might be standing around. These are provocative findings and quite stimulating that such work is actually possible. They must also offer some avenues for investigating peak-experiences, some clarification about their occurrence.

Furthermore neuroscientists, physiologists, biochemists and others like them have conducted various experiments on the make-up of the human brain. These experiments speak directly to the experience of peak moments. Some of the rather miraculous results are: that it takes 10 to 20 milliseconds of processing before small electrical shocks applied from the outside world can actually reach the level of consciousness; that the brain continues to process towards a further developing awareness after the first shock registers; that all behaviour is initiated unconsciously; that FMRIs (functional magnetic resonance imaging) and EEGs (electroencephalography), together provide a glimpse of the unconscious (Tallis 2002, pp. 110–129). Some even argue that they provide a total view of the unconscious. Of course this is a regrettable abbreviation of what neurologists have produced. Most neuroscientists readily confess that the studies of the brain hardly touch the problem of 'mind', while others, the must pure-minded among them, might well ask 'what is mind?'

The contributions of neuroscientists to the explanatory discourses about peak-experiences offer many narratives that revolve around the notion of 'shock'. They note the changes in attention that follow the shock; the 'daze' that can be observed; the narrowing of consciousness and of concentration, the detachment, the depersonalization, the disorientation. The corresponding physiological symptoms of the central nervous system are readily produced. Mention might be made of an 'adrenalin rush' or the role of epinephrine, the hormone and neurotransmitter, the palpitations and tremors that could be involved. Almost always, there is the reference to the autonomic and central nervous systems, the electrical activity of the brain, blood pressure, heart rate, muscle responses and other signs. This is but a small recognition of the multiple contributions of the scientific community.

Fascinating as the propositions from the scientists are, they create gaps that can only be addressed by the humanists. One humanist narrative, in particular, has always intrigued me. I have been watching for some decades how Romanticism has endured while being seen as a term of derision in the social sciences, a term of theoretical abuse, used pejoratively and treated as a correctible in seminars. To be accused of a romantic interpretation of some situation was an intellectual belittlement. Presumably the implications of high emotion, the lack of reason and constraint often found in Romantic texts are among the elements leading to this denunciation and the apparent embarrassment. Yet how can one see the whole tourist enterprise as anything but a romantic quest? The seeking for ruins, monuments, relics, the past, the picturesque, the sublime, the aesthetic, the exotic, the strange, the primeval, the supernatural and occult, the feeling-good are characteristics of this quest. Indeed travelling itself has been a large part of the literature deemed Romantic. Certainly peak-experiences are right out of the handbook for Romanticism. Feeling supersedes rationality. Awe, fear and sentimentality triumph over the restraints of reason. Expressive individuality is supreme. Imagination is revered. The spirits of Wordsworth, Thoreau, John Muir,

Joseph Wood Krutch, Caspar David Friedrich and Aldo Leopold stand over us. Tourism, and peak-experiences, appear to be an antidote to the world of labour, the Industrial and Computer Revolutions, the crush of urbanism and materialism, and boredom. The unconscious, of course, is also a product of Romanticism.

Perhaps the most noteworthy romantic characteristic in peak-experiences is the reaction to wilderness. The majority of accounts I have collected seem to refer to encounters with wilderness. Whether this is simply conditioned by the fact that most of the reported responses came from those whose daily lives were spent in cities, in complex work situations, is hard to say. It seems that perhaps the more isolated, the more chaotic the wilderness, the more prone to inspire such peaks of emotion. The wish to be removed from the crush of population and from the usual self and its environs appears to characterize all of us (Aldous Huxley in Shorto 1997, p. 230). Solitude. Silence (Manes 1996). Being dwarfed by natural forces – looming islands of ice, towering mountains, bottomless crevices, threatening skies. Human insignificance is overpoweringly a variable of the emotion.

> As I looked at that absolutely gigantic tree, absurdly large, and all the others around it, I was struck by the thought of oneness with the whole earth and how we actually manifest that oneness every day of our lives, by passing the earth through our bodies every single day. (Visitor to Sequoia Redwoods of California, interview)

Interesting in examining peak-experiences there arises the seeming undoing of one of the major tenets of western philosophy. Cartesian dualism seems to disappear. A space and time chasm is evident. The rethinking of space is forced upon one by the extreme depth, height and width differentials. Time ceases to exist, overcome by a sense of universality and eternity. Another reality entirely engulfs one, the happiness of having risen above the harried world. As Philip Whalen puts it:

> I was kneeling over the edge of this raft in my underwear, holding this horse under the chin … It was two o'clock in the morning and it was a beautiful summer night, and the mountains were all around, and the lake, and this horse, and me – and I suddenly had a great weird kind of *satori*, a sort of feeling about the absolute connection between me, and the horse, and the mountains, and everything else. And you can't describe it very well – the feeling – because the feeling is a feeling. But it was … a big *take* of some kind. (Suite 2002, pp. 109–11)

Self falls away. The burden of the self – it has been called the 'mountain of the self' (Marshall 2003, p. 15) – that self carried around in everyday life, is something that a tourist hopes to escape. The self is the repository of expectations, obligations, personal history, psychic energy, intentions, feelings and all thoughts – the stronghold of the reality of who we are. A heavy burden indeed. Tourism is a symbolic allegory of the escape from the prison of ego and self. But, more importantly, peak experiences are major shifts in reality that bring about a loss of this self and a euphoric union with the environment. They are major turning points. A physiology professor notes:

> The sense of having a small, isolated self disappeared, and in its place was the delicious sensation of flowing out into everything I beheld. I felt a sense of complete fullness contained in my own silence... (Shear 1990, p. 236)

The demands of interaction with others also fall away. The old self, and its partner, identity, which connect us to the world, is now dead, and has lost control over the new reality now overwhelming all thoughts. This change in perception of self and reality is described in a letter from Einstein to Queen Elizabeth of Belgium:

> there are moments when one feels free from one's own identification with human limitations and inadequacies. At such moments, one imagines that one stands on some small spot of a small planet, gazing in amazement at the cold yet profoundly moving beauty of the eternal, the unfathomable: life and death flow into me, and there is neither evolution nor destiny; only being. (quoted in Shear 1990, p. 4)

Of course I cannot forget the discipline into which I have been reared. As guardians of the intellectual property of culture, anthropologists direct themselves to the presumed contents of the unconscious, the cultural scripts that reside there. Clearly the tourist is evoking the imaginary, the scripts hidden in memory, and seeking the route to actualize what Julia Harrison refers to as 'making the make-believe real' (Harrison 2003, p. 200). Clearly any visions of the outer spaces rely entirely on the visions in the inner spaces. Take the Grand Canyon, for example. An infinite number of scripts converge (Nye 1997). Crowding into consciousness are cultural reactions to depth, to space, to the beautiful, to residual notions of *Sturm und Drang,* to risk, to religion, to solitude and to historic time. These may include the echoing words of those who had visited in earlier times such as Mark Twain, John Wesley Powell and John Muir. Visiting the Grand Canyon is visiting one's imagination, as well as touching the past. Of course anthropologists are wont to note the similarities between peak-experiences and what we have long known about and called 'spirit possession' and 'vision quest'. These important accomplishments of the spirit that claim the attention of the anthropologist seem to have many similarities to seeking and having a peak-experience.

Peak-experience has a rather charming dated quality. It is as if they were inspired by the 1930s and 40s novels of James Hilton and Somerset Maugham where heroes travel to find spiritual awakening, an epiphany which then comes to be the moral foundation of their later lives. 'Those are the novels my mother used to read', observed a colleague, 'about utopian heroes'. Incidentally, the popularity of these novels also led to award-winning films. There still appears to be a slight reluctance by social scientists to show enthusiasm for research in emotional issues. Despite a three-decade history of involvement with emotion in anthropology and sociology (Kemper 1990; Lutz and White 1986; Lutz and Abu-Lughod 1990; Thoits 1989 and others) there still seems to be a slight embarrassment associated with it. Is this the positivist monkey that still sits on the backs of many of us? And is it because, in thinking about emotion, no positivists need apply? Work in this area continues to remain rare and is relegated to philosophy, humanistic psychology, clinical psychology and psychiatry. Of course, one must admit, not everything that matters should be studied and analysed, and equally, not everything actually studied matters. A graduate student admitted to me recently that she had wanted to do a dissertation on love. Her adviser blanched. And mumbled. She ended up doing ethnography on a law firm with an international clientele involved in international trade. Of course she also multiplied her chances of a future faculty position.

Similarly, the culture of emotion in tourism is seldom tapped, but like love it promises great riches. Emotion is central to tourism, the thrills of anticipation and of daydreaming, the accumulation of travel accounts and advice, the excitement and dread of departure, the disappointment of having to return. There are also the passions of meetings with hosts and strangers, discoveries made about them, and about oneself. The awe of beauty and of complexity. The reverence for elsewhere and those living elsewhere. Consider also the narratives that we, the various analysers, have proposed? Do we merely simplify something as complex as peak-experiences? Or do we invalidate and even destroy the experience itself? Will the magic be lost? Some have suggested, never trust the theorist, but always trust the basic experience. Should peak-experiences thus remain ever a mystery? Mysteries may well be great motivators. To finish with the wisdom from that knower of all things, Oscar Wilde: We can have in life but one great experience at best, and the secret of life is to reproduce that experience as often as possible.

Acknowledgements

An earlier version of this chapter was presented as the keynote address at the International Conference on Tourism and Emotion, Leeds Metropolitan University, Leeds, United Kingdom, July 5, 2009. I am grateful to Lelia Kennedy and Neil Eaton for many conversations about Abraham Maslow.

Bibliography

Adams, M.V. (2001) *The Mythological Unconscious*, New York: Karnac.
Apter, M.J (1992) *Dangerous Edge: the Psychology of Excitement*, New York; Free Press.

Bar-El, Y., Durst, R., Katz, G., Zislin, J., Strauss, Z. and Knobler H.Y. (2000) 'Jerusalem Syndrome', *British Journal of Psychiatry*, 176, pp. 86–90.

Csikszenthihalyi, M. (1990) *Flow: The Psychology of Optimal Experience*, New York: Harper & Row.

Csikszenthihalyi, M. (1997) *Finding Flow: The Psychology of Engagement in Everyday Life*, New York: Basic Books.

Csikszentmihalyi, M. (1996) *Creativity: Flow and the Psychology of Discovery and Invention*, New York: Harper Collins.

Harrison, J.D. (2003) *Being a Tourist: Finding Meaning in Pleasure Travel*, Vancouver: UBC Press.

Kemper, T.D. (ed.) (1990) *Research Agendas in the Sociology of Emotions*, Albany, NY: SUNY Press.

Lutz, C. and Abu-Lughod L. (eds) (1990) *Language and the Politics of Emotion*, Cambridge: Cambridge University Press.

Lutz, C. and White G.M. (1986) 'The anthropology of emotion', *Annual Review of Anthropology* 15, pp. 405–436.

Manes, C. (1996) 'Nature and silence', in Cheryll Glotfelty and Harold Fromm (eds), *The Ecocriticism Reader*, Athens: University of Georgia Press, pp. 15–29.

Marshall, I. (2003) *Peak Experiences: Walking Meditations on Literature, Nature, and Need*, London: University of Virginia Press.

Maslow, A.H. (1954[1970]) *Motivation and Personality*, New York: Harper.

Maslow, A.H. (1964[1994]) *Religions, Values, and Peak-Experiences*, New York: Penguin Arkana.

Muir, J. (1979) *John of the Mountains: The Unpublished Journals of John Muir*, edited by Linnie Marsh Wolfe, Madison: University of Wisconsin Press.

Nunavut Tourism (2009) (advertisement) Walrus 6, pp. 3:55.

Nye, D.E. (1997) 'De-realizing the Grand Canyon', in Gerhard Hoffmann and Alfred Hornung (eds), *Emotion in Postmodernism*, Heidelberg: Universitätsverlag C. Winter, pp. 75–94.

Privette, G. and Bundrick C.M. (1991) 'Peak experience, peak performance, and flow: Correspondence of personal descriptions and theoretical constructs', *Journal of Social Behavior and Personality*, 6, pp. 169–188.

Scheese, D. (1996) 'Desert solitaire: Counter-friction to the machine in the garden', in Cheryll Glotfelty and Harold Fromm (eds), *The Ecocriticism Reader: Landmarks in Literary Ecology*, Athens: University of Georgia Press, pp. 303–322.

Shear, J. (1990) *The Inner Dimension: Philosophy and the Experience of Consciousness*, New York: Peter Lang.

Shorto, R. (1997) *Saints and Madmen: Psychiatry Opens its Doors to Religion*, New York: Henry Holt.

Suite, J. (2002) *Poets on the Peaks: Gary Snyder, Philip Whalen and Jack Kerouac in the North Cascades*, Washington, DC: Counterpoint.

Tallis, F. (2002) *Hidden Minds: A History of the Unconscious*, London: Profile Books.

Thoits, P.A. (1989) 'Sociology of emotion', *American Review of Sociology*, 15, pp. 317–342.

Viala, A., Ota, H., Vacheron, M.N., Martin, P., Caroli, F. (2004) 'Les Japonais en voyage pathologique à Paris: un modèle original de prise en charge transculturelle', *Journal de Psychiatric* 17(5), pp. 31–34.

Chapter 5

Affect and Moral Transformations in Young Volunteer Tourists

Émilie Crossley

Travel has long been associated with ideas of self-transformation. Through travelling, there is a sense in which we can see our lives with renewed clarity, recognize desires and callings that previously appeared hidden from us, and ultimately forge new identities. Journeys have a 'capacity for mirroring the inner and outer dimensions that makes possible the "inner voyage", an archetypal form in which movement through the geographic world becomes an analogue for the process of introspection' (Stout 1983, p. 13). This transformative potential of travel is perhaps most significant for young people who, already finding themselves in a transitional period between adolescence and adulthood, are expected to participate in often *spatial* rites of passage such as moving away from home or undertaking a period of solo travel (O'Reilly 2006). Therefore, for young people travel provides valuable experiential and narrative resources that can be used to construct adult biographies and identities (Desforges 2000). This chapter explores the idea that the imperative for young people to be transformed through their travel practices is taking on an increasingly moralized character as ethical discourses become pervasive throughout the tourism industry (Butcher 2003). This has implications for the way in which spaces of tourism in developing countries, such as those involved in volunteer tourism, are interpreted and used by tourists as well as for our understanding of the formation of contemporary moral subjectivities. Furthermore, I argue that emotions and affects[1] play a crucial role in enabling moral transformations of the self and that in order to grasp these dynamics it is necessary to go beyond a purely discursive reading of tourists' accounts.

To date, most of the research looking at youth travel narratives and identities has focused on backpackers and independent travellers in developing countries (e.g. Elsrud 2001; Desforges 2000, 1998; Noy 2004; O'Reilly 2006). However, this model of casual, independent, 'round-the-world' travel is increasingly under attack from discourses emerging from the marketing of alternative, supposedly

---

1 The distinction between the terms 'emotion' and 'affect' is contested, but here I use 'emotion' to refer to the culturally recognizable patterning of feelings that leads to discrete emotions such as happiness and sadness (Blackman and Cromby 2007). I use 'affect' as a broader term that expresses emotional *flows*, which may be less clearly defined than emotions, intersubjective and involve unconscious dynamics.

more ethical tourism products (Butcher 2003) and from bodies such as the Year Out Group, which advises young people to plan 'structured' and 'worthwhile' activities for their time out from education or employment. Therefore, whilst being encouraged to have an enjoyable time, young people are also faced with what Cremin (2007) refers to as the 'enterprising injunction' and the 'ethical injunction'. The enterprising injunction destabilizes the dichotomy of work/leisure by subjecting leisure time to the concerns of the labour market, meaning that travel becomes dominated by the need for activity, productivity, and contributions to one's CV. At the same time, the ethical injunction obliges travellers to engage in responsible tourism and in activities of moral value. In this context, volunteer tourism is becoming a hugely popular option for young people wanting to combine the hedonism of travel, the productivity of volunteer work, and the virtue of helping poor communities. As a more interactive, enduring and reciprocal practice, volunteer tourism is recognized as having the potential to affect and develop the selves of its participants more profoundly than with mainstream tourism experiences (Wearing 2001). However, relatively little academic attention has been devoted to how these personal transformations take on a decidedly moral character in volunteer tourism and how the increasing popularity of such programmes is gradually changing the landscape of youth travel and subjectivity.

Transformation of the self through travel is frequently characterized as a discursive accomplishment; it is part of the narrative identity-work that takes place through storytelling after a trip, elements of which then become inserted into the traveller's broader life-story. As part of a culturally available resource for recounting travel experiences, the discourse of personal change takes several recognizable forms. Self-discovery or transformation can form part of a plot in which travellers overcome adversity, such as the physical and mental endurances of climbing (Neumann 1992), can be precipitated through meaningful encounters with Other people and cultures (Desforges 1998), or by engaging in risky activities in an attempt to break with the mundane (Elsrud 2001). The resulting changes are framed as predominantly positive, with travellers claiming to have achieved personal improvement and maturation (Noy 2004). However, rather than such transformations being a spontaneous occurrence, Noy (2004, p. 88) recognizes personal change as an 'inherent feature of the rhetoric' surrounding youth travel. This begs the question of whether the self (conceived of as a narrative construct or otherwise) actually changes as a result of travel experiences or whether this claim is made because of the cultural expectation surrounding youth travel as a rite of passage. Part of the difficulty in answering this question lies in the fact that there is a lack of longitudinal research in this area, which leaves us reliant on tourists' retrospective accounts, making it difficult to ascertain whether narratives of self-change have a processual basis and possibly obscuring the role of extra-discursive features of subjectivity in these processes.

The affective and experiential aspects of self-transformation remain relatively unexamined. This seems especially surprising in the case of ethical tourism products such as volunteer tourism, which not only promise the chance of a 'life-changing experience' but are marketed through highly emotive means; for example, by showing images of smiling local children joyous at the help that they have received or the sad faces of those still in need. Leigh (2006) draws on the concept of 'reverse culture shock' to suggest that volunteer tourists' long-lasting immersion in another culture can lead to changes that make them susceptible to difficulties when re-adjusting to life in their home society; difficulties which are implied to go beyond narrative in having a psychological and embodied basis. Following in this vein, Zahra and McIntosh (2007) have explored the profound and enduring changes that can arise in young people as a result of volunteer tourism. By re-interviewing their participants several years after the 'cathartic' volunteer experiences, Zahra and McIntosh show the lasting impact of sustained contact with cultural and economic difference. Former volunteer tourists talk of personal transformations that include transcending their materialistic attitudes, learning to put others before themselves, and becoming a better person, all of which have a distinctly moral quality. However, despite alluding to emotional and even spiritual experiences elicited by encounters with poverty in their host countries, the links between these responses and the narratives of self-change remain underdeveloped. In what follows, I hope to build on this work and show that the moral transformations of young people that are required by volunteer tourism are deeply intertwined with emotions and affective processes, and that in understanding these we can gain insights into the relationship between tourism and the shaping of morality in young people.

Researching Transformations

The broader project from which this research is taken aimed to investigate the subjectivities of ten young British people, aged 18 to 24 years, who undertook a structured volunteer programme in Kenya of between one and three months' duration in the summer of 2010. The programme, offered by a commercial provider, consisted of a mixture of environmental conservation and community projects run in rural locations experiencing high levels of socio-economic deprivation, and also offered more mainstream touristic activities such as safaris and days on the beach. I conducted in-depth interviews with my participants at three stages: prior to, during, and after the volunteer placement, across a period of approximately nine months. This longitudinal methodology was opted for because retrospective accounts inevitably refract the past through the lens of the present, containing omissions and exaggerations of certain elements, and because these accounts give little away in terms of the processual nature of (self-)change. Repeated, longitudinal interviewing, on the other hand, has the advantage of allowing the researcher to examine how opinions, identities and experiences fluctuate, metamorphose and are actively negotiated by participants through time and space. Supplementary to the core data generated through these interviews, I joined my participants for one month in Kenya in order to conduct participant observation and gain a first-hand perspective on volunteer tourism.

In order to explore the role of affects in the volunteer tourists' self-transformations, the research adopted a 'psychosocial' framework. A psychosocial approach understands subjects as constituted through interpermeating 'social' and 'psychic' processes (Frosh 2003), foregrounding the roles of socio-cultural discourses, unique biographies, and unconscious affective mechanisms. Accordingly, an interview format was used that would allow narratives to emerge relatively undirected by the interviewer so that links and disjunctions in the interviewee's speech could be examined for evidence of unconscious or emotional associations (Cartwright 2004; Hollway and Jefferson 2000). Interviews were initiated using a broad, open-ended question and subsequent questions were guided mainly by the flow of the participant's narrative. The second and third wave of interviews were used to explore new material based on events that had occurred since our last conversation, as well as to follow up salient themes from previous interviews. Following a process inspired by the 'three levels of analysis' developed by Walkerdine et al. (2001), analysis of the interview transcripts commenced with a basic discursive/narrative reading before attempting to explain participants' investments in particular identity or attitudinal positions by exploring affective mechanisms such as desire and defence against anxiety. The third stage of analysis involved reflecting on the effects of my own subjectivity throughout the research process. Further to these steps, I tried to incorporate spatio-temporal sensitivity into my analysis in order to comprehend how narratives changed over time and how the construction of meaning was spatially dependent.

Moral Inner Journeys

Having looked briefly at some of the socio-cultural norms placed upon young people's travel practices, especially regarding the onus to undergo self-change and develop a moral awareness, I now want to examine how such discourses are lived, experienced and negotiated. Taking the cases of three of my participants, Sarah, Tess and Lisa, I will explore three different transformative trajectories that originate from similar starting points and which all implicate emotions and affects differently. I want to show that emotions play a pivotal role in narratives of moral self-transformation and that unconscious affects can temper and diminish the effect of such personal changes.

Sarah: Thwarted by the 'Happy Poor'

The first time I met Sarah she was keen to justify her decision to travel to Kenya by referring to its ethical benefits, both in terms of the effect that volunteering would have on the host community and on her. From the start, Sarah expects that travelling will have a positive impact on her:

Sarah: I know I'm gonna, sometimes it's g- I'm gonna be so homesick, but, and like miss my boyfriend and everything, but I'll ab- I know I'll love it and I'll come back and I'll be like a better person for it and everything. (Interview 1, 06:59)

Despite anticipating some hardships such as the separation from her family, Sarah judges that these will be worth it because she will become a 'better person' through travelling. That Sarah feels the need to justify her actions in these terms demonstrates the pervasiveness of the moral discourse that infuses volunteer tourism. Furthermore, Sarah sees this moral transformation as something that will be precipitated by emotional experiences in relation to encounters with poverty in Kenya:

Sarah: I'll cry. I'll be like oh! (*laughs*) [Émilie: Really?] It'll be sad, won't it, to see everyone like that. But it'll be really good as well, so I'm like excited and anxious altogether. All the emotions (*laughs*)

Émilie: Yeah (.) So, um, you think you'll be quite emotional about it then.

Sarah: I imagine so, yeah. Because I, like I'll realize how lucky I am. Because I like, I live in like the countryside, but I've got like a big house, a swimming pool, a big garden. I've got everything I could need. ... So, going to see them like that will be a bit like (.) you'll realize everything that you've got and feel bad (*laughs*) ... It's nice, like it's, if, I know I'm gonna come back and be really pleased that I did it but I know that sometimes it's gonna be like heartbreaking to see how everything is. (Interview 1, 12:27)

Sarah expects to be 'heartbroken', 'sad' and to 'feel bad' about the poverty that she will witness, implying that the local people will not only be poor, but miserable with it. However, in her account these negative emotions are portrayed as catalysts that will enable Sarah to transform morally by allowing her to realize her material wealth and 'luck', and attain a more appreciative state of mind. There are resonances here with the concept of 'redemptive suffering' found in Catholicism, in the sense that Sarah believes that her endurance of emotional suffering will yield personal (in place of spiritual) rewards and deliver her from ignorance and ingratitude.

However, once we had arrived in Kenya it became difficult for Sarah to follow through with this personal transformation because she found that the local people, although very poor, appeared happy and contented in their way of life. This confrontation with a vision of the 'happy poor' therefore deprived Sarah of the crucial emotional experiences that, according to her account in the first interview, would have permitted her to achieve moral betterment:

Émilie: last time I spoke to you um (.) you, you said that you're quite an emotional person, that you thought you might get upset [*Sarah*: Yeah] and so, is that something that you've found or?

Sarah: Not, not really 'cause everyone seems, like I haven't spoken to anyone that's not happy. (Interview 2, 04:09)

Despite this, Sarah did not completely give up on the search for emotional experiences. Later in the interview, she told me of her suspicions that this happiness was an act put on by the locals for the 'white people', meaning the volunteer tourists. This implied that the suffering Sarah had expected and hoped to see *did* exist but was concealed from view for foreign visitors, leaving open the possibility that she could still encounter it at some point. Sarah also expressed an interest in volunteering at an orphanage for part of her stay. I believe that this was an extension of Sarah's pursuit of emotions, as before we left for Kenya she had talked about wanting to work with people within the host communities rather than doing a lot of construction work because she felt that 'you can't get all the absolute emotions from building'. However, despite these efforts, by the time we had returned to the UK for the third interview this part of Sarah's narrative that had featured so strongly in her original account as a motivating factor for her volunteering in Africa had completely disappeared.

Tess: Placing Poverty, Containing Emotion

The following passage from the first interview with Tess is strikingly similar to my initial conversation with Sarah. Again, Tess anticipates having strong emotional reactions to the cultural differences and poverty in Africa and frames these responses as a medium through which she will develop a sense of 'gratitude' for what she has:

Tess: I think I'm gonna cry a lot. [Émilie: Really?] I'm quite an emotional person. I cry at practically everything like, I'll be quite overwhelmed I think [Émilie: Yeah] and I'll probably get a little bit emotional …

Émilie: When you say you'll feel overwhelmed, by what?

Tess: By like, just like how differen-, just like culture shock, like how different um like it is for them but then I think like (.) that what I've heard from people who've done this kind of thing, they're so happy. [Émilie: Yeah] They're so happy, it's not like they're there and they're sad because they don't have like a t-, like tv. [Émilie: Yeah] And like they're just happy in like their way of life. I suppose they're not used to anything else so I think I'll be overwhelmed to think, so much gratitude for everything we have. (Interview 1, 45:21)

One difference in Tess's account is her portrayal of the host community. From the outset, Tess invokes the image of the 'happy poor' that destroyed the possibility of emotional transformation for Sarah and in doing so seems to imply that there would be something inherently moving about poverty regardless of the feelings of those living under such conditions. I want to suggest that this representation of the 'happy poor' provides a defensive function for young volunteer tourists. Poverty is a potentially problematic 'object' for those embroiled and invested in a culture that celebrates affluence, materialism and consumption, signifying instead lack, failure and Otherness. Therefore, thinking of poor people as contented has the potential to lessen feelings of anxiety or guilt (either on a conscious or unconscious level) that can arise as a result of the volunteer tourist's position of privilege and affluence. This allows Tess to anticipate strong emotional responses to poverty whilst at the same time maintaining control over its threatening potential.

Unlike Sarah, Tess did find herself affected by the poverty that she witnessed in Kenya. Here, she is telling me about an occasion when she became upset after meeting a sad young boy who was not able to play with the other children from the village because he was ill and his family could not afford to take him to a doctor:

> *Tess*:   I didn't want to cry, I <u>hate</u> crying near them 'cause they like just must think like, I don't know, I don't want to look like they're a sob story, d'you know what I mean? [Émilie: Yeah] I don't want them to think like, it's fine, they're happy, 'cause they <u>are</u>, most like the majority of people are <u>so</u> happy here like I'm sure they didn't (.) ask for mo-, some ask for more but [Émilie: Hmm] you know they all seem quite happy but I really just had to walk away and just kind of collect myself but that's the only thing that really got to me 'cause it just, they're so <u>young</u> I suppose and like (.) don't know, they deserve more I suppose. (Interview 2, 13:54)

Tess struggles to reconcile her emotional reactions with the defensive conceptualization of the 'happy poor' that she deploys. The sick boy was clearly not happy and yet Tess tries to reassure herself that he is an exception and that the 'majority of people' there are. Perhaps it is these defences that lessen the potential of this emotional episode in her travels to have a more profound, transformative impact on Tess. Indeed, during the third interview, Tess celebrates the fact that she has not changed 'dramatically' as a result of her trip:

> *Tess*:   I was worried I was gonna come back and be like completely different. [Émilie: Yeah] Not worried n- but a bit like god I hope I don't change too dramatically as a person and I'll have all these different views and [Émilie: Yeah] but I think I've changed for the better. You know, I'm a lot more independent, I'm <u>so</u> much better with money now ... and I'm much more grateful for everything back home now (Interview 3, 53:13)

Tess has achieved her objectives, including undergoing a moral transformation, but since she at no point explicitly links this newly found gratitude to her emotional encounter with poverty we are left to wonder what role this played in the process. What is certain from the rest of Tess's retrospective account is that she no longer feels troubled by what she saw in Kenya; because *that* was the place that she identified as poor and because she had anticipated being emotional *there*, we can understand Tess's emotions as having been spatially contained. The narrative of self-change that she brings back is a simple one of moderate change, satisfaction and moral betterment, and because the transformative and redemptive emotional 'work' has been performed and completed, this narrative has a sense of closure.

Lisa: Tears and Redemption

As with Sarah and Tess, Lisa initially anticipated a transformation of her perspective, although in her case this was configured as a refutation of Western materialism rather than in finding gratitude for her wealth:

> *Émilie:*   What sort of different view (.) on things [*Lisa:* Yeah] what d'you, what sort of view d'you mean?

> *Lisa:*   Um, I dunno like (.) like kind of the materialistic side of things like that (.) you like here you, you don't really (.) you take for granted like what you have and then [*Émilie:* Hmm] I think a lot of it's gonna be (.) to do with coming back with a different perspective on it, just [*Émilie:* Hmm] thinking it's just stuff it doesn't matter. (Interview 1, 27:32)

What differs from the other volunteer tourists is that emotions as a vehicle for these changes do not feature in Lisa's account, nor does she describe herself as a particularly emotional person. However, once we were in Kenya Lisa had an emotional experience that would allow her to apprehend the discourse of moral betterment in a meaningful way and which would instigate her own self-transformation. Here, Lisa is recounting having what she describes as 'a bit of a mental breakdown' after learning that some of pupils at a local primary school that we visited were not in school uniform because their families could not afford it:

> *Lisa:*   I just cried and cried and cried, and I just, I- like it just, it's just, I like as much as it was upsetting I think it was a <u>really, really</u> good like lesson for me? [*Émilie:* Yeah] Because like I, I was sat, I was sat there like just getting so upset thinking about what I'd spend £2 on – that's not even a coffee (.) and yet there's a child that can't afford a school uniform because they, like they don't have £2 and it just, oh god it just hit me like I got the <u>biggest</u> reality check in the world at that point … I know it sounds silly but when I look back on it now I actually like smile about it 'cause it's made me realize that like (.) stuff's not that important anymore. [*Émilie:* Yeah] It's like obviously it's not, you're not gonna change

everything, it's just the lifestyle isn't it but [Émilie: Hmm] it like, even if you
just think about it like. (Interview 2, 16:30)

What is telling about this passage is the satisfaction that Lisa is able to draw from
a seemingly traumatic episode during her time in Africa. Her tears form part of a
redemptive process which instils in her a new sense of 'realization', allowing her
to look back on this upsetting time and 'smile'. However, despite this apparently
significant self-transformation, the final part of Lisa's account demonstrates the
inertia and continuity of lifestyle that it permits. Lisa accepts that her materialistic
lifestyle is unlikely to 'change' drastically as a result of her experience, but insists
that it is enough to simply have a changed state of mind and be able to 'just think
about it'. These defences allow Lisa to retain her Western lifestyle with diminished
guilt and in the process poverty again becomes transformed from a threatening,
anxiety-inducing object into one associated with moral redemption.

For Lisa, the process of returning to the UK was far messier emotionally than
in the case of Tess, for whom the anxiety and sadness educed by the poverty
she had seen was safely spatially contained in Kenya, leaving her only with the
positive derivatives of the transformative experience. In the following passage,
Lisa describes her attempt at resisting the culture of consumerism that she had
supposedly achieved a new perspective on, at the same time as having accepted
that she would be reintegrated into:

> Lisa: I kept getting really upset when like all of my friends were like 'oh d'you
> wanna come shopping' and everything … and then like I caved and went and
> did it. And after I'd done it I felt so bad about (.) like going and spending all this
> money after like all the poverty you'd seen and everything. [Émilie: Yeah] And
> then like I just came home and like cried. (Interview 3, 24:46)

This time Lisa's tears are less directly connected to poverty and more self-
referential as she expresses possible feelings of regret and guilt. They may also be
evidence of a deeper, more lasting transformation which goes beyond the purely
discursive, as Lisa seems to have developed a new, embodied potential for being
affected by unjust global disparities in wealth. Yet despite this, Lisa wishes that the
change in her had been more profound:

> Lisa: I would've hoped it would've changed me more in the sense that I
> would've thought about it more? [Émilie: Really?] Like but then again you are
> coming back to a culture where it's, like you're looked upon strangely? if you,
> if you go 'no I don't want that, there's starving kids in Africa' … It's just not the
> culture here like people do spend money here (Interview 3, 41:24)

With a personal transformation that puts her in opposition to the materialistic
culture of the West, Lisa depicts herself as powerless, unable to turn down offers of
shopping sprees from her friends and not wanting to appear 'strange'. Lisa is thus left

living with the uncomfortable contradiction between her 'internal' transformation and 'external' behaviour. We then see a reoccurrence of Lisa's statement during the second interview in Kenya, where she anticipated that her transformation would probably not affect her lifestyle upon returning home because of dominant cultural norms. Appealing to these norms again has the effect of renouncing Lisa's agency, making her submission to Western society seem inevitable and acceptable, and in the process lessening the possible anxiety surrounding this conflict in her subjectivity. As with Tess, the operation of defences protecting Lisa has the effect of diminishing the potential impact of her self-transformation, although in this case the narrative seems less closed and continues to be adjusted.

Conclusion

The three case studies discussed above give us an insight into the complexities of the relations between youth travel, discourses of morality, and affective processes. Taking part in volunteer tourism places an onus on young people to become a 'better person', to develop 'gratitude' and 'appreciation', and to return from their experience with a reformed, morally superior 'perspective' on life. Instead of travelling to 'find themselves', implying a personal and unique journey, young people are now encouraged to travel ethically in order to construct a version of the self that fits a particular moral mould. Through moralized tourism practices, youth travel is becoming transformed from an arena in which young people can experiment and be carefree before settling into the 'roles of responsible adulthood' (O'Reilly 2006) into one which is itself regulated by the concerns of adulthood, such as work, responsibility and morality. For Sarah, Tess and Lisa, the path that results in moral self-transformation is one that implicates poverty and emotions as transformative catalysts: encountering destitution is narrated as an unpleasant yet necessary experience that one must go through in order to trigger emotions such as sadness and guilt, which in turn facilitate the positive change in the self. This process has similarities to travel narratives of physical hardship and endurance that allow narrations of the self (Elsrud 2001; Neumann 1992), and to religious motifs of suffering in order to attain redemption. Clearly then, these moral self-transformations are rooted in narrative and take shape through being recounted to others but, in some instances at least, volunteer tourists must experience (negative) emotions in order to actualize these narratives.

The case studies also allow us to glimpse the defensive processes that are set in motion when volunteer tourists face uncomfortable situations or conflicts within the self. For Tess, this came in the form of a constant reassurance to herself that the host community was 'poor but happy' despite having had strong emotional reactions to the damaging effects of poverty that she witnessed first hand. This may have been a way of protecting Tess against poverty as a threatening object, with its potential to throw into relief the stark and unjust inequalities in wealth between people living in developing countries and the tourists that visit them. In the case of Lisa, a disavowal of her agency in the face of the dominant cultural norms of her home society allowed her to ease the tension that she felt between her personal transformation and her Western lifestyle by effectively removing the element of choice in this dilemma. What is particularly interesting about these defences is the extent to which they seemed to be pre-emptive. Tess had anticipated becoming emotional in the face of poverty and so deployed the discourse of the 'happy poor' before we had even arrived in Africa. Similarly, Lisa talked about how her lifestyle would probably not change after returning to the UK while we were still in Kenya. One effect of these defences is that the radical potential of the transformative emotional moment is lessened. Instead of coming away with a sense of the unacceptability of poverty, Tess reassures herself that it is not all that bad. And instead of reforming her lifestyle in light of a new perspective on Western materialism, Lisa accepts that she has no choice but to continue to follow the norms of her society.

Deciphering the nature of moral transformations in young volunteer tourists may prove to be a problematic task as they appear to have a narrative basis, with an element of rhetorical inevitability (Noy 2004), at the same time as involving emotions and affective processes. Some may argue that very little changes in the tourist self (Bruner 1991) and that emotional reactions to poverty are simply sentimental responses to the emotive call issued by volunteer tourism, which have as much predictability to them as the narrative of self-change in youth travel more generally. However, the lasting impressions left on volunteer tourists shown by Zahra and McIntosh (2007) suggest to me a more complex picture in which something does become imprinted on young people through these experiences, whether spontaneous or premeditated, and that either way understanding the role played by affects in this process is important. We should also recognize that continuities may be as significant as changes in tourist subjectivity, as shown in the defensive tempering of self-transformations and in the way that changes framed as 'internal' allow a person's separate, 'external' lifestyle to continue unmodified. Affects therefore have a dual potential – to bring about self-change through emotional encounters and to lessen the effects of these changes through defence against unconscious anxieties. I suggest that a closer examination of these affective processes not only has relevance for studies of contemporary tourism, but may also have broader implications in terms of understanding the normative processes of change faced by young people and the spatial and emotional expression through which moral subjectivity is supposedly attained.

Acknowledgements

The research for this chapter was supported financially by the UK Economic and Social Research Council. I am also grateful to my supervisors, Prof Valerie Walkerdine and Dr Gabrielle Ivinson and to Sarah, Tess and Lisa for sharing their thoughts and feelings with me.

Appendix

Transcription Notation

(.)	Short, untimed pause in the flow of speech
<u>text</u>	Emphasized word(s)
text?	A question or raised intonation at the end of a phrase
te-	Preceding sound is cut off
(01:00)	Time at which excerpt begins in interview

References

Blackman, L. and Cromby, J. (2007) 'Affect and feeling', *The International Journal of Critical Psychology*, 21, pp. 5–22.

Bruner, E.M. (1991) 'Transformation of the self in tourism', *Annals of Tourism Research*, 18(2), pp. 238–250.

Butcher, J. (2003) *The Moralisation of Tourism: Sun, Sand... and Saving the World?*, London: Routledge.

Cartwright, D. (2004) 'The psychoanalytic research interview: preliminary suggestions', *Journal of the American Psychoanalytic Association*, 52(1), pp. 209–242.

Cremin, C. (2007) 'Living and really living: the gap year and the commodification of the contingent', *Ephemera*, 7(4), pp. 526–542.

Desforges, L. (1998) 'Checking out the planet: Global representations/local identities and youth travel', in T. Skelton. and G. Valentine (eds), *Cool Places: Geographies of Youth Cultures*, London: Routledge, pp. 175–194.

Desforges, L. (2000) 'Travelling the world – identity and travel biography', *Annals of Tourism Research*, 27(4), pp. 926–945.

Elsrud, T. (2001) 'Risk creation in travelling: backpacker adventure narration', *Annals of Tourism Research*, 28(3), pp. 597–617.

Frosh, S. (2003) 'Psychosocial studies and psychology: is a critical approach emerging?', *Human Relations*, 56, pp. 1547–1567.

Hollway, W. and Jefferson, T. (2000) *Doing Qualitative Research Differently: Free Association, Narrative and the Interview Method*, London: Sage.

Leigh, D. (2006) 'Third cultured volunteer tourists and the process of re-assimilation into home environments', *Australian Journal on Volunteering*, 11(2), pp. 59–67.

Neumann, M. (1992) 'The trail through experience: finding self in the recollection of travel', in C. Ellis and M.G. Flaherty (eds), *Investigating Subjectivity: Research on Lived Experience*, London: Sage, pp. 176–201.

Noy, C. (2004) 'This trip really changed me: backpackers' narratives of self-change', *Annals of Tourism Research*, 31(1), pp. 78–102.

O'Reilly, C.C. (2006) 'From drifter to gap year tourist: mainstreaming backpacker travel', *Annals of Tourism Research*, 33(4), pp. 998–1017.

Stout, J.P. (1983) *The Journey Narrative in American Literature: Patterns and Departures*, Westport, CT: Greenwood.

Walkerdine, V., Lucey, H. and Melody, J. (2001) *Growing Up Girl: Psychosocial Explorations of Gender and Class*, Houndsmills: Palgrave.

Wearing, S. (2001) *Volunteer Tourism: Experiences that Make a Difference*, London: Cabi.

Year Out Group. 'Choosing a worthwhile project', http://www.yearoutgroup.org/Choosing-a-worthwhile-project.html (accessed on 20 December 2010)

Zahra, A. and McIntosh, A.J. (2007) 'Volunteer tourism: evidence of cathartic tourist experiences', *Tourism Recreation Research*, 32(1), pp. 115–119.

Chapter 6

Overwhelmed by Divinity in Jerusalem

Eliezer Witztum and Moshe Kalian

Introduction

Travelling has been explained by a variety of underlying motives such as curiosity, adventure, status and emotional needs. Stressing the multiple determinations of tourist motivation, Pearce (1982), for example, drew on fields as wide apart as self-actualization, achievement motivation and cognitive attribution to explain individual differences. However, it has become clear that these motives usually remain similar to those driving our daily lives. They thus cannot fully explain the emotional condition of travel which, in many cases, is not related to the very act of travel *per se*, but to conditions stemming from the everyday lives of tourists which are revealed and often amplified by the act of travel.

What does differentiate tourism from daily life is that, as tourists, we alter our quotidian routines (Machils and Burch 1983).[1] We sleep in different beds, eat different food, meet different people and are exposed to different environments. These changes sometimes have a tremendous impact on our mental state, especially where travelling reflects a deep emotional involvement with specific sites or objects encountered during the journey. In some cases, such involvements represent a main goal of travel, for instance in forms of religious pilgrimage or cultural tourism to places considered spiritual centres of social life (Turner 1973), e.g. to a religious shrine, a place of venerated origin, an artistic masterwork, or a place of sublime beauty.

In this chapter we will examine the dramatic impact such spiritually or aesthetically heightened places can have on the emotional state of specific tourists. We will focus in particular on what has been called 'The Jerusalem syndrome', a psychopathology involving religiously-themed obsessive ideas, delusions and psychosis-like experiences observed in certain types of tourists visiting the city

---

1 Travelling has been explained by a variety of underlying motives such as curiosity, adventure, status and emotional needs. Stressing the multiple determinations of tourist motivation, Pearce (1982), for example, draws on fields as wide apart as self-actualization, achievement motivation and cognitive attribution to explain individual differences. However, it has become clear that these motives usually remain similar to those driving our daily lives. They thus cannot fully explain the emotional condition of travel which, in many cases, is not related to the very act of travel *per se*, but to conditions stemming from the everyday lives of tourists which are revealed and amplified by the act of travel.

of Jerusalem (Kalian and Witztum 1998). Contrary to certain received ideas about this and similar 'tourist syndromes' (cf. Bar-el et al. 2000), we will argue that the phenomenon does not occur spontaneously in people with no previous signs of psychopathology (who are supposed to become psychotic after arriving in Jerusalem), but that the large majority of subjects had previous conditions. However, we suggest that, as an extreme case, the phenomenon can help us to understand the cognitive stress and processes all tourists undergo in a much milder way and actually quite consciously research as part of the tourist experience.

'Travel Syndromes': The Psychopathology of Tourism and Travel

Psychiatric literature scarcely refers to mental symptomatology related to tourism. However, during the last 50 years there have been some medical reports on morbidity referring to long-distance travelling, or visiting other countries. McIntosh et al. (1988) studied mental and physical morbidity in 238 air travellers and found that about 40 per cent of the travellers experienced situational anxiety upon take-off and landing. Jauhar and Weller (1982) investigated the psychopathological phenomena at Heathrow Airport from the perspective of time-zone change. They found that depression was seen more in travellers moving from East to West and hypomania in travellers going in the opposite direction. Travellers to the Far East are susceptible to developing a psychotic breakdown due to additional factors such as the consumption of mefloquine (an anti-malarial agent) or due to drug abuse. Lange and McCune (1989), Flinn (1962) and Singh (1961) listed some of the causes for psychotic breakdowns of travellers: unfamiliar surroundings, the presence of strangers, inactivity, monotony, a sense of isolation, and the shock of cultural re-transplantation. Hiatt and Spurlick (1970) identified a population of patients who are on the move in order to seek a 'geographical solution to internal problems'. Stewart and Leggat (1989) put a special emphasis on the issue of 'culture shock', suggesting that the phenomenon should be brought to the awareness of travel health advisors, 'who can in turn advise travellers, especially longer term travellers, about having realistic expectations of their travel and life in new cultures'. The model of accumulated precipitating factors could also be applied to the somewhat anecdotal 'Honeymoon Psychosis' – a phenomenon observed in 16 cases among newly-wed Japanese couples, who suffered from a psychotic breakdown shortly after their arrival to a honeymoon holiday in Hawaii (Langen, Streltzer, Kai 1997).

The Emotional Impact of 'A Significant Place'

One of the earliest professional observations relating to the impact of a significant earthly site on specific mental symptomatology was documented by Sigmund Freud. Being an enthusiastic admirer of the Hellenistic culture and a keen self-observant, Freud documented his personal experience of de-realization upon arriving at a unique place, referring to his visit to the Acropolis in 1904. Writing home he stressed that the unique experience there had surpassed anything he had ever seen or could imagine (Jones 1955). The emotional impact of that single incident was so profound and overwhelming, that more than 30 years later in a letter to Romain Roland (Freud 1962) Freud still remembers in detail his curious mental experience. It was a peculiar disbelief in the reality of what was before his eyes. He had puzzled his brother by asking him if it was true that they were really standing upon the grounds of the Acropolis. He felt himself being split into two persons, one who was in fact on the Acropolis and the other who could not believe that it was so. Another skilled self-observant traveller was the famous 19th-century French writer Stendhal (Marie Henri Bayle) who gave a vivid description of his sudden 'fainting' upon observing the frescoes painted by Giotto Di Bondone at the church of Santa Croce in Florence. Self-description of intense emotional reaction related to the sight of Jerusalem can be traced as far back as the middle-ages in the autobiography of Margery Kempe who describes:

> And when this creature saw Jerusalem, riding on an ass, she thanked God with all her heart, praying him for his mercy that like as he had brought her to see this earthly city Jerusalem, he would grant her grace to see the blissful city Jerusalem above, the city of Heaven. Our Lord Jesu Christ, answering to her thought, granted her to have her desire. Then for joy that she had and the sweetness that she felt in the dalliance of our Lord, she was in a point to a fallen off her ass, for she might not bear the sweetness and grace that God wrought in her soul. The twain pilgrims of Dutchmen went to her and kept her from falling, of which one was a priest. And he put spices in her mouth to comfort her, weaning she had been sick. And so they helped her forth to Jerusalem. And when she came there, she said Sirs, I pray you be not displeased though I weep sore in this holy place where our Lord Jesu Christ was quick and dead. (Kalian and Witztum 2002)

Florence (Stendhal) Syndrome

This syndrome was first described by the two Italian psychiatrists, Magherini and Zanobini in 1987, and was named in homage to Marie-Henri Beyle whose pseudonym is Stendhal, a French writer who travelled in Italy. Magherini (1989) conceptualized the syndrome as an outcome of profound emotional reaction aroused in tourists intensely captivated by the overwhelming classical beauty of environments they visit. The name she has chosen reflects the emotional reaction reported by Stendhal during a visit to Florence in 1817. Between 1977 and 1983 psychiatrists at Santa Maria Nuova Hospital treated 106 foreign tourists with the same psychic affliction. They believed that exposure to Florence's great works of art served as a catalyst for some sensitive, psychically charged foreign visitors, plunging them into mental turmoil. Suddenly, they were confronted by mental distress that could be successfully internalized at home, but not in a provocative foreign setting. The majority of the foreign tourists who attended the Santa Maria

Nuova Hospital presented acute psychological disturbances that lasted from two to eight days or longer. Magherini classified the 106 cases observed between 1977 and 1986 into three types:

Type 1: Patients with predominantly psychotic symptoms ("*troubles de la pensée*"), representing 70 of the 106 cases;

Type 2: Patients with predominantly affective symptoms, of which there were 31;

Type 3: Patients whose predominant symptoms are somatic expressions of anxiety, (e.g. Panic attacks), of which there were only five.

Only 38 per cent of 'Type 1' patients had a prior psychiatric history, while 53 per cent of 'Type 2" patients presented report some sense of disintegration or fragmentation of self. The psychological profile of such patients was of single persons who were relatively young, sensitive, impressionable and travelling on their own (or perhaps with one other person), and were confronted by the sight of great works of art without the mediation of a professional guide. Furthermore, it was argued by Magherini that the discovered "malady" was not a new phenomenon in the Capital of Renaissance art, whose wealth of artistic beauty has attracted travellers throughout the ages.

Paris Syndrome

Paris syndrome is a transient psychological disorder encountered by some people visiting or vacationing in Paris. Japanese visitors are considered to be especially susceptible. The syndrome was first detected in 1986 by Prof Hiroaki Ota, a Japanese psychiatrist consulting afflicted Japanese visitors to France. He reported that some Japanese tourists visiting Paris encountered significant emotional distress when their fantasy and idealization of Paris turned into culture shock. However, in the European psychiatric literature the syndrome was first described in 2004 (Valia et al. 2004). It was found that around 20 Japanese tourists per year exhibit the syndrome. The afflicted individuals are characterized by a number of psychiatric symptoms such as acute delusional states, hallucinations, feelings of persecution (delusions of being a victim of prejudice, aggression, or hostility from others), de-realization, depersonalization, anxiety, as well as somatic manifestations of dizziness, tachycardia, sweating, etc. The authors identify two types of the syndrome:

Those who have a previous history of psychiatric problems, and may travel from Japan to Paris due to 'strange' or delusional motivation, and those without morbid history who exhibit the delayed-expression type. (Nam 2010)

The scenario of Japanese tourists in Paris is a fairly clear-cut demonstration of significantly diverse cultures coming into contact, most significantly in terms of an Asian culture meeting a Western culture. The Japanese vision of foreign countries is often based upon romantic perception rather than reality. Tourists arriving at Paris with highly romanticized expectations (at times after long years of anticipation) seem to be unprepared for the clash with reality. The language barrier, the pronounced cultural differences in communication styles and public manners, and the quotidian banalities of contemporary Paris – characterizing any other 21st-century Western-World city – induce profound culture shock which, according to the authors, triggers the syndrome (Halim 2010).

The 'White House Syndrome'

The 'White House Syndrome' is related to phenomena of eccentric visitors to the White House in Washington D.C. or to other government offices (often demanding a personal interview with the President). After being questioned by the Secret Service, and if considered mentally ill and potentially dangerous to themselves or others, they are referred to psychiatric hospitalization. Hoffman described in 1943 a variety of characteristics observed among the hospitalized visitors: Mainly single white males with poor vocational, social, and educational histories. Their median age was 44 years, most of them with a long history of psychiatric morbidity. The majority were described as passive, delusional paranoid schizophrenic patients; some were manic or 'organically confused'. They generally came to the White House or other government offices 'to give advice', obtain money, or demand redress of grievances or relief from alleged persecution (Hoffman 1943). Sebastiani and Foy (1965) described the typical non-forensic White House Case as a paranoid schizophrenic suffering from grandiose or persecutory delusions. For such patients, current national events had become incorporated into delusions that were persistent and tenaciously held. The patients were described as 'petitioners', seeking an 'authoritative judgment from the President' that would confirm their paranoid beliefs. Very few were violent at the White House, and the authors believed that none of these patients posed a real threat to the Presidency. The President was generally 'incorporated as a benevolent and necessary agent' in these patients' delusions. Sebastiani and Foy noted that while some of these patients were 'preoccupied with impending disaster and violence [...] a great many persons so preoccupied did not act with violence or any exceptional hostility during their White House visit or during their subsequent hospitalization'. The number of such cases mounted from less than ten per year during the 1940s to almost 100 per year during the early 1970s. A survey of the demographic characteristics and diagnoses of 328 of these 'White House Cases' hospitalized between 1970 and mid-1974 showed that most of these single white males were diagnosed as paranoid schizophrenics. Although 22 per cent of this group have threatened some prominent political figure, to date none of this study's patients has attempted to assassinate any such government official

(Shore et al. 1985). Shore and his associates (1985) conclude that the preeminent role of the President in American society has led to the inclusion of the President in the delusional system of so many psychiatric patients. Most of those labelled as 'White House Cases' considered the President a benevolent authority, and typically came to ask for some intervention on their behalf or to advise or warn the President in some way. Only a few delusional patients had thought that the President was a threatening authority who must be removed at all costs. None of the 328 patients in the study were known to have made an attempt on the life of any prominent political figure during follow-up, although one of them (who had threatened the President) shot and killed a Secret Service Agent in 1980. Another former White House Case patient later assaulted a security officer at a US Treasury Department office, and a third later assaulted a woman she mistakenly believed to be the First Lady.

Differences between the Phenomena

Differences between the three syndromes are related to the symbolic significance of each site. Florence is perceived as the shrine of renaissance arts, exhibiting an overwhelming wealth of colossal classical works which symbolize a turning point in the history of Christian humanism. The 15th-century renaissance works of art reflect a religious philosophy viewing life no longer as a vale of tears but as a quest for enlarging man's powers, and so his awareness of God. Thus the Florentine art treasures, apart from their impressive physical dimensions, symbolize the adherence of pagan antiquity and unorthodox thinking to the spirit of Christian faith. Paris syndrome, contrarily, represents an emotional shock derived from significantly diverse cultures coming into contact. Japanese tourists arrive in Paris with high romanticized expectations, sometimes after years of anticipation, and are unprepared for the reality of the city. The language barrier, the profound cultural differences both in communication styles and public manners 'trigger' feelings of de-realization, depersonalization, anxiety, as well as physical symptoms of dizziness, tachycardia, and even delusional states, hallucinations and feelings of persecution in severe psychiatric cases. The White House syndrome reflects a view by those who regard it as representing the establishment of mightiest earthly powers in recent political history. It symbolizes a modern philosophical political thought, where a mortal is elected by the people for the people, and is granted the power to influence global affairs. It is a symbol of a human superpower. However, the symbolism of Jerusalem is spiritual and embedded in the history of both Jewish and Christian messianic traditions. The uniqueness of this sacred place is derived from being perceived religiously as well as emotionally as 'the centre of the world'. Jerusalem is not just the 'axis mundi' of faith, but also the site where the last episode of a highly emotionally charged event, the end of times, is believed to occur. The syndrome in its modern transformations has been studied and has been described since the eighties and early nineties of the 20th century. However, there is evidence pointing at the existence of the syndrome since the early Middle-Ages.

Exploring the 'Jerusalem Syndrome'

Jerusalem is regarded a sacred space for all three monotheistic religions (in our studies we were focused upon Judaism and Christianity). The custom of Jewish pilgrimage to Jerusalem goes back to the days of the first temple, and exists in Christianity since its early days. It became an established model of worship by Christians during the fourth century AD. Turner (1973) defines this phenomenon as a 'prototypical' pilgrimage, in which the spiritual content of the act is directly related to the life of the founder of the faith and to geographical sites where central events in the history of the religion took place. Jerusalem, apart from being a place of crucial importance in the history of the religion, is regarded in religious eschatology as the arena where future events are believed to occur, encapsulated in messianic ideas of the forceful return of a founding figure that will initiate a new era for humankind.

Messianic Ideas and Millenarism in Judaism and Christianity

Messianic ideas have been observed in a great many religious contexts (e.g. Oceania, West Africa). However, the Judeo–Christian tradition is constructed around traditions in which the Holy City – Jerusalem, considered the *axis mundi* of faith (Eliade 1959) – is perceived as the arena where great dramatic events are about to occur. It is based on the belief that the Messiah – considered a descendent of Kind David – will be revealed and shall break the regime of foreigners, will revive the kingdom of Israel and gather its children from the Diaspora, the temple will be rebuilt and the work of sacrifice re-established. (Licht 1972) Born during the post Biblical era, Messianism reappears repeatedly throughout history with each generation reflecting a new set of ideas. Defining the Messiah as an eschatological figure originates from the apocalyptic literature of the second temple contemporaries. There is no unified relation to the Messiah in the Talmud and the Midrash, and references regarding his appearance are varied (Licht 1972). The everlasting search for a Messianic revival throughout human history appears to reflect a conjoint individual and communal craving and desire for consolation over deep emotional distresses along the human ages. Calculations and speculations of the date of redemption has become an unrepeated part of Jewish culture since the Middle-Ages in the Diaspora, as well as in modern times.

Similarly, the central element in the Christian eschatology is the expectation of the Second Advent of Christ and the establishment of the Kingdom of God on earth. This belief is based on interpretations of the book of Daniel and the book of the vision of John. According to Christian faith, due to the evil rule of the Antichrist the world will suffer a set of disasters, at the end of which redemption will occur, with its climax in the fall of the Great Babel, and the overthrow of Satan and his aids, who will be doomed to incarceration in Hell for a thousand years (the millennium). At the end of the millennium there shall be the war of Gog and Magog with the triumph of Good over Evil. The results will lead to the resurrection of the dead and the establishment of the New Jerusalem. Millenaristic movements are known to have existed since the Middle Ages (Cohn 1970). Towards the year 2000, millenaristic movements and apocalyptic expectations were rising in North America and throughout the world. Even after the disappointments that neither apocalyptic catastrophe nor redemption happened, the 'millenial myth' ingrained in Western culture is still continually generating new movements, which draw upon the myth and at time reshape and reconstruct it. Millenarists tend to adopt the 'method' of adhering biblical quotations to contemporary events, thus 'proving' current events to be significant 'markers' of the soon-coming redemption. Nineteenth century Jerusalem became an active arena for such believers and, even in today's Jerusalem, one can spot among tourists visiting the Holy city eccentric individuals dramatically expressing apocalyptic ideation, enhanced by current global events e.g. global warming or catastrophic events such as floods, hurricanes, draught or volcanic eruptions, exhausting multi-national wars, and world-wide acts of terror. The historical travel narratives by pilgrims who had gone to Jerusalem is overloaded with anecdotal descriptions of eccentric travellers, who upon arrival in the city regarded themselves as unique historical and religious figures, and acted accordingly (Witztum and Kalian 1999, p. 12). Systematic accounts of these unusual phenomena have been well documented since the mid-nineteenth century. To illustrate the phenomenon, we have selected a few significant examples.

Bertha Spafford-Vester

In her book of memoirs, *Our Jerusalem*, Bertha Spafford-Vester describes the saga of her family, as well as the foundation of the American Colony in Jerusalem by her parents (Spafford-Vester 1950). Fate navigated them through great personal suffering until empowered by faith they managed to fulfil their tremendous altruistic mission. A special chapter in Bertha's memoirs is dedicated to cases of eccentric characters among the various visitors, at times tenants, who came to the American Colony. 'Jerusalem attracts all kinds of people', she writes. 'Religious fanatics and cranks of different degrees of mental derangement seemed drawn as by a magnet to the Holy City. Some of those who particularly came into our lives were men and women who thought themselves the reincarnation of saints, prophets, priests, messiahs, and kings' (1950). As it occurs with other written accounts of her time, Bertha's descriptions are very vivid and picturesque. She even adds bits of her own subtle humour. In the first character she remembers 'old Mr. Benton', who 'thought he had invented perpetual motion'.

> Why he came to Jerusalem on that account is hard to tell, except that people less cranky than he believe Jerusalem to be the centre of the universe and he may have thought his discovery would get a better start from this point. He was sure his theory was plausible, yet it was quite evident Mr. Benton was not right in his mind. He bought a small bit of property in the open fields beyond the city limits […]. In those days it was considered dangerous to live so far outside the

city limits, but because Mr. Benton was noticeably simple even the peasants of the village of Lifta, the notorious thieves of that time, would not molest him. The Arabic conviction that God has touched his head established Mr. Benton as a holy man or dervish, and assured him safety. (Spafford-Vester 1950, p. 127)

She then writes that one day

> his wife and son Frank arrived. They had hunted for him everywhere and at last traced him to Jerusalem. They bought a small bit of property adjoining his […]. Their intention was to look after Mr. Benton, but he thought differently. Soon after his wife and son settled in their small house Mr. Benton vanished, and as far as I know was never heard from again. Later his poor abandoned wife and son went through a series of horrible troubles and people at the Colony had to nurse and protect them. (Spafford-Vester 1950, p. 128)

Another dramatic character was 'Elijah, as he called himself'. A converted Jew who arrived with his wife and son from America, and whose first disappointment in the Holy Land was to find out there were other compatriots already living in the Jerusalem. Nevertheless he began fasting, and 'on the third day was so weak he had to keep to his bed'. Bertha's mother inquired about him and found out he thought himself 'Elijah, who must come first and prepare the way to the Lord'. 'Mother understood and pitied his poor, unbalanced mind', Bertha writes, and then she explains: 'By this time we knew several like him, who thought they were John the Baptist or Elijah or another of the prophets. There were several Messiahs, too, wandering about Jerusalem'. Then Bertha gives a vivid description of a sequence of events (which seems almost inevitable in the eyes of a modern mental health professional), starting with a called for, humane act, done by her bountiful mother:

> She saw how physically weak the man was, so she prevailed on him to take a little milk. […] Later, they learned that her charitable act turned to be a devastating error. He rose early the next morning and left the house, and as we learned later, went to the top of the Mount of Olives. He had fasted three days and expected the hill to 'cleave in two' before him. I'm afraid he had his prophecies slightly mixed, but as no two people agree on them, that part was not important. He had been so positive, that when the prophecy was not fulfilled, his disappointment was terrific. The poor man could believe only that his failure was owing to breaking his fast, and that Mother was the evil spirit who had tempted him. He came back from his unsuccessful pilgrimage in an excited state, shouting, gesticulating, and condemning everyone in the Colony, especially mother, to outer darkness. We did not have to ask him to leave, he had already arranged for that. (Spafford-Vester 1950, p. 131)

However, later on 'Elijah' did return to their house in an acute paranoid state, acting violently and physically endangering Bertha's family. Eventually he recovered, and the Colony members bought him and his family tickets back to America. However, few years later he returned to the Holy City, this time as a salesman of hand operated vacuum cleaners. 'He sold only one, to our family', Bertha writes 'and so it happened that a second time we had to pay Elijah's passage back to the United States, for he had settled down in the American Colony with every apparent intention of remaining with us for the rest of his life'.

Another strange incident happened with a group of Germans who 'stalked into the living room without invitation and seated themselves without being asked'. It turned out, as their leader announced 'in a form of proclamation', that 'he had a spiritualistic mission in Jerusalem [...] and had been led by the Spirit from Germany to Palestine, to Jerusalem, and to this house, to take possession'. It took the intervention of the German Consul to drive the uninvited visitors out. Still, the leader of the group forced his flock to dwell in most dreadful unsanitary conditions, under the city walls in Solomon's Quarries, awaiting the 'spirits' to drive the Colony's tenants out of their homes. The German Consul was asked to intervene again; still he could not prevent the tragic end of the leader's wife and two other old women. The three could not endure the hardships and died in the local German hospital. And as for the head of that unfortunate group, in Bertha's words: 'The mad leader was sent back to Germany by his government.'

She concludes the chapter by stating that

> During our lives in Jerusalem we witnessed many tragedies caused by religious
> frenzies and fanaticisms, and followed the course of numerous unbalanced cranks.
> There is a thread of similarity in all their stories of the same sad, exaggerated
> egotism. Something in the brain suggests the idea of their uniqueness as chosen
> by God, or reincarnated to fulfil some tremendous purpose. I could continue
> indefinitely, for the simples in Allah's Garden were many, seeming to gravitate
> to the Holy Land to enter our lives for long or short periods of time, sometimes
> with direful consequences. The few I have told about are typical. (Spafford-
> Vester 1950, p. 141)

Adela Goodrich-Freer

Adela Goodrich-Freer, an English lady who travelled the country at the turn of the twentieth century, gives in her book *Inner Jerusalem* (1904) an enthusiastic account, full of praise and admiration, of the 'American Colony Overcomers'. However, she dedicates a large part of Chapter III to the issue of the city's 'cranks'. As she points out at the beginning of that chapter:

> It is a recognized fact that a large proportion of insanity takes the form of
> religious mania, and as Jerusalem, more even than Rome herself, is a gathering-
> place of creeds, the holy place alike of Christian, Jew and Moslem, nay more,
> as she unites the still wider disparities of sect and sect, it is hardly surprising
> that all the more striking eccentricities of Christianity seem to have been, at

some time or other, represented with her walls, from the self - tortured ascetics of the earliest Christian centuries, down to the latest extravagances fresh from America. (Goodrich-Freer 1904, p.35)

While Spafford-Vester (1950) chose to arrange the descriptions of her encounters with eccentric figures on a time-span axis, Goodrich-Freer gives an account of the 'cranks' on a geographical continuum. She puts a special impetus on the role of the Mount of Olives – at that time full of hectic activity of various Christian groups, since this is the location considered to be the arena for the announcement of the coming end of times:

To the east, we have the mount of Olives, geographically the rallying place of an extraordinary variety of enthusiasts, including a worthy English woman who is alleged (probably with some exaggeration) to be in constant readiness to welcomes Our Lord's return thither with a cup of tea. We have Adventists and Lydites, and Seventh Day Baptists, and Mormons, and votaries of Christian Science. We have had a penitent Englishman who did penance for his sins by beating his wife because it was the punishment which caused him the most pain. We have a worthy Englishwoman who at over fifty years of age converted a modest competence into portable property, and wandered out to Jerusalem alone, with fifty six pounds of luggage and one hundred and fifty pounds of money, upon which, with the kindly help of foreigners of another creed, she has lived for over twenty five years, convinced of the justice of her undertaking by the fact that she had travelling companions whose relation to each other permitted her to suppose her journey a fulfilment of Jeremiah iii,14: "I will take you one of a city, and two of a family, and I will bring you to Zion". We have had a well-intentioned pilgrim who, deciding somewhat hastily that her turn of mind was ascetic, presented herself at a strictly enclosed convent, entreating to be accepted as a novice, and insisting (immediately upon gaining admission, in spite of all representations as to the length of novitiate required) on cutting off her hair. Having discovered, however, in a few days, that she had no vocation, she was next observed at the door of the hospice, where her fellow-pilgrims had been received, imploring the advice of some young theological students as to where in Jerusalem she could get a wig – a situation that probably afforded them considerable amusement. (Goodrich-Freer 1904 p. 36)

Goodrich-Freer goes on describing all sorts of 'cranks', and then tells fantastic stories about groups of various Christian schools who tied their fate with the Holy City. A less fortunate group which suddenly appeared in 1885, and are documented in her book, were

a party of Saxons under the guidance of a miner who had received information from the Evil C-no as to the immediate incarnation of the Anti-Christ, whom they were directed to await in Jerusalem. Unfortunately their finances were tarried, and the party was soon reduced to extreme poverty, whence they were rescued, as many in need have been rescued, by the kindness and benevolence of the American Colony.[2] (Goodrich-Freer 1904, p. 41)

Dr Haim (Heintz) Herman

Dr Herman was a Jewish immigrant to Palestine from Germany. Director of the Ezrat-Nashim Psychiatric Hospital Institute between 1924 and 1948, he was a pioneer psychiatrist in Israel.

In a paper drawing attention to his personal experiences published in 1937 (Herman 1937), he stressed the difficulties to distinguish between normal and pathological psyche within the socio-geographical milieu of Jerusalem. He mentioned in particular the hectic believers of the numerous religions and sects attracted to the city, and pointed out the various messiahs and prophets that can be seen in the streets of Jerusalem. Herman further elaborates on 'the unique atmosphere of Jerusalem' and gives descriptions of several patients whose messianic ideas can be seen as core element of an emotional breakdown. Some of them, he noticed, claimed to have invented a new religion, consisting of an admixture of all existing religions of their time. His clinical observations (Hermann 1937) remain strikingly similar to those described in the writings of Spafford-Vester and Goodrich-Freer.

Recent Psychiatric Research on the Jerusalem Syndrome

Between 1979 and 1995, Kfar-Shaul Psychiatric Hospital has admitted all foreign tourists in need of psychiatric hospitalization in the Jerusalem area. During the first year 25 tourist-patients were admitted. In recent years, this number increased to an average of around 50 patients per annum. Comprehensive statistical data about these patients was gathered throughout the years. In addition, a more extensive and focused study was carried out between 1986 and 1987, gathering data on 89 patients (Bar-El, Witztum, Kalian et al. 1991). The two series of data – one based on 177 patients hospitalized between 1979 and 1984, the other on 89 hospitalized between 1986 and 87 – were then compared. Astonishingly, no significant differences were found with regard either to the method of referral or the age, gender, marital status, religion, country of origin, or the number of previous visits to Israel of the patients. Therefore we assumed that the patients analysed here[3]

---

2   It seems that the above mentioned group matches the descriptions given by Spafford-Vester of the German 'invading stalkers'.

3   The group studied comprised 32 women and 57 men whose mean age was 32.4 years. 74% were single, 15% divorced and only a minority (11%) married. 52% had received 13 or more years of education, 36% had between 8 and 12 years of education, while 7% had an education of less than five years. Most tourists came from North America (40%)

merely represented a normal distribution of people with psychological pathologies among the total of about one million tourists per year at that time. The examination of the behaviour of the patients before their admission to the hospital showed that behaviour such excessive preaching and vagrancy was found in 33 per cent of the cases. Manifestations of aggression, such as physically attacking people or threatening them with a weapon, led to the admission of 11 per cent. Another 11 per cent were walking around naked when apprehended and referred to hospital. Thirteen per cent were admitted after attempting suicide and 33 per cent did not show any specific behaviour.

While recent years saw the increase of a practice among eccentric tourists who quite literally enacted the idea of being 'Naked before God', dramatic episodes of 'religious violence' by affected individuals remained relatively rare. However, considering the sensitive relations between the various religious groups that attach spiritual and emotional values to significant sites within the Holy Space of Jerusalem, local violent acts can yield global reactions. Such was the uproar of the Muslim world in 1969 when Michael Dennis Rohan, an Australian Christian tourist and a member of the 'Church of the World' organization, tried to burn down The Dome of the Rock (El-Aqsa Mosque) 'so that the Jews will restore their temple upon the ruins, and the Messiah will return'. It turned out that shortly before committing his 'messianic mission' in Jerusalem he had been released from psychiatric hospitalization in Australia where he had been treated for schizophrenia. Other cases motivated by similar religious folly caused less harm and limited public distress, such as those from recent years, described below.

The Case of the 'Purified Giuseppe'

Giuseppe, a 40-year-old single male from a European country came to Jerusalem with a group of Catholic pilgrims. On their eighth day, after visiting most of the holy places, he suddenly busted into shouting, 'Thank you Jesus' and 'Ave Maria', stripped himself naked and ran along Via Dolorosa with his arms lifted up in the air. Members of the group ran after him trying to cover his naked body with their coats but he managed to push them away, ran into a street outside the walls and suddenly lay naked on the ground, causing havoc and a traffic jam. He was captured and taken to the nearest emergency room, where he became more agitated, and was referred to psychiatric hospitalization. He was then treated with anti-psychotic medications and recovered dramatically. The next day he was able to give some coherent rapport. Being an intelligent person with some insights gained in previous treatments, he tried to make sense of what was happening to

---

and Western Europe (44%); the remainder were from Eastern Europe, South America, South Africa or elsewhere. Among the analysed sample, various motifs to travel to the city were observed. 38% came for recreational purposes, 15% to visit relatives, 7% to do volunteer work, 26% for reasons of a mystical-religious nature, and 11% to experience the city considering the option to stay and settle.

him. It turned out that he had a previous psychiatric history. Since his early thirties, he experienced several short psychotic breakdowns which were treated in a day-hospital, with quick remissions. During remissions he continued outpatient care and worked as a technician in a communication company. He lived with his parents and was regarded as a devout Catholic. The lengthy suffering of his mother, who had died from cancer two years before, affected him deeply. According to peers in his group, he became spiritually devout to the Virgin Mary since his mother's death. They mentioned he had been very excited about going to Jerusalem but had shown no alarming signs during the first days. Giuseppe reported that on the day of his hospitalization in Jerusalem, while walking in the streets of Old City, 'in the footsteps of Jesus' he suddenly felt profound emotions and an unusual sense of an elated mood that exceeded anything he ever experienced before. Then, fuelled by an unimaginable sense of joy, he felt 'chosen', 'incarnated', and both 'purified' and 'canonized' for a most sublime mission, worthy of the love of the Virgin Mary. When running through the streets and finally laying 'naked before God' he felt totally immersed in the unique experience of humbleness and purity, worthy of the Holy Mother and 'deprived of any intent of the flesh'. Later, while being 'persecuted by the mob' and brought before the doctor, he thought he was facing Satan who tried to dismantle his 'purity' and jeopardize his 'sublime mission'. Though time was too short for therapeutic interpretations, Giuseppe managed to tie, with some ambivalence, his recent extraordinary experience with previous feelings of agony and distress experienced in his personal past which until then had not been worked-out with professional help.

The Case of 'John the Disappointed Emissary'

A case almost fatal was that of 'John', a 41-year-old tourist who was wounded by gun shots while trying to stab the guards at the Church of the Holy Sepulchre. Born to an upper middle-class family, John was the younger of two children in a family that moved through several locations within the British Commonwealth due to senior jobs taken by his father. His parents, retired and living for years in different locations, had led a disharmonious marriage life during his childhood and adolescent years, and finally got divorced when he was 20. John attended private schools where he had difficulties in maintaining relationships with his peers, was described as rather timid, solitary, and had learning difficulties. At times it was questioned whether he was dyslexic while there was no formal diagnosis. At the age of 16 he entered an apprenticeship as a boat-builder, but soon some alarming signs were spotted in his behaviour. His family doctor described a significant decline in concentration and inability to hold logical conversation. He left the apprenticeship and took temporary jobs. A few years later he suffered a full-blown paranoid psychotic episode. One night he called a friend of the family and told him he was convinced that the rock singer Ozzy Osbourne was involved in a plot to assassinate Tony Blair and urged him to deliver a warning to Downing Street. He explained that he identified characterizations of 'Nero', which are representations of 'Satan', in the appearances of the singer. His mother subsequently urged him to seek professional help. He refused claiming that 'all doctors are like Dr Shipman' (a family physician who turned out to be an infamous serial-killer of his patients). Two attempts to establish meaningful relations with women were terminated with heavy disappointment and distress. He then became over-indulged with religious scripts, living solitarily and becoming more estranged. At times he threw articles and pieces of furniture out of the window, claiming that they had been used by hostile entities to spy on him and other family members. He then gathered financial resources and travelled abroad. He went to China, Turkey, South Africa and Israel, at times carrying with him missionary pamphlets of Christian religious content. He visited Jerusalem four times. On his third visit he found a simple job in a small hostel in East Jerusalem and stayed there for three months. During that visit he started experiencing elated emotions, being convinced that he was 'one of the four emissaries' who would bring tidings of redemption to mankind. However, he was forced to return to England once he ran out of financial resources. Back home he gathered money once again, 'waiting for his day to come'. Six months before his fourth and last visit to the Holy City, a chain of global events made him see that 'The End was coming soon' and 'that God had chosen him to go to Jerusalem again'. He believed that he was to take the role of the emissary that would be killed by Satan – an act that would initiate the apocalyptic process at the end of which the evil powers would be defeated, Satan would be thrown to hell for a thousand years and good was to prevail. John noticed several satanic disruptions aiming to 'jeopardize his mission'. His flight was delayed due to a heavy volcanic cloud over the skies of Europe. Once landed, it took several hours until his luggage was found. However, in spite of all these obstacles, he was determined to reach the Church of the Holy Sepulchre and carry out his messianic mission. There, inside the Holy Place, he thought, his life would be sacrificed for the sake of mankind, since Satan – trying to prevent him from spreading the announcement – would kill him, the emissary, and by committing such an act would initiate the millennial apocalyptic process. Yet, when John eventually reached the holy site, in spite of all satanic tricks, the gates of the church were about to be closed for further visits that afternoon. He rushed to a shop in the Old City and bought a big knife. Determined to overcome Satan's tricks and diversions, he returned to the church, running towards the gates and aiming to stab an armed policeman located in front of the site, in spite of all warnings. He was shot and wounded. While being interviewed later in the surgical ward he expressed remorse for his foolish act, claiming that he should have understood that Satan was cunning and tricky enough to avoid 'the death of the emissary', since he knew that such act would eventually lead to his own defeat.

Concluding Remarks

The phenomenon of overseas visitors to Jerusalem who demonstrate highly emotional and eccentric acts, and attract attention by presenting themselves publicly as biblical or messianic figures, is not a new one. Cases of 'Jerusalem syndrome' can be traced back to the beginning of pilgrimage and tourism to the Holy city. There is a striking similarity between the clinical reports of tourists hospitalized in modern day Jerusalem, and the accounts documented throughout history since the Middle Ages. Contrary to some speculations about the syndrome, the city of Jerusalem is neither a pathogen, nor a precipitating factor. Studying the psychological profile of those who demonstrated the syndrome reveals a common emotional denominator. Almost every affected visitor – whether evaluated in modern times or studied through documents from the past, had a history of significant unresolved psychological distress. Either conscious or unconscious, personal motivation to travel to Jerusalem by the affected visitors exceeded ordinary needs based upon an individual's religious and cultural background. The personal, intimate experience of being chosen for a unique mission germinated prior to arriving in the Holy city, representing an initial stage in a voyage by an individual in need of solace. Once those fragile individuals reached Jerusalem their emotionally charged behaviour vividly demonstrated publicly their idiom of distress. Their eccentric conduct, at times a bizarre and psychopathological performance, became dramatically overt once they reached the Holy City – a geographical locus containing the *axis mundi* of their religious belief.

Tourism reflecting the de-contextualization, accompanied by environmental and cognitive stress, could be related to the need to order the unusual space of encounter through which tourists travel. It also reflects a desire to produce positive encounters with venerated realms such as 'Paris', 'high art in Italy', 'political mighty power', as well as sacred religious sites. It should be noted that in reference to holy spaces pilgrimage throughout the ages was considered prototypical to the phenomena of ordinary tourism. Being intrigued by the different and the desire to experience a particular significant place are probably essential parts constituting travel tourism, as well as modern pilgrimage to a unique place. However, mentally vulnerable people (probably due to prior psychiatric background) are at times susceptible to reacting in most extreme ways. These phenomena may raise curiosity by itself, yet in its extreme forms may delimit a social phenomenon most tourists live and actually research in much milder ways. It seems that the phenomena demonstrated by the so-called 'Jerusalem syndrome' represent a failed attempt by the afflicted individual to overcome personal distress germinated elsewhere, by utilizing a high emotionally-charged sacred place as an arena where the performed act, beyond its 'universal mission', represents a deep need for individual solace.

References

Amâncio, J.E. (2005) 'Dostoevsky and Stendhal's syndrome'. *Arquivos de Neuro-Psiquiatria*, 63(4), pp. 1099–1103.

Bar El, I., Witztum, E., Kalian, M., Brom, D. (1991) 'Psychiatric hospitalization of tourists in Jerusalem', *Comprehensive Psychiatry*, 32(3), pp. 238–244.

Bar-el, Y., Durst, R., Katz G., Zislin, J., Strauss, Z., Knobler, H.Y. (2000) 'Jerusalem syndrome', *British Journal of Psychiatry*, 176, pp. 86–90.

Cohn N. (1970) *The Pursuit of The Millennium*. Oxford: Oxford University Press.

Eliade, M. (1959). *The Sacred and The Profane, the Nature of Religion*, New York: Harcourt Brace Jovanovich.

Flinn, D.B. (1962) 'Transient psychotic reactions during travel', *American Journal of Psychiatry*, 119, pp. 173–174.

Freud, S. (1964) *A Disturbance of Memory on the Acropolis*, Standard Edition, Vol. 22, London: Hogarth, pp. 239–248.

Goodrich-Freer A. (1904) *Inner Jerusalem*, New York: E. P. Dutton & Co.

Halim, N. (2010) 'Mad tourists: The "Vectors" and meanings of City-Syndromes', www.inter-isciplinary.net/ptb/persons/madness/m1/halim%20paper.pdf (accessed on 24 December 2010).

Herman, H. (1937) 'Psychiatrisches aus Palastina', *Folia Clinica Orientalia*, 1, pp. 232–237.

Hiatt, C.C. and Spurlick, R.E. (1970) 'Geographical flight and its relation to crisis theory', *American Journal of Orthopsychiatry*, XL, pp. 53–57.

Hoffman, J.L. (1943) 'Psychotic visitors to government offices in the national capital', *American Journal Psychiatry*, 99(1), pp. 571–575.

Jauhar. P. and Weller, M.P.I. (1982) 'Psychiatric morbidity and time zone changes: A study of patients from Heathrow Airport', *British Journal of Psychiatry*, 140, pp. 231–235.

Jones, E. (1955) *The Life and Work of Sigmund Freud*, Vol. 2, New York: Basic Books.

Kalian M. and Witztum E. (2000) 'The quest for redemption: reality and fantasy in the mission to Jerusalem', in P. Hare and G.M. Kressel (eds), *Israel as Center stage: Setting for Social and Religious Enactment*, Westport, CO: Bergin & Garvey.

Kalian, M. and Witztum, E. (1988) 'Facing a Holy space: Psychiatric hospitalization of tourists in Jerusalem', in *Sacred Space: Shrine, City, Land*, Jerusalem and London: Israel Academy of Sciences and Humanities, and Macmillan.

Kalian, M. and Witztum, E. (2002) 'Jerusalem Syndrome as reflected in the pilgrimage and biographies of four extraordinary women from the 14th century to the end of the second millennium', *Mental Health, Religion and Culture*, 5(1), pp. 1–16.

Lange, W.R. and McCune, B.A. (1989) 'Substance abuse and international travel', *Advances in Alcohol and Substance Abuse*, 8, pp. 37–51.

Langen, D., Streltzer, J. and Kai, M. (1997) '"Honeymoon psychosis" in Japanese tourists to Hawaii', *Cultural Diversity* and *Mental Health*, 3(3), pp. 171–174.

Licht, J. (1972) 'Messiah', *Encyclopaedia Judaica*, 11, pp. 1407–1417.

Machils, G.E. and Burch, W.R. (1983) 'Relations between strangers: Cycles of structure and meaning in tourist experiences', *Sociological Review*, 22, pp. 666–692.

Magherini, G. (1989) *Le syndrome de Stendhal*, trans. Françoise Liffran, Florence: Uster.

Magherini, G. and Zanobini, A. (1987) 'Eventi e psicopatologia: Il perturbante turistico: nota preliminare', *Rassegna Studio Psichiatrici*, 74, pp. 1–14.

McIntosh, I.B. Swanson, V., Power, K.G. and Dempster, C. (1998) 'Anxiety and health problems related to air travel', *Journal of Travel Medicine* 5(4), pp. 198–204.

Nam. J. (2010) 'Paris Syndrome: Reverse homesickness?' www.mecon.nomadit. co.uk/./conference_epaper_download.php5 (accessed on 24 December 2010).

Pearce, P. (1982) *The Social Psychology of Tourist Behaviour*, Oxford: Pergamon Press.

Sebastiani, J.A. and Foy, J.L. (1965) 'Psychotic visitors to the White House', *American Journal of Psychiatry*, 122, pp. 679–686.

Shore, D, Filson, C.R., Davis, T.S., Olivos, G., Delisi, L. and. Wyat, G.R. (1985) 'White House cases: Psychiatric patients and the Secret Service, *American Journal of Psychiatry*, 142(3), pp. 308–312.

Singh, A.A. (1961) 'A case of psychosis precipitated by confinement in long distance travel by train', *American Journal of Psychiatry* CXVII, pp. 936–937.

Spafford-Vester, B. (1950) *Our Jerusalem. An American Family in the Holy City. The American Colony*, Lebanon: Middle East Export Press.

Stewart, L. and Leggat, P.A. (1989) 'Culture shock and travelers', *Journal of Travel Medicine*, 5(2), pp. 84–88.

Turner, V. (1973) 'The center out there: the pilgrims' goal', *History of Religion*, 12, pp. 191–210.

Viala, A., Ota, H., Vacheron, M.N., Marti, P. and Caroli, F. (2004) 'Les Japonais en voyage pathologique à Paris: un modèle original de prise en charge transculturelle', *Nervure* (supplement), 17(5), pp. 31–34.

Witztum E. and Kalian M. (1999) 'The Jerusalem Syndrome: Fantasy and reality. A survey of accounts from the 19th century to the end of second millennium', *Israel Journal of Psychiatry*, 36, pp. 260–271.

Chapter 7

Passionate Movements: Emotional and Social Dynamics of Padre Pio Pilgrims

Michael A. Di Giovine

Out of all the forms of travel and tourism, pilgrimage may best be associated with emotion, with a captivating and all-encompassing sense of passion that undertakes a participant's very being, often changing his very cosmology. Many scholars have attempted to posit a satisfactory definition of pilgrimage, but, like tourism, it is an activity whose meaning varies not only from culture to culture and epoch to epoch, but from person to person. Fundamentally, however, a pilgrimage is a ritual journey from the quotidian realm of profane society to a sacred centre, a passion-laden, hyper-meaningful voyage both outwardly and inwardly, which is often steeped in symbols and symbolic actions, and 'accrete[s] rich superstructures' of mythological representations (Turner and Turner 1978, p. 9, 23) that passionately captivate their practitioners. Upon reaching their destination, pilgrims mourn, leaving *immortelles* as Elvis devotees do at Graceland (Jasud 2009). They celebrate, singing songs, clapping and whistling as *peregrinos* do during Mass at the basilica of Santiago de Compostela, marking the completion of their *Camino* by wildly swinging an immense incense-spewing censor. They inflict penitential pain upon themselves, as Marian supplicants do when they crawl on their stomachs to the chapel in Fátima whose construction was requested by the Virgin Mary in an apparition to the *tres pastorhinos* in the early 20th century. Sometimes they are even moved to death, as some Hindu pilgrims aspire to do at the mansions of *moksha* in Varanasi, India (Parry 1995; Justice 1997).

While each of these examples regard a different kind of passion, all can be considered 'emotions in motion'. That is, the touristic form of interaction with a hyper-meaningful place – an action which we call pilgrimage – moves one not only physically, but also socially. Drawing on the studies of religion conducted by early social scientists such as Arnold van Gennep (1909[1960]), Emile Durkheim (1912[1995]), and Mircea Eliade (1959), Victor Turner pointed out that pilgrimage involves the movement from a society's profane centre to a sacred 'centre out there' (1973). It is a liminal place, 'betwixt-and-between' realms, wherein one is temporarily removed from his or her daily life. In the interaction with a place that is decidedly out-of-the-ordinary, peripheral to the profane, and hyper-meaningful, emotions that have often been cultivated for longs spans of time effervesce, creating formative passions that move people towards or away from each other (cf. Di Giovine 2009a).

As Turner contends (1973, 1974a, 1974b), such interior movements at a liminal pilgrimage centres marks a temporary reorganization of one's cosmology, in the way one perceives the outside world, its structures, and his or her place in it. As Turner and Turner write,

> Major liminal situations are occasions on which a society takes *cognizance of itself*, or rather where, in an interval between their incumbency of specific fixed positions, members of that society may obtain an approximation, however limited, to a global view of man's place in the cosmos and his relations with other classes of visible and invisible entities. (1978, p. 239–240, emphasis in original)

Anthropologists such as Anthony F.C. Wallace (1956), Claude Levi-Strauss (1974, p. 17), and Marshall Sahlins (2000) have argued that it is precisely this integration of the Other into one's cosmology, this shift in one's worldview and his place in it, through which society replicates itself. 'Every culture is a cosmological order', Sahlins points out, 'and in thus including the universe within its own cultural scheme ... people accord beings and things beyond their immediate community a definite place in its reproduction' (2000, p. 489).

However, the sentiment of unity between self and the Other seems to vary in accordance with the place that an object of pilgrimage occupies within the pilgrim's cosmology. In the pages to follow, I will examine three broad typologies of *'communitas'* or social movement among pilgrims to the Southern Italian towns of Pietrelcina and San Giovanni Rotondo. To many people, Pietrelcina and San Giovanni Rotondo are hyper-meaningful sites because they are intimately associated with the life and works of the newly canonized Catholic saint Padre Pio of Pietrelcina, a Capuchin monk who has become one of the 'world's most popular saints' (Wilkinson 2008) for his Christ-like suffering, poverty alleviation initiatives, and supernatural visions and stigmata, which he suffered until his death in 1968. Considered a 'living saint' during his lifetime (cf. Frank 2000), masses flocked to this remote monastery for a glimpse of his stigmata, to petition for help in their daily lives, and to celebrate the Sacrament of Reconciliation; Pio was said to know people's transgressions before they confessed them. Spurred on by worldwide prayer groups and a mass media conglomerate that effectively raised awareness of the supernatural abilities of the monk, these devotees formed a pilgrimage route and a new sacred center in the corpus of the small mountaintop town – which continued to grow after his death. Today, San Giovanni Rotondo nets 120 million Euros per year from its mix of hotels, restaurants, souvenir shops and media outlets. Since April 2008, when the Capuchin monks made the controversial decision to exhume and exhibit Pio's body (the monstrance concluded on Pio's feast day of September 23, 2009 after extending it for a year), an estimated nine million pilgrims have visited the town (Di Giovine 2009b, p. 483, cf. ANSA 2008). Featuring a new basilica designed by noted architect Renzo Piano and decorated by the famed sculptor Arnoldo Pomodoro and the Vatican's premier mosaic artist

Marko Ivan Rupnik, SJ, it is the second largest and second most-visited Catholic shrine in the world, surpassing even that of Lourdes.

Old Testament Identity in Pietrelcina: The Kinship-Heritage Typology

However, the sentiment of unity between self and the Other seems to vary in accordance with Padre Pio's understood place in the pilgrim's cosmology. Local pilgrims in Pietrelcina, Padre Pio's birth town, view the saint through a kinship-heritage idiom that is specifically defined against San Giovanni Rotondo – a direct response to the competition between the two towns, exacerbated by the unequal distribution of pilgrims (and the material benefits of pilgrimage and other forms of tourism) to the towns. Pilgrimages largely eschew a visit to the locations associated with Padre Pio's childhood, a holdover from the days in which they would travel to communicate directly with the 'living saint'. One Italian devotee and tour sponsor, who takes upwards of 50 pilgrims four times a year on Padre Pio-centered pilgrimages, informed me that she includes Pietrelcina on less than a quarter of her trips, and of her 45 pilgrims on a July 2009 tour I accompanied, only a handful had ever visited Pietrelcina. Indeed, when a passenger realized that the name of Pietrelcina was spelled incorrectly on the itinerary, a great discussion ensued on the bus on how to pronounce the name of the town; even the accompanying priest thought it was spelled differently until he read it in the *Guida Rossa* he brought with him on the journey, a red-bound guide which is culturally deemed obligatory for all Italian domestic tourists.

The geographic location of the town is also an issue for foreign and domestic tourists. One youth from the provincial capital of Benevento, 10 km away from Pietrelcina, explained, 'up until recently, people thought Pietrelcina was in the Province of Foggia', which, lying 165 km away from Pietrelcina, is the province in which San Giovanni Rotondo is found. Indeed, many Italians (who have not been to Pietrelcina) assume that San Giovanni Rotondo – the site of Pio's ministry, death, and sanctuary – naturally would be located near the place of his birth. This sentiment was actually confirmed by a group from central Italy, who were surprised at the two hour drive between Pietrelcina and San Giovanni Rotondo. 'I thought it was nearby', one remarked as the bus ambled through the winding roads of three regions (Campania, Molise and Puglia) to San Giovanni Rotondo.

On the whole, *Pietrelcinesi* share a communal sentiment that is founded – as so many other social groups are – in opposition to outsiders. Such a feeling of unity is particularly cultivated when *Pietrelcinesi* themselves engage devotional pilgrimages of their own, both when they visit San Giovanni Rotondo and when they engage in devotional or pilgrimage practices in and around their hometown. This particular sense of unity *Pietrelcinesi* feel seems to correspond with Old Testament spirituality. That is, one's identity is largely ascribed in an *a priori* society of moral hierarchies created by God; he is born into it and will die out of it. The ascriptive – rather than acquired – aspect of social status is evident in the

Old Testament's constant re-iterating of lineages, illustrated by its famous lists of 'begats' (cf. Reagen 2008). In this form of community, birthright and social institutions regulate one's status, and one 'proves' or acquires the privilege of being a full member of the group through socially sanctioned rites of passage. Physical markers aimed at distinguishing insiders from outsiders are important, from the tattoo God gives the exiled Cain to show that he is nevertheless a Hebrew and under God's protection from outsiders (Genesis 4:13–15) – in much the same way nomadic Bedouins do to indicate their tribal affiliations today (cf. *NAB* 1995, p. 11) – to circumcision which God requires the descendants of Abraham to practice as a sign of His new covenant (Genesis 10:11–14). But as the story of the rape of Dinah reveals (Genesis 34:1–26), the acquisition of such outward markers is not enough; kinship must nevertheless be ascribed.

When Pio became famous and his cult began to spread internationally, *Pietrelcinesi* began to feel their marginalization at the hands of San Giovanni Rotondo. Frustrated, *Pietrelcinesi* who visited the monk asked him why he allowed San Giovanni Rotondo to reap the material benefits of pilgrimage – including wealth, infrastructural development, and 'traffic' – while his hometown suffered poverty and anonymity. Pio reminded them that his visions of Jesus and Mary occurred first (and some would say 'only') when he was a child in Pietrelcina, and not San Giovanni Rotondo ('*A Pietrelcina c'è stato Gesù, e tutto è avvenuto là*' – 'Jesus was in Pietrelcina, and everything happened there'). He also promised, 'I have valorized San Giovanni in life, Pietrelcina I will valorize in death' (Da Prata and Da Ripabottoni 1994, p. 160,163).

Pietrelcinesi have begun to understand this as a special promise to protect them by virtue of their shared kinship and heritage, a familial 'story of love' (Mastronardi 2008) that continues to be written through the interactions between Padre Pio the saint and local *Pietrelcinesi*. They enjoy an ascriptive affinity to the saint and the benefits he bestows, over and above any assistance acquired through a conscious embracing of the cult. The emotional words of one poetic *Pietrelcinese*, Enrico Medi, speak volumes to this end:

> Padre Pio is from Pietrelcina.
> I'm sorry for S. Giovanni Rotondo.
> But he's from Pietrelcina.
> His first air, his first breath, his first little desire,
> his first milk, he took these all in Pietrelcina.
> And this can't be taken away by anyone.
> ...
> Why are you blessed, O Pietrelcina?
> Because Padre Pio, this man who one day will become,
> as he is already, one of greatest Saints of the Church,
> breathed his first air, his first oxygen, his first nitrogen,
> his first milk, his first smile, his first light, his first birdsong here in
> Pietrelcina.

This land was the first land his feet touched.
These rocks were the first rocks his little hands
collected. These images were the first images his eyes collected.
You are a holy city.

(qtd. Montella 2008: inside cover)[1]

And just as *Pietrelcinesi* have begun to re-write their version of Pio's narrative in text and image, so too are they re-inscribing it onto the appearance of their town itself. Collapsed buildings in the *centro storico* have been rebuilt; structures that were owned by Pio's family have been museumified and re-populated with period furniture. During the years between Pio's beatification and canonization, plaques commemorating places in which Pio or his family interacted seem to pop up every day. 'Soon it'll come out that every building is related to Padre Pio', scoffed one resident of Benevento, the nearby provincial capital, at what she perceived as Pietrelcina's invention of tradition (7/14/2009).

These elements seem to be effective for those pilgrims who do come to Pietrelcina, for they fulfil expectations of a 'classic Southern Italian village' that has been developed in the media. Numerous pilgrims state not only that 'it was just as I imagined', but, in the words of one pilgrim from Pesaro, 'with a little imagination, you can know how it was back them. The structures are all the same' (6/27/2009). Although the management of these sites makes no comparisons to San Giovanni Rotondo, many tourists have been overheard favourably comparing Pietrelcina's aesthetics to that of modern San Giovanni Rotondo. 'I like Pietrelcina better than San Giovanni Rotondo', one Italian declared as he rested with two women of the same age; they agreed that it was 'enchanting' (7/24/2009), as opposed to San Giovanni Rotondo, which is 'very, very modern with respect to who Padre Pio was' (Italian, 6/27/2009). Indeed, even pilgrims who correctly figured that 'it was more rustic back then', nevertheless positively recognized the heritage dimension: 'It [Pietrelcina] needs to be cleaned and organized. To maintain it, to let the future see how it was, for the people who will come – you have to maintain it like that' (Italian, 6/27/2009).

If heritage is, as I have argued elsewhere, a specific narrative claim about a place's ability to 'temporally mediate between an individual's lineage and society's history as a whole' (Di Giovine 2009a, p. 34), then such efforts to create Pietrelcina into a distinctive heritage site – where locals are the curators – is indicative of a revitalization movement, one that includes a conscious rediscovery, and revalorization, of their own selves in relation to the saint (Di Giovine 2010). Yet heritage is precisely what is being contested. While *Pietrelcinesi* boast a particular kinship link to Padre Pio, the Capuchin 'brothers' of Padre Pio counter with their own spiritual heritage claims – claims which, by virtue of their strong media enterprise, have reached the ears of outsiders. According to Christopher McKevitt, since Padre Pio was so materially helpful to San Giovanni Rotondo

---

1   Translation is my own.

during his lifetime, locals in San Giovanni Rotondo have 'recognized Pio as one of their own' (1991, p. 86; cf. Coleman and Elsner 1991, p. 66). When Pope Benedict XVI made his monumental first visit to Padre Pio's shrine on June 21, 2009, he began his homily by addressing the Capuchin brothers, San Giovannesi, and devotees from prayer groups as the *erediti* – the descendants – of Padre Pio. Notably absent was any mention of *Pietrelcinesi*.

Pietrelcina seemed to counter this pervasive conceptualization with a high-budget, televised media campaign of its own. On a night before the Pope's visit, the city hosted a nationally televised music festival which interspersed performances by top Italian pop artists and testimonials by devotees who experienced a miraculous intercession by the saint. (In actuality, the festival was planned much earlier than the Pope's visit, but the symbolism was not lost on residents). Crowds of locals – many of them youths singing along to popular songs and holding up banners for their favourite singers, many of whom were Southerners such as Gigi D'Alessio and Luca Napolitano – crammed the streets as dignitaries from the region enjoyed front-row tickets. The concert thus served as a double proselytization: on the one hand, it connected Padre Pio and his hometown to a nation that associates him with San Giovanni Rotondo; on the other hand, it instilled a revitalized sense of pride in the youth of the region, who come to Pietrelcina 'out of curiosity' (as one informant stated, 6/19/2009) but stay to learn about their special connection as 'descendants' (*erediti*) of Padre Pio – above and beyond their immediate position in the quotidian social structure of the town.

The town has also created a *Via del Rosario* – a mini pilgrimage route modelled after the steps of the Catholic rosary ritual, which connects the various locales in the region that are associated (or imagined to be associated) with Pio's life. In its very form, description and usage, this route calls upon San Giovanni Rotondo to create a sense of local unity. Dug into the mountainside between Padre Pio's sanctuary and the Casa Sollievo della Sofferenza, and boasting monumental sculptures at regular intervals along its tree-lined pathways, San Giovanni's *Via Crucis*, or Stations of the Cross, is one of the major religious sites for pilgrims to San Giovanni Rotondo. Pietrelcina's *Via del Rosario*, on the other hand, follows pre-existent pathways from the centre of the town into the countryside of Piana Romana, three kilometres away. While this route may have been created as a *Via Crucis* for visiting pilgrims, locals are the primary devotees who use this trail. Townspeople from all ages, genders and social positions (fieldnotes 9/7/2009) move *en masse* through the rocky natural trail on September 7, the anniversary of Pio's 'invisible stigmata' – a sharp pain on Pio's hands, side and feet that occurred after Pio underwent a mystical experience under an elm tree in the country outside of Pietrelcina. Though Pio did not manifest any external signs of the stigmata, *Pietrelcinesi* consider this the first occurrence of the stigmata, which would occur several years later while Pio was praying before a crucifix in San Giovanni Rotondo's monastery. Reciting the rosary, reflecting on Pio's letters, and carrying a replica statue of their patroness, the Madonna della Libera, hundreds of locals – elderly walking with canes, school children in shorts and sneakers, nuns and monks, and civic leaders – depart from their cathedral and make the hike through the wooded hillside to Piana Romana's new sanctuary to 'Blessed Padre Pio' (it was dedicated before Padre Pio was canonized). The pilgrimage ends with a Mass in Pio's honour, typically said by a visiting archbishop flanked by military police, Capuchin monks and Pietrelcina's mayor dressed in full regalia. These townspeople walk the *Via del Rosario* not (necessarily) out of penitence or thanksgiving to Padre Pio, but out of a communal celebration of a particular historical moment that definitively placed Pietrelcina on the map, setting its townspeople apart as a sanctified people.

Although two visiting Padre Pio prayer groups joined in the 2009 pilgrimage I attended, it is clear that the *Via del Rosario* is a local affair, a local pilgrimage route for those whose identity is constructed through a very local narrative of Padre Pio – one that imprints important elements of *Pietrelcinesi* life onto Pio's biography. One advertisement that was plastered on walls in Pietrelcina during the summer of 2008 describes the *Via del Rosario* in just this way:

> The Via del Rosario is a route that connects Pietrelcina with Piana Romana, which Padre Pio walked while reciting the Holy Rosary. Who knows how many graces he obtained for our souls through the many rosaries he recited along this very path. It is up to us to re-walk [this path] to obtain from our heavenly *Mamma* all of the graces we need for ourselves, for all those we hold dear, for our Church and for the world.[2]

As this quote reveals, Pietrelcina creates a particular biography of Padre Pio that is intensely local, and easily shared by those who imaginatively walk in the saint's footsteps. It recalls the special kin-based relationship they have with Padre Pio and the Virgin Mary: Pilgrimage at Pietrelcina – especially by those in the Benevento region who straddle both categories of 'hosts' and 'guests' – goes beyond mere *dulia*, or salvific Catholic veneration; it is an act of familial bonding. Padre Pio mediates between locals and the Madonna who is not simply the spiritual *Madre* (Mother), but *la mamma* – familiar, caring and nurturing; one to whom a child calls out in love, in devotion, in suffering.

New Testament Identity among Pilgrims: The Ecumenical-Catholic Typology

Devotees of Padre Pio, however, view the saint as a communal 'intimate, invisible friend' (cf. Brown 1981, pp. 50–51) – one who intercedes on their behalf without regard to birthright or geographic region – and their act of pilgrimage often elicits a distinctive sense of 'fellow-feeling', as Adam Smith once called it (2000, p. 241), a 'sympathetic' recognition of another social organism's humanity, a sense

---

2   Translation is my own.

of unity in diversity. Pilgrimage fosters not only a religious experience with a liminal destination, but what Turner calls *communitas*. *Communitas* is more than merely a sense of 'community' – a term which itself is imbued with a geographical sense of common living within a social structure. Rather, occurring in the liminal phase of rituals wherein individuated statuses are suspended as individuals pass from one state to another, or from one structure to another, *communitas* is social anti-structure, a transcendence of social statuses that serve to order a social community. A convert to Catholicism from atheistic communism, one can sense liberation theology at work in Turner's theory: *communitas* is social 'anti-structure', 'not a structural reversal, but the liberation of human capacities of cognition, affect, volition, creativity, etc., from the normative constraints incumbent upon occupying a sequence of social statuses' (1982, p. 44).

But the notion of *communitas* is not relegated solely to 1960s socialist Catholicism; St Augustine of Hippo, writing nearly 1600 years earlier, invokes a similar concept in his theological treatise *De Civitas Dei* (*The City of God*), in which he frequently utilizes the metaphor of pilgrimage to describe the unifying, yet individually-instantiated, interior journey all Christians must take from the *civitas terrena*, or 'city of man',[3] to the heavenly city of God, *civitas Dei*. These are not (necessarily) tangible cities (which would be written as *urbs* in Latin), but rather moral orders, or communities; ruled by individual desires over oneself – which he calls the enjoyment of *libido dominandi* (cf. Milbank 1990, p. 390) – the *civitas* of man is a single community composed of individuals who are bound by the universality of human nature to seek out individual pleasure and to avoid pain (Augustine 1958, p. 224). This is the height of disorder, the height of division and chaos; and for Augustine, God enjoins good Christians unify in a pilgrim band which 'pursues' Him through love (1958, p. 191). 'The City of God invites all people from all nations and races together and unites them into a single pilgrim band', Augustine writes; 'she takes no issue with customs, laws and traditions, which on earth were used to foster peace. Rather, she takes and appropriates whatever is best from these diversities of diverse races, to use for maintaining everlasting peace' (458).

Augustine's theories are rooted in the Catholic doctrine of *communio*, the communion of believers who make up the Church (George 2009, pp. 18–20), which is based on the turns of thought evident in the Gospels, particularly that of Matthew. Commonly called the 'Gospel of Obedience', Matthew's account was probably written for nascent Christians in Antioch, a community boasting a large mix of Greek-speaking Jewish and gentile converts (Spivey and Smith 1995, pp. 97–98; *NAB* 1995, p. 1009), and thus he had to appeal to, and integrate, both Hebrew 'insiders' and Gentile 'outsiders'. Textually, Matthew accomplished this by beginning his book with Jesus' genealogy, a clear reference to the ascribed

---

3   The original Latin text can be found online at www.thelatinlibrary.com/augustine/ civ11.shtml. This particular phrase is found in, for example, Book XI: 1 (or, in the English, pp. 205–206).

nature of Hebrew sociality, yet transforming it in Jesus' liminal Sermon on the Mount, acclaimed as the 'heart and centre of Christian faith' (Spivey and Smith 1995, p. 107) precisely for its exposition of *communitas*. In this sermon, Jesus lays out a new moral contract for the Church in the form of the Beatitudes; kinship or heritage is superseded by universal human ethics: 'Blessed are the poor in spirit, theirs is the kingdom of heaven' (Matthew 5:3). This form of belonging, of being under the 'protection' or beneficence of God through moral action (including 'obedience'), is quite different from the kin-based heritage conception in the Old Testament, as illustrated by God's statement to Noah after He destroys all but Noah's family in the flood: 'With you I shall establish my covenant; you and your sons, your wife and your sons' wives' (Genesis 6:18). God revitalizes this covenant to Abraham in similar kinship idioms: 'My covenant with you is this: you are to become the father of a host of nations ... I will maintain my covenant with you and your descendants after you throughout the ages as an everlasting pact, to be your God and the God of your descendants after you' (Genesis 17:4, 7). In the Sermon on the Mount, on the contrary, Jesus breaks with Old Testament sociality as a basis for salvation and preaches a new form of *communitas*, or 'anti-structure' (Turner 1974b, pp. 202–203) which exists above and beyond temporal social orders; the 'kingdom of heaven' can belong to anyone – regardless, or in spite of, their social status, kinship or social network – so long as they follow a particular moral code that is theoretically accessible to all.

St Augustine discusses this supplanting of temporal social structure – and the imagined kinship that goes along with it – in favour of a universal communitas precisely through the idiom of pilgrimage. This pilgrimage is another *civitas*, another group composed of diverse individuals, albeit oriented in a very specific and standardized direction, in which each must 'pursue' Him with love (1958, p. 191). As with any sort of pursuit, whether it be a race or a pilgrimage, the velocity and time that it takes varies from person to person. Yet participation in this pilgrimage has a distinct origin and a distinct endpoint: in Augustine's case, it bridges the community of man and the community of God. Renouncing the divisive chaos of the earthly community wherein individuals act in individual ways to satisfy their personal pleasures, Augustine's pilgrims set off on a communal interior movement wherein all proceed separately yet in unison with virtue: avoiding sin and thereby directing action towards the same goal, which is existence in a perfect and ordered community where all Creation is in spiritual, intellectual and material unison with the Creator – and, through this, with each other. In doing so, the very act of pilgrimage, the very act of unifying above and beyond traditional social structures, creates what Augustine calls the *civitas Dei supra terram* – the city of God on earth – the Church. It is this conceptualization of the Church that St Paul calls the body of Christ in his oft-cited letter to the nascent community of believers in Corinth: 'Do you not know that your bodies are members of Christ? ... [W]hoever is joined to the Lord becomes one spirit with him' (1 Corinthians 17–18). In response to Paul's letter to the Ephesians, which states, 'For no one hates his own flesh but rather nourishes and cherishes it, even as Christ does the church, because we are members of His body' (Ephesians 5:29–30), the parish priest of Pietrelcina, a Capuchin monk, referred to human agency in the construction of Augustine's *civitas Dei supra terram* through pilgrimage when he said in a recent homily, 'We create our own society' (fieldnotes 8/23/2009). Individuals become the totality that is the metaphysical Christ precisely through this iterative, and emulative, interior pilgrim movement – which, like contemporary tourism, must be undertaken voluntarily.

Indeed, Augustine points to another aspect of Catholic pilgrimage, which is fundamental to creating Turner's emotional sense of *communitas*: its iterative, and emulative, quality (Barry 2008, p. 63). Much has been written on the iterative quality of pilgrimage – and by association, tourism (cf. Cohen 1972; De Kadt 1972, p. 44; Turner and Turner 1978; Graburn 1983; Sivan 1988; Eade and Sallnow 1990; Honey 1991, p. 91; Williams 1998; Elsner 2000, p. 181; Di Giovine 2009a, pp. 145–185). In particular, Dean MacCannell argues that the tourist 'attraction' is created at the confluence of person-place-marker (1976, p. 41), where a marker any type of information about the site, such as images, texts, oral narratives, and relics – what I have elsewhere termed 'reproducible re-presentations' for their ability to present the site across multiple geographies and temporalities simultaneously (2009a, pp. 376–396). It is precisely through this process that 'site sacrality' is created (MacCannell 1976, pp. 43–45) – drawing a constant flow of tourist-pilgrims to the same place. Locals, whose businesses are increasingly tailored to tourism, are quick to notice broad trends in groups' itineraries, and often complain about the relatively short time (and little money) pilgrims spend in Pietrelcina.

While they may spend only a few short hours in the town, pilgrims who have heard about Pietrelcina are genuinely interested in visiting the sites associated with the stories they have heard about Padre Pio; favourite places are Padre Pio's house, the *torretta* atop '*a morgia* (about which Pio often spoke), and the famous '*olmo*' (elm tree) in Piana Romana where Pio experienced his invisible stigmata and well-noted ecstatic visions of Jesus and Mary (it is now behind glass inside a small country chapel, rubbed smooth and petrified from the hands of thousands of pilgrims). Like at other tourist sites, pilgrims on the narrow streets of Pietrelcina are overheard exchanging stories of the places they visited, and frequently a visitor will scramble to see a site others spoke about but he or she mistakenly skipped over.

As Augustine conveys, pilgrimage is also phenomenologically iterative, which creates deep emotional and moral implications. Augustine's pilgrim joins with others who have come before him, and leads the way for others who will come later, on a common pilgrim trail. Likewise, one must recall that Matthew's account of the Sermon on the Mount concludes with Jesus making the clarification that, although salvation is open to all through God's justified, unmerited Grace, obedience is still required; one can enter the kingdom only if he performs 'the will of my Father in heaven' (Mt. 7:21). That saints' shrines are primary objects of pilgrimage is fitting, for, in the words of the Catechism of the Catholic Church, a saint is a 'disciple who has lived a life of exemplary fidelity to the Lord' (United States Catholic

Conference 1994, p. 2156). Collective and institutionalized veneration (*dulia*) of saints ultimately stems from the pagan cult of the dead (Cunningham 2005, pp. 10–11; Delooz 2005, p. 191; cf. Thurston 1911), practices by extended family to 'care for the dead' though elaborate burial customs and graveside rituals (Brown 1981, p. 24). Peter Brown contends that these practices translated into veneration by early Christians, especially when the grave contained martyrs, who, 'because they had died as human beings, enjoyed close intimacy with God. Their intimacy with God was the *sine qua non* of their ability to intercede for, and, so, to protect, their fellow mortals' (1981, p. 6). Writing at roughly the same time as Augustine, St John Chrysostom explicitly states that 'veneration of the martyrs is imitation of the martyrs' (cf. Marx 1842, pp. 60–61, qtd in Barry 2008, p. 63). This imitation of the saints' obedience to God's moral tenets forms the interior movement in an Augustinian pilgrimage, and joins all together in a *communitas* that transcends the social structures of the temporal world. One should not forget that the term *(h)agios* (saint), as St Paul frequently invokes in his greetings to various communities (for example, Romans 1:7; 2 Corinthians 1:1; Ephesians 1:1), was thus originally intended to denote members of the early Christian community (Cunningham 2005, pp. 8–9). In short, the 'communion of saints' (as the Nicene Creed calls it) is those, living and dead, who are recognized to be close to God through measurable obedience (Cunningham 2005, p. 9).

Turnerian *communitas* is the transcendence of traditional boundaries that mark daily social life, a recognition among individuals temporarily stripped of their social trappings that they are all the same – precisely because they are all engaged in similar moral and material actions, irrespective of their position in society, the proverbial speed in which they engage in such action. '*Communitas* is universalistic', Turner writes (1974b, p. 217). At the same time, the structure never passes away; Turner recognizes that 'seeking oneness is not … to withdraw from multiplicity; it is to eliminate divisiveness, to realize non-duality' (217). All creation is ultimately the fruit of God's work; *communitas* is the fleeting, yet emotionally striking, recognition of this (cf. George 2009, pp. 17–18). For St Augustine and other Catholic theologians, the Church gives structure to this realization of universal *communitas* (cf. Starkloff 1997); pilgrimage thus serves to continually refresh such sentiments. Fostering *communitas*, fostering a sense of oneness with self and Other, pilgrimage is thus integral to not only the creation of a community of faith, but to the replication of the entire devotional society as a whole.

Arguments have been levelled against Turner's analysis (cf. Eade and Sallnow 1991), however, and the most compelling concern the evident, and seemingly omnipresent, sense of competition both among pilgrim groups and between pilgrim centres. One sees this in many different places across the world, not the least of which at my field sites of Pietrelcina and San Giovanni Rotondo, the birthplace and sanctuary, respectively, of St Padre Pio. Like so many others, groups of pilgrims come to these two sites adorned with markers denoting their devotional affiliations; they often sport matching T-shirts, baseball caps, badges or bandannas inscribed with the name of their parish or prayer group, and some may carry large flags or banners with the name of their prayer group and place of origin written on it. But while these exterior signs may seem to index competition, from the interior, contemplative point of view, a unity nevertheless seems to be created – a certain, temporary non-duality, a shedding of external social trappings that are so viscerally indexed in the manifestation of such outward symbols.

The 2009 visit of Pope Benedict XVI to Pio's shrine was particularly imbued with external markers of division and stratification. Papal visits, like other visits of heads of state, are heavily symbolic events which often reaffirm the socio-political structure. Secular leaders at San Giovanni Rotondo jockeyed for public 'face time' with the Pope, while members of the Capuchin order, lay youth groups, and other political figures were valorized through brief, private encounters with their highest spiritual leader before he returned to the Vatican. 'Hundreds of thousands from all over the world' (Asian News 2009) showed up for a rainy papal Mass outside Pio's new basilica, and for security purposes this large crowd had to be divided into 'digestible' pieces to maintain order. Pilgrims had to obtain tickets through their parishes or prayer groups in advance, and seating for the Mass was divided hierarchically in terms of sectors. That morning, volunteers from San Giovanni Rotondo handed out yellow and white bandannas commemorating the papal visit, special missals for the Mass, and prayer cards with the Pope's image on it. These relics were to be distributed only to ticket holders – which may seem to reinforce a sense of division among pilgrims – and crowds of non-ticket-holders would press against the railings, their hands outstretched, begging, like prison inmates, for 'just one image' of the Pope. In the spirit of *communitas*, the volunteers would buck their orders not to give the objects out to ticketless pilgrims and occasionally launch a confection of banners to the crowd, who would scramble like chickens at feeding time to grab one or two. Even the ticket holders who were able to take their fill would pass the relics to the poor masses on the other side of the gate. For their part, the non-ticket-holders who caught these confections did not greedily hoard the spoils they caught, but would distribute them among their neighbours, whom they did not know but who were united, along with everyone on the other side of the railing, in a common pilgrim devotion to the saint. This *communitas* persisted not only despite such outward procedures of division and hierarchization, but *was elicited precisely through such processes.*

'A pilgrim is half a tourist if a tourist is half a pilgrim', Victor and Edith Turner once wrote, and this is ever the more the case considering modern-day pilgrimage utilizes the same global infrastructures as mass tourism (cf. Meyer 2007, pp. 145–146) – including tour operators, hoteliers, bus drivers, tour guides, and other entities within the 'field of touristic production' (Di Giovine 2009a, pp. 42–48). When instances of divisiveness among groups or group members did emerge, in fact, they were nearly always of a 'touristic' kind, having more to do with unfulfilled expectations concerning the quality of the hotels, the taste of the food, or the organizational abilities of the tour manager. Hotels, for example, garner the largest number of complaints among cultural tourists for a variety of reasons that concern their liminal position as an oasis-like 'home away from home'

(Di Giovine 2009a, pp. 177–178); theoretically, this perception of the nature of hotels should differ from the traditional understandings of pilgrim accommodations, which were low-cost hostels (*ospezie*) and hospitals (*spedali*). But in the summer of 2009, hostilities initially flared among members of an Irish prayer group who have stayed in the same hotel for decades, when they discovered that some of their fellow travellers were placed in a lower-quality hotel by the tour operator. They manifested their anger against the leader of a second group, whose members were added to their own by the same agency because of insufficient sales but received better rooms. While politics may also underlie this situation (the larger group was from Northern Ireland while the second was from Ireland), the discontent was directed primarily towards a perceived lack of interpersonal 'fellow feeling' by the second group leader – who never thanked them – and unbalanced treatment by the operator. But even in this situation, a sense of 'fellow felling' poked out, as a traveller who was placed in the better hotel finally offered her room to the group's accompanying priest, who was particularly dissatisfied with his hotel.

Communitas is also publicly articulated, particularly by spiritual leaders and the tour guides who frequently work with them. In particular, they urge their travellers to think differently. 'This is a pilgrimage not a leisure trip' one guide told her group, echoing the words of an Italian priest who began his welcome speech as the bus left home, 'Remember, this is a pilgrimage not tourism'. Even pilgrimage leaders, particularly those who had been accompanying travellers for many years, are quick to invoke unity among their groups. At the end of the tour, the third Irish group leader, 'Brendan', (who was in another hotel and out of the fray) invited the two other groups to a festive farewell dinner. He evoked pilgrim *communitas* and a shared purpose, and complemented the unity they eventually experienced even as he chastised them:

> The most important thing is that we are a family ... we're a family of pilgrims
> – so what if your pillows aren't right, your room isn't right, the food isn't right .
> We are all pilgrims, not holidaymakers; think of St Francis walkin' – we are not
> holidaymakers but pilgrims – it's harsh but that's what I have to say.

Following his speech, all three groups finished their cake – which read 'Grazie Padre Pio' – and began singing mournful Irish ballads together.

Modernistic Intimacy: The Existentialist-Individualistic Typology

While both the heritage paradigm espoused by *Pietrelcinesi* locals and the ecumenical *communitas* felt by the masses unify individuals from different levels of society together, there is also a third category of pilgrim that comes to venerate Padre Pio. They are devotees who experience an intimate, personal relationship with the saint, a passionate movement that not only exists above and beyond the social milieu in which the pilgrim finds himself, but which actively sets the practitioner apart from the pilgrim masses. It is a small but vocal group of people, who often testify to this miraculous individualization in print, as one American devotee named Kevin did when he published his unique pilgrim experience online. It turns out that he is an usher at my own parish in Chicago, and I asked him to recount the story after Mass to me one day.

The year was 1965, less than three years before Padre Pio would pass away. On his 21st birthday Kevin made the pilgrimage to San Giovanni Rotondo to witness Mass by this living saint. Because Kevin didn't speak Italian, he had reluctantly foregone the usual cue to confess his sins to Padre Pio directly. But, remembering that Padre Pio would often say, 'send me your guardian angel',

> Well, I remembered that and I just, I was laying in bed one night and so I decided that, ok, I ask my guardian angel to go to Padre Pio to discuss with him whatever I needed for my spiritual life. There was nothing in particular. And then ... the following night, I went to where he cell was, because people used to gather in the garden area there, and he would come to the window and say goodnight and talk to the people. And he started talking to the people staying there. And there was woman was standing next to me, and I said, 'please could you tell me what Padre Pio said?' and she said, 'Yes, he just said he was kept awake last night by a guardian angel from America!' (laughs). And oh, that was amazing there. That was amazing!

After (and perhaps in spite of) this direct, existential experience with Padre Pio, Kevin has actively involved himself in communal pilgrimage and devotional experiences. He has gone back to San Giovanni Rotondo three more times (but only one included a trip to Pietrelcina), and was present in Rome for both Pio's beatification in 1999 and canonization in 2002, for the latter bringing a fellow usher with him. Kevin is currently the co-moderator of a 200-person online Padre Pio prayer group that boasts members from all over the world.

While Kevin's formative, emotional and individual experience occurred while Pio was still alive, many enjoyed a similar type of experience on pilgrimages after he died. In particular, they attest to sensing a sweet-smelling odour, which is characteristic of many saints since late antiquity (cf. Brown 1981, p. 82), and particularly for Padre Pio. (Indeed, locals at San Giovanni Rotondo sell artificially rose-scented holy water, too – much to the chagrin of the Capuchin monks who tell devotees 'there is no such thing as Padre Pio holy water – if someone tells you they have it, tell them to go away!' (fieldnotes 8/29/2009)). One telling example, out of many, is a story recounted to me on a train from Benevento by a devotee on her way to join a pilgrimage to Medjugorje. As a local from the province of Benevento, she strongly conformed to the kinship-heritage paradigm of a local pilgrim – although she prefers Medjugorje to San Giovanni Rotondo in terms of the sentiment that she gets from it, she is 'obviously' devoted to Padre Pio by dint of his associated kinship. Indeed, when her friend asked her to go to San Giovanni Rotondo she did not get any heightened sensation, and was let down. In particular, her friend had said she once smelled Padre Pio's famous perfume, and though she hoped (and perhaps expected to) smell it, she didn't.

> I was really disappointed about not smelling the perfume as we left. And then – I remember we got gas at the Agip [a gas station right outside San Giovanni Rotondo]. And I smelled the perfume! I asked Michele [her husband], and he said he smelled nothing. I looked around and said, 'There must be something in this car.' 'I don't smell anything,' he replied! Well, that smell was with me from San Giovanni Rotondo all the way until San Giorgio del Sannio [a town outside Pietrelcina].

Such occurrences are of an existential nature; they single an individual out from the masses for special treatment by the saint. This is not *communitas* – 'anti-structure' or 'fellow-feeling' – but nor is it a conformity to deeply rooted social structure or kinship claims. Rather, individualism is privileged over any particular *communio* or social group – Padre Pio does not simply communicate to an individual in prayer, in the privacy of one's own home, but actively singles a faithful devotee out from the masses during a pilgrimage. Padre Pio made reference to the special attention he paid to Kevin's guardian angel, which was conveyed through the mediation of other pilgrims listening, with Kevin, to the monk's nightly predications. Likewise, Padre Pio made his post-mortem presence known to the second informant only after she left the pilgrim group and began traveling home; furthermore, he explicitly did not manifest himself (in the form of the perfume) to her companion.

And along with an existential experience, a pilgrim may also suffer an existential crisis, as in the case of one devotee from Belfast, Ireland, who met Padre Pio with her aunt and cousin in 1968. She recounted the event:

> Forty years ago, I came with my cousin a few months before he [Pio] died. We met him and my cousin got to shake his hand. And I was always a little jealous, and thought, 'why her and not me? Did I do something [that made him not shake my hand]?' But maybe it was because I had short hair, but she had short hair too—but I *was* shorter ... (8/28/2009)

This speaker did not receive special treatment from Padre Pio, yet nevertheless felt singled out by the saint through her very exclusion. She interpreted this exclusion in existential terms, as a personalized message from Padre Pio that needed to be deciphered. This clearly created a crisis for the narrator, evoking questions of physical and moral inadequacy which she repeatedly turned over in her head throughout the years. In her account, she eventually makes recourse to logic, though she remains unconvinced: 'I guess I should consider myself fortunate to have ever met him.'

As Kierkegaard points out in his Existentialist treatise, *Fear and Trembling*, such occurrences ultimately require an act of faith by the devotee – which he considers the greatest of passions, the most genuinely human factor in life (2006, pp. 149–150). Because Man can only make meaning of the world through the standard communicative symbols and rules of understanding that the ethical community presents (53), this movement seems to rest on the 'strength of the absurd' (65,146) that is absolutely incomprehensible and unable to be humanly articulated – to his fellow citizens and his own consciousness alike (70). Thus, this 'movement of faith' (54) necessarily pits 'the singular individual ... [as] the particular in opposition to the universal' (72). Yet according to Kierkegaard, faith is the greatest of passions, the most genuinely human factor in life (149–150). Unlike Smith's passionate, intersubjective fellow-feeling that constitutes the bonds of community, or Turner's anti-structural *communitas* that temporarily constructs a new order among pilgrims, Kierkegaard's is an *intra*-subjective movement, an intensely individual call to action that occurs privately and interiorly, and thus separates (81). It does not occur between two human actors, but rather between an individual and the supernatural,[4] who requires him to act in purely personal virtue in contradiction to the community's ethical norms (69). This poses a particular problem to the Catholic community, predicated as it is on *communio*. While the catholic paradigm as espoused by Turner and Augustine is an on-going, progressive pilgrimage that an individual joins, this existential paradigm is a momentary leap of faith. That is, an ecumenical pilgrim joins a universal movement – an unchanging river flowing across space and time – while Kierkegaard's individualistic pilgrim leaps like a salmon out of this river, and, once the move to higher ground is made, the individual re-integrates himself back into the eternal flow of the ethical.

If one of pilgrimage's most meaningful effects is to induce a communal sense of 'fellow-feeling', to unify at least a select group of men and women together, and to endow them with a heightened understanding of their shared humanity, such existential spiritualism – if it occurs in lieu of, or supplants, this *communitas* – troubles some pilgrimage sponsors. As one Italian priest and pilgrimage spiritual director stated,

> The problem with [spiritual] intimacy and not including everyone together is that you become too individualist – everyone has a personal relationship with God; He means something different to each person. And you lose religion. Remember, religion comes from the Latin *religio*, to bind. *Rilegare* is what you do to a book, it means to put pages together. If you don't have that, you just have scattered pieces of paper; you don't have a book. (6/23/2009)

Although this priest was talking about certain strands of modern Protestant spirituality, his words can easily be applied to discourses concerning pilgrimage, and the Church's often reticence to embrace charismatic saints such as Padre Pio. In

---

4   'Supernatural' is my word, used to denote a category of beings; throughout the book, Kierkegaard uses the term 'Absolute', which is not a category but a precise supernatural individual (namely, God).

life, as in death, Pio had the charisma – which in the Catholic faith literally means 'grace' or 'free gift' (cf. 1 Corinthians 12:10) – to attract others, to communicate with them, to stir their passions and their emotions. Such charisma, when recognized by the Church, can lead members on a proper ethical path, in service to the 'communal good' (Leon-Dufour 1970, pp. 152–155). As the aforementioned priest explained, 'The charisma of sainthood, like beauty, draws people towards the beauty of sanctity. The saint and sainthood is the instrument that brings others towards God.' *Communitas* is therefore an integral product of Catholic pilgrimage, a passionate recognition of one's non-duality with Others, who are united together in an unceasing interior journey along which they are drawn by the saint's charisma. Yet in the case of Padre Pio, how the saint is understood in relationship to the practitioner determines the direction of this movement, and how the Other will be integrated – or marginalized – in it.

Bibliography

ANSA (2008) 'Padre Pio set to beat Lourdes', *ANSA English Media Newswire*, May 7, 2008. Accessed from Lexis Nexis on May 7, 2008.

Augustine of Hippo (1958) *The City of God*, trans. G. Walsh, D. Zema, G. Monahan and D. Honan, New York: Doubleday.

Barry, K. (2008) 'On site: Pilgrimage and authorship in Goethe's "Third Pilgrimage" and *Italian Journey*', in J. Zilcosky (ed.), *Writing Travel: The Poetics and Politics of the Modern Journey*. Toronto: University of Toronto Press, pp. 57–78.

Brown, P. (1981) *The Cult of the Saints*, Chicago: University of Chicago Press.

Cohen, E. (1972) 'Towards a sociology of international tourism', *Social Research*, 39(1), pp. 89–103.

Coleman, S. and Elsner, J. (1991) 'Contesting pilgrimage: Current views and future directions', *Cambridge Anthropology*, 15(3), pp. 63–73.

Cunningham, L. (2005) *A Brief History of Saints*, Malden, MA: Blackwell Publishing.

Da Prata, L. and da Ripabottoni, A. (1994) *Beata Te, Pietrelcina*. Pietrelcina: Convento 'Padre Pio'—Frati Minori Cappuccini.

De Kadt, E. (1979) 'Social planning for tourism in the developing countries', *Annals of Tourism Research*, Jan/March, pp. 36–48.

Delooz, P. (1983) 'Towards a sociological study of canonized sainthood', in S. Wilson (ed.), *Saints and their Cults: Studies in Religious Sociology, Folklore and History*. Cambridge: Cambridge University Press, pp. 189–215.

Di Giovine, M. (2009a) *The Heritage-scape: UNESCO, World Heritage, and Tourism*, Lanham, MD: Lexington Books.

Di Giovine, M. (2009b) 'Re-Presenting St. Padre Pio of Pietrelcina: Contested ways of seeing a contemporary saint', *Critical Inquiry*, The Curious Category of the Saint, Vol. 35, No. 3.

Di Giovine, M. (2010) 'Rethinking development: Religious tourism as material and cultural revitalization in Pietrelcina, Italy', *Tourism: An International Interdisciplinary Journal*. Special edition, 'Tourism, Religion, Culture', 58(3), pp. 271–288.

Durkheim, E. (1912[1995]) *The Elementary Forms of Religious Life*, New York: The Free Press.

Eade, J. and Sallnow, M. (eds) (1991) *Contesting the Sacred: The Anthropology of Christian Pilgrimage*, London: Routledge.

Eliade, M. (1959) *The Sacred and the Profane*, Orlando: Harcourt.

Elsner, J. (2000) 'The *Itinerarium Burdigalense*: Politics and Salvation in the Geography of Constantine's Empire', *Journal of Roman Studies*, 90, pp. 180–194

Fisher, I. (2008) 'Italian saint stirs up a mix of faith and commerce', *New York Times*. Section A, Column 0, page 9, April 25, 2008. Accessed from Lexis Nexis on August 27, 2008.

Frank, G. (2000) *The Memory of the Eyes*, Berkeley: University of California Press.

Fulton, R. (2002) *From Judgment to Passion: Devotion to Christ and the Virgin Mary, 800–1200*, New York: Columbia University Press.

George, F. (2009) *The Difference that God Makes: A Catholic Vision of Faith, Communion, and Culture*, Chestnut Ridge, NY: Herder and Herder.

Graburn, N. (1977) 'Tourism: The Sacred Journey', in V. Smith (ed.), *Hosts and Guests: The Anthropology of Tourism*, Philadelphia: The University of Pennsylvania Press.

Graburn, N. (1983) 'The anthropology of tourism', *Annals of Tourism Research*, 10, pp. 9–33.

Honey, M. (1991) *Ecotourism and Sustainable Development: Who Owns Paradise?*, Washington, DC: Island Press.

Jesud, L. (2009) 'St. Elvis', *Critical Inquiry*. The Curious Category of the Saint, Vol. 35, No. 3.

Justice, C. (1997) *Dying the Good Death: The Pilgrimage to Die in India's Holy City*, New York: State University of New York Press.

Kierkegaard, S. (2006) *Fear and Trembling*, trans. A. Hannay, New York: Penguin.

Leon-Dufour, X. (ed.) (1970) *Vocabulaire de Théologie Biblique*, Paris: Les Éditions du Cerf.

Lévi-Strauss, C. (1974 [1966]) *The Savage Mind*, London: Weidenfeld & Nicolson.

MacCannell, D. (1976) *The Tourist: A New Theory of the Leisure Class*, Berkeley: University of California Press.

Marx, J. (1842) *Das Wallfahrten in der katholischen Kirche. Historisch-kritisch dargestellt nach den Scriften der Kirchenvälter un den Concilien von den ersten christlichen Jahrhunderten bis auf die nuere Zeit*, Trier: Fr. Linz'sche Buchhandlung.

Mastronardi, D. (2008) *Storia d'Amore*. Reprinted by the author from the first edition, *Padre Pio, il Santo di Pietrelcina* (2002) Pietrelcina (BN): Edizioni Padre Pio S.r.l.

Mauss, M. (1954) *The Gift*, London: Cohen and West, Ltd.

McKevitt, C. (1991) 'San Giovanni Rotondo and the shrine of Padre Pio', in J. Eade and M. Sallnow (eds), *Contesting the Sacred: The Anthropology of Christian Pilgrimage*, Urbana and Chicago: University of Illinois Press, pp. 77–97.

Meyer, J.W., Boli, J., Thomas, G. and Ramirez, F.O. (1997) 'World society and the Nation-State', *The American Journal of Sociology*, 103(1), pp. 144–181.

Milbank, J. (1990) *Theology and Social Theory*, Oxford: Blackwell.

Montella, C. (2008) *Padre Pio Pietrelcinesi*, Benevento: Flash Print.

Neirotti, M. (2008) 'Fede e show l'esposizione della salma. Gli occhi del mondo su Padre Pio. Quindicimila persone in attesa, a San Giovanni anche una troupe di Al Jazeera. Dopo 40 anni si rivedrà il corpo del Santo', *La Stampa*, Section CRI, pg. 11. Accessed from Lexis Nexis on August 28, 2008.

New American Bible (NAB) (1995) Wichita, KS: Catholic Bible Publishers.

Parry, J. (1995) *Death in Benaras*, Cambridge: Cambridge University Press.

Reagen, D. (2008) 'Those "Boring Begats"', *The Christ in Prophecy Journal* (Blog). Thursday, August 14, 2008. Accessed from www.lamblion.us/2008/08/those-boring-begats.html on July 24, 2009.

Sahlins, M. (2002) 'Goodbye to Tristes Tropes', in *idem, Culture and Practice: Selected Essays*, New York: Zone Books.

Smith, A. (2000) *The Theory of Moral Sentiments*, Amherst, NY: Prometheus Press.

Spivey, R. and Smith, D.M. (1995) *Anatomy of the New Testament: A Guide to its Structure and Meaning*, Englewood Cliffs, NJ: Prentice Hall.

Thurston, H. (1911) 'Relics', *The Catholic Encyclopedia*, Vol. 12, New York: Robert Appleton Company. Accessed from www.newadvent.org/cathen/12734a.htm on August 27, 2008.

Turner, V. (1973) 'The center out there: Pilgrim's goal', *History of Religions*, 12, pp. 191–230.

Turner, V. (1974a) 'Pilgrimage and communitas', *Studia Missionalia*, 23, pp. 305–327.

Turner, V. (1974b) 'Pilgrimages as social processes', in *idem, Dramas, Fields and Metaphors: Symbolic Action in Human Society*, Ithaca: Cornell University Press, pp. 166–229.

Turner, V. (1982) 'Liminal to liminoid in play, flow, and ritual', in *idem, From Ritual to Theatre: The Human Seriousness of Play*, New York: Performing Arts Journal Publications, pp. 20–60.

Turner, V. and Turner, E. (1978) *Image and Pilgrimage in Christian Culture*, New York: Columbia University Press.

United States Catholic Conference – Libreria Editrice Vaticana (1994) *Catechism of the Catholic Church*, Ligouri, MO: Ligouri Publications.

Urry, J. (2002) *The Tourist Gaze*. London: Sage.

van Gennep, A. (1909[1960]) *Rites of Passage*, Chicago: University of Chicago Press.

Wallace, A.F.C. (1956) 'Revitalization movements', *American Anthropologist*, n.s., 58(2), pp. 264–281.

Wilkinson, T. (2008) 'Padre Pio exhumed for a second life', *Los Angeles Times*, April 25. Accessed from http://articles.latimes.com/2008/apr/25/world/fg-padre25 on August 26, 2008.

Williams, W. (1998) *Narrative and Pilgrimage in the French Renaissance*, Oxford: Oxford University Press.

PART II
The Emotions of Attractions

Chapter 8

Religious Devotion and Sublime Experience during the Procession of the Romería in El Rocío, Spain

Eddy Plasquy

The yearly celebration in honour of the patron saint of the Andalusian village of Almonte, the *Virgen del Rocío*, is by all reasonable standards exceptional. Not only because of the unique location and the amplitude of the *romería*,[1] but also due to the way the tumultuous procession takes place, and especially the extremely belligerent attitude of the Almontese men during its course. The excessive tension which surrounds the statue seems to go against all that is normally associated with a formal procession in a Roman Catholic context. Instead of a respectful and peaceful carrying around of a holy statue, the spectacle has much more in common with a never-ending melee during a rugby game. Non-villagers are not allowed to approach the patron saint and are firmly kept away. Continuous discussions with angry bystanders, who do not accept the leading role of the Almontese men, often escalate into short fist fights. At the same time, people are anxiously watching the passing image and are visibly moved by what is happening. Passions boil up while both men and women burst out in tears. Violence and emotions are inextricably connected in this idiosyncratic ritual which is recognized as one of the most emblematic expressions of local religion in this South Spanish region.

Viewing such a baffling and unique spectacle makes one even more puzzled, thinking: what the hell is going on there. In order to feel at least some firm ground, Terence Turner's assertion that ritual is activity that frames itself as ritual, comes to the fore as a good starting point to approach the remarkable events in El Rocío (Turner 2006). It draws attention to framing as a key dynamic of ritual and makes the activity that occurs within the frame significant as ritual action (Kapferer 2006). This framing involves, according to Turner, signs and patterns of behaviour, usually but not necessarily repetitive and commonly recognized.

---

1 A *romería* in Spanish or *romaria* in Portuguese is a religious pilgrimage. The word *romería/romaria* comes from *romero/romeiro*, meaning those travelling towards Rome. It is a Catholic celebration that consists of a trip or peregrination (in cars, floats, on horseback or on foot) that ends at a sanctuary or hermitage. It is not necessarily always a trip, but in some cases a celebration that lasts for several days.

The way a statue is moved around forms a crucial element in the framing of a procession. It sets aside the object as special and plays a key role in triggering the specific emotional flow which characterizes the celebration. When carried around, the transcendental saint is not merely symbolized but actualized during the course of the procession. For the people present it becomes nothing less than the concrete manifestation of the saint or holiness itself (Gell 1998; Sax 1990; Schieffelin 1985). For David Parkin, the rules by which these movements take place are vital, because a ritual is not just performative but performative-for-some goal and for-someone:

> ritual tends towards a performative pour-soi, conscious, through its participants, of its power to make or break life depending on the directions and, literally, the steps it takes and so entrusted with that good faith, yet forever experimenting with these spatial forms. (Parkin 1992, p. 17)

João Pina-Cabral (1986) and Jon Mitchell (2004) offer pretty convincing examples of how important directionality is within the context of Catholic processions. Pina-Cabral documents the *romaria* in Alto Minho in Northern Portugal and describes the processions associated with saints' feasts as nothing less than rituals of correct motion. Mitchell focuses on a *festa* in the Maltese city of Valetta and, after clarifying the importance of the saint's cult as a locus for the exercise of popular lay control, illustrates how, within a structure of correct spatiality, the agency of this lay authority is publicly demonstrated.

The presence of human agency in such a 'framing' mechanism can hardly be overestimated. Especially when this involvement implicates potential trauma, and the physical and symbolic subjection of the body can be interpreted as the literal and figurative subjection of the person to the power of the saint (Mitchell 2004). In such instances, the emotions during the procession not only stem from the presence of the moving statue but also from the experience of those who are directly involved with it. As if the resulting emotional expression achieves significance 'both for those whose bodies are actively, expressively involved and also those who do not physically participate' (Lüddeckens 2006, p. 569).

The peculiar manner in which the procession in El Rocio takes places stresses these theoretical insights. When, following Parkin, it is accepted that directionality and spatial qualities are seen as the basis of a 'proper', 'hallowed' or 'effective' ritual, the question rises how this directionality and these spatial qualities are to be interpreted in a context which has more in common with a tempest than an ordered liturgical event. The same counts for the startling movements the holy statue undergoes in the eye of this human cyclone where, at first sight, the contrast with a respectful handling can hardly be more pronounced. At the same time and within the same context, clear differences between the ritual actors and the spectators are constantly blurred. When the latter engage in a fight with the former, one can indeed ask how this physical violence plays a role in the arousal of an emotional vein which ultimately fuels both the religious devotion and the peculiar sublime experiences during the procession.

All these questions came to mind while doing fieldwork in Almonte from 2001 on.[2] Since then, I have spent several months a year in the village and have participated at every *romería*. This long term presence meant that, during the procession, observation gradually shifted to active participation. The initial puzzlement as well as the core ideas of this contribution occurred to me during these intense moments beside the Almontese men.

The Confusing Attitude of the Almontese Men

The highly unusual honouring of the Virgin Mary starts with a chaotic assault on the altar verge after which the statue of the *Virgen* is brought out of the chapel by the Almontese men. For more than twelve hours, the heavy stretcher with the image is surrounded by hundreds of Almontese men. All seem to be more engaged in either a continuous fight to get under one of the beams or in keeping foreigners away, than in keeping it upright. Seen from afar, the statue seems to be floating on a sea of heads, never stable and always uncertain about the way it will proceed. Its course depends on the collective force generated by the ever-changing endeavour of the men around the stretcher and those who have put their shoulder under it. The statue can suddenly change direction, turn around, accelerate, stay put, incline and even slide down to the ground. When this happens, it often takes several attempts before the stretcher – weighing more than 800 kg – can be brought upright again.

It stands without any doubt that the unique way in which the procession takes place and especially the aggressive conduct of the Almontese men, provide some good arguments to explain the presence of the tens of thousands of spectators during the event. Year after year, their bewildering attitude is broadcast live on several regional and national TV channels and commented on in popular magazines, newspapers and documentaries. Commentators and social scientists have interpreted their brutal behaviour in different ways. Their opinions range from theologically inspired authors who see in their conduct an incomprehensible and pure love for their patron saint, comparable with the early Christian martyrs (Diaz de la Serna 1998); to anthropologists who perceive it as a relic of an authentic rural way of life, mysteriously kept alive in this village (Rodriguez Becerra 1986, 2000; Cantero 2002); an example of symbolic robbery (Comelles 1984, 1995; Moreno 1990, 1993), or a case of extreme sociocentrism, referring with this concept to the quite fanatic way in which villagers, by definition, view

---

2 The fieldwork is part of a PhD program in anthropology at the University of Leuven (Belgium), IARA department of Social Sciences. The initial focus of the research was centred on the repercussions of the highly popular cult for, and in, this village. Later on, this interest was complemented with a focus on the ritual changes the *romería* in El Rocío underwent during the last fifty years (Plasquy 2006, 2010).

themselves as better than all the neighbouring ones. Still others approach it as an epiphenomenon due to the presence of the TV media or the large number of spectators (Zapata 1991; Comelles 1995; Crain 1992, 1997). Finally, more ironic observers, such as the Sevillian columnist Antonio Burgos, even give the whole scenery a globalizing twist, portraying the Almontese as the Basques of Andalusia, fearlessly defending their local rights against an advancing globalizing cultural crushing (ABC, 26/5/1985).

These are all very interesting observations and descriptions. However, they all have in common a very restricted focus on the attitude of the Almontese men. As a consequence, questions which relate their conduct to the popularity of the image stay largely out of sight. Given the immense appeal of the cult of the Virgen del Rocío, one can indeed ask whether the violent attitude of the Almontese men has something to do with this rather exceptional upswing in popularity. While it is undeniable that the devotion in El Rocío can look back on a rich history, sprinkled with moments of regional, political and economic importance, it is also true that the image as such has never been gifted with exceptional miracles, visions or appearances. In this respect, it is not different from the tens of other local images in the region. Nevertheless, the presence of the huge number of pilgrims and spectators during the *romería*, not to mention those around the world who, in one way or another, are inspired by that image, leaves no doubt about the agency attributed to this specific Virgin.

The relation between this remarkable increase in popularity and the tumultuous way the procession takes place forms the core subject of this contribution. The topic shall be approached from two different angles. In the first part, Gell's theory on art and agency will be used as a starting point to explore the impact of the unforeseeable movements on the anthropomorphic qualities of the statue and the nature of the agency which can be related to these. Next, attention is drawn towards the impact of the frenzied Almontese behaviour on the experience of the spectators. This will be done using Kant's insights on the sublime. However, before tackling these peculiar aspects of the celebration, some general background is needed. Firstly about the cult of the Virgen del Rocío and the singular relation the Almontese have with their patron saint. Secondly, about the course of the yearly celebration, or *romería*, in El Rocío.

History of the Cult of the Virgen del Rocío and the Almontese Village

The cult of the Virgen del Rocío, which literally means 'the Virgin of the dew', spans more than seven centuries. The first historical references to the chapel appear halfway through the 14th century, in a time when the region was reconquered from the Moors (Infante Galan 1971; Murphy and Gonzales Faraco 2002). The chapel stands right in the middle of the hostile marshlands bordering the Guadalquivir River, in an area deep in Southern Spain, nowadays belonging to the province of Huelva. Partly due to this location in a true no-man's land, it took until the last quarter of the 16th century before the spot officially became part of the Almontese territory (Ojeda Rivera 1987).

In contrast to the scarcity of historical manuscripts to document the foundation of the chapel, a highly popular legend explains in detail the presence of the image of the Virgin Mary as a miraculous event.[3] The story goes that in the course of the 15th century a solitary hunter encountered, pointed towards it by his dog, a statue in a little bush deep in the marshland. He took it out of the tree and left with the idea to taking it to the village. However, since he was too far from Almonte to get there before night, he decided to camp outdoors. The next morning he found to his surprise that the image was no longer with him but back at the spot where he first encountered it. Completely upset, he ran to the village to tell his odd experience to the priest and the mayor. After bringing them to the site where the image still stood, they agreed that this could only be interpreted as a holy sign. As a consequence they decided to construct a chapel for this wonderful and miraculous statue.

The geographical location where the Virgen is venerated is known as '*Las Rocinas*' which meant that, until the middle of the 17th century, the statue was referred to as *La Santa Maria de las Rocinas*. Then the name changed to *La Virgen del Rocío*. A good half century before, the statue of the Virgin Mary underwent an even more radical transformation. The polychromatic wooden statue was mutilated and transformed into a substantially taller doll-like image, dressed in the aristocratic style of that epoch.[4] From a *Virgen Hodegetría*, representing a humble Virgin Mary with a little Jesus on her arm, it became all of a sudden a *Virgen Majestad*, raised upright with the little Jesus holding a globe and a sceptre between his outstretched hands (Carrasco Terriza 2002). It is in this representation that the Holy Mother is still venerated today.

From around 1600 it is documented that the Almontese relied on the Virgin Mary in El Rocío to protect them against natural calamities. When famine, drought or plagues scourged the villagers, the statue was brought from the remote chapel into the village. In 1656, this protective reliance became formalized with the recognition of the Virgen del Rocío as the patron saint of Almonte (Flores Cala

---

3   The first version of this story appears halfway through the 18th century in the first publication of the rules of brotherhood of Almonte. It is clearly one of the countless versions of the so-called discovery legends which, from the 15th century on, played a crucial role in the dissemination of the Marian cult throughout Spain (Christian 1981).

4   The adaptation of a statue was, according to the Spanish art historian Manuel Trens (1946), quite common in the Counter Reformation. Not only did the infantile habit to dress these dolls give way to an increase in devotion, but the offered mantles, crowns and jewels were also seen as a way to gain an indulgence. In the case of El Rocío, both changes are barely documented. Nevertheless, several clues point to the influence of a Franciscan order from Almonte. Not only were they, at the turn of the century, in charge of the chapel, but they also had a theological interest in the onomastic and iconographic change of the statue. With the name 'Rocío', which refers both to the holy dew and the Holy Spirit, the biblical connotation is obvious (Infante Galan 1971); see also Christian (1976) on the role of the Monastic orders in the spreading of the Marian cult in Southern Spain.

2005; García García 2007). From then on, the statue is also brought to the village on exceptional occasions, such as for example the end of a war or the crowing of a king. When, halfway through the last century, the means to deal with natural calamities became greater and, as a consequence, the necessity to bring the statue to the village lessened, it was decided to take the statue to the village for a stay of nine months every seven years.[5] Throughout that time the Virgin Mary is guarded in the parochial church and all the celebrations which normally take place in El Rocío happen in the village.

The fomenting and the propagation of a local cult is traditionally the mission of a brotherhood, or *hermandad*.[6] When the fame of the venerated statue exceeds the village boundaries and brotherhoods are founded in the vicinity or in locations further away, their influence and responsibility increase accordingly. In the highly exceptional case of the cult of the Virgen del Rocío, 107 officially affiliated brotherhoods have been recognized so far. Eighty per cent of these brotherhoods are situated in the Western provinces of Andalusia, the rest of them are spread out over the other Andalusian provinces and several other Spanish regions (Cháves Flores 2004). In the year 2000 the first brotherhood outside of Spain was recognized: the brotherhood of Brussels, founded by a group of eurocrats working at the European institutions in Brussels (Plasquy 2010).

The reasons why such a network came into existence are diverse. According to Muñoz Bort (2002) the first impetus for this offset was given in the 17th century. Although situated in a hostile and abandoned area of Almonte the chapel was constructed at the crossroads of two important trade routes and meant that, at that time, the *romería* was already attended by brotherhoods from the neighbouring villages and cities. In 1913 the supra-local significance of the cult of the Virgen del Rocío was further underlined with an official crowning, backed up by influential and eminent personalities from Sevilla and Huelva. Meanwhile, the polarizing and escalating political climate of that time turned the brotherhoods into bastions in defence of the Catholic cause. In the turbulent years before the outbreak of the Civil War, more than ten new brotherhoods were founded. During the harsh decades after the war, this increase slowed down. But, halfway through the sixties, a new spectacular enlargement of the network began, largely due to an impressive master plan which envisioned not only the opening up of the economically

---

5   For this occasion, the whole village is beautifully decorated with huge wooden arches and white paper flowers. The statue of the Virgin Mary undergoes a complete change for this procession. No longer dressed as a queen but rather as an aristocratic traveller, she is brought to the village during an enigmatic night on the shoulders of the Almontese men. Meanwhile, her crown and golden ornaments are carried by a group of older women (Rodriguez Ramirez 2006).

6   With a history that goes back to the 16th century, the Spanish brotherhoods are still influential local actors and a true backbone for the expression of popular religion. As a lay-organization they form a crucial link between the ecclesiastical authorities on the one hand and the local folk beliefs and interests on the other (Bennassar 1979; Agudo Torrico 1999).

backward region but also the reactivation of the Christian devotion. The former would be realized through the building of a beach resort on the nearby coast and the construction of a new road which facilitated the access to El Rocío, the latter by the erection of a brand new chapel and a profound amplification of urbanization (Ojeda Rivera 1989). At the same time a huge part of the marshland was recognized as a national park while the rest was opened up for fruit growing.

The increasing popularity, or so-called 'massification', of El Rocío does not moderate the privileged position the Almontese claim vis-à-vis their patron saint. On the contrary: the Almontese brotherhood firmly remains the primary agent in the fomenting of the cult. Firstly, as the head of the extended network of brotherhoods and with the authority to decide whether or not a brotherhood is accepted as a formal member. Secondly, as the proper organizer of the yearly collective pilgrimage at Pentecost. Meanwhile, the Almontese people leave not the slightest doubt that, despite the immense fame of the Virgin Mary of El Rocío, she is still their patron saint. This is all the more apparent during the *romería*, and especially during the procession.

The Procession during the Romería

In the days before Pentecost tens of thousands of pilgrims and spectators arrive at El Rocío. Many of these pilgrims are members of one of the brotherhoods who officially participate at the *romería* and with which they have been on the road for several days. The size of these brotherhoods varies significantly. The prestigious brotherhoods from the cities of Seville, Huelva and Cadiz can count on tens of thousands of pilgrims. Those from more humble locations, the recently founded ones, and the ones coming from further away, are significantly smaller and in many cases number below a hundred. Regardless of their size all follow one of the four historical paths which lead to the emblematic site. The majority of the brotherhoods, which are not located within the triangle formed by the aforementioned cities, join in along the trail. Travelling on horses, carts or walking, they all accompany their unique pilgrimage banner, or *simpecado*, as a symbol of unity and their commitment to endorse this specific cult in honour of the Virgin Mary of El Rocío. During the night they join together around big camp fires, evoking an idyllic atmosphere of conviviality and fraternalism.

Their arrival transforms the sleepy hamlet on the borders of one of Spain's most cherished national parks, *el Parque National de Doñana*, into a reverberant city, dominated by the different religious acts and an equally important festive atmosphere. Bordering the marshlands, where troops of wild horses graze and flamingos incessantly search for shrimps, the scenery has much in common with an out of time town in a Western movie. There are no paved roads. Through the wide sandy streets stroll proud horse riders while beautiful carts carry excited people from one inviting porch to another. People wander around in colourful flamenco dress. The air is filled with guitar music and enthusiastically sung *coplas* in honour of the Virgin. On the terraces people dance, in bewildering spirals, the different modes of the popular *sevillanas*. Beer and other alcohol as well as endless plates of food are offered to the guests who come by and turn the *romería* into one big feast. This highly playful atmosphere goes hand in hand with the different official acts of the *romería* during which the Virgin is officially honoured by the brotherhoods, and the more intimate visits of the individual pilgrims.

The ceremonial acts start on Saturday at noon with an official reception of all the brotherhoods at the main entrance of the chapel. One by one, starting with the most senior of them, the brotherhoods approach the delegation of the Almontese brotherhood with their *simpecado*. Most of the time they are located on a beautifully decorated cart, pulled by a pair of impressive oxen or mules. Given the number of brotherhoods this highly formal event continues until midnight. The next morning an impressive outdoor mass is celebrated by a prominent member of the clergy and all the present priests of the brotherhoods. At midnight on Sunday a rosary brings all the brotherhoods together on a huge square a few hundred metres from the chapel. Once the praying begins the brotherhoods leave the site in reverse order of seniority, thereby following a track which brings them ultimately before the open front door of the chapel. The final act consists of a procession which starts in the early hours of Whit Monday. It takes off shortly after the end of the impressive rosary, and more precisely, at the moment when the banner of the Almontese brotherhood is brought into the chapel and towards the statue of their patron saint.[7]

At that moment the esplanade around the chapel is filled with tens of thousands of spectators. The pilgrims, who were already present, are then joined by tourists who are attracted by the bewildering pictures and documentaries that have gone around the world in recent decades. In their midst photographers try to capture the increasing nervousness, while radio journalists are wandering through the crowd, commenting and interviewing the excited onlookers. TV cameras, set up on a flat roof right in front of the huge entrance door, transmit images of the scenery, intermingled with shots from within the chapel and the waiting statue on the altar.

Inside the overcrowded sanctuary the tension is almost unbearable. In the hours before, hundreds of Almontese men have gathered around the verge which surrounds the presbytery. Tense and nervous, they guard their place, while keeping an eye on their patron saint on the other side. The statue, which normally stands in a niche high in the middle of the impressive golden retable, is now almost

---

7   The impressive beginning of the procession underwent profound changes in recent decades. Halfway through the seventies, the starting hour was, year after year, pushed back. Between 1972 and 1989 by more than six hours. As a consequence the masses which were traditionally celebrated before the procession, needed to be suspended. In the early nineties, the rosary, which at that time still entered the church, also became altered. The Almontese brotherhood anticipated this by relocating its course. At the same time, the bringing in of the Almontese *simpecado* was introduced as a new act. From then on, the starting hour became stabilized and could even be brought forward (Plasquy 2006).

within reach. It is standing in the middle of the altar, placed on an impressive and beautifully decorated stretcher with four beams in the front and the rear and covered with an embellished top, resting on six decorated silver bars.

When the word is spread that the banner of the brotherhood is approaching, the youngsters in the front rows can hardly be kept under control by the guarding sacristans. Hanging over the verge, they are more than ready to jump on the altar. Bystanders pull them back by their shirts and try to calm them down. Serious, furious discussions follow, intermingled with enthusiastic clapping from further down the chapel. There, hundreds of spectators try to get a glimpse of what is happening. Hundreds of cameras are held up high in the air in an attempt to capture this thrilling moment. Once the banner enters the chapel the soothing words of the sacristans are no longer heard. Hell truly seems to break loose. After the first ones have jumped over the fence, it takes only a fraction of a second before the first rows start to climb in the most chaotic way over the verge. At the same time the gate of the altar enclosure is opened. Scrambling and jostling over each other, a real human avalanche seems to overflow the altar. Apparently without any form of organization, all of the men fiercely try to get as close as possible to the statue in order to participate in the lifting of the weighty stretcher. When the statue starts to move and is finally taken off the altar, overwhelming applause fills the chapel. Once in the spotlights which illuminate the main entrance, the excitement is shared by the thousands on the esplanade. The Virgin Mary is finally outside. The long-awaited procession can start.

Figure 8.1   Surging the tempest © Eddy Plasquy, 2009

Figure 8.2   Praising the Virgin Mary © Eddy Plasquy, 2009

After the statue is brought into the crowd, it is carried around a huge square at the back and side of the chapel. From there the procession proceeds to a large, wide street near the other side of the old nucleus of the hamlet. The whole circuit is hardly one kilometre long but it takes almost 12 hours to cover it. During that time all of the brotherhoods are greeted by the statue of the Virgin. The greeting consists of bringing the stretcher as close as possible to the banner of the brotherhood. Those among them who, during the *romeria*, reside in a house on the track, bring their banner to the front for this occasion. The others bring their *simpecado* nearby and hold it up high at a site along the way. When the stretcher is approaching, the members of the brotherhood lift their accompanying priest on their shoulders. Gesticulating with his arms, he tries to capture the attention of the folks who are carrying the statue. When the statue is close enough, he starts to praise the image of the Mother of God and ends his honouring with a Hail Mary, prayed together by all the bystanders. Once finished the scramble under and around the stretcher increases and the statue continues its bizarre course, directed towards the next banner in sight.

In between the greetings, children are lifted over the heads of the crowd towards the statue. From more than ten metres away, fathers lift up their child and hand it over to the person standing in front of him, who in his turn, passes it to the one before him. After arriving in this rough and bumpy way at the stretcher, the children, sometimes even babies, are placed on top of it and pushed against the mantle of the Virgin Mary. Most of them are, of course, anxiously crying. After a short time, they

Figure 8.3   Bringing children close © Eddy Plasquy, 2009

are brought back to their parents in the same, but reverse way. As has already been mentioned, non-villagers are not allowed to come close to the stretcher. However, exceptions are made for those who can convince an Almontese in a polite way to help him to get near the image. This happens more than one would expect at first sight. Most of the time as a fulfilment of a special promise made to the Virgin Mary. When granted, a couple of tough guys take the petitioner under their protection and escort him towards the statue and eventually even under it.

The authority of the Almontese brotherhood ceases to exist once the statue is off the altar. When a member of the board takes off his full dress and approaches the stretcher, he does this just as one more Almontese, dressed in work wear and, most importantly, heavy steel-capped shoes to protect his feet in the jumble around it. The stretcher is carried by at least 30 men. All are situated at both sides and in between the beams at the front and rear. Around them a cordon of tall men firmly hold the bars of the stretcher and the ends of the beams. Although it seems as if they are pulling, they are instead protecting those who have their shoulders under it. The suffocating heat and the weight make it impossible to stay under the stretcher for more than ten minutes. When asphyxia and exhaustion become visible, one is pulled out and dragged backward. Meanwhile, someone else slips under the arms of the protecting guy into the gap. The heavily perspiring, heaving and groaning men regain, bit by bit, their breath and calm, often assisted by their wife, girlfriend or mother who hangs a warm blanket or coat around their shoulders. After refreshment or a warm cup of coffee, served in the lodgings of the

Figure 8.4   Tension around the stretcher © Eddy Plasquy, 2009

Almontese brotherhood, or picked up in one of the houses of Almontese families nearby, they are ready for another round of duty.

The exceptional way in which the procession takes place, qualifies the whole situation for the persons present, as a unique event. In the first place for the participating Almontese men, but also for the spectators. While the former play a crucial role as protagonists in the whole situation, it is obvious that the latter are not passively watching but are profoundly moved by what is going on. In the first place by viewing how the statue is moved around and secondly by experiencing the presence of a physical, brutal and frightening force once they pass a visible threshold. In what follows, the attention is drawn to these two specific aspects of the procession.

The Captivating Potential of a Moving Image

In order to get a better grip on the way the perception of the movement influences the agency which is attributed to an image, Gell's (1998) theory on art and agency comes to the fore as a fairly interesting starting point.[8] Not in the least

---

8   In his posthumously published book *Art and Agency: an Anthropological Theory* (1998), Gell draws attention to the context of social relations that are objectified in the art object and which 'social objects' constitute. In order to support such a description, he

because his concept of agency is relational and context-dependent, and as such not classificatory or context-free. Within a network of social relations, an object, be it an art-object, an idol or artefact, is seen first and foremost as an index of agency. This index itself is the outcome, and/or an instrument of social agency. As such, these art-objects or idols are not 'self-sufficient' agents, but only secondary ones, in conjunction with certain specific 'human' associates.[9]

In dealing with anthropomorphic images Gell points out that, whenever images have to be touched, rather than merely looked at, there is an imputation that an inherent agency is present in the material index. This line of reasoning finally boils down to the crucial question of how a material entity can possess such an intentional psychology without being biologically alive. And how, in practice, this agency becomes attributed to this specific image. In order to tackle this question Gell focuses on the distinction between the external relations and the inner structure of an image. While the former refers to the way its role as a social other is stipulated, the latter implicates the presence of some 'homunculus' hidden inside the object. Both dimensions are clearly present in this case: The first, by the aforementioned discovery legend which imbued the image with a miraculous aura; the second, by being the holy protectress of the village over centuries, to give just one example.

Despite the attention Gell pays to the anthropomorphic qualities of an image, it is surprising how he treats his idols and images as unmovable. They generally just stand there. The idols do not apparently 'do' anything. They are immobile. The central mechanism by which a connection is made between the object and the observer is basically by seeing it. The strength of the object lies solely in its capacity to captivate, as it were, the eye of the observer. In doing this, the seer is frozen in a binding relationship. The eye contact with the image plays a crucial role. However, things become more complicated when the idol is carried around. When in El Rocío the image is taken off the altar and brought out of its chapel, a radical shift takes place. From a static and passive idol, it changes into a moving and active one. Mediated of course by the joint forces of those who carry it, but nevertheless interacting in a direct way with the visiting brotherhoods which are greeted and the pilgrims who receive her blessing for their children.

---

devises a four-term model. The main players in any action-context in the vicinity of objects are identified and related as follows: a material Index made by an Artist 'represents' a Prototype and appears before a Recipient. Gell uses 'index' in the sense of a 'natural sign', in the meaning which goes back to Charles Saunders Peirce. Indices have the effect of drawing the attention of the interpreter/user/addressee (Recipient) to the object of the index (Prototype) or its maker (Artist). This 'attention' is theorized by Gell and made to cover many kinds of cognitive processes – 'abductions' or 'abductive inferences' – that surround the artefactual index.

9   Gell defines idolatry as physical interaction with inanimate entities (such as sculptures) which represent divinities for the purpose of receiving the blessings those supernatural beings supposedly confer (Gell 1981, p. 135).

While bringing out a sacred image is not an unusual event in itself, and as a matter of fact can be seen as the core business of every procession, the way it is taken out and carried around can vary significantly. It suffices to compare the organized processions during Holy Week, or *Semana Santa*, with the hectic turbulence during the procession in El Rocío to illustrate this. During *Semana Santa*, the highly formal movements of the statues are directed by a captain. He orders and instructs in a meticulous way the exact moves of the participating carriers, who all have a fixed position under the stretcher. The movements of the images are studied in advance and practiced in the days before the procession. Highly detailed instructions are communicated by short commands and signals. At regular intervals the stretcher is set down in order to change a number of carriers. In El Rocío, on the contrary, there is no formal, hierarchical structure. The statue is carried around in a highly disorderly manner. While every participating Almontese man knows the trajectory and the next brotherhood to be visited, the movement of the stretcher is always uncertain. It is even unsure whether the statue will stay upright or will slide to the ground. Getting under the stretcher is, to a great extent, a rough individual endeavour.

The modalities by which the statue is carried around influence, in a profound manner, the way the movement of the image is perceived by the spectators. In the case of *Semana Santa* the movements are set and the image of the Virgin Mary always follows another image of Jesus, of secondary importance. Both images first and foremost illustrate a biblical scene which is carried around during Holy Week. Within this context the strength of the image of the Virgin Mary lies, besides its intrinsic artistic qualities, in the way it visualizes the sorrow of the Mother of Christ. The importance of the movement basically lies in the fact that the image is brought to a specific neighbourhood, the one to which it belongs and where it is often venerated as the patron saint. During the procession in El Rocío, the movement of the statue is at any time uncertain and a permanent source of inquiry for the spectators. How shall She move? Forward, backward, slowly, rapidly? Accelerating at one moment, inclining to one side and sliding to the ground at another. Lifted up in a shaky way, never certain it will come down again. All this uncertainty brings the focus to the movement of the image itself. It gives the statue a highly dynamic modality. Looking at the image from a distance, it seems to move 'organically', slowly, sometimes seemingly hesitating about where to go to next, at other times rushing forward.

At the same time this illusion of physicality is complemented by the fact that the statue is not moved arbitrarily, but always with a certain point in view. Most of the time this point is the next brotherhood that needs to be greeted. At other moments it is a band which wants to bring an honour song to the Virgin and in response will be thanked by moving up and down. In a more reproving way and as an unmistakable sign of holy discontent, the back of the Virgin can be turned towards a brotherhood with which the Almontese had difficulties during the past year. As a consequence all these different elements create the illusion that the statue is not only moving organically, but also intentionally. This intentionality is further enhanced by the fact that no visible order is present under and around the stretcher. All that is visible is a chaotic mess from which from time to time someone is pulled out. The exact handling of the statue stays largely out of sight. Instead of individuals, a frightening and always changing conglomeration of bodies is seen. As such it becomes uncertain whether these bodies are moved by the statue or the statue is moved by them.

Finally, when the focus is brought towards the violence with which the Almontese men prohibit, by all means, access of non-villagers to their patron saint, this protective human barrier becomes almost literally the sociological skin of the statue. Very significant in this respect is the open space which is spontaneously created between the spectators and the swarm of men who are either under the stretcher or intending to get close to it. Again, the amorphous nature of the group of men around the stretcher makes this impression all the more real. This nucleus seems to move by itself and changes permanently. At the same time, the nucleus has a clear frontier which means that you literally have to go into it, or as the Almontese says it: '*Vamos pa' dentro*' (We go inside). Although this space might not be wider than half a metre and in many occasions even less, one senses immediately when this line is crossed. Aggressive, non-Almontese who try to break through that barrier are immediately and efficiently neutralized. Only non-threatening, accompanied individuals and children who are passed over the heads, are allowed through.

These observations make it possible to extend Gell's ideas on the nature of the agency of an anthropomorphic image. While his focus is primarily on the materiality of the statue, the case of the procession in El Rocío illustrates that the way the image is carried around significantly increases its anthropomorphic quality. The way it is moved is thereby crucial. It creates the illusion of a proper physicality and intentionality. The image does not only move, but seems to do this with intention: the Virgin is not only 'seeing', but 'visiting', 'greeting', 'receiving', 'punishing' and 'reconciling' in a public and observable way. The manner in which the statue is violently protected and made accessible to harmless individuals even gives it a figment of sociability. As the patron saint of the Almontese she moves around like a true mother, surrounded by her children. Children who feel protected by her and are even willing to give their lives to protect her.

The highly unusual way in which the statue is carried around profoundly enhances the anthropomorphic quality of the image. On a regular basis, people collapse and start to cry, overwhelmed by emotions, not only when seeing the statue as it moves around in an almost organic way, but also by the awe-inspiring presence of the Almontese men around it. This distinctive mixture of beauty and fearfulness comes very close to what Immanuel Kant referred to as the sublime, or more specifically, to what he defines as the dynamic sublime.

The Procession as a Sublime Experience

In the first part of his *Critique of Aesthetic Judgment* (1790) Kant explains his concept of the sublime by differentiating it from three other possible reflexive judgments: namely the agreeable, the beautiful, and the good. These reflexive judgments differ from determinative ones in the sense that with the former we seek to find unknown universals for given particulars, while with the latter one, we subsume given particulars under universals we already know. The agreeable is a purely sensory judgment, based on inclination alone and thus purely subjective. The good is essentially a judgment that something is ethical, that it conforms with moral law, by which Kant refers to a coherence with a fixed and absolute notion of reason. The beautiful and the sublime are situated between the agreeable and the good and are referred by Kant as being 'subjective universal' judgments. With this oxymoronic term he means that, in practice, the judgments are subjective, and as such not tied to any absolute and determinate concept. However, the judgment is made with the belief that other people ought to agree with this judgment – even though it is known that many will not. In other words, it refers to a *sensus communis*, a community of taste.

The judgment that something is beautiful is a claim that it possesses a 'form of finality': it appears to have been designed with a purpose, even though it does not have any apparent practical function. The judgment that something is sublime is a judgment that it is beyond the limits of comprehension, and as such primarily an object of fear. Kant further divides the sublime into a mathematical and a dynamical form. The mathematical sublime stands for a type of experiences that is occasioned by things that appear to be absolutely large, such as mountains, oceans or a sky full of stars. The dynamic sublime deals with the type of experience that is occasioned by those things that appear to be absolutely powerful, such as overhanging rocks, tornados or lightings.

Kant maintains that the experience of the sublime is rather complex. Firstly, it is a painful experience, basically due to a failure on our part to comprehend with our imagination the experience in its totality. In other words: we simply cannot imagine it. The mountain is too high, the ocean is too wide and the storm is so powerful that you simply cannot grasp it with your imagination. However, it would be a mistake to say that many of the objects that give rise to an experience of the sublime are indeed infinite in size or power. It just depends on the perspective of the observer. Whether seeing the pyramids is a sublime experience changes with the distance from which they are seen. The same counts for a tornado when seen from far away or on the contrary, almost frighteningly close. Importantly, Kant insists that, in order to preserve the aesthetic effect of such experiences, it is crucial that we view them from a proper distance. In the case where we are overwhelmed with real fear, as for example in a really frightening storm, it is difficult to qualify this experience as sublime: you do not think about it, you just want to save your life and limbs.

It has already been underlined that an important aspect of the peculiar behaviour of the Almontese is their explicit violence towards spectators who come too close, or worse, who intend to get under the stretcher. As such, a crucial factor in this setting is the distance from where one is confronted with this violence. Viewing the movements of the statue from a porch, 50 metres away, is different than watching it from a closer but still safe distance, for example, 10 metres and surrounded by other spectators, and again different when situated at the edge, at a couple of metres from the stretcher, where the tension is eminently and visibly present, and again different when one crosses this line and intends to get into the swarm of struggling bodies, knowing that the Almontese do not hesitate to use violence to keep non-villagers away from their patron saint. From each of these positions the perspective changes dramatically. In the same way distance makes viewing the pyramids or a tornado a sublime experience or not, this distance is a crucial factor in understanding what makes the violence during the procession for so many people an abstract or invisible one, a truly fearful experience or a sublime one: overwhelmed by a bombardment of sensorial impressions, of what is seen, heard, smelled and felt, but at the same time not extremely scary. Indeed, it is an experience which fairly matches the description of Kant's dynamic sublime.

Closely related to these different experiences is the degree of involvement of the individual spectator. From a passive observing position at a safe distance he can move towards the stretcher, thereby increasing his personal involvement in the actual turbulence, up to the point where he crosses a line and is actually willing to engage in a confrontation. In this gradual shift, the differences between a spectator and a participant become increasingly blurred. Confronting the Almontese men in a straightforward, if not to say aggressive way, is precisely what the Almontese need in order to be able to demonstrate the protective mission they attribute to themselves. While it cannot be excluded that such a confrontation can also be seen as a sublime experience, for example if you like a good fight, it is clearly of another kind than the one experienced by those who watch the spectacle from a safe distance.

Finally, it is worth mentioning that an analogous situation is noticeable when focusing on the Almontese who actually put their shoulders under the stretcher. When they are not actively involved, they often choose a spot at a certain distance to keep a close eye on what is going on around the stretcher, a distance which is kept when the statue moves slowly forward. This distance makes it possible to open oneself to the experience of the sublime. However, when they go 'inside', they don't do this with the intention of having a sublime experience. When they go towards the stretcher, they go there first and foremost 'to work'. To work, not to meditate: '*Vamos a dentro para trabajar*'. To work means in this context, fulfilling a task they see primarily as a collective one. And when looking closer at the way this 'work' is carried out, it becomes clear that this does not take place either in a chaotic or in a plain individualistic way. On the contrary, it happens in a surprisingly structured way, or as they themselves describe it: 'it is an ordered chaos', governed by rules which are known and respected by the Almontese. In this 'ordered chaos', unwritten rules mean not only that the procession actually follows its proper course and completes its goal of greeting all of the 107 brotherhoods, but also that most of the non-Almontese who succeed in slipping through the ranks, are quickly detected and pushed backward.

Bringing the focus to the way the procession takes place, and especially the conduct of the Almontese men during that time and the reactions of the spectators towards the statue and the violence, does not only reveal the importance of the enhanced anthropomorphic qualities of the statue but also the importance of the interaction between the Almontese and the bystanders. Locked in a mutual relation the former need the latter in order to protect their patron saint against someone. At the same time, the latter see in the former a highly idiosyncratic and attractive example of what devotion to a local saint can mean. In this way, violence, mostly seen as an aberration within the context of a Christian pilgrimage where penance and remission are core concepts, becomes redefined within a unique framework wherein this local anchoring is first and foremost a seductive constituent. Being in El Rocío is therefore, for more than one reason, an extraordinary experience. Not only for the highly unusual location in which one can participate in an atmosphere that reasonably matches Turner's (1969) description of *communitas*, but also, if not more, by the way one can be enchanted by seeing the Holy Virgin being moved around by, and on top of, a frightening and terrifying local collective.

Conclusion

The ethnographic data in this study reveal that, despite the highly complex and organic way in which the image is carried around, the procession is far from chaotic but surprisingly well 'organized'. Both the Almontese men and the outsiders either know the 'rough' rules or come to know them very quickly. Parkin's insistence on the importance of movement for the efficacy of ritual thus stands. However, the unique case in El Rocío stretches the meaning which is attributed to this movement when dealing with religious processions.

While Pina-Cabral (1986) insists on the importance of directionality in *romarias* and Mitchell (2004) stressed the structure of the *festa* as a central opportunity for the laity to demonstrate their agency within a structure of correct spatiality, the opposite seems to be the case in El Rocío. Here the movement literally emerges out of the dynamic interplay around and under the elevated statue. Instead of a performance by a selected group of carriers whose individual qualities can be evaluated afterwards, it is the collective endeavour of an unknown number of men which is at stake and the attitude of the 'Almontese' which is commented on in the days after.

Their frightening and direct demonstration of collective agency plays a crucial role in the actualization of the Virgin Mary of El Rocío. It enhances the attributed agency and creates an image that goes beyond imagination. Seeing the statue of the Virgin Mary surging within a tempest of furious men, while at the same time peacefully looking down on these human creatures who, like a swarm of bees, are willing to give their lives for her, can hardly be more suggestive and indexical, of the hidden powers which reside in this celestial queen.

References

Aguda Torrico, J. (1999) 'Hermandades y tiempos rituals: viejos y nuevos significados', in S. Rodriguez Becerra (ed.), *Religión y Cultura. Volumen 1*, Consejería de Cultura y Fundación Machado: Signatura, pp. 353–376.

Bennassar, B. (1979) *The Spanish Character. Attitudes and Mentalities from the Sixteenth to the Nineteenth Century*, Berkeley: University of California Press.

Cantero, P.A. (2002) *Tras el Rocío*, Almonte: Ayuntamiento de Almonte.

Carrasco Terriza, M.J. (2002) 'La iconografía de la Virgen del Rocío y su proceso de fijación', in D. Gonzáles Cruz (ed.), *Ritos y Ceremonias en el Mundo Hispano durante la Edad Moderna*, Huelva: Universidad de Huelva Publicaciones, pp. 353–372.

Cháves Flores, F.J. (2004) *Hermandades del Rocío*, Madrid: Cháves Flores.

Christian, W.A., jr. (1976) 'Panorama de las devociones a sanctuarios españoles desde el principio de la edad media hasta nuestros dias', in C. Lisón Tolosana (ed.), *Temas de antropología española*, Madrid: Akal, pp. 49–105.

Christian, W.A., jr. (1989) *Apparitions in Late Medieval and Renaissance Spain*, Princeton, NJ: Princeton University Press.

Comelles, J.M. (1984) 'Los caminos del Rocío', in S. Rodríguez Becerra (ed.), *Antropología cultural de Andalucía*, Sevilla: Consejería de Cultura de la Junta de Andalucía, pp. 755–770.

Comelles, J.M. (1995) 'Rocíos', *Demófilo*, 17, pp. 13–39.

Crain, M. (1992) 'Pilgrims, "yuppies", and media men: The transformation of an Andalusian pilgrimage', in J. Boissevain (ed.), *Revitalizing European Rituals*, London: Routledge, pp. 95–112.

Crain, M. (1997) 'The remaking of an Andalusian pilgrimage tradition: debates regarding visual (re)presentation and the meanings of "locality" in a global era', in A. Gupta and J. Ferguson (eds), *Culture, Power, Place. Explorations in Critical Anthropology*, Durham, NC: Duke University Press, pp. 291–312.

Diaz de la Serna, A. (1998) *El Rocío de siempre* (2nd edn), Cordoba: Publicaciones CajaSur.

Flores Cala, J. (2005) *Historia y documentos de los translados de la Virgen del Rocío a la Villa de Almonte 1607–2005*, Almonte: Ayuntamiento de Almonte. Centro de Estudios Rocieros.

García García, F. (2007) 'La Virgen del Rocío en el marco medioambiental de Doñana', in D. Gonzáles Cruz (ed.) *Virgenes, Reinas y Santas. Modelos de mujer en el mundo hispano*, Huelva: Universidad de Huelva Publicaciones, pp. 377–394.

Gell, A. (1998) *Art and Agency. An Anthropological Theory*, Oxford: Clarendon Press.

González Faraco, J.C. and Murphy, M.D. (1999) El Rocío: 'La evolución de una Aldea Sagrada', *Aestuaria*, 6, pp. 89–132.

Infante Galán, J. (1971) *Rocío: La devoción mariana de Andalucía*, Sevilla: Editorial Prensa Española.

Kant, I. (1790) *Critique of Judgement*, trans. W.S. Pluhar, 1987, Indianapolis: Hackett Publishing.

Kapferer, B. (2006) 'Dynamics', in J. Kreinath, J. Snoek and M. Stausberg (eds), *Theorizing Rituals. Issues, Topics, Approaches, Concepts*, Leiden: Brill, pp. 507–522.

Lüddeckens, D. (2006) 'Emotion', in J. Kreinath, J. Snoek and M. Stausberg (eds), *Theorizing Rituals. Issues, Topics, Approaches, Concepts*, Leiden: Brill, pp. 545–570.

Mitchell, J. (2004) 'Ritual structure and ritual agency. 'Rebounding violence' and Maltese Festa', *Social Anthropology*, 12(1), pp. 57–75.

Moreno Navarro, I. (1974) *Las hermandades andaluzas. Una aproximación desde la antropología*, Sevilla: Universidad de Sevilla.

Moreno Navarro, I. (1990) 'Niveles de significación de los iconos religiosos y rituales de reproducción de identidad de Andalucía', in *La fiesta, la ceremonía, el rito*, Granada: Universidad de Granada y Casa de Velásquez, pp. 91–103.

Moreno Navarro, I. (1993) 'El Roció: de Romería de las Marismas a fiesta de identidad andaluza', in A. Fraguas (ed.), *Romerías y Peregrinacions. Simposio de Antropoloxia. X.*, Santiago de Compostela: Consello de Cultura Galega, pp. 121–141.

Muñoz Bort, D. (2002) 'Ritos y ceremonias rocieras en la Edad Moderna' in D. Gonzáles Cruz (ed.), *Ritos y Ceremonias en el Mundo Hispano durante la Edad Moderna*, Huelva: Universidad de Huelva Publicaciones, pp. 419–428.

Murphy, M.D. and Gonzáles Faraco, J.C. (1996) 'Masificación ritual, identidad local y toponimia en El Rocío', *Demófilo*, 20, pp. 101–120.

Murphy, M.D. and Gonzáles Faraco, J.C. (2002) *El Rocío: análisis culturales e históricos*, Huelva: Diputación Provincial.

Ojeda Rivera, J.F. (1987) *Organización del territorio en Doñana y su entorno proximo (Almonte). Siglos XVIII–XX*, Sevilla: Icona.

Parkin, D. (1992) 'Ritual as spatial direction and bodily division', in D. de Coppet (ed.), *Understanding Ritual*, London: Routledge, pp. 11–25.

Pina-Cabral, J. (1986) *Sons of Adam, daughters of Eve*, Oxford: Oxford University Press.

Plasquy, E. (2006) '"¡El Salto a las 02.45!": ¿Un ritual establecido o atemporal? Cambios rituales durante el inicio de la procesión en honor a la Virgen del Rocío', *Anduli*, 6, pp. 133–146.

Plasquy, E. (2010) 'El Camino Europeo del Rocío: A Pilgrimage towards Europe?', *Journal of Religion in Europe*, 3, pp. 256–284.

Rodríguez Becerra, S. (1989) 'La *romería* del Rocío, fiesta de Andalucía', *El Folklore Andaluz*, 3, pp. 147–152.

Rodríguez Becerra, S. (2000) *Religión y Fiesta. Antropología de las Creencias y Rituales en Andalucía*, Sevilla: Signatura Demos.

Rodríguez Ramirez, M.F. (2006) *Nueve meses con Ella. Venida, Estancia e Ida de Ntra. Sra. del Rocío 2005–2006*, Almonte: Ayuntamiento de Almonte.

Sax, W.S. (1990) 'The Rannagar Ramlila: Text, performance, pilgrimage', *History of Religions*, 30, pp. 129–153.

Schieffelin, E.L. (1985) 'Performance and the cultural construction of reality', *American Ethnologist*, 12, pp. 707–724.

Trens, M. (1946) *María. Iconografía de la Virgen en el arte español*, Madrid: Editorial Plus Ultra.

Turner, T. (2006) 'Structure, process, form', in J. Kreinath, J. Snoek and M. Stausberg (eds), *Theorizing Rituals. Issues, Topics, Approaches, Concepts*, Leiden: Brill, pp. 207–246.

Turner, V.W. (1969) *The Ritual Process: Structure and Anti-structure*, The Lewis Henry Morgan lectures, 1966, Chicago: Aldine Pub. Co.

Zapata Garcia, M. (1991) *El Rocío. Estudio psicoanalítico de la devoción mariana en Andalucía*, Sevilla: Rodríguez Castillejo.

Chapter 9

Emotional Memory Formation at Former Nazi Concentration Camp Sites

Jessica Rapson

Introduction

This chapter discusses and revises various existing ideas about how contemporary tourists experience former Nazi concentration camp sites in Europe, with a specific focus on the way in which encounters with both testimonial literature and natural elements of these landscapes may impact tourist emotions. Initially, I will chart my work's theoretical position in the existing field and outline the model of tourist emotion under consideration. In consideration of Auschwitz–Birkenau in Poland, I will then discuss how natural elements shape emotion. In the final section on Buchenwald Concentration Camp Memorial in East-central Germany, I will demonstrate how elements of the landscape and related literature can play a potentially important role in emotional experiences at former camp sites.

A central aim of this chapter is to consider how and why tourist experience might be affected by the sharing of geographical co-ordinates with sufferers of the past, and to ask what role landscape and nature may play in increasing visitor understanding of this past and its victims. This second question is complex in the context of the Holocaust. Much discourse around the Holocaust suggests that the experiences of its victims were so extreme as to transcend normal representational limits and thus challenge our ability to understand or empathize with people from this past. This debate stresses the importance of avoiding totalizing over-identification. This is in part due to the common perception of literature as an aestheticizing form that transforms experience into linear narrative, and the idea that personal accounts invite personification.[1] However, Dominick LaCapra's concept of 'empathic unsettlement' supports the argument that appropriate emotional engagement with others through testimony is possible.[2] LaCapra argues

---

1   Berel Lang, for example, explores the moral consequences of literary representation and argues that 'where impersonality and abstractness are essential features of the subject, as in the subject of the Nazi genocide, then a literary focus on individuation and agency "contradicts" the subject itself' (Lang 1990, reproduced in Levi and Rothberg 2003, p. 330). See Amy Hungerford (2003) for a full discussion of personification in this context.

2   LaCapra's original discussion focuses on responses to viewing video testimony. This idea is developed here specifically in relation to literary testimonial works.

that, whilst no-one can provide a how-to model of response to the Holocaust, empathy necessarily plays a central role:

> Empathy is bound up with a transferential relation to the past, and is arguably an affective aspect of understanding which both limits objectification and exposes the self to involvement of implication in the past, its actors, and victims ... Desirable empathy involves not full identification but what might be termed empathic unsettlement. (LaCapra 2001, p. 102)

This statement acknowledges the necessity of resisting full identification, a state LaCapra considers to be an overextension of original traumas experienced by victims to those secondary onlookers who attempt to contemplate this trauma. He argues it to be 'blatantly obvious that there is a major difference between the experiences of camp inmates or Holocaust survivors and that of the viewers of testimony videos' (2001, pp. 102–103). Accordingly, this text contends that testimony also plays a part in the way landscapes at camp sites are experienced by visitors. Related research, for example by Kathryn Jones (2007) on visits to battlefield and concentration camp sites, suggests that encounters with testimonial literature subsequently inform and frames visitor expectations and experiences of place in this context. In addition, the exhibitions that now form part of the topography at these memorials increasingly feature testimony, whether in text, audio or video form. Bearing this in mind, I am particularly interested in the way that landscape and testimony may come together at the sites in question in a way which prompts a form of empathic unsettlement.

I also take up the question of the way that natural elements of landscape in particular are symbolized, manipulated and interpreted in commemorative environments. Whilst rationally we know nature responds to human death in a 'strictly organic sense' (Pogue Harrison 2003, p. ix), in doing so landscapes' capacity for 'decay and endless renewal' frequently become seen as either sympathetic to lost humanity or consoling in their capacity for regeneration (Dixon Hunt 2001, p. 22). Thus whilst nature is fundamentally neutral to human suffering, it retains significance in commemorative landscapes. Elaine Scarry contextualizes assumptions about nature as emotionally responsive as misconceptions which are yet fundamental to human structures of perception:

> The naturally existing external world [...] is wholly ignorant of the 'hurtability' of human beings. Immune, inanimate, inhuman, it indifferently manifests itself in the thunderbolt and hailstorm, rabid bat, smallpox microbe, and ice crystal. The human imagination reconceives the external world, divesting it of its immunity and irresponsibility not by literally putting it in pain or making it animate but by, quite *literally, 'making it' as knowledgeable about human pain as if it were itself animate and in pain.* (1985, pp. 288–289)

In Scarry's argument, the natural world is constantly subject to re-creation in the human imagination, and the imagination is of primary concern in this investigation. The exploration of Auschwitz–Birkenau in the first half of this chapter will consider that in addition to the factors discussed by Dixon Hunt, nature can potentially prompt feelings of empathic unsettlement, of a reflexive distance that situates the self in relation to the past.

Since 1945 many former Nazi concentration camps have been transformed into primarily commemorative landscapes. In some cases this transformation began immediately after camp inmates were liberated, with spontaneous gestures such as the erection of rudimentary monumental forms. In others official bodies have instigated more formal memorial projects. In all cases, the original sites have changed over the years according to the respective shifting political and cultural climates in which they exist. Much illuminating commentary has examined how these changes have found representational manifestation in landscape (James Young 1994; Claudia Koonz 1994; Sarah Farmer 1995). I argue here for a more phenomenological consideration of memorial spaces, which changes emphasis from political representation to the mediation of these sites in the eyes of the visitor by the literary testimony of former concentration camp victims. In this argument, memory is conceptualized as dynamic, constantly affected by different experiences and new sources of information. The role of space is important in this; places affect feelings, and subsequently play a part in the construction of emotional memory. The model of memory suggested here attempts to interrogate this process by focusing on the tourist and the space in which their activities are performed, for 'collective memory is not a matter of collecting, but of continuously performing. It is constantly in process' (Rigney 2008, p. 93).

The model also emphasizes the dialogical metamorphosis of memorial sites, an idea which is becoming popular in memory studies as a discipline. Alon Confino and Peter Fritsche (2002) suggest that a one-dimensional approach to cultural artefacts has been too frequently assumed, and assert that culture cannot and should not be perceived 'as an autonomous sphere disconnected from social experience' (2002, p. 4), thus neglecting crucial issues of mediation and reception. Emphasis has frequently been placed 'on how memory *represents* social relations, but not how *memory shapes them*' (2002 p. 4, my emphasis). Such a perspective constitutes a significant revision of authoritative existing approaches, such as Pierre Nora's concept of *lieux de mémoire* in French culture (2001), which has had considerable implications for the study of commemorative sites and texts. Nora conceptualized memory as embodied in loci; these loci are seen to 'bear memory' (Nora 2001, p. xx). In such a model, symbols or sites take on the role of repositories of memory, and can thus be seen as direct representations of it. Nora's project, despite its significance in challenging pre-existing conceptualizations of notions of memory object or text arguably set in motion a tendency in others to overlook the way in which memorial sites are subject to continuous evolution.[3] It could be argued that Nora's project is ultimately *nostalgic* – that is, it mourns the loss of the past and clings to remnants that seem to fix or embody it. A more progressive approach suggests that memory may be created through social and emotional processes which are affected by, and not divorced from, memory 'texts'. Whilst Confino and Fritsche's 2002 collection of essays made a key development by focusing on taking memory 'out of the museum and away from the monument' (Confino and Fritsche 2002, p. 5), I return to these 'sites'; not as places which *embody* memory, but as co-ordinates in dialogical social processes such as tourism.

Existing work on concentration camp tourism is to some extent characterized by concerns about inappropriate visitor motivations (Lennon and Foley 2000; MacCannell 1992; Urry 1995), and implies that sites such as former camps have become consumer-driven environments. Although some commentators have provided alternative perspectives which allow a more nuanced exploration of individual experience (see, for example, Dalton 2009), academic work has largely conceptualized 'dark tourism' (Lennon and Foley 2000) as a commoditized experience with pre-determined outcomes. It is possible to revise fixed assumptions about the consumer via the work of Michel de Certeau, who offers a more nuanced understanding. De Certeau has proposed that consumption, rather than being completely pre-determined, is a form of behaviour open to subversion. Theoretically, he notes, the process of consumption is akin to language; just as a sentence must be constructed with pre-existing words, their order can yet be entirely original. Consumers to de Certeau are 'unrecognized producers, poets of their own acts, silent discoverers of their own paths … their trajectories trace out the ruses of other interests and desires that are neither delimited or captured by the systems in which they develop' (1984, p. xviii).

With these arguments in mind this study is concerned, not as such with the political motivations that have guided representational shifts, or in fact with why people might chose to spend leisure time there - although this is indeed a fascinating question. Rather, it attempts to speculate on how visitors actually *feel* when they travel through these spaces, and how their emotions may be affected by them. This relies on a fundamentally phenomenological understanding of space. As Christopher Tilley's discussion of such models notes, the phenomenological approach is indebted to Martin Heidegger's generation of a '*topological* model' to better understand the relationship 'between people and landscape as a matter of "thereness" of the self-disclosure of Being of and in the world' (Tilley 1994,

---

3   Nora himself, in fact, was aware of the necessarily evolutionary nature of memory sites, stating that their capacity for metamorphosis is central to their existence (2001, p. 19) – although, even with this qualification, in Nora's thesis memory is still *attached* to sites, whether material or immaterial. The notion that that such sites were thus rendered 'static' is to some extent a misreading by those who have used his work since, hence this is a trend that may have originated with Nora's work, but which was not, strictly speaking, instigated by him.

p. 13), and Maurice Merleau-Ponty's conceptualization of the human body as mediator between thought and the world:

> Any perception of a thing, a shape or a size as real, any perceptual constancy refers back to the positing of a world and a system of experience in which my body is inescapably linked with phenomena. But the system of experience is not layed before me as though I were God, it is lived by me from a certain point of view; I am not the spectator, I am involved. (Tilley 1994, p. 13 cites Merleau-Ponty 1962, pp. 303–304)

Space, once approached as coherent, neutral and atemporal, has gradually come to be seen by many as contextualized in human history (Tilley 1994, p. 9). With the arrival of a more phenomenological approach, abstract considerations of space have begun to appear irrational, idealist, and divorced from activities and events. A phenomenological approach thus provides an alternative which sees space as 'experienced and created through life-activity, a sacred, symbolic and mythic space replete with social meanings wrapped around buildings, objects and features of the local topography, providing reference points and places of emotional orientation for human attachment and involvement' (Tilley 1994, p. 16).

The experience of being in space necessarily organizes perspective, requiring an acknowledgement of where the self stands in relation to landmarks. Perspective is not only a positioning of the self in space, however, and it is particularly a sense of *historical perspective* that is arguably a central factor in the context of the Holocaust. Ulrich Baer provides a useful discussion of the relationship between people and landscape which has been prevalent since the dawn of Romanticism; specifically, the tendency to *locate the self in response* to landscape: 'Looking at landscapes as we do today manifests a specifically modern sense of self-understanding, which may be described as the individual's ability to view the self within a larger, and thus potentially historical context' (Baer 2002, p. 68). In relation to the Holocaust, Baer asks what the 'proper position' may be for the individual to face the 'stark truth' of the Holocaust, for '[p]rior to all efforts at commemoration, explanation or understanding, I would suggest, we ... must find a place and position from which to gain access to the event' (Baer 2002, pp. 67–68). Whilst Baer rejects the phenomena of visits to places of former atrocity as a way of accessing the past, based on the objection that 'the Holocaust's empty sites are radically inhospitable and ... attempts to inhabit them through empathic identification and imaginary projection via transferential bonds, is illusory at best' (2002, p. 83), I pursue an alternative view influenced by phenomenological writers such as Edward Casey, who has argued that '[t]here is no knowing or sensing a place except by being in that place, and to be in a place is to be in a position to perceive it' (Casey 1996, p. 13). Whilst wary of suggesting that phenomenological experience foregrounds *identification*, this at least allows place to become the starting point for investigations into a less totalizing form of empathy. Similarly, rather than become pre-occupied with the question of visitor motivation, I take the optimistic view presented in Derek Dalton's discussion of tourism at Auschwitz – that there is at least some evidence to suggest that many visitors' experiences are characterized not by voyeurism but by 'intense concern' for the victims of the past (Dalton 2009, p. 211). With this in mind, I now turn to a discussion of the ways in which nature is encountered and interpreted at Auschwitz II Birkenau.

Auschwitz–Birkenau: Nature and Ruins

Auschwitz and the corresponding site at Birkenau are the most visited of all the former Nazi camps. Auschwitz–Birkenau was visited by 1.3 million people in 2009 alone,[4] and the director of the memorial, Piotr Cywiński, reported that visitor numbers had tripled since 2002. Auschwitz I is a collection of former barracks and other camp buildings containing exhibits and reconstructions. Auschwitz II Birkenau is a wide expanse of primarily grassed landscape containing the ruins of barracks and, at the far side of the site, crematoria. There are monuments erected in this area, but the vast space often seems empty and abandoned to visitors, and many consider it to be a place for quiet contemplation (Keil 2008).

At the Auschwitz–Birkenau International Preservation Conference *Preserving for the Future* (2003), natural vegetation at Birkenau was discussed at some length. Two particularly suggestive approaches to nature are revealed in the conference proceedings. Firstly, despite prevalent impressions of Birkenau as an abandoned landscape, this vegetation is in fact very carefully controlled, and beyond protecting architectural structures this is also done to create a particular atmosphere. Attempts to curate the site at Birkenau are balanced between the demands of authenticity and emotional signification; nature must be allowed to start the inevitable process of reclaiming the landscape. According to curators, 'lush vegetation … lends peace to what was once a malevolent landscape' (Bohdan Rymaszewski 2004, p. 24). Thus careful control of vegetation both 'gives visitors access to the Museum grounds and shapes their emotions' (Zając 2004, p. 62). Secondly, the trees at the site, many of which were between 60 and 100 years old at the date of the conference, are considered to be witnesses of past atrocities at the site, and are protected by memorial staff accordingly (Zając 2004, p. 60).

The curatorial approach at Auschwitz certainly raises questions. Since original buildings must be preserved – and thus vegetation controlled – nature will never completely take over. Whether curatorial manipulation of the landscape either contributes to or interferes with the overall rubric of maintaining 'authenticity' seems uncertain. Chris Keil's discussion of curatorial activity at Birkenau suggests that '[t]he attempt to halt time at Birkenau, to sidestep processes of decay and dilapidation … involves the artful and conscious construction of illusion, the elaboration of

---

4   Visitor numbers as announced by the Auschwitz Birkenau Memorial and Museum on their website on Tuesday, 26 January 2010 http://en.auschwitz.org.pl/m/index. php?option=com_content&task=view&id=737&Itemid=7

mimetic effects which are designed to conceal themselves, in a discourse, certainly of aesthetics, and in some cases also of ethics' (Keil 2008, p. 491).

The designation of natural forms as witnesses also raises issues. The capacity of nature to witness human suffering and slaughter is often assumed. Simon Schama's extensive *Landscape and Memory* (1995), a landmark text for the discussion of topology and narrative, frequently raises the compelling metaphorical idea of landscape as witness. In Poland, where he reports first having made sense of the concept of linking landscape to memory, he recalls his impression that the 'fields and forests and rivers had seen war and terror, elation and desperation' (1995, p. 24). Yet, as Pogue Harrison has suggested, nature's response to human death is purely organic. But curatorial approaches at Birkenau embrace the potential of the imaginative re-construction of nature as outlined by Scarry in which nature assumes a structure of perception (although as Keil hints, there may be ethical issues at stake here). The way nature and ruins interact is also central to the manipulation of the atmosphere at Birkenau. Nature may be a culturally constructed concept (Wolscke-Bulmahn 1997, p. 6), yet elements perceived as 'natural' are particularly affective in certain contexts. At Birkenau, natural symbolism can usefully be unravelled alongside the affectivity of ruins. Clearly specificity must be maintained; ruins are the remains of deliberately constructed human structures. They are often worn down by the encroachment of 'natural elements' such as plant matter and meteorological conditions, but should not be conflated with them. Ruins are constantly diminishing, whilst nature 'grows'. Nevertheless the two are intimately related, as Gustave Flaubert has suggested:

> I saw some ruins, beloved ruins of my youth … I saw them and I thought about the dead I have never known and on whom my feet trampled. I love above all the sight of regeneration resting upon old ruins; this embrace of nature, coming swiftly to bury the work of man, the moment he is no longer there to defend it, fills me with deep and ample joy. (M. Roth 1997, p. 62, cites Flaubert)

Similarly, Susan Stewart notes that 'inert matter is made increasingly meaningful by its juxtaposition to living forms. When we find the encroachment of moss on a brick or thyme on a rock appealing, we are pleased by the contrast between the fixity of the inert and the mutability of its natural frame' (1998, pp. 111–112). At Birkenau, the 'work of man' in question is associated with events of atrocity, and in this instance the growth that overtakes them may be considered particularly appealing.

Throughout discourses around what Young has called the 'rhetoric of ruins', it is often suggested that these structures take us *closer* to the events of history.[5] I would like to refine this and propose instead that both ruins, and the encroachment of nature on these structures, force us to realize the unbridgeable gap between

---

5   Young, for example, remarks on the common habit of 'mistaking the piece [the artefact or ruin] for the whole, the implied whole for unmediated history' (1993, p. 127).

the present and the past. Charles Merewether has suggested that 'ruins collapse temporalities' (1997, p. 25); it would, I suggest make more sense to say that ruins *reassert* temporality. Furthermore, natural materials play a role in this, unique as they are in their ability to record the passing of time in ways that we can 'read' (Spirn 1993, p. 17); more so than the ruin, which is at the mercy of nature's whims. Roth has argued that ruins 'embody the dialectic of nature and artifice' (1997, p. 5); ruins are often the 'work' of nature. The traditional romantic appeal of the ruin, however, is far from straightforward in the commemorative context:

> The total wars of the twentieth century have shaken our framing of ruins and shattered the notion that culture can exist as an innocent, floating fragment in a powerful sea of violence. In the wake of World War II, culture itself came to be cast as a ruin, as a troubled witness to the violence of humanity rather than as a spectator of the sublime powers of nature ... the sentimental attachment to the ruin, *the contemplative gaze that finds some sign of renewal in nature's growth in a broken stone, has been shaken, diverted.* The promise of understanding the past and of the renewal or even redemption that this might provide seems empty or a lie in the wake of extremities (and the threat of nuclear annihilation) that turned a world into (potential) ruins . The regular rhythms of nature have been replaced in our time by the enormity of our capacity for ruination. (Roth 1997, p. 20, my emphasis)

The disruption of Romantic perception is also apparent in the landscape of Auschwitz. Young's work on the ruins at Auschwitz and Majdanek suggests that visitors experience an initial sense of 'shock: not because of the bloody horror these places convey, but because of their unexpected, even unseemly beauty. Saplings planted along the perimeters of the camps, intended to screen the Germans' crimes from view, now sway and toss in the wind (Young 1993, p. 120).

Young's description of the landscape suggests, beyond their beauty, that these places seem unsettlingly *pastoral*; 'local farmers, shouldering scythes, lead their families through waist-deep fields to cut and gather grass into great sheaves' (ibid). According to Terry Gifford, the term pastoral – originally defined as 'idealized' or 'celebratory' approaches to the countryside and nature (Gifford 1999, pp. 1–2) – has come to encompass a new scepticism: ' "pastoral" as pejorative, implying that the pastoral image is too simplified, and thus an idealization of the reality of life in the country' (ibid.). The original pastoral if often disrupted in this way when problems such as rural pollution poverty are acknowledged. Young's comments imply that the integration of concentration camps into pastoral landscapes causes a similar sense of unease.

A further uncomfortable juxtaposition may also arise when literary material is introduced into visitors' structures of perceptions. Dalton's account of his visit to Auschwitz provides a pertinent example of this. Much of Dalton's discussion is explicitly grounded in Holocaust literature encountered prior to his visit, demonstrating the affective impact of such work on experience of place. On seeing the expansive grassed area that now constitutes the remains of Birkenau, Dalton experiences an awareness of 'the presence of absence' (2009, p. 202) when he recalls the testimony of former inmate Kitty Hart. Hart describes her impressions of the Birkenau site when returning for the first time after the end of the war: 'You see grass. But I don't see any grass. I see mud; just a sea of mud. Outside the "meadow" is green with grass. That's something I can't get used to. It was never like that. men collapsed and died in the mud.' (Dalton 2009, p. 202, cites Hart[6]). For Dalton, the result was to make him 'painfully aware of [a] sense of privilege … [of] the presence of this absence' (Dalton 2009, p. 202). He returns to this feeling in his conclusion, as he works through the 'experimental failure' of his visit as a 'dark tourist', as '[o]ut-of-wartime temporality cannot capture the multitude of true horrors and loss embedded in the camp complex' (2009, p. 218). And yet:

> the very relics and remnants of Auschwitz-Birkenau provide a powerful backdrop – a type of *mise en scène* – that helps animate the imagination. I thought back over the many moments of imaginative reflection that had prevailed during my visit … the so-called 'material evidence of crimes' … are, despite their plurality – able to invoke a powerful affective sense of individual loss if one is prepared to engage in imaginative contemplation. This small paradoxical triumph struck me as something worth celebrating. And as I prepared to finally depart Birkenau, I reflected on the fact that whilst I cannot 'live their loss' … I can pause to imagine their suffering. (Dalton 2009, p. 218)

From this perspective, it becomes possible to conceive of the tourist as engaging in a relation with past 'others' founded on a fundamentally ethical premise, which demonstrates intense concern yet avoids an over-extended sense of complete identification. Although the degree to which visitors are generally acquainted with literary material is an unknown factor, given the extent to which certain texts have been embraced by popular culture and education in many national contexts in recent years, this angle is certainly worthy of further scrutiny, and will be more fully developed in the second half of this chapter.

Buchenwald: Literature and Landscape

Many of the factors described above in relation to Auschwitz are also central to Buchenwald Concentration Camp Memorial. The site is a reasonably representative example of how the landscapes of such sites are commonly shaped: formal indoor exhibition space is surrounded by primary outdoor spaces, with commemorative monuments, and often markers and signage to clarify how each particular area

---

6   The extract from Kitty Hart's testimony is cited by Dalton from a reproduction in Charlesworth and Addis (2002: 231).

was used in the past. As applies to parts of Auschwitz II Birkenau, there are also secondary outdoor spaces, not apparently being used for anything in particular and where there is less of an obvious curatorial presence or designation of space, for example as commemorative or educational. The camp is situated on the slopes of the Ettersburg, within the Thuringian forest, which in itself attracts tourists for its idyllic rural scenery and the wildlife supported by the ancient woods; Baedeker's guides from the inter-war period describe the Thuringian Forest as 'full of interest for the pedestrian' (1925, p. 266), and grant the area an asterisk designating it as of notable interest to the traveller. Weimar has a profoundly traditional German history, and Johann Wolfgang von Goethe regularly strolled in the area, along with his plays being performed there in an amateur theatre.

The German name of the camp, *Buchenwald*, translates to mean 'beech wood' in English, referring to the local area which was partly deforested in order to build the site. A scrutiny of former inmate testimony suggests that the camp's location within the forest had an impact on the way it was experienced by a number of the prisoners held there throughout the National Socialist regime. Survivor Ernst Weichart's memoir *The Forest of the Dead* [*Der Totenwald*] (1947) refers constantly to memories of the surrounding landscape and emphasizes the author's difficulty in reconciling the 'golden fields ... verdant meadows' and 'wooded acres' of the Ettersburg with the immediate hardship of the camp: to Wiechart the view 'always seemed like a mirage, treacherous and unreal ... reality close at hand was such as to forbid the eye to turn to all that distant beauty' (Weichart 1947, p. 74). Weichart also recalls how this 'lovely' name sparked an immediate mistrust to those familiar with the Nazi's use of misleading natural signifiers (1947, p. 59). Spanish author Semprun spent two years in Buchenwald after being arrested for his activities in the resistance movement. Semprun similarly recalls the German Army's 'revealing military tradition' of using poetic name codes such as *Meerschaum* [Sea Foam] and *Frülingswind* [Spring Wind] for mass deportations of French prisoners in 1944 (Semprun 1997, p. 40).

Semprun's testimonial oeuvre presents a series of reflections about the position Buchenwald occupied within the larger cultural and geographic landscape. Bella Brodzki's recent work on Semprun (2007) suggests the value of pursuing a reading of the Buchenwald site alongside Semprun's testimony and highlighting the parallel significance of Buchenwald, both throughout Semprun's narratives and within the larger context of Holocaust commemoration. To Brodzki, Buchenwald 'resonate[s] as a defining site for considering the Holocaust, cultural memory, and the conflation of physical landscape and catastrophic event' (2007, p. 170). However, as Brodzki's own thesis is primarily concerned with translation and forms of survival, she does not herself undertake such a survey of landscape and literature. Various discussions of Semprun's work have also suggested that his work, particularly his first Buchenwald text *The Long Voyage*, constitutes a particular form of travel writing that potentially places the experience of deportation within a common, shared frame of reference; that of travel (Silk 1992; Jones 2007).

Both on his journey and upon arrival at the camp, Semprun explicitly describes the landscape of his deportation and internment in terms which could indicate a phenomenological and informed engagement with space. Throughout, an awareness of his geographical position and the cultural and historical heritage of specific topographies around him can be noted. In the cattle truck, Semprun looks out a window as the train travels through the Moselle valley and, contemplating its contours 'fashioned by the work of centuries', lovingly describes a landscape with its 'dazzling certainty of grey tints, the tall pines, the prim villages, the calm smoke in the winter sky' (Semprun 1963, p. 15). At Buchenwald he continues to scrutinize the aesthetics and cultural history of the space around him. In *What a Beautiful Sunday!* (1983), his second Buchenwald memoir, he describes walking over to the edge of the camp on most Sunday afternoons at sunset to admire the view across the Ettersburg (1983, p. 237), just as many locals in the past would have walked the same slopes to visit a favourite natural beauty spot before the inauguration of the camp.

The descriptions of the landscape sit uneasily against Semprun's discussions of the horrendous conditions in the part of the camp where he stood to admire this view. Indeed this area, known as the Little Camp, was mainly used for the internment of Jewish prisoners who reputedly suffered most of all the groups held at Buchenwald. By bringing these two elements together in the reader's imagination – the peaceful view over the rural Ettersburg with the atrocities of the Little Camp – Semprun's work is suggestive of the pastoral disruption Young remarked upon in relation to Auschwitz. Semprun also demonstrates a pre-occupation with issues of perspective, particularly the potential of landscape to frame shared perspective. He imagines others, including the guards in their watch towers, sitting looking over the landscape, and remarks 'Even Goethe could not have had such a fine view, for the trees that were cut down to build the camp must have blocked the view in his day' (1983, p. 34). He frequently considers, in this way, the way others would perceive the views he looks upon. His knowledge of the cultural history associated with the Weimar area is also evident, suggesting a particular interest in Goethe's association with the area. In discussing this connection he indicates the existence of another uncomfortable juxtaposition; that of Germanic Enlightenment alongside Nazi atrocity. Amongst the landmarks that Semprun discusses, several notable examples are connected to the life of Goethe. These include a large oak tree in the centre of the camp itself, which the writer used to visit regularly. It was preserved when other trees were deforested to build Buchenwald. Semprun comments extensively on the oak, and speculates on how the writer himself would have reacted to the continued protection of his favourite tree (1983, pp. 206–207). He also visits Goethe's house on in Weimar after Buchenwald was liberated in Spring 1945 (Semprun 1997, pp. 78–105).

Finally, there is to be found in Semprun's work a nuanced interrogation of commemorative politics. In *The Long Voyage*, he also anticipates the way nature might one day change the site:

I would like to see that: the grass and the bushes, the roots and brambles encroaching as the seasons go by, beneath the persistent Ettersburg rains ... obstinately encroaching, this camp constructed by men, the grass and the roots repossessing the place where the camp had stood. (Semprun 1963, p. 189)

Such sentiments are grounded in a rejection of the idea of Buchenwald one day becoming a memorial space; certain passages from his texts suggest that the site itself has, for Semprun, no place in the contemporary world. After the camp had been liberated but before the inmates had left, Semprun gets into a discussion with another inmate, the camp librarian, about the future of the site. The librarian predicts that it will soon be used as a camp to re-educate the Nazis (which, in fact, does happen for six years after the end of the war). He questions Semprun in frustration when the other rejects this idea:

'What do you want to do with Buchenwald? Turn it into a place of pilgrimage, of meditation? A vacation resort?

'Absolutely not!' [Semprun replies] 'I'd like the camp to be abandoned to the erosion of time, to nature.I'd like it to be engulfed by the forest'. (Semprun 1997, p. 63)

Semprun's literature provides a way into thinking about the landscape of Buchenwald and the surrounding area in the present day. There certainly remains the disruption of a pastoral landscape with atrocity. Travel writer Michael Gorra visited Buchenwald in 1993, and his journey through the landscape to the main memorial features in his later account of his time in Germany. He recalls a sense of uneasiness about the location of the camp: 'We went north through the hills, and each curve in the road seemed to open up a pastoral landscape, with distant fields gone yellow in flower. The woods here are full of beech trees still' (Gorra 2004, pp. 15–16). He articulates the 'trouble' he faced in integrating an appropriate literary representation of Buchenwald alongside a more straightforward appreciation of the landscape.

The uncomfortable but compelling juxtaposition of the high culture of Germany's literary past with Nazi destruction is also embedded in recent tourist experiences of the area. In 1999 Weimar became the first former Eastern bloc city, and the smallest to date, to be awarded Europe's City of Culture title. The media delighted in mentioning 'the dark side' of the area's history in their commentary on the decision. Silke Roth has argued that Weimar is an important *lieu de mémoire* for German national identity, a cultural and political homeland for numerous important movements in history, including Romanticism, Classicism, the Bauhaus, the Weimar Republic, and National Socialism. In an assessment of the events organized throughout the year known as Weimar 1999, Roth observed that many of these histories were downplayed; Classicism and National Socialism emerged as clear priorities in the schedule. An opening speech by then President of the Federal Republic of Germany, Roman Herzog, stressed a model of German culture defined by a 'contrast between Enlightenment and National Socialist terror' (S. Roth 2003, p. 95). The Nazi past was acknowledged, but not over-emphasized, throughout Weimar 1999; 'It will not do [.] to pride oneself on Goethe and deny Hitler. There is only Goethe *and* Hitler, humanity *and* bestiality' (von Plessen et al. 1999, p. 137, cite Richard Alewyn 1949, p. 333).

Thus despite all Weimar's many legacies, it seems to have been Buchenwald and Goethe that took precedence in the cultural landscape of Weimar 1999. As a result, many tourists that year followed, inadvertently, the trajectory between Buchenwald and Goethe's house traced out by Semprun in 1945, a path that meanders along a dialectical opposition between creativity and destruction, evolution and fixity. Contemporary tourists visit many of the same landmarks within the Buchenwald landscape that also feature significantly in Semprun's narratives. The stump of Goethe's oak tree, for example, remains a prominent feature at the memorial site today, fully signposted, mentioned in the museum guidebooks, and integrated into the most frequented walking tour of the site. According to Young, monuments are always fixed points of reference amongst others; together they create meaning, orientation and linear narratives for the visitor to a memorial landscape (1994, p. 7). Young indicates the existence of a dialogical relationship between objects in memorial landscapes. Contemporary visitors who do attempt to unravel the significance of the Goethe Oak at Buchenwald are faced with the problem which, according to Gorra, confronts 'any student of German culture': they must 'worry at the question of how one might get from the poet to the prison. of their coincidence in something more than space' (Gorra 2004, p. 16).

It serves as a testament to the extent of Semprun's knowledge about the construction and history of Buchenwald that he presents readers of *What a Beautiful Sunday!* and *The Long Voyage* with the same information that can now be found in the camp exhibition official guidebook (published some ten years later in 1993).[7] His impeccably sourced information provides as worthy and detailed an account as any of the official literature available. Goethe's oak, as Semprun suggests, was indeed the only tree left standing in the main area of the Buchenwald camp after the deforestation of the designated Ettersburg area. One contemporary Buchenwald guide book suggests that the tree was significant for the camp prisoners, representing 'unspoilt nature' and 'the positive world' outside the camp (Sabine and Harry Stein 1993, p. 33). Gorra speculates that this 'bit of greenery' could, in fact, have sustained or mocked the prisoners, depending on their perspectives (2004, p. 16). In 1944 the tree was reduced to a stump when it caught fire during an Allied bombing attack; however the attempt to preserve it continued. The camp authorities filled the centre of the stump with concrete in order to prevent erosion (Kattago 1998, p. 275). Its meaning as a commemorative monument remains in flux; the suggestion of a straightforward respect and

---

7   See, for example, a discussion of the Goethe Oak (*LV* 119–120) and of the deforestation of the Ettersburg (Semprun 1983, pp. 7–8).

honour for this era of German cultural history cannot but be undermined, even retrospectively, by National Socialism's lack of 'Goethean humanism'.

Semprun's Sunday visits to the border of the Little Camp to admire the view of the Ettersburg can be re-enacted in the camp's present landscape. The barracks of the main camp area have been marked out for perpetuity. Razed not long after liberation their foundations are demarcated with different coloured stones. Other buildings in this area have been preserved, including the crematorium. The site of the former Little Camp is comparatively untouched. A small sunken plot has been paved, and here a memorial plaque describes the conditions faced by prisoners interned there, concluding:

> After liberation, although the main camp was preserved and various memorials established, the Little Camp was totally obliterated and allowed to be overgrown with trees and bushes. The site was neglected by the German authorities until the mid-1990s. Some of the survivors settled in the United States; they and their descendants have supported the creation of this memorial.

Sunken as it is, this area is not visible when a visitor looks across the site. Facing one way, preserved buildings and monuments spread across the landscape as far as the eye can see; but if you turn around there is nothing but a forest of beeches and birches stretching towards the horizon.

Given Semprun's long-standing desire to see the camp overgrown by nature, it is worth straying even further from the main memorial. Away from this area are the remains of the SS complex. Buchenwald was a space of internment, but also a centre for training. By the end of the war over 6,000 SS men and women, and often their families too, were housed in the area directly around the main camp. Of four walking tours suggested by the Buchenwald guidebook, one takes the visitor through some, but not all, of these areas. This walk, nearly 5km long, is less frequented than the others for obvious reasons; the terrain is often uneven and at times rendered inaccessible by (not infrequent) extreme weather conditions. There is comparatively little sign posting, and it requires some effort to stick to the path suggested by the map. The area is scattered with the ruins of buildings which are, for the most part, not sign-posted or labelled on the map, their original function undisclosed. Tree roots have worked their way through concrete foundations, and in the field that was once the military garage thick layers of moss and dense grass disguise the remnants of original structures.

Semprun himself questions:

> Has one really experienced something that one is unable to describe, something whose minimum truth one is unable to construct in a meaningful way – and so make communicable? Doesn't living, in the full sense of the term, mean transferring one's personal experience into consciousness – that is to say, into memorized experience that is capable at the same time of integration into the future? But can one assume any experience without mastering its language?

> The history – the stories, the narratives, the memories, the eyewitness accounts
> in which it survives – lives on. The text, the very texture, the tissue of life.
> (1983, p. 39)

I propose that despite the commemorative transformation of the camp which Semprun himself rejected, the landscape of the Buchenwald memorial is meaningfully transformed for readers of Semprun's testimonial literature just as the meaning of the space was originally mediated and textualized, for Semprun himself, by its German literary legacy. Through a phenomenological appreciation of space the contemporary subject can begin to approach the task of confronting the difficulties of attaining a shared experience so inherent to empathic unsettlement. And in this model, it is the *attempt* to engage, rather than the achievement of a vicarious sense of illusory identification, which renders the subject an ethical participator in the essential work of memory demanded by the atrocities of the past.

Conclusion

The examples discussed here highlight the way in which landscape can place different people, at different times, in a position which unites their perspectives. At the same time, the combination of nature and ruins at the site make contemporary visitors aware of the time scale separating them from those who experienced the landscape many years before.

Quotes from Semprun's work about his desire to see the camp overgrown by nature were used by historian Robert Jan van Pelt (2009) when he argued that, after the death of the last surviving internee, the remains of the former Nazi camps should be left to decay; in his view the remains of these places in themselves do not communicate anything of sufficient value to recommend their continued preservation for future generations. However, as the curators at Auschwitz II Birkenau have discovered, the encroachment of nature and gradual decay is actually a part of what affects visitors' feelings about the sites themselves when they do visit. As the curators are also discovering, over time, increasingly expensive and time-consuming measures must necessarily be put in place to retain a desirable balance of nature and human structures. As previously mentioned, the approach taken at Auschwitz raises questions to which there are no clear-cut answers. And yet, given the argument outlined here, these attempts are of value in one sense, for they may allow visitors to experience a kind of empathic unsettlement as LaCapra has defined it. By standing in the place where the victims of the past stood, visitors may gain, albeit temporarily, a view that was also that of the victims, an opportunity to place ourselves in their perspective. As I have suggested in a brief scrutiny of Semprun's work about Buchenwald, literature can play a central role in guiding this process. Many factors can be seen to suggest that emotional responses at such sites are tied up with the way people feel about their relationship with the landscape around them and the natural world. Because nature is constantly changing the view, and the ruins at the sites of memory are gradually decaying, the passing of time is always visible. This could be understood to reasserts our inevitable temporal difference from past victims. In short, it has been argued here that these sites potentially take visitors closer to experiencing a form of genuine empathy, whilst elements within them act as a constant reminder that full identification will always be impossible.

References

Auschwitz-Birkenau Memorial Museum (2010) 'Museum Report 2009', http://en.auschwitz.org.pl/m/index.php?option=com_content&task=view&id=737&Itemid=7 (accessed on 10 April 2010).

Baer, U. (2002) *Spectral Evidence: The Photography of Trauma*, Cambridge, MA: MIT Press.

Brodzki, B. (2007) *Can These Bones Live? Translation, Survival and Cultural Memory*, Stanford, CA: Stanford University Press.

Casey, E. (1996) 'How to get from space to place in a fairly short stretch of time: Phenomenological prolegomena', in S. Feld and K. Basso (eds), *Senses of Place*, Santa Fe, NM: School of American Research Press, pp. 13–52.

Certeau, M. de. (1984) *The Practice of Everyday Life*, trans. S. Rendall, Berkeley: University of California Press.

Confino, A. and Fritsche, P. (2002) *The Work of Memory: New Directions in the Study of German Society and Culture*, Champaign: University of Illinois Press.

Confino, A. (2006) *Germany as a Culture of Remembrance: Promises and Limits of Writing History*, Chapel Hill: University of North Carolina Press.

Dalton, D. (2009) 'Encountering Auschwitz: A personal rumination on the possibilities and limitations of witnessing/remembering trauma in memorial space', *Law-Text-Culture*, 13, pp. 187–226.

Dixon Hunt, J. (2000) 'Come into the Garden, Maud': Garden art as a privileged mode of commemoration and identity', in J. Wolschke-Bulmahn (ed.), *Places of Commemoration: Search for Identity and Landscape Design*, Washington, DC: Dunbarton Oaks.

Gifford, T. (1999) *Pastoral*, Abingdon, Oxon and New York: Routledge.

Gorra, M. (2004) *The Bells in their Silence: Travels through Germany*, Princeton and Oxford: Princeton University Press.

Hungerford, A. (2003) *The Holocaust of Texts: Genocide, Literature and Personification*, Chicago and London: Chicago University Press.

Jones, K. (2007) *Journeys of Remembrance: Memories of the 2nd World War in French and German Literature, 1960–1980*, London and Leeds: Legenda.

Kattago, S. (1998) 'Narrating the histories of Buchenwald', *Constellations*, 5(2), pp. 266–282.

Keil, C. (2008) 'Sightseeing in the Mansions of the Dead' *Social and Cultural Geography*, 6(4), pp. 479–494.

Koonz, C. (1994) 'Between memory and oblivion: Concentration camps in German memory', in J.R. Gillis (ed.), *Commemorations: The Politics of National Identity*, Princeton: Princeton University Press, pp. 258–280.

Koshar, R. (2000) *German Travel Cultures*, Oxford and New York: Berg.

LaCapra, D. (2001) *Writing History, Writing Trauma*, Baltimore and London: Johns Hopkins University Press.

Lang, B. (2003) [1990], 'The moral space of figurative discourse', in N. Levi and M. Rothberg (eds), *The Holocaust: Theoretical Readings*, New Brunswick and New Jersey: Rutgers University Press, pp. 329–334.

Lennon, J.J. and Foley, M. (2000) *Dark Tourism: The Attraction of Death and Disaster*, New York and London: Continuum.

MacCannell, D. (1992) *Empty Meeting Grounds: The Tourist Papers*, London and New York: Routledge

Nora, P. (2001) *Rethinking France: Les Lieux de Memoire, Volume 1: The State*, trans. M. Trouille, London and Chicago: Chicago University Press.

Pelt, R.J. van. (2009) 'Cash crisis threat to Auschwitz', http://news.bbc.co.uk/1/hi/world/europe/7827534.stm (accessed 20 February 2009).

Pogue Harrison, R. (2003) *The Dominion of the Dead*, Chicago and London: Chicago University Press.

Rigney, A. (2008) 'Divided pasts: A premature memorial and the dynamics of collective remembrance' *Memory Studies*, 1, pp. 89–97.

Roth, M. et al. (1997) *Irresistible Decay: Ruins Reclaimed*, Los Angeles: Getty Publications.

Roth, S. (2003) 'Goethe and Buchenwald: Reconstructing German national identity in the Weimar Year 1999', in P.M. Daly et al. (eds), *Why Weimar? Questioning the Legacy of Weimar from Goethe to 1999*, McGill European Studies Series 5, New York and Baltimore: Peter Lang Publishing.

Rymaszewski, B. (2004) 'The limits of intervention in museum and conservation Practice at the Auschwitz Memorial and Museum', trans. W. Brand, in K. Marszalek (ed.), *Preserving for the Future: Material from an International Preservation Conference, Oświęcim, June 23–25, 2003*. Oświęcim: Auschwitz Birkenau State Museum, pp. 24–34.

Scarry, E. (1985) *The Body in Pain: The Making and Unmaking of the World*, Oxford and New York: Oxford University Press.

Schama, S. (1995) *Landscape and Memory*, London: Harper Collins.

Semprun, J. (1963) *The Long Voyage* [*Le Grand Voyage*], trans. R. Seaver, Paris: Gallimard.

Semprun, J. (1983) *What a Beautiful Sunday!* [*Quel beau Dimanche!*], trans. A. Sheridan, London: Abacus.

Semprun, J. (1997) *Literature or Life* [*L'écriture ou la Vie*], trans. L. Coverdale, London: Viking (Penguin).

Silk, S.M. (1992) 'Writing the holocaust/writing Travel: The space of representation in Jorge Semprun's *Le Grand Voyage*', *CLIO: A Journal of Literature, History, and the Philosophy of History*, 22(1), pp. 53–65.

Sprin, A.W. (1998) *The Language of Landscape*, New Haven and London: Yale University Press.

Stein, S. and H. (1993) *Buchenwald: A Tour of the Memorial Site*, trans. T. Gohlke, Weimar: Buchenwald Memorial.

Stewart, S. (1998) 'Garden Agon', *Representations*, 62, pp. 111–143.

Tilley, C. (1994) *A Phenomenology of Landscape: Places, Paths, and Monuments*, Providence, RI and Oxford: Berg.

Urry, J. (1995) *Consuming Places*, London and New York: Routledge.

Von Plessen, M.-L. et al. (eds) (1999) *Walking through Time in Weimar: A Criss-cross Guide to Cultural History – Weaving between Goethe's Home and Buchenwald*, Ostfilden-Ruit: Hatje Verlag.

Weichart, E. (1947) *The Forest of the Dead [Der Totenwald]*, trans. U. Stechow, London: Victor Gallancz.

Young, J.E. (1994) *The Texture of Memory: Holocaust Memorials and Meanings*, New Haven and London: Yale University Press.

Zając, B. (2004) 'Grey or green? Problems with the maintenance of the vegetation on the museum grounds', trans. W. Brand, in K. Marszalek (ed.), *Preserving for the Future: Material from an International Preservation Conference, Oświęcim, June 23–25, 2003.* Oświęcim: Auschwitz-Birkenau State Museum, pp. 57–62.

Chapter 10

World War II Tourism in France

Bertram M. Gordon

This chapter explores the emotions, passions and movement that characterize World War II-related tourism in France, both during the war and in the occasionally contentious development of war-related tourist sites and what are often called *lieux de mémoire* [sites of memory] thereafter. The reaction, in the *Daily Mail*, a British tabloid newspaper, and elsewhere, to Queen Elizabeth's non-invitation to the 65th D-Day anniversary events in Normandy in June 2009 speaks eloquently to the emotions aroused by wartime tourism (Hickley and English 2009; Burns 2009; Delasalle-Stolper 2009).

Tourism is sometimes considered a relatively new phenomenon, with some dating it to the English aristocratic Grand Tour of the sixteenth century and later, but its history goes back far earlier (Lfier 1977, p. 7). Evidence for ancient tourism includes the graffiti dating to the middle of the second millennium BC found on walls in tombs in Sakkharah, Ghizeh, and Abusir in Egypt. Herodotus, who in Lionel Casson's words, 'spent the better part of his life as a tourist', described large swaths of the Persian Empire and was, according to Casson, the world's first travel writer (Casson 1994, pp. 32 and 96). Based on the ancient notion of *curiositas*, Petrarch wrote, 'I know that in men's minds resides an innate longing to see new places' (Thubron 1999, p. 12). Maurice Dupuy considers tourism, 'from pre-history to our days', as based on 'a desire to know' and 'to discover' (Dupuy 1994, p. 18). Emphasizing that 'far from being born a tourist, man became one', Pascal Cuvelier argues that tourism began with the Roman *otium*, a cultured retreat for the optimates (Cuvelier 1998, pp. 19–20). More recently, Mike Robinson, a British specialist in tourism studies research wrote: 'If one strips away much of the hardware of tourism and travel we find that the human imagination is at its core' (Robinson 2005, p. xix). As a cultural expression, the tourist 'gaze', a term popularized in 1990 by John Urry, has taken on the signification of the ways in which people encounter, assimilate, and understand ideas, material objects, and other people as they move around the world, observing and studying (Urry 2000, pp. 1–2; Crawshaw and Urry 1997, p. 176).

Too often, however, the history of tourism in the twentieth century is depicted as stopping in 1939 only to resume again after 1945. Despite the extensive literature on cultural tourism and on warfare and its history, there has been relatively little study of the inter-relationships between the two. Anthologies of studies of specific times and places in tourism history include works edited by John K. Walton, Gilles Bertrand, and the collection edited by Hermann Bausinger, Klaus Beyrer, and

Gottfried Korff, to name only a few (Walton 2005; Bertrand 2004; Bausinger, et al. 1991). More broadly themed historical studies of the development of tourism include studies by Jean-Didier Urbain, the work by Maurice Dupuy cited above, Catherine Bertho Lavenir, Maxine Feiffer, and Cindy Aron (Urbain 1993; Dupuy 1994, p. 18; Lavenir 1999; Feiffer 1986; and Cindy Aron 1999). In Germany, Hasso Spode's, 'Zur Geschichte der Tourismusgeschichte', includes a picture of bathers at the Baltic Sea in 1941, 'in the middle of the war', (Spode 2009, p. 20) but these and other general works on tourism history rarely address its relationship to war.

Occasional linkages may be found in a study of urban tourism by Marc Chesnel (Chesnel 2009, p. 8) and in a presentation by Josette Mesplier-Pinet, who, in addressing a conference entitled '*Tourisme Culture Patrimoine*' [Tourism, Culture, Heritage] in 2004, noted that cultural tourism, formerly concentrated on the beaux-arts, had become increasingly less 'elitist' and was opening more to "new themes" that included military heritage [*patrimoine militaire*] (Mesplier-Pinet 2009, pp. 12–13). Magazines for enthusiasts, such as *After the Battle*, published in Britain, are devoted to the retrospective description of battlefield sites. The Dutch website WW2Museums.com, an initiative of STIWOT (*Stichting Informatie Wereldoorlog Twee* [World War II Information Foundation]), with listings of battlefields and other war monuments throughout Europe, states:

> WW2Museums.com is the place to plan your own battlefield tour along WW2 museums, monuments, cemeteries and other sights of interest in and outside Europe. Through WW2Museums.com you will be introduced to WW2 sights [*sic*] of interest that still can be visited today! (STIWOT 2010)

In many ways, tourism was attenuated during the war but it continued, even if altered in significant ways, and planning for post-war tourism continued as well. One of the pillars of post-war tourism became the sites and circuits linked to the memory of the battles, the concentration camps, the Resistance and the collaboration in France. Post-war tourism in memory became big business and people in the tourism industry recognized it, contributing to making France one of the largest receivers of tourists in the world. Wartime and war-related, tourism, sometimes known as 'battlefield tourism', is now occasionally referenced as 'thanatourism', or 'dark tourism', linked to death, atrocity, or disaster, with visits to battlefields, cemeteries, and memorials, notably the Holocaust (Seaton and Lennon 2004, pp. 63–64). The economic exploitation of three sites of memory connected to World War II in France is addressed by Henning Meyer (Meyer 2006, p. 529), whereas Wiebke Kolbe notes in her study of post-war German battlefield tourism that distinctions among pilgrimages, battlefield tourism, and tourism in general are difficult if not impossible to draw as reactions of visitors to *lieux de mémoire* vary. The same visitor to a battlefield or war cemetery might also visit other sites (Kolbe 2009, p. 47). As a field, World War II tourism study is hardly new but its publishing history and many of the related details still need to be elaborated. My own earlier efforts linking war and tourism include studies of the

Germans in occupied France during World War II as well as wartime sites in their role as tourism attractions in the post-war period (Gordon 1996; Gordon 1998; Gordon 2001).

This chapter points to some of the emotion generated by World War II tourism and makes a hypothetical foray into the assessment of its significance in the larger tourism context using France as a case study. France is an important case in examining the connections between tourism and war especially in regard to World War II for three significant reasons: first, France's role as the current world leader in tourist visits; secondly, the development of the field of cultural memory following the work of French scholars such as Maurice Halbwachs and more recently Pierre Nora; and thirdly, the production of an extensive historical literature relating to the war and its interpretations in France since 1945.

People often think of World War II tourism in France as visits to the Moulin Rouge and Maxim's restaurant in Paris, where German occupation soldiers spent leisure time; or the grand hotels in the Alps and beach resorts near Nice, many of which remained open during the war years. Just as a larger view of curiosity in motion is needed to analyse generic tourism, a more extensive view of World War II tourism is necessary to understand its history in France during the war and in the more than 60 years since. This chapter re-examines World War II tourism in France by focusing first on the most significant sites of tourist curiosity, namely the Atlantic Wall and subsequent Normandy battlefield sites, before turning briefly to tourism during the 1940–1944 German occupation in France, and lastly to the post-1944 expansion of tourist sites that, in addition to the Normandy beaches, became *lieux de mémoire*.

Tourist Gazes during and after the War: Normandy and the Maginot Line

In sheer numbers, tourist gazes inevitably followed the major military sequences of the war with attention drawn to the Battle of Britain, the Great Patriotic War in Eastern Europe, the Atlantic and Pacific Theatres, and, D-Day. What focused the tourist gaze during the war in France was surely newsreel films of General Erwin Rommel on tour along the Atlantic Wall coastal defences, aerial reconnaissance photographs taken by all sides during the war – arguably among the most photographed sites – the gawkers on the streets as German, and later Allied, tanks rolled by, and the theatres, movie houses, cafés, and hotels, the romantic sites for French as well as foreign visitors. To this list should be added historic sites that became *lieux de mémoire* after the war.

How many aerial photographs and gazes were directed during the war toward the Atlantic Wall, or how many in France watched newsreels of General Rommel touring the fortifications will never be known. Although one might hesitate to call Rommel a tourist in the sense of a participant in a Cook's tour, Scott McCabe in an essay on the concept of the tourist notes that the American Heritage dictionary offers as one of its definitions: 'a brief trip through a place, as a building or a site, in order to view or inspect it: The visiting prime minister was given a tour of the chemical plant.' (McCabe 2009, p. 31). Tourist curiosity is invariably involved in military campaigns and the interest in the coast can only have been intense as Allies, Germans, military and civilians, looked toward the Atlantic Wall in anticipation of the outcome of the war with intense aerial photography focused on it (Desquesnes 2009b, pp. 74–75). As early as October 1940, the German high command expressed concern about a possible English landing on the French coast and called for continual vigilance there (Rundstedt 1940). Ernst Jünger, a German officer and writer stationed in Paris, wrote on 4 May 1944, 'the landing occupies everyone's attention; the German command, as well as the French, believe it will take place one of these days.' (Jünger 1965, p. 315). A mammoth undertaking that employed thousands of workers and was run by the Organization Todt, the Wall was described by the magazine *L'Illustration* in 1943 as comparable in history only to the Great Wall of China (cited in Desquesnes 2009b, pp. 22–23). With some 15,000 concrete fortifications of varying sizes, the Atlantic Wall was never completed (Quellien 2004, pp. 6–7).

Described as the last great fortified system, the Atlantic Wall was to be an impregnable series of fortifications along the coast of western Europe extending from Norway's North Cape to the French-Spanish border and was based on a

Figure 10.1   Pointe du Hoc, France © Bertram Gordon, 2009

directive of Hitler's on 14 December 1941, a week after the entry of the United States into the war (Desquesnes 2009a, pp. 9 and 17). Ultimately, the Atlantic Wall failed for reasons that included Allied surprise in the Normandy invasion of 6 June 1944, their overwhelming air and naval superiority in materiel, and German indecision and their expectation that the Normandy invasion was a feint, especially as the Allied operation Fortitude was designed as an ersatz invasion intended for the Pas-de-Calais further north (Grandhomme 2009, pp. 108–109).

Aerial photographs to glean military intelligence both over the Atlantic Wall and Normandy, as elsewhere, were among the earliest expressions of World War II 'battlefield tourism', even if directed toward military purposes. 'Battlefield tourism' or 'memory tourism' [*tourisme de mémoire*] is especially evident in Normandy, where the post-war proliferation of *lieux de mémoire* as tourist sites attests to French success in exploiting the tourist potential of the battlegrounds (Meyer 2006, p. 529). In *La Mémoire désunie* [Divided Memory], Olivier Wieviorka traces the history of ways in which war-related sites were given Resistance signification after 1944 as succeeding governments, following the suggestion of General Charles de Gaulle, portrayed a France united in resistance to the Nazis (Wieviorka 2010). The French had long before begun to classify military fortifications as official historic sites with the Amiens citadel in 1840. In 1946 and 1947, they moved to protect the town of Oradour-sur-Glane, scene of a massacre of the villagers by a unit of the Waffen-SS on 10 June 1944; the Struthof concentration camp in Natzweiler in Alsace, and Omaha Beach in Normandy (Raffray 1999, pp. 6–7).

The Loi Triboulet of 21 May 1947, named for the first sub-prefect of liberated territory in Normandy, created an annual celebration of the landings there (Chapron 2009). Michelin published its first battlefield map, number 102, of the region in 1947. By 1953, a 'Liberation Circuit' tour focused on the Allied landing beaches (Horizons 1953, pp. 1–2; Gordon 2001, p. 250). In the 1950s there were two museums in Normandy devoted to the landings, whereas there are presently more than 30.

Anniversaries also played a part in the development of war-related tourism, as exemplified in the case of the Normandy invasion sites. A guidebook to these locales, prepared for the twentieth anniversary of the invasion in 1964, contained a preface by General Pierre Kœnig, who had commanded the Free French military contingent participating in the 1944 expedition. In the preface Kœnig claimed the 1964 guidebook to be the first of its kind. 'No longer', he wrote, 'would those wishing to tour the battlefield need to do extensive preparatory research as now all was put together in one accessible guidebook intended especially for war veterans, families coming to pay respects to their dead', and 'naturally, tourists traveling these regions heavy with history' (Kœnig 1964, pp. 5–6). In addition to a brief history of the events leading up to the Normandy invasion, the guidebook listed seven touring itineraries, one focusing on the British parachute troops' landings, another devoted to the events from the battle of Cherbourg to that of Caen, plus five other tours, each visiting one of the landing beaches: Sword, Juno, Gold, Omaha, and Utah. The book concluded with a chronology and a bibliography.

As of 2009, a 'Normandie Pass', offered discounts for visits to 26 D-Day museums in the region (Normandie Pass 2009). Normandy has many other tourist attractions, such as the Bayeux tapestry, which, according to Philippe Chapron, the Director of the *Musée Mémorial de la Bataille de Normandie* in Bayeux, also draw people toward the D-Day story. The *Musée Mémorial* was inaugurated officially on 14 July 1981. As of 2009, the museum employed eight people who staffed the equivalent of eleven positions, according to M. Chapron (Chapron 2009). One display in the museum is a telegram sent by the American War Department to the parents of a 20-year old soldier killed in action in Normandy on 30 July 1944. The picture of the soldier, one of four brothers serving in the war at the time, is just below. 'At that moment 'Saving Private Ryan' was very close to me', wrote one visitor to the site, illustrating the role that cinema often plays in the creation of tourism images (van den Bogert 2010).

In the British landing sector, the *Musée du Débarquement* in Arromanches-les-Bains, the site of an artificial harbour constructed to facilitate the landings, was one of the first D-Day museums.

Established as a private venture in 1953, it was inaugurated officially the following year, on the tenth anniversary of D-Day, by President René Coty (Arromanches 2009, p. 30; Lorrain 2009, p. 70; Meyer 2006, p. 210). By the early 1960s, the *Musée du Débarquement* was attracting over 200,000 visitors

Figure 10.2   Musée du Débarquement, France © Bertram Gordon, 2009

annually, according to paid entrance figures. The figures, gathered by the *Institute National de la Statistique et des Études Économiques* [INSEE], were 213,500 in 1962, 258,000 in 1963, and 284,000 in 1964, according to the *Annuaire Statistique de la France 1965* (Annuaire 1965, p. 396). Frédéric Sommier, Director of the *Musée du Débarquement*, indicated that it drew about 400,000 visitors in 2004, the sixtieth anniversary of D-Day, but that it normally attracts some 300,000 annually. The war, Mr Sommier noted, transformed Arromanches-les-Bains from a spa town – hence its name – to a *lieu de mémoire*. He described his museum's clientele more as "tourists" in quotes, than the visitors to some other places, such as the *Mémorial Cité de l'Histoire pour la Paix* at Caen. As of 2009, the Musée employed 17 people with an additional six or seven seasonal workers for the summer. A third of the visitors came in groups, the remaining visitors as individuals. Some 40,000 students, half French and half English, visited annually. Plans were underway in 2009 to enlarge the museum on some adjacent land available to it (Sommier 2009).

The Caen *Mémorial* has been depicted as a museum with a scenography 'based on emotion, the mise en scène seeking to mobilize passions, sentiments, emotions – in this case the memories of the spectators – while the historical content seeks to mobilize reason.' (Perissière 1998, p. 189; Sherman 1995, p. 50).

The *Mémorial* in Caen, a city heavily damaged in 1944, was established in 1988. According to paid entrance figures, it receives approximately 380,000 to 400,000 visitors each year. In 1994, the 50th anniversary of the D-Day landings, some 600,000 persons visited the *Mémorial*. Comparing the Caen *Mémorial* to other World War II sites in Normandy, Marc Pottier, its educational and research director, stated: 'we are more oriented to reflection, more demanding of the visitors.' (Pottier 2009). To Shannon L. Fogg, an American historian of France, 'A month spent studying at the *Mémorial de Caen* and visiting war sites throughout Normandy cemented my love for the period and for France.' (Fogg 2009, p. xiii). The Caen *Mémorial* is also situated on a tourist access route to Mont Saint-Michel, so it attracts a substantial '*tourisme d'autoroute, de passage*' [passing motorway tourism] in Pottier's words. Foreign visitors, Pottier noted, tended to go more to the cemeteries than to the *Mémorial* and they generally frequented sites closer to the sea, so that Arromanches received more foreign visitors than did the *Mémorial*. (Pottier 2009; Tobelem and Benito 2002, p. 269). It was said to be just behind Mont-Saint-Michel as the second most visited tourist site in the Normandy region (Gautier-Desvaux 1998, p. 311).

The proliferation of Atlantic Wall, D-Day related museums, and related tourist sites has given rise to debate regarding their purpose and the historical messages they send to the public (Davallon 1998, pp. 351–356). On one hand, a German guidebook, published in 1997, noted that much of the former Atlantic Wall had been turned into memorials to specific military actions, mile markers, and cemeteries for the fallen on both sides. In addition to the remembering, came the reconciliation, expressed in signs along the tourist route that bore German as well as British names (Schauseil 1997, p. 157). On the other hand, Elisabeth Raffray expressed concern in Lower Normandy about 'accusations made against all development of such a *patrimoine* that would promote "war tourism"' (Raffray 1999, p. 5). Tourist revenue potential of *lieux de mémoire* in France, however, is significant, although statistics regarding tourist visits are often subject to question and multiple interpretations. In one estimate, some 3,000,000 visitors toured the battle sites of Normandy in 2003, placing them arguably among the top 25 most frequented tourist sites in France (ORT-CRT 2003). The French *Observatoire national du tourisme* [ONT], which listed the 44 most visited sites in France for 2006, had war tourism tied for sixth and seventh place with three listings each. In first place were 16 'general' or unclassifiable destinations, such as the Saint-Ouen flea market near Paris and the Eiffel Tower; followed by religious and pilgrimage tourism sites with eight destinations. These included the Notre-Dame cathedral and the Sacré-Cœur basilica in Paris. Picnics, nature, and what might be called "environmentalist" locales, such as the Fontainebleau forest and the park at the Versailles château, were tied for fourth and fifth places with science and technology sites, including the *Cité des sciences de La Villette* in Paris and the Borély botanical gardens in Marseille (Vacances 2006). Because of problems with any statistics attempting to measure where people tour and how they spend their time, together with questions concerning who compiled the ONT list, the methodology used, and the fact that the list available came from a secondary source, a Wikipedia article, this attempt to place war tourism into the larger context must be regarded as hypothetical, awaiting further research. Marc Pottier's comment that the Caen *Mémorial* attracts *touristes de passage* exemplifies the multiplicity of reasons for which people visit sites (Pottier 2009). A breakdown of tourist numbers by age and gender would also help analyse tourism in general and the place of war tourism in particular. According to Frédéric Sommier, of the 300,000 visitors drawn annually to the *Musée du Débarquement* in Arromanches, some are 40,000 students who are split roughly half and half between France and the UK (Sommier 2009). Approximately one-third of the annual visitors to the Mémorial at Caen are students (Pottier 2009). Neither set of figures addresses the ages of the students, pre- or post-puberty.

Nonetheless, war-related sites comprised a significant segment of the tourist trade in the estimation of some. General Secretary of the *Conseil national du Tourisme* [National Council of Tourism] in 1996, Alain Monferrand estimated some 15 million visitors drawn to fortifications, battlegrounds, and military or historical museums of various kinds in France annually, but this was ten years prior to the *ONT* figures and it is not clear how he derived his numbers (Monferrand 1998, p. 335). These tourists, Monferrand emphasized, visited 'spontaneously', without an organized advertising campaign, which, he believed, might have doubled the numbers of visitors. With some 60 million international visitors per year, he argued, France was dependent on tourism's economic revenue, which employed a million persons, and constituted one of the last forms of economic development still possible for the then coming millennium. Culture and history were fundamental to this growth and many regions still had the potential, he wrote, to exploit their *patrimoine* for tourist expansion (Monferrand 1998, pp. 335–336 and 340–341). Monferrand also warned that local historical museums needed to avoid duplicating their exhibits (Monferrand 1998, p. 337), an issue also raised by Frédéric Sommier (Sommier 2009).

If the Atlantic Wall and Normandy together comprise the primary cluster of battlefield sites in France, the next would be the sites relating to the German victory in the West in 1940, in particular the fortresses of the Maginot Line. Bitterly described as a 'useless bastion', by one of its French defenders, the fortifications had cost an estimated five billion francs in the 1930s (Masson 1985: title page). With the German victory in 1940, the Maginot Line changed in meaning almost overnight from an expensive state of the art network of defensive fortifications to a site of touristic curiosity on the part of the victors. The newly taken fortifications were said to be 'all the rage' among the Germans in June 1940 and Hitler himself visited on the 30th (Kemp 1981, p. 101). Following the war, the fortresses were opened to tourists after 1964 when the French opted for nuclear rather than conventional military defense. The fort at Fermont, for example, was repaired by the French army shortly after the war and then abandoned in 1964. It subsequently came into the possession of private societies. From 1964 through 1970 French military engineers used several of the fortifications for study. The army maintained the Simserhof fortifications and established a museum there in 1966 with an extensive collection of artillery, shells, and related military materiel (Pallud 1988, p. 35).

A sequence of television programmes in 1965 brought the Maginot Line's new status to the attention of the French public. In 1973, the publication of Roger Bruge's book, *Faites Sauter la Ligne Maginot* [Blow Up the Maginot Line] that maintained that the forts had served France well in 1940, forcing the Germans to circumvent rather than attack them directly, gave a boost to tourism there. The Bambesch fort, near Metz, then recently opened to tourists, received nearly 10,000 visitors that year. The Marckolsheim fortress was opened to tourism in 1972 (Soudagne 2006, pp. 117–118). At Fermont, the *Association de l'Ouvrage du Fermont* [Fermont Fortress Association] obtained access to the fort in 1976 and opened it to the public the following year (Pallud 1988, p. 19). Two Maginot fortresses were given official protection in the 1980s (Raffray 1999, p. 7). Those open in 2009 were estimated to receive some 300,000 visitors annually (Fortified military architectures in Europe 2009; Seramour 2007; Gordon 2001, p. 255). A group of tourists ascending from the French Maginot Line fortifications was seen to be more solemn than the same people earlier entering the site (Gordon 2001, p. 239).

Changes and Continuities: Tourism in France – 1940–1944

War and occupation, not surprisingly, brought significant changes to the pre-war tourism models and itineraries in France. Beyond the tourist curiosity directed toward invasion sites in Normandy – both prior to and following the 1944 landings

– and the transformed symbolism of the Maginot Line after 1940, a significant, if immeasurable, manifestation of tourist curiosity has to have been the numbers of those who watched the various tanks, trucks, and wagons of all types roll down highways and village lanes, often depicted in the German newsreels of 1940 and their American counterparts of 1944. A hint of the magnitude of this kind of tourism can be seen in the 510 documentary films produced in France between 1940 and 1944. The list, taken from the *Brochure du premier congrès du Film Documentaire*, CARAN, Paris, F42/114 and F42/132, and "Le Nouveau Film", January 1943, is reproduced in an appendix in Steve Wharton's book, *Screening Reality: French Documentary Films during the German Occupation* (Wharton 2006, pp. 209–228).

Lastly, the cinemas, theatres, hotels, cafés, and restaurants, and related romantic sites that attracted French as well as foreign visitors form a significant component of wartime tourism both during the war and in the years thereafter. Many of these sites, such as the Eiffel Tower, had drawn tourists from within France and abroad prior to the war and would resume their role as popular sites afterward, the continuities in German perspectives on tourist France represented by the journalist Friedrich Sieburg (Gordon 1996). On 23 June 1940, Hitler was one of the first Germans to tour occupied Paris. He is seen standing at Trocadéro with the Eiffel Tower in the background in the well-known photo taken by his personal photographer, Heinrich Hoffmann. *Der deutsche Wegleiter*, a bi-weekly

Figure 10.3   Mont Valerien (inaugurated 1960), France © Bertram Gordon, 2009

German language guide to Paris, similar to today's *Pariscope*, was published in Paris and made available to military and civilian personnel there who were given tours by the tens of thousands by a special military unit, in occupied France during World War II (Gordon 1998, p. 618).

The German Tourist Office [*Deutsches Verkehrsbüro*] also began offering travel suggestions in the occupied zone in France as well as information regarding travel from France to Germany beginning in September 1940 (Deutsches Verkehrsbüro 1940). The *Pariser Zeitung*, a German-language daily newspaper, and the *Guide Aryen*, a bilingual brochure in French and German, steered the Occupation soldiers to tourist attractions that included the re-opened Louvre, Moulin Rouge, and Longchamps race track. In addition, the Germans created an organization called '*Jeder einmal in Paris*' [Everyone in Paris once], with offices in the Palais Bourbon, the former (and future) home of the French Chamber of Deputies. The mission of *Jeder einmal in Paris* was to offer all the troops a holiday in Paris, arranged in rotational visits to the city by German army units (Perrault and Azéma 1989, p. 17). Descriptions in the *Wegleiter* (Hönig 1942, pp. 16–17) of German tourist sites in and outside Paris are echoed in the memoirs of the German officers, such as Jünger and Gerhard Heller, whose accounts also provide a good sense of what they did in France. In preparation for an exhibition of Arno Breker's sculptures at the Orangerie in May 1942, Heller was sent to Collioure, a small Catalan town in southern France, to accompany Breker's old master Aristide Maillol who lived there, to Paris. As in the case of so many business trips, before, during, and since the war, Heller combined work with tourism. He stopped off at Toulouse, where he had studied in 1934–1935, and also visited the Côte Vermeille, the Catalan coast along the Mediterranean in southern France where he was enchanted with 'a little fishing port whose picturesqueness had been completely preserved' (Heller 1981, p. 123).

As Ahlrich Mayer writes, the quotidian bureaucratic activities of Germans such as Jünger and Heller, combined with the attractions of Paris, enabled them to avert their gazes from the German occupation policy in France that dictated privations for most of the French population, the rounding up of Jews to be sent to the extermination camps, and the war against the Soviet Union (Mayer 2002, p. 29). Gerhard Heller's post-war memoir is a telling example of a self-serving apologia for living the good life in occupied Paris while Germany carried out its belligerent policies (Heller 1981, p. 168). German tourist itineraries can also be followed in the post-war films that are copious in their descriptions of occupied France, such as: 'Is Paris Burning?' 'The Longest Day', or '*Les visiteurs du soir*'. To these may be added the accounts of witnesses such as Jean-Paul Sartre and Simone de Beauvoir.

American soldiers after 1944 were equally likely to be tourists, as indicated by the guidebook, *For You*, published, as had been the *Wegleiter*, by locals in France. Many young Americans, British, Canadians, Australians, and New Zealanders first saw France as soldiers in uniform, as had so many of the Germans in 1940. The excitement described by Arthur Frommer upon seeing Europe for the first time from the confines of a military transport plane was by no means unusual and the many Allied soldiers who came to France to fight in 1944 and in peacetime during the years that followed contributed to the surge in tourism that characterized the post-war landscape and played so large a role in post-war European prosperity.

Essentially, French tourism was little changed from the advent of the bus and train touring pattern in the early 1920s to the coming of the Common Market in the late 1950s. The wartime Germans strove to preserve this infrastructure, which served them as it did others. Their documents show an interest in keeping top Parisian restaurants, often reserved exclusively for them, well stocked. As of August 1941, the restaurants categorized as '*hors classe*' [unclassified] and, therefore not subject to rationing, were Carton, Drouant-Gaillon, Laperouse, Maxim's, and La Tour d'Argent in Paris, and Le Coq Hardi in Bougival, the last so designated in November 1941 (État Français 1942; Guy 1985, p. 132). Heller asked rhetorically in his memoir how many meals he had taken with the French publisher Bernard Grasset at Lipp (Heller 1981, p. 132). German documents also show a lively interest in maintaining clean brothels for their soldiers (Brauchitsch 1941). Within a month of their arrival in Paris, German officials determined that local French brothels lacked proper hygiene and were insufficiently supervised by the governing authorities. Selected brothels in larger cities and under medical supervision were made available to German military personnel with access to them forbidden to French civilians, other than the prostitutes themselves. Germans were forbidden to frequent bordellos other than those especially designated for them. Jewish and other 'alien race' prostitutes were not allowed to serve German personnel, nor were bordellos allowed to serve as hotels for travellers (Schreiber 1940; Müller 1940).

For the French during the Occupation years, however, tourism continued but not always in the normal pre-war manner. The creation of the *Commissariat au Tourisme* and the Popular Front's paid holidays program in the mid-1930s had given a new impetus to tourism in France. Although only a minority of eligible workers took advantage of their paid vacations to travel, Marc Boyer, a historian of tourism in France, notes that the paid vacations after 1936 came to be considered as a right by the public (Boyer 2007, p. 130). Despite the economic hardships of the Occupation and its own moralistic agenda of '*Travail, Famile, Patrie*', with its emphasis on work, the Vichy government extended the paid holidays, set at 15 days in 1936, by an additional day for those on the job five years or more (Boyer 2007, p. 96).

The division of occupied France into several military zones meant German permission was required to travel within much of France. Students were allowed to go on vacations, but only if visiting family members in other parts of France (Isoré 1942, p. 4). Parisians continued to take vacations but the Atlantic coast was off limits to them, so they headed inland instead. As Boyer points out, however, many in France during these years experienced mobility, even if not of their own choosing and under severe conditions of transport restrictions. Hiding places and pilgrimage sites could be agreeable, as in the case of the Côte d'Azur, which served as a refuge for many but was also a prized tourist area. The French countryside was rediscovered by many hungry urban dwellers sometimes finding good food in the rural homes of previously neglected parents or other relatives. Health benefits of the countryside were also rediscovered. Despite the hardships, many of the French, Boyer argued, retained pleasant memories of these experiences, which encouraged them to tour in ever larger numbers when conditions improved after the war. The stunning success of the first post-war *Salon de l'Automobile* [Automobile Exposition] in 1946 and the increase in automobile touring in the years that followed, were due in no small part to the experience of so many of the French during the war (Boyer 2007, pp. 151–152).

Some in the tourist trade saw optimistic trends despite the wartime restrictions under the Occupation. According to Monsieur Clauzel, the head of Vichy's *Comité d'organisation de l'industrie hôtelière* [Hotel Industry Organization Committee] some 400,000 pensioners with paid vacations, dating from the French legislation of 1936, found lodgings in 2,000 hotels recommended by his service in 1942 and an additional 500,000 vacationers were helped as well. He anticipated an expanding opportunity for the French hotel trade amongst retirees with pensions in 1943 (Bouis 1942). On the other side of the tourism equation, Suzanne Sauvan, writing in a geography periodical in 1942, excoriated the effects of tourism that she believed was turning France's rural areas into suburban developments with garish red corrugated metal rooftops (Beauguitte 2007, p. 84). The last pre-war *Guide Michelin* appeared in 1939. In the spring of 1944, a special edition of the guidebook, based on the 1939 edition, was published in Washington by the Allies to provide their forces with maps of French towns. The Michelin series was resumed only in 1945 with its stars rating system reappearing in 1946 and 1947, as the French hotel-restaurant system returned to its pre-war norms (Blandin 2009; Michelin 2009).

Emotion, Trauma, and Thanatourism in Post-war France

Following the war, the list of sites expanded to include those associated with trauma, such as Oradour-sur-Glane; the Drancy concentration camp in the suburbs of Paris; and Mont Valerien, also close to Paris, where some one to two thousand people were tortured and executed during the Occupation. Focusing on the attempts to preserve the ruins of Oradour-sur-Glane, destroyed during the 10 June 1944 Nazi massacre, Sarah Bennett Farmer evaluated the problems of trying to preserve the town exactly as it had been when destroyed, in order to convey the horror of the atrocity, as opposed to the inevitable deterioration of the ruins, caused by time and weather, necessitating intervention to create something other than the wreckage of the 1944 massacre. Analysing the layout of the various sites: the ruined town, a cemetery still in use, and a new town, Farmer constructed a 'topography' of memory (Farmer 1995, p. 35). She described plans to make the site available to 'pilgrims', 'visitors', and 'tourists', situating the pilgrims in a tradition of Christian visitors to holy sites (Farmer 1995, p. 40; Pearson 2008, p. 174).

Figure 10.4   Le Mémorial des Martyrs de la Déportation, Ile de la Cité, Paris (inaugurated 1962), France © Bertram Gordon, 2009

Mont Valerien was inaugurated as a *lieu de mémoire* by General de Gaulle on 17–18 June 1960, the twentieth anniversary of his first radio address from London to occupied France, underscoring again the importance of anniversary commemorations in the construction of war-related tourism (Barcellini 1998, p. 53).

Places related to the deportation of both French and non-French and Jews and non-Jews to the Nazi camps in Central and Eastern Europe also became tourist sites, referenced in a geography of Resistance sites in Paris, by Jean-Louis Goglin and Pierre Roux (Goglin and Roux 2004). The *Mémorial des Martyrs de la Déportation*, a monument to those deported from France to concentration camps in Germany and Eastern Europe during the war, directly behind the Notre-Dame cathedral on the Ile de la Cité, which I first visited when I began my research on World War II France in 1973, was inaugurated on 12 April 1962, by General de Gaulle.

Specific to the Holocaust in France is the Shoah Memorial, an entire building that holds an archive and library, which I also visited in 1973 and where I was first able to locate documents related to the Second World War in France.

In the post-war years, birth or death sites of prominent personalities also became tourist spots. Some were official, such as the many monuments to General de Gaulle, including the naming of an airport for him, and the *Historial Charles-De-Gaulle*, inaugurated in 2008 at the *Invalides*. Others were not, such

Figure 10.5 Birthplace of Marshall Petain, Cauchy-à-la-Tour, Pas-de-Calais, France © Bertram Gordon, 2009

as the acquisition and preservation of Marshal Philippe Pétain's birthplace in the village of Cauchy-à-la-Tour, in the Pas-de-Calais, by a private organization, the *Association pour Défendre la Mémoire du Maréchal Pétain* [The Association to Defend the Memory of Marshal Pétain] that seeks to restore his name.

In conclusion, it may be argued provisionally that war tourism is in a second tier of destinations by popularity, but that it continues to generate significant revenue at least in France. Battlefield tourism for one side or another appears to be the most significant element in war tourism both during and after the war. There is a timeline for meaningful attention to a tourist site, whether for a specific purpose or for incidental curiosity, that arguably might be quantified. Between the fall of France in 1940 and the Battle of the Bulge in 1944, one could estimate that virtually the entire adult population of France virtually craned their necks with curiosity over the Atlantic Wall and related military sites. Highs in interest may be established by examining the publication peaks of the World War II related documents in the listings of the French publication catalogues '*Biblio*', *Bibliographie de la France*, and *Bibliographie Nationale Française*, from 1939 through the present. The publication statistics peak during the war years and again in the mid-1990s, reflecting the fiftieth anniversary of the liberation, some of the last trials of those involved in the war, and in general a higher ratio of World War II themes in the more recent series. A recent decrease in World War II related publications may indicate a decline in tourist interest as well but the hundreds of thousands of visitors to the Atlantic Wall and Normandy sites, as well as the Maginot Line, reflect an interest and emotional involvement at least in the battlefield *lieux de mémoire* whose history decisively affected the outcome of the war. The dust-up over the failure of the French government to invite the Queen to the 2009 Normandy anniversary commemoration reflected a continuing, if limited interest in and passion for the World War II sites in France (Hickley and English 2009).

References

Annuaire Statistique de la France (1965) Paris: Imprimerie Nationale and Presses Universitaires de France.

Aron, C. (1999) *Working at Play: A History of Vacations in the United States*, New York: Oxford University Press.

Arromanches (2009) *Arromanches Histoire d'un Port*, Cully [Calvados]: OREP Éditions.

Barcellini, S. (1998) 'Les commémorations', in M-H. Joly and T. Compère-Morel (eds), *Des Musées d'histoire pour l'avenir*, Paris: Éditions Noêsis, pp. 43–56.

Bausinger, H. et al. (1991) *Reisekultur: von der Pilgerfahrt zum modernen Tourismus*, Munich: C.H. Beck.

Beauguitte, L. (2007) *Un champ scientifique à l'épreuve de la seconde guerre mondiale : les revues de géographie françaises de 1936 à 1945* [online thesis, Master de Géographie (M1), Université Paris 7, 2006–2007]. Available at http://www.cybergeo.eu/index19853.html [accessed 4 April 2009].

Bertho Lavenir, C. (1999) *La Roue et le Stylo, Comment nous sommes devenus tourists*, Paris: Odile Jacob.

Bertrand, G. (2004) *La Culture du Voyage, Pratiques et discours de la Renaissance à l'aube du XXe siècle*, Paris: L'Harmattan.

Blandin, N. (2009) 'Guide Michelin', *La République des Lettres* [Online 2 March 2009] Available at http://www.republique-des-lettres.fr/10674-guide-michelin.php [accessed 15 June 2009].

Bouis, P. (1942) 'Le bureau de renseignements de l'hôtellerie/Plus de 500.000 Parisiens ont déjà été aiguillés vers d'agréables "séjours de remplacement"', *Paris-Midi*, 29 August 1942, in Archives nationales. AJ/40/784, Folder 4.

Boyer, M. (2007) *Le Tourisme de Masse*, Paris: L'Harmattan.

Brauchitsch, W. von (1941) Der Oberbefehlshabers des Heeres, Gen. Qu. Gen St d H/Nr. 18 497/40, Anlage 1 zu Ob d H Nr. 8840/41, PA 2 (I/Ia) vom 6 September 1941. H. Qu den 31 Juli 1940. In Archives nationales. AJ/40/451 (Folder 2, #109).

Burns, J.F. (2009) 'Left out of D-Day events, Queen Elizabeth is fuming', *New York Times.* 27 May [Online]. Available at http://www.nytimes.com/2009/05/28/world/europe/28queen.html?_r=1&ref=world.

Casson, L. (1994) *Travel in the Ancient World*, Baltimore and London: Johns Hopkins University Press, [originally published 1974].

Chapron, P. (2009) Directeur du Musée Mémorial de la Bataille de Normandie, Bayeux. Author's interview, 19 May.

Chesnel, M. (2009) *Le Tourisme Culturel de Type Urbain: Aménagement et Stratégies de Mise en Valeur*, Paris: L'Harmattan [originally published 2001].

Crawshaw, C. and Urry, J. (1997) 'Tourism and the photographic eye', in C. Rojek and J. Urry (eds), *Touring Cultures: Transformations of Travel and Theory*, London and New York: Routledge, pp. 176–195.

Cuvelier, P. (1998) *Anciennes et Nouvelles Formes de Tourisme, Une approche socio-économique*, Paris: L'Harmattan.

Davallon, J. (1998) 'Conclusion du colloque', in M-H. Joly and T. Compère-Morel (eds.) *Des Musées d'histoire pour l'avenir*, Paris: Éditions Noêsis, pp. 351–356.

Delasalle-Stolper, S. (2009) 'La reine privée de D-Day', *Libération*, 28 May. [Online]. Available at http://www.liberation.fr/monde/0101569854-la-reine-privee-de-d-day?xtor=EPR-450206.

Desquesnes, R. (2009A) *Le Mur de l'Atlantique du Mont-Saint-Michel au Tréport*, Rennes: Éditions Ouest-France.

Desquesnes, R. (2009B) *Normandy 1944: The Invasion and the Battle of Normandy*, trans. J. Lee, Rennes: Éditions Ouest-France.

Deutsches Verkehrsbüro (1940) Reichsbahnzentrale für den Deutschen Reiseverkehr (1940). Paris, 38 Avenue de l'Opéra, Paris, note, 20 September; in Archives nationales. AJ/40/878 [Folder 2] C. 6 4III Ic 6; #434 in German, #435 in French.

Dupuy, M. (1994) *1000 Ans de Tourisme*, Montreal: Proteau.

État Français (1942) Secrétariat d'État aux Communications et au P.T.T. et au Tourisme, Comité d'Organisation Professionnelle de l'Industrie Hôtelière/ Hôtels – Restaurants – Débits de Boissons, note to Dr. Gehrhardt, Conseiller Supérieur de Guerre, Hôtel Majestic, Paris, 3 February, Annexes 1 and 2; Archives nationales. AJ/40/784, Folder 7, MBF 35, 22105E.

Farmer, S.B. (1995) 'Oradour-sur-Glane: Memory in a preserved landscape', *French Historical Studies*, 19(1), 27–47.

Feiffer, M. (1986) *Tourism in History, From Imperial Rome to the Present*, New York: Stein and Day.

Fogg, S.L. (2009) *The Politics of Everyday Life in Vichy France: Foreigners, Undesirables, and Strangers*, Cambridge: Cambridge University Press.

Fortified military architectures in Europe: conflicts and reconciliations (2009) European Institute of Cultural Routes, prepared in the framework of the Luxembourg chairmanship of the Council of Europe [Online]. Available at http://www.culture-routes.lu/php/fo_index.php?lng=en&dest=bd_pa_det& rub=57 [accessed 24 June 2009].

Gautier-Desvaux, E. (1998) 'Musées d'histoire et aménagement culturel du territoire, Le "cas" du Mémorial de Caen', in M-H. Joly and T. Compère-Morel (eds) *Des Musées d'histoire pour l'avenir*, Paris: Éditions Noêsis, pp. 311–315.

Goglin, J-L. and Roux, P. (2004) *Souffrance et Liberté: une géographie parisienne des années noires (1940–1944)*, Paris: Paris Musées.

Gordon, B.M. (1996) '*Ist Gott Französisch?* Germans, tourism, and occupied France, 1940–1944', *Modern and Contemporary France*, NS4(3), pp. 287–298.

Gordon, B.M. (1998) 'Warfare and tourism: Paris in World War II', *Annals of Tourism Research*, 25(3), pp. 616–638.

Gordon, B.M. (2001) 'French cultural tourism and the Vichy problem', in S. Baranowski and E. Furlough (eds), *Being Elsewhere: Tourism, Consumer Culture, and Identity in Modern Europe and North America*, Ann Arbor: University of Michigan Press, pp. 239–272.

Grandhomme, J-N. (2009) *La Seconde Guerre mondiale en France*, Rennes: Éditions Ouest-France.

Guy, C. (1985) *Histoire de la Gastronomie en France*, Paris: Éditions Fernand Nathan.

Heller, G. (1981) *Un Allemand à Paris 1940–1944*, Paris: Seuil.

Hickley, M. and English, R. (2009) 'D-Day snub to Queen: Palace fury as Sarkozy refuses to invite royals to 65th Anniversary', *Daily Mail*, 27 May [Online]. Available at http://www.dailymail.co.uk/news/article-1188515/D-Day-snub-Queen-Palace-fury-Sarkozy-refuses-invite-royals-65th-Anniversary--Brown-wont-act.html.

Hönig, H.O. (1942) 'Paris und Frankreich', *Der Deutsche Wegleiter*, 59(16–17).

Horizons (1953) 'Itinéraire No. 1100, Le Circuit de la Libération', in *Horizons de France et d'Europe*, Paris: Compagnie Française de Tourisme.

Isoré, P. (1942) 'Chef du Service des Voyages de Vacances, Secrétariat d'État, L'Éducation Nationale et à la Jeunesse, Office du Tourisme Universitaire. Rapport sur les convois interzones de Pâques 1942, to Monsieur le Ministre de 'Éducation Nationale, undated (probably early 1942)', in *Archives nationales*. AJ/40/561, Folder 1, Verwaltigungsstab Abt. Verwaltung, betr.: Vorgänge betr. Passierscheine, Band Nr. 1, Akten Nr. V kult 408A.

Jünger, E. (1965) 'Entry, Paris, 4 May 1944', *Journal de Guerre et d'Occupation 1939–1948*, trans. H. Plard, Paris: René Julliard.

Kemp, A. (1981) *The Maginot Line: Myth and Reality*, London: Frederick Warne.

Kœnig, P. (1964) 'Préface', in P. Boussel (ed.), *Guide des plages du débarquement*, Paris: Librairie Polytechnique Béranger/Département Technique des Presses de la Cité.

Kolbe, W. (2009) 'Reisen zu den Schlachtfeldern des Zweiten Weltkriegs', *Nachrichten aus der Forschungsstelle für Zeitgeschichte in Hamburg (FZH) 2008*. Hamburg: FZH, 44–54.

Lfier, D.A. (1977) *Pokusaj dijalektickog objasnjenja pojave turizma, Zbornik radova*. Dubrovnik: FTVT, 1977 [Online]. Available at http://216.239.53.100/search?q=cache:wntAHG1nfCoJ:www.eh.net/XIIICongress/cd/papers/4Hitrec185.pdf+history+of+tourism+antiquity&hl=en&ie=UTF-8 [accessed 28 May 2003].

Lorrain, F-G. (2009) 'Obama à Omaha, un must', *Le Point*, 4 June, p. 70.

Masson, C-A. (1985) *La veille inutile*, Paris: Sercap.

Mayer, A. (2002) *L'occupation allemande en France.* Translated from the German by P. Hervieux, e. al., Paris: Privat.

McCabe, S. (2009) 'Who is a tourist? Conceptual and theoretical developments', in J. Tribe (ed.), *Philosophical Issues in Tourism*, Bristol: Channel View Publications.

Mesplier-Pinet, J. (2009) 'Culture et patrimoine aujourd'hui, peuvent-ils contribuer au développement touristique?', in *Patrimoine et Tourisme*, Bordeaux: Presses Universitaires de Bordeaux.

Meyer, H. (2006) *Der Wandel der französischen 'Erinnerungskultur'des Zweiten Weltkriegs am Beispiel dreier 'Erinnerungsorte': Bordeaux, Caen und Oradour-sur-Glane.* Doctoral dissertation, History Faculty, University of Augsburg and Université Michel de Montaigne Bordeaux 3. 14 November.

Michelin (2009) *Le Guide MICHELIN: 109 ans d'histoire d'aide à la mobilité.* 2 March [Online]. Available at http://www.viamichelin.fr/viamichelin/fra/tpl/mag6/art200903/htm/tour-saga-michelin.htm [accessed 15 June 2009].

Monferrand, A. (1998) 'Le tourisme culturel', in M-H. Joly and T. Compère-Morel (eds) *Des Musées d'histoire pour l'avenir*, Paris: Éditions Noêsis, pp. 335–341.

Müller (1940) Der Generalquartiermeister. Geheim. Oberkommando des Heeres, Generalquartiermeister, Az.: 265 IVb Nr.: 11244//40 geh., Betr.: Prostitution und Bordellwesen in Belgien und im besetzten Gebiet Frankreichs. 29 July, in Archives nationales. AJ/40/451, [Folder 1, #5], Akte Nr. 130 geh.

Normandie Pass (2009) Normandie Pass, Des réductions sur vos visites. *Tourist office, Basse-Normandie,* No. SIRET Normandie Mémoire: 444 116 453 00036.

ORT-CRT Normandie (2003) [Online]. Available at http://sig.cr-basse-normandie.fr/atlas/cartes/dday.jpg [accessed 25 May 2009, courtesy of Daniel Letouzey].

Pallud, J-P. (1988) 'The Maginot Line', *After the Battle*, 60(19, 35, 39).

Pearson, C. (2008) *Scarred Landscapes: War and Nature in Vichy France*, Basingstoke: Palgrave Macmillan.

Perissière, M. (1998) 'Le Mémorial de Caen: Un Musée pour la Paix', in M-H. Joly and T. Compère-Morel (eds), *Des Musées d'histoire pour l'avenir*, Paris: Éditions Noêsis, pp. 183–190.

Perrault, G. and Azéma, P. (1989) *Paris under the Occupation*, trans. A. Carter and M. Vos, New York: Vendome [originally published 1987].

Pottier, M. (2009) Directeur du pole Educatif et Recherche Mémorial – Cité de l'histoire, Caen, Author's interview, 18 May 2009.

Quellien, J. (2004) *Les Plages du Débarquement*, Caen: Le Mémorial de Caen.

Raffray, E. (1999) *La Protection du Patrimoine Militaire de la seconde guerre mondiale en Basse-Normandie: Le Mur de l'Atlantique et le Port Artificiel d'Arromanches.* Thesis. École du Louvre/Muséologie – 1998–1999.

Robinson, M. (2005) 'Foreword', in M. Novelli (ed.), *Niche Tourism: Contemporary Issues, Trends and Cases*, Amsterdam: Elsevier.

Rundstedt, General G. von (1940) Der Oberbefehlshaber West/Ia Nr. 1323/40 geh., Abschrift, 30 October 1940; in Archives nationales. AJ/40/451, AG. 104, Folder 1, No. 27.

Schauseil, A. (1997) *Normandie*, Cologne: Vista Point Verlag.

Schreiber (1940) Oberarzt. Der Heeresarzt, Oberkommando des Heeres, Gen. St. d. H./Gen. Qu., Az. 265, Nr. 17150/40, "Betr.: Prostitution und Bordellwesen im besetzten Gebiet", 16 Juli, in Archives nationales. AJ/40/451, folder M.B.F. C. 59 L. VIII. A. G. 104.

Seaton, A.V. and Lennon, J.J. (2004) 'Thanatourism in the early 21st century: Moral panics, ulterior motives and alterior desires in T. Singh (ed.), *New Horizons in Tourism: Strange Experiences and Stranger Practices*, London: CAB [Commonwealth Agricultural Bureaux] International, pp. 63–82.

Seramour, M. (2007) 'Histoire de la ligne Maginot de 1945 à nos jours', in *Revue historique des armées*, 247, 86–97 [Online]. Available at http://rha.revues.org/index1933.html [accessed 18 April 2009].

Sherman, D.J. (1995) 'Objects of memory: History and narrative in French War Museums', *French Historical Studies*, 19(1), pp. 49–74.

Sommier, F. (2009) Directeur du Musée du Débarquement, Arromanches les Bains, Author's interview, 18 May 2009.

Soudagne, J.P. (2006) *L'histoire de la ligne Maginot*, Rennes: Éditions Ouest-France.

Spode, H. (2009) 'Zur Geschichte der Tourismusgeschichte', *Voyage: Jahrbuch für Reise- & Tourismusforschung 2009*, Munich and Vienna: Profil Verlag.

STIWOT (2010) *Stichting Informatie Wereldoorlog Twee*. [Online]. Available at http://www.ww2museums.com/article/62/Musée-Mémorial-de-la-Bataille-de-Normandie.htm [accessed 17 July 2010].

Thubron, C. (1999) 'Both seer and seen: The travel writer as leftover amateur', *Times Literary Supplement*, 30 July, p. 12.

Tobelem, J-M. and Benito, L. (2002) *Les musées dans la politique touristique urbaine*, Paris: L'Harmattan.

Urbain, J-D. (1993) *L'idiot du voyage, Histoires de tourists*, Paris: Payot.

Urry, J. (2000) *The Tourist Gaze, Leisure and Travel in Contemporary Societies*, London: Sage [originally published 1990].

Vacances (2006) Vacances – Tourisme en France. *Observatoire national du tourisme* [Online]. Availabe at http://tourisme-reservations.com/index2. php?option=com_content&do_pdf=1&id=67 [accessed 26 June 2009].

van den Bogert, D. (2010) Musée-Mémorial de la Bataille de Normandie *ww2museums.com, STIWOT (Stichting Informatie Wereldoorlog Twee)* [Online] Available at http://www.ww2museums.com/article/62/Musée-Mémorial-de-la-Bataille-de-Normandie.htm [accessed 17 July 2010].

Walton, J.K. (2005) *Histories of Tourism: Representation, Identity and Conflict*, Clevedon, UK: Channel View Publications.

Wharton, S. (2006) Appendix 2, in *Screening Reality: French Documentary Films during the German Occupation*, Bern: Peter Lang.

Wieviorka, O. (2010) *La Mémoire désunie, Le souvenir politique des années sombres, de la Libération à nos jours*, Paris: Éditions du Seuil, collection "L'Univers historique".

Chapter 11

Tourist Attractions as Sites of Suicide: The Case of Beachy Head, England

Angelina Karpovich

The topography, morphology, and indeed history of natural environments have an impact on the kind of tourist experiences they produce (Wong 1993). In this chapter, I focus on tourist sites at which there is a high incidence of suicide, exploring the relationship between landscape and location, and the act of suicide. The study will primarily focus on Beachy Head, a striking range of chalk cliffs located just outside the seaside resort of Eastbourne in Sussex, in southern England. At 530 ft above sea level, Beachy Head is notable as the highest chalk sea cliff in Britain. It is also notorious for being the single most popular location for suicide attempts in the United Kingdom and even in Europe; many of those who end their lives at Beachy Head come from distant places and travel there specifically to commit suicide, despite there being many other locations which have similar topography and potential for fatal falls. Similar phenomena have been noted in Japan, the USA and Canada, with incidences of suicide greatly concentrated at touristic landmarks. This begs the question, what makes a tourist location suitable or attractive to suicidal people? In this study, I shall explore the geographical and material aspects of popular suicide spots and examine how the notion of authenticity within touristic discourse may have parallels in the decision-making processes of those with suicidal impulses.

Beachy Head

Eastbourne's tourist industry has long suffered from the town's proximity to the much larger and more vibrant seaside resort of Brighton, with its well-developed attractions and exciting nightlife. Where Brighton has developed a reputation as a resort catering to the young and fashionable, Eastbourne, in contrast, has been primarily associated with the elderly – the climate had long made it a popular retirement destination. Seeking to establish a new and distinct identity for Eastbourne, the local council and tourist office have sought to promote Beachy Head as a local attraction, an area of natural beauty offering spectacular views and healthy walking trails for sightseers. In this respect, Beachy Head is an ideal example of a 'geomorphological feature … [as an attraction in its] own right, rather than the resource upon which other tourist activities can develop' (May 1993, p. 6), which is particularly characteristic of coastline attractions in southern England (ibid., p. 5). As Sternberg (1997, p. 960) notes, natural features of the landscape have undergone a substantial shift in public perception as tourist attractions:

> [I]n the pre-modern era, strange geological scenery like mountains and cataracts were thought to be pockmarks on the face of the earth – frightening places frequented by ogres and witches. By the 19th century, it was landscape paintings and travel books that predisposed visitors to have a sense of [nature's attractions] as sublimely awe-inspiring or delightfully picturesque. But if nature's sublimity probably once had a big market, it has a much smaller one now that nature has been scientifically explicated and re-engineered. There is still some touristic mileage in the picturesque, but very many parks now compete for that designation and, in any case, picturesqueness can be a weak thrill in these times of electronic entertainment.

Nevertheless, given the scarcity of other tourist attractions in the immediate area, the Beachy Head cliffs remain one of the main highlights of the local touristic experience. They are a regular stop on the sightseeing bus tour of Eastbourne, and tourist amenities on the clifftop include a countryside centre with a small museum, gallery, and gift shop, and a pub. In the summer, a local bus service between Eastbourne and Brighton runs through Beachy Head every 30 minutes, making the cliffs even more accessible to sightseers.

One of the Most 'Popular' Suicide Spots in the World

Yet Beachy Head is a curious, ambiguous, complex, and even somewhat menacing attraction. On a sunny day (which is by no means a regular feature of a British summer), it does have a certain sparse beauty, though the views from it (Eastbourne to the east, the sea to the south, and fields to the north and west) are not by any means extraordinary. The flatness and sparseness of the landscape dominates the site; it is palpable even if one is visiting with a group; a single visitor would feel very isolated indeed. The openness of the landscape also means that any wind feels stronger, chillier, and louder than it does down in Eastbourne. On a non-sunny day, Beachy Head is not a particularly attractive, or comfortable, attraction.

Paradoxically, the most picturesque aspect of the cliffs, the striking chalk cliff face rising from the sea, which forms the image of Beachy Head in all tourist publications, can't really be seen or appreciated by those actually on top of the cliffs. On the clifftop itself, short grass stretches as far as the eye can see, so that the ground at the edge of the cliff looks indistinguishable from the fields in the distance, before rapidly giving way to a sheer and dizzying drop. There is no change in the visible topography, no natural warning sign that the ground underfoot is about to come to an end. There are a few official warning notices dotted around, which mention the dangers of cliff erosion and advise caution. In places, thin lengths of rusty wire are stretched along the edge of the cliffs, serving very much as a symbolic, rather than physical, barrier between the ground and the drop on the other side. At any given time, the wire barrier will have bouquets of flowers, cards, small toys, and handmade crosses attached along its length. These tributes vary in age (some look weathered, others very recent), and in number (on three separate visits to Beachy Head between 2007 and 2009, I counted, respectively, 9, 14, and 12 individual tributes), but cumulatively, they suggest that Beachy Head is not only a tourist site, but also a consistent and active site of commemoration.

The floral tributes are a result of Beachy Head's other, morbid, claim to fame; one which never appears in tourist brochures, yet provides a uniquely dark undercurrent for Eastbourne's tourist industry: Beachy Head is one of the most 'popular' suicide spots in the world, and the most 'popular' not just in the UK, but in all of Europe. Beachy Head has been a site of suicide for decades, though, as suicide had been criminalized in the UK until 1961, many if not most of these deaths used to be officially recorded as accidents or open verdicts, rather than suicides (Surtees 1982). Since the 1970s, on average 20 people a year end their lives by jumping from these cliffs (ibid.).[1] Even more travel to Beachy Head to make the attempt, but are persuaded not to, by members of the emergency services, the Chaplaincy team who regularly patrol the cliffs, and even local taxi drivers and staff at the Beachy Head Pub. In other words, Beachy Head is an active tourist site at which, on average more than once a fortnight, someone attempts to end their life. The frequency of suicides typically increases in the summer, at the height of the tourist season. Surtees speculates that this increase may possibly be due to 'the strange attraction in the beauty of the summer scene, but the main reason appears to be that Beachy Head is even more accessible in the summer for both locals and visitors. The weather is less inclement and the bus service more frequent' (1982, p. 323). Many of the suicide attempts and most of the emergency services' operations to recover the bodies happen in the daytime, in full view of any passing holidaymakers, who would certainly not be prepared for the potentially-traumatic 'spectacle' if their expectations of Beachy Head had been based solely on official tourist marketing of the place.

Significantly, relatively few suicide cases are native to Eastbourne or even Sussex. Surtees' 1982 study of Beachy Head suicides between 1965 and 1979 showed that only 28 per cent of suicides came from Eastbourne. Sixty-one per cent came from outside East Sussex, including five individuals who had come from abroad (1982, p. 322). This ratio has persisted, and indeed increased, in more recent statistics, between 1993 and 1997, 81 per cent of Beachy Head suicides had been 'visitors' (King and Frost 2005, p. 25). Gross et al. (2007) term this phenomenon 'suicide tourism', but in doing so, they refer to people who travel to

---

1   John Surtees' seminal analysis of Beachy Head suicides is, as far as I am aware, the only academic text which deals directly with the subject. Evidence from local Sussex newspapers suggests that the regularity of Beachy Head suicides has not diminished since the publication of Surtees' report.

any distant location to end their lives, rather than focusing on suicides which take place at particular sites more usually associated with tourism.

What makes Beachy Head even more unusual, both as a tourist site and a suicide spot, is that many people travel for hundreds of miles, some even from abroad, specifically to end their lives there.[2] Indeed, some data suggests that Beachy Head may be a statistical anomaly even when it comes specifically to the method of suicide by jumping, Reisch et al. cite Wohner and Schmidtke's (2005) finding that 'persons who kill themselves by jumping tend to use sites close to their place of residence' (2008, p. 98), while Ross and Lester's (1991) study of suicides at Niagara Falls concluded that most of those who jumped had lived within a 10-mile perimeter of the Falls. Johnson (2009) discusses suicides at the Cold Spring Arch Bridge in California specifically in terms of a localized act, 'Leaping from the bridge is [partly] a statement that taps into local memory and the very palpable meaning of this bridge in this community' (2009, p. 145). Moreover, while King and Frost's (2005) study of suicides in the New Forest produced anecdotal evidence in the inquest files which 'suggested that some suicides had previously spent holidays in the New Forest and wanted to die there' (2005, p. 25), there is no suggestion in any of the literature which concerns itself with Beachy Head that those who chose it as a suicide site did so because of a particular prior emotional or sentimental attachment to the place.

Suicide 'Tourism'

The phenomenon of suicide at tourist attractions is certainly not new. Perhaps understandably, given the sensitivity of the topic, there has been relatively little published work dealing with it, and virtually no work has addressed the phenomenon from the perspective of tourism. Academic work in the area has tended to take the form of qualitative studies rooted in the disciplines of psychology and public health (cf. Mann et al. 2005, for a comprehensive overview of available clinical literature), where the role of location 'remains a neglected issue within the wider literature' (Owens et al. 2009), while non-academic publications have mainly been fascinated with the suicide taboo and its social implications (cf. Friend 2003; Hunt 2006), rather than the role of, or impact on, the location.

Some sites are convenient for would-be suicides for some of the same reasons as they are attractive to tourists (accessibility and, in the case of suicide by jumping, height). For example, the Eiffel Tower, the Empire State Building (Reisch et al.

---

2   Gross et al. (2007) examined suicide statistics in Manhattan to suggest that those who chose to end their life away from their home area are more likely to use public spaces. Owens et al. (2009) state that public spaces accounted for nearly a third of all suicide sites in a 4-year study of a large English county. In both cases, the definition of a public space includes multiple varied sites. What sets Beachy Head apart from these general statistical patterns is the very intensive concentration of suicides within a single narrow area.

2008) and the Niagara Falls (Ross and Lester 1991; Sternberg 1997) were initially 'popular' suicide spots until barriers and nets were installed. Other kinds of tourist sites, such as parks and forests, are also easily accessible, and yet offer many secluded spots, where someone who has chosen a more time-consuming method of ending their life is unlikely to be interrupted (thus, the more remote car parks in the New Forest in England used to be a regular site for suicide by car exhaust fumes (King and Frost 2005), and the Aokigahara Forest in Japan is notorious as a site for suicide by hanging (Takahashi 1988). There may also be something in the beauty or distinctiveness of the tourist site which makes it attractive not just to tourists but to those who want to spend their last moments there, though all currently-available evidence for this is anecdotal. As Hunt (2006) notes, more people are killed in a day in New York than in a year at Beachy Head, but 'New York City isn't a beautiful place. Beachy Head is interesting because it's tragic *and* beautiful' (2006, p. 35, emphasis in original).

Neither accessibility nor height, nor indeed beauty, however entirely explain the peculiar and enduring 'appeal' of Beachy Head. As Surtees (1982) pointed out,

> On the cliffs at Dover, which are structurally similar and at least as famous as Beachy Head, there was only about one suicide a year over the 22 years from 1956. The Dover cliffs are less accessible ... [but] [o]ther cliffs, either of a similar nature or associated with holiday resorts, also have a much lower incidence. (1982, p. 323)

There are certainly parallels to be drawn between Beachy Head and its counterpart as the 'most popular' suicide spot in North America (and indeed, the world), the Golden Gate Bridge in San Francisco. Both are sites which are simultaneously very well known for tourism and notorious for suicide. Both have seen strong official opposition to the installation of suicide barriers (for various reasons, including cost, engineering/geological difficulties, 'spoiling the view', and the argument, thoroughly debunked in clinical literature, that a suicide barrier would force suicidal people to take their lives elsewhere, rather than preventing suicides).[3]

Here, the idea of the relative 'symbolism' (Reisch et al. 2008) of certain public sites may also be worth noting. Tourism studies have paid a great deal of attention to the way in which tourist sites are constructed, represented, mediated, and perceived. Urry (2002) has introduced the notion of 'the tourist gaze' as a way of conceptualizing the role of visual perception in the tourist experience. Urry's emphasis on visuality resonates with Jenks (1995) and Rojek (1997), among others, but perhaps the clearest expression of ideas about the relationship between tourist sites and visuality is to be found in MacCannell's (1999) conception of the touristic experience, in which tourists encounter a succession of sights mediated

---

3   For evidence of the effectiveness of suicide barriers, see, for example, Bennewith et al. 2007; Pelletier 2007; Seiden 1978.

through 'markers' (the most picturesque and recognizable elements of the sites); the touristic experience is thus bound up with representation and reproduction of the 'original' sight. Ultimately, some sites acquire what Hayden (1995) termed the 'power of place', 'the power of ordinary urban landscapes to nurture citizens' public memory, to encompass shared time in the form of shared territory' (1995, p. 9). The impact of place on public memory can extend to metonymic associations, where the mere mention of a placename becomes significantly evocative. As Cohen stated, 'Neutral words such as place-names can be made to symbolize complex ideas and emotions; for example, Pearl Harbor, Hiroshima, Dallas and Aberfan' (1980, p. 40). The association between Beachy Head, the Golden Gate Bridge, the Aokigahara Forest, and suicide, is a shared public memory, which persists, and is particularly resonant for local residents and for those preoccupied with the topic of suicide.

Much of the literature in tourism studies is concerned, in one way or another, with the notion of 'authenticity'. As MacCannell (1999) points out,

> The rhetoric of tourism is full of the manifestations of the importance of the authenticity between the tourists and what they see, this is a *typical* native house; this is the *very* place where the leader fell; this is the *actual* pen used to sign the law; this is the *original* manuscript. (p. 14, emphasis in original)

However, 'authenticity' is a complex term; as Taylor (2001) points out, the centrality of 'authenticity' as an issue in tourist studies 'has set the agenda for lively and diverse debate and analyses. As a result of these, there are at least as many definitions of authenticity as there are those who write about it' (2001, p. 8). Taylor identifies a range of dialectics ('between object and subject, there and here, then and now' [ibid.]) within which the authenticity of a particular site or experience may be determined. Similarly, in his discussion of the touristic appeal of authenticity, MacCannell immediately draws a distinction between 'minimal' 'sub-minimal' 'pseudo' and/or 'tacky' tourist attractions (such as a giant Fiberglas statue of Jesus in a Biblical amusement park) and 'true sites' (such as the Statue of Liberty or the Liberty Bell), whose supposed authenticity is only enhanced by the existence of the 'pseudo' sites, '[m]odern society institutionalizes these authentic attractions and modern life takes on qualities of reality thereby' (1999, p. 14).

There is some indication that the dynamics of touristic 'authenticity' may also play a part in the appeal that certain locations, but not others, have as sites for suicide. Seiden and Spence (1983) asserted that about 50 per cent of those who had jumped from the Golden Gate had actually crossed the equally-high Oakland Bay Bridge in order to get to it. The Oakland Bay is less than ten kilometres away from the Golden Gate, it was built at around the same time, and while it is admittedly less accessible, accessibility alone does not explain why at least five times as many people have jumped off the nearby Golden Gate (Glenn 2003). Friend (2003) refers to the Golden Gate's 'fatal grandeur', and cites a San Francisco historian's assessment of the bridge's legacy as 'a monument to death'. According to Glenn

(2003, p. 37), an Oakland Bay Bridge suicide is considered by some to be 'kind of tacky' as 'all the famous, well publicized suicides use the Golden Gate. The Oakland Bridge simply doesn't have the same mystique'. The echoes between this description and MacCannell's distinction between 'tacky' and 'true' tourist sites are striking. Glenn goes on to draw a direct parallel between the Golden Gate Bridge, Beachy Head, and Toronto's suicide hotspot, the 'oddly romantic' Bloor Street Viaduct, all of which offer 'breathtaking' views, or at least 'an enticing glimpse of nature', with the notion of 'nature' once again positioned here as something 'authentic'. Glenn notes that 'it's not uncommon for out-of-town suicides to drive over several other suitably high and equally convenient bridges to get to the one with the beautiful view, the one all the other jumpers use' (ibid.).

A number of possible, and perhaps interdependent, reasons for the enduring 'popularity' of certain tourist locations as sites of suicide, emerge from the comparison between Beachy Head and the Golden Gate Bridge. Aside from the intrinsic 'picturesqueness' of the place, and perhaps a related aura of 'authenticity', there is a common element of notoriety, and with it, perhaps the idea that a site which has already witnessed multiple suicides offers some guarantee of a fast and painless death to those who seek it.[4] At the same time, there are significant differences between Beachy Head and the Golden Gate Bridge, which may also have some impact on the ways in which the sites are popularly perceived.

Most obviously, there is the difference in setting, one quasi-rural and the other urban. Correspondingly, one is a natural feature of the landscape, and the other is man-made. Thus, the two sites have entirely different historiographies, the Golden Gate is inscribed into public consciousness through extensive, but comparatively recent, photographic and cinematic representations, its myth a very modern iconography.[5] In contrast, Beachy Head's history traces back through centuries, the darker side of its mythology tied up with ghost stories, medieval plagues, and paganism. In this respect, Beachy Head is much closer to Asia's most 'popular' suicide site, Aokigahara Forest, which also has a long and complex folk history. In the case of Beachy Head, according to Hunt (2006, pp. 18–19), 'Legend has it that in the seventh century, a shipwrecked Christian missionary named Saint Wilfrid observed the natives throwing themselves off the cliff to placate the gods for years of crop failure. The first documented death off Beachy Head is found in the Eastbourne Parish Register of 1600'. Some contemporary adherents of paganism believe that Beachy Head was a site of ritual sacrifices, and is also a powerful intersection of ley lines, underground flows of positive and negative energy, which results in a heavily negative atmosphere 'that lures vulnerable people to the edge' (ibid., pp. 73–74).

---

4   In fact, there are numerous survivors of jumps at both sites, more often than not left paralysed as a result of the jump.

5   Seiden (1978) claims that the Golden Gate Bridge is the most photographed structure in the US.

Beachy Head is a conceptually very complex, and therefore difficult-to-manage, site. Its prime purpose, and its public face, is tourism, but leisure activities, and tourist marketing, have to coexist with its parallel notoriety as a regular site of violent self-inflicted death, without ever publicly acknowledging it. Moreover, as a result of the suicides, Beachy Head is also a site of commemoration and public grieving. The memorial tributes are a problem for the management of the tourist site, they are a persistent public reminder of the site's association with suicide, far more prominent and visible than the single small sign displaying the Samaritans' phone number which is situated relatively far from the cliffs' edge.[6] The tributes, and particularly their sheer number, contradict the official construct of Beachy Head as a beautiful bucolic natural attraction. Yet, propriety and respect for the families' grief would not allow the tributes to be removed. These visual reminders of suicide and resultant grief are as much 'markers', to use MacCannell's term, of Beachy Head, as the picturesque images of the chalk cliffs which adorn tourist brochures.

Yet, the impact of suicide on Beachy Head and the surrounding areas goes even beyond the fortnightly suicide attempts and the mass of small memorial displays at the edge of the cliff. The impact is felt perhaps most closely on the fringes of the tourist service industry, be it the taxi drivers who routinely notify the police after dropping off lone passengers at the top of the cliff (Hunt 2006), or, in my own experience, an Eastbourne bus driver who responded to my request for a one-way ticket to Beachy Head (the kind of request which would be unremarkable virtually anywhere else), with a pointed question, 'And how will you be getting back?' The Beachy Head Pub is surely one of the few, if not the only, leisure spaces in the world whose staff are instructed to constantly watch out for patrons who may be suicidal (Hunt 2006). Long-time residents, meanwhile, go to some lengths to avoid talking about Beachy Head's, and by extension, Eastbourne's, unfortunate notoriety (ibid.).

The avoidance is understandable, and in the case of tourist marketing, twofold, to acknowledge Beachy Head's dark side in any way may be both off-putting to regular holidaymakers and might even prompt an increase in the suicide rate (Surtees mentions the case of a man who read a report about Beachy Head suicides in a newspaper and remarked, 'Fancy putting something like that in the paper for people like me to see'. Two weeks later, he jumped from Beachy Head [1982, p. 323]). Indeed, Beachy Head is by no means the only tourist spot whose official promotional materials seem the result of extremely careful editing, rather than an attempt at an 'authentic' representation of the location. Sternberg, for instance, focuses on the immediate surroundings of Niagara Falls,

---

6   King and Frost (2005) describe the single Samaritans sign at Beachy Head as 'very environmentally discreet, white lettering on a dark green background, and almost invisible from the main car park, particularly at night' (2005: p. 32).

long a city in decline, [which] further exposes tourists to empty storefronts, vacant lots, and industrial relics. Yet the guidebooks, brochures and tour itineraries pretend that these surroundings do not exist. ... [T]ourists must contend with the jarring incongruity between the spectacle at stage centre and the urban decay located just off stage. (1997, p. 960)

Conclusion

Certain other sites have embraced what might be termed the 'gruesome' aspects of their history and turned them into somewhat unusual, but nonetheless popular tourist attractions; the London Dungeon and Jack the Ripper walking tours are among some of the most obvious and successful examples. On a more sombre note, cemetery tours and Holocaust memorial sites also function as particular kinds of tourist 'attractions'. Collectively, these and some other instances of sites associated with death, disaster, and suffering, have become known as sites of 'Dark Tourism' (Lennon and Foley 2000; Sharpley and Stone 2009). Dark tourism focuses on macabre 'attractions', many of which re-package and re-present their history as 'dark' entertainment or straightforward education. Neither option is available or indeed feasible at Beachy Head, as long as it continues to be an ongoing and active site for suicide. Thus, the site continues to present a highly constrained and sanitized public history (focusing on the natural features of the landscape), rather than the more distinctive and perhaps even potentially far more lucrative 'dark' history of paganism, ghosts, and tragic legacy. There is little evidence that Beachy Head functions as an unofficial site of dark tourism; the cliffs are not associated with celebrity, and the few suicides which receive attention from national, rather than local, media, tend to be stories of personal tragedy, rather than salacious sensationalism. Perhaps one has to be interested in suicide in a very particular, partly-abstract and yet partly-vaguely-personal, way, as Hunt (2006) had been, in order to conceive of Beachy Head as a viable site for dark tourism.

A necessary question arises: why have the local authorities not been more proactive in suicide prevention? The relatively recent Chaplaincy team initiative, which regularly patrols the cliffs, may have led to a reduction in the annual suicide rate, but has not been operating for long enough for any long-term effect to be statistically valid. More permanent and visible measures, such as putting up a greater number of Samaritans' signs or even building a permanent suicide barrier, face a range of objections, from charges of ineffectiveness, to high economic costs, to arguments that any such measures would diminish the aesthetic qualities of the landscape. In addition, Beachy Head is subject to cliff erosion, which means that installing a permanent barrier near the edge of the cliffs would be unusually difficult, if not impossible.

Therefore, Beachy Head remains caught up in a tense set of circumstances and intensely 'inauthentic' representations. Its public, but rarely locally-acknowledged, reputation as a notorious suicide site continues to grow, leaving a physical impact on the landscape in the form of memorial tributes and affecting both locals and visitors. At Beachy Head, the tourist gaze can be subjected to a huge and potentially-unsettling disjuncture between the official representation and the reality of presence at the site/sight. There are tangible reasons for the omission of the topic of suicide from both the tourism publicity materials and the landscape of the cliffs. Partly, these are to do with promoting the site as a 'regular' tourist attraction, and partly they are to do with trying to avoid the link between Beachy Head and suicide in the minds of those who might be vulnerable or sensitive to that association. I return to Wong's (1993) observation on the relationship between tourism and the environment referred to in the opening lines of this chapter. Beachy Head, I would argue, is a dramatically unusual case in which the respective demands of the environment and tourism are revealed to be constantly at odds with each other. The needs of tourism demand that the environment is re-packaged as something intrinsically inauthentic; the particular features of the history and topography of the environment, in turn, constantly undermine the constructed touristic experience. Beachy Head shares common features with multiple sites around the world which serve both as tourist attractions and 'attractions' for people who wish to end their lives, and exemplifies the tensions and difficulties involved in managing such sites, from the perspectives of tourist authorities, local inhabitants, visitors, and mourners.

References

Bennewith, O., Nowers, M. and Gunnell, D. (2007) 'Effect of barriers on the Clifton Suspension Bridge, England, on local patterns of suicide: Implications for prevention', *British Journal of Psychiatry*, 190, pp. 266–267.

Cohen, S. (1980) *Folk Devils and Moral Panics: The Creation of the Mods and Rockers* (2nd edn), Oxford: Martin Robertson.

Friend, T. (2003) 'The fatal grandeur of the Golden Gate Bridge', *The New Yorker*, 79, pp. 48–59.

Glenn, W.M. (2003) 'The Magnet and the Veil', *MD Canada*, May/June, pp. 36–42.

Gross, C., Markham Piper, T., Bucciarelli, A., Tardiff, K., Vlahov, D. and Galea, S. (2007) 'Suicide tourism in Manhattan, New York City, 1990–2004', *Journal of Urban Health*, 84(6), pp. 755–765.

Hayden, D. (1995) *The Power of Place: Urban Landscapes as Public History*, Cambridge, MA: The MIT Press.

Hunt, T. (2006) *Cliffs of Despair: A Journey to the Edge*, New York: Random House.

Jenks, C. (1995) 'The centrality of the eye in Western culture', in C. Jenks (ed.), *Visual Culture*, London: Routledge.

Johnson, B. (2009) 'Last chances', *Injury Prevention*, 15(3): pp. 145.

King, E. and Frost, N. (2005) 'The New Forest Suicide Prevention Initiative (NFSPI)', *Crisis*, 26(1), pp. 25–33.

Lennon, J. and Foley, M. (2000) *Dark Tourism: The Attraction of Death and Disaster*, Andover: Thomson.

MacCannell, D. (1999) *The Tourist: A New Theory of the Leisure Class*, Berkeley, CA: University of California Press.

Mann, J.J. et al. (2005) 'Suicide prevention strategies: A systematic review', *Journal of the American Medical Association*, 294(16), pp. 2064–2074.

May, V. (1993) 'Coastal tourism, geomorphology and geological conservation: The example of south central England', in P.P. Wong (ed.), *Tourism vs. Environment: The Case for Coastal Areas*. Dordrecht: Kluwer.

Owens, C., Lloyd-Tomlins, S., Emmens, T. and Aitken, P. (2009) 'Suicides in public places: Findings from one English county', *European Journal of Public Health*, 19(6), pp. 580–582.

Pelletier, A.R. (2007) 'Preventing suicide by jumping: The effect of a bridge safety fence', *Injury Prevention*, 13, pp. 57–59.

Reisch, T., Schuster, U. and Michel, K. (2008) 'Suicide by jumping from bridges and other heights: Social and diagnostic factors', *Psychiatry Research*, 161, pp. 97–104.

Rojek, C. (1997) 'Indexing, dragging and the social construction of tourist sites', in C. Rojek and J. Urry (eds), *Touring Cultures: Transformations of Travel and Theory*, London: Routledge.

Ross, T.E. and Lester, D. (1991) 'Suicides at Niagara Falls', *American Journal of Public Health*, 81, pp. 1677–1678.

Seiden, R.H. (1978) 'Where are they now? A follow-up study of suicide attempters from the Golden Gate Bridge', *Suicide and Life-Threatening Behaviour*, 8(4), pp. 203–216.

Seiden, R.H. and Spence, M. (1983) 'A tale of two bridges: Comparative suicide incidence on the Golden Gate and San Francisco Oakland Bay Bridge', *Omega*, 14, pp. 201–219.

Sharpley, R. and Stone, P.R. (eds) (2009) *The Darker Side of Travel: The Theory and Practice of Dark Tourism*, Bristol: Channel View.

Surtees, J. (1982) 'Suicide and accidental death at Beachy Head', *British Medical Journal*, 284, pp. 321–324.

Sternberg, E. (1997) 'The iconography of the tourism experience', *Annals of Tourism Research*, 24(4), pp. 951–969.

Takahashi, Y. (1988) 'Aokigahara-jukai: suicide and amnesia in Mt. Fuji's Black Forest', *Suicide and Life-Threatening Behavior*, 18(2), pp. 164–175.

Taylor, J.P. (2001) 'Authenticity and sincerity in tourism', *Annals of Tourism Research*, 28(1), pp. 7–26.

Urry, J. (2002) *The Tourist Gaze* (2nd edn), London: Sage.

Wohner, J. and Schmidtke, A. (2005) 'Ist die Verhinderung von Hotspots suizidpräventiv?' *Suizidprophylaxe*, 32, pp. 114–119.

Wong, P.P. (1993) 'Introduction', in P.P. Wong (ed.), *Tourism vs. Environment: The Case for Coastal Areas*, Dordrecht: Kluwer.

Chapter 12

The Affective Life of the Spa

Jill Steward

In a retrospective memoir of a pedestrian tour through Central and Eastern Europe of a journey made as a young man in the 1930s, Patrick Leigh Fermor (1986) describes how, suddenly, he came across an 'ornate and incongruous watering place called the Baths of Hercules'. In its faded glory this provincial, little spa appeared as an 'an echo of the Austro-Hungarian empire at its farthest edge.'

Still splendid, with *fin-de-siècle* stucco, terracotta balustrades, Grand Hotels, pump-rooms, gardens and woodland walks, it was redolent of everything that the words 'spa', 'casino' and '*villeggiatura*' conjured up, evoking images of a past when the place was host to 'ailing burghers in crinolines and stove-pipe hats, sabre-taches and *czapkas*, or mutton-chop sleeves and boater' (Fermor 1986, pp. 210–212). For me, far more vividly than anything else I have read, this piece creates an image of a certain kind of landscape and a 'lost world', sometimes referred to as the 'golden age of the spas', now vanished for ever (Wechsberg 1979).

**Figure 12.1   Postcard c. 1905. Herculesbad/Herculesfürdo in Transylvania.
Collection of author**

The spa as a concept and an institution is still very much with us however, since the term is currently deployed across a wide variety of contexts to refer to many different types of places, institutions and facilities that include old-fashioned spa towns, modern hotels in far-flung and exotic destinations and urban beauty salons of which are in the business of marketing sensory experiences, therapies and products designed to induce health and well- being and rejuvenate and restore minds and bodies (O'Dell 2005). Like their predecessors, they promote themselves as extraordinary and distinctive kinds of space (Mansén 1998), therapeutic landscapes (Kearns and Geslar 1998; Smyth 2005) and sites of healing and pleasure (Kos 1991), existing in a world 'out of time' in which the motion of weary travellers is temporarily suspended and life is regulated according to rhythms and rituals distinct from those of everyday life in the world outside. Implicit in this image of the spa is the notion of affectivity for the rationale of the spa is to induce some kind of change, whether transformative or merely temporary, in the people who go there since the spas are (and always were) regarded as places where visitors seek relief from pain, unhappiness, stress and anxiety, to engage in sensory activity and pleasurable distractions, and to achieve states of state of inner peace and tranquillity.

The 'imaginary space' of the spa and its material realizations constitutes a rich source of material for scholars. For ethnologists with an interest in magic, pilgrimage and liminality, there are links to be made between ancient rites and customs related to the use of water and many of the practices and rituals associated with spa medicine (Nolan 1986; O'Dell 2005), particularly since spas were often founded on sites once regarded as sacred (Steward 2002). For medical and cultural historians, the history of the spas is bound up with changes and shifts in the discourses and practices relating to sickness and health and the care of the mind and the body (Brockliss, 1990; Steward 2002; Wood 2004); as well as to popular and elite cultures of leisure, consumption and display (Mackaman 1998; Fuhs 1998; Borsay 2000; Chambers 2002, and to aspects of colonialization 2006). More recently, changes in the economic and cultural role of the spas involving their decline and renaissance are regarded as important components of the global tourist industry (Erfurt-Cooper and Cooper 2009) while on a wider front, spa history continues to interest historians, sociologists and ethnologists, not least because the spa trade (and its associated rhetoric) is maps onto to a wide range of discourses, practices and issues relating to attitudes to health and the body, gender behaviours and sexuality, consumption habits and leisure practices (Durie 2006) and the affective categories and emotional economies with which they are associated (Lempa 2002; Cossic 2006; Herbert 2009).

In what follows, this chapter will, briefly, consider some general features of spa history focusing on the role of affectivity in the relationship between the idea of the spa and in its material realizations, and then, drawing on real and imaginary representations of spa life, it will examine some examples of the influence of feeling and emotion on experiences of spa life.

The Concept and Reality of Spa Life

The spas (or health resorts) of the past were as numerous and diverse and diverse as contemporary ones. Individual spas were (and are) differentiated by their size, medical functions, social profiles and the extent to which they embraced forms of holistic and alternative medicine (Steward 2000; Wood 2004), but were united by the claims they made for the therapeutic and salubrious properties of their waters, airs and climates. Early modern establishments often consisted of little more than a few springs, baths and wooden huts while urban settlements, such as Bath, Spa, Carlsbad/Karlovy Vary and Aachen, functioned as seasonal leisure resorts for the social elites and were well-equipped with hotels, shops and places of amusement. In the modern period the spa trade expanded to include colonies like Marienbad/ Mariánské Lansky (founded in the wake of the enlightened interest in the medical and economic benefits of the mineral waters), as well as those which were redeveloped or re-discovered, such as Baden-Baden or Vichy. It also encompassed seaside spas such as Scarborough, Nice and Abbazia as well health resorts in the mountains like the Semmering (near Vienna) and Davos which became popular with consumptives.

In the past people were often advised to take a spa cure not just for its physical effects on the body, but also for the psychological affect it might have (Steward 2002). The belief that travel, a change of scene and removal from the home environment could be good for the health (particularly in the case of some kinds of mental disorders) goes back to the ancients (Andrews 2000), while the idea that the spa environment could directly influence emotional states also has a long history. In the pre- modern period, spa visits were recommended for melancholy and forms of depression (Guerini 2000; Ingram and Sims 2011) because of the opportunities they offered for sociability and other pleasurable forms of distraction, while in the modern period the spas were popular with 'nervous' patients suffering from hysteria, neurasthenia and other disorders attributed to the effects of the stresses and traumas of modern life: many of whom were catered for in luxurious private clinics (Gijswijt-Hofstra and Porter 2001; Steward 2012). As this indicates, changes to the medical and social profile of health travellers were bound up with shifts in medical theory and practice since diagnoses of emotional pathologies were historically contingent and culturally situated, as well inflected by gender and class relations (Alberti 2009, p. xiv).

The way that people respond to the spa environment is (and was) mediated not only by their physical condition, but also by the state of their inner lives and feelings. One source of information about the way that people in the past were affected by their experiences of spa life comes from the letters and journals of the many famous travellers and writers who visited them. These, rather than standard spa guides and medical hand books offer cultural historians, and others interested in the historical dimensions of 'emotional geography', an insight into the particularities of the way that people were affected by the spa environment. The narratives of spa literature are structured by many of the standard tropes of travel writing – pilgrimage, displacement, migration and exile, arrival, departure and return, absence and loss – which in the past have also functioned as allegories (Todorov 1996, pp. 292–293) and metaphors for the interior journeys of embodied subjects as well mapping out their movements through material landscapes (Duncan and Gregory 1999, p. 5). As such, they offer material for the analysis of the link between the cognitive experiences offered by spa life and the 'raw feels' with which they are associated (Alberti 2009, p. xv).

Interest in the history of the emotions (or the 'affective categories' as Thomas Dixon (2009) prefers to call them (pp. 24–25) is still relatively new (Rosenwein 2002). As Alberti (2009) notes that 'emotions are physical and lived experiences' yet 'they are also learned and behavioural systems, revealed through gestures, postures and a series of display codes' (p. xvii). Terms such as 'passion' and 'emotion' carry meanings (and are performed) in ways which are historically and cultural specific rather than referring to trans-historical or pre-cultural experiences (Alberti 2009, p. xv). At the same time they operate in ways that articulate and describe sets of phenomena occupying different but overlapping semantic fields (Dixon 2009, p. 25)'. For historians, therefore, any attempt to use affective terms to map out and interpret the way that sensate subjects interact with particular environments is a complex and difficult enterprise.

Thinking about the affective dimensions of 'spa' life I was reminded of Alain Renais' film, *Last Year in Marienbad* [*L'anneé dernière à Marienbad*] (1961) which, despite its title, was shot in several different locations, none of them in the Bohemian spa of Marienbad. It has been suggested that the deceptiveness of the title and its evocation of a 'fictional, intertextual space' is one of the things that has continued to fascinate people about this film (Pauly 2000, p. 327) and it is certainly true that this (together with the various devices used to disrupt the continuity of the narrative) has gene rated a great deal of writing about illusion and allusion. What is of interest here however, is the way that the name '*Marienbad*' immediately conjures up (for me at least) a 'sense of place' that functions as a *mise-en-scène* in its own right, constituting a setting that is directly related to the idea of the spa as an extraordinary kind of space, given substance in the film by the ornate and baroque décor which could well be that of a grand, fin-de-siècle spa hotel or private clinic, with its elegant mirrored interiors, salons, bars, and formal gardens in which the inmates appear to while away the hours with cards, concerts and affairs against a constant background of conversation. The film theorist Guiliana Bruno (2002), has written of the way that camera movements through the architectural settings of particular films chart 'the motion of emotion' in a way that is integral to the construction of 'narrative journeys', in the course of which places are linked to affect, rendering the latter visible in ways that elicit emotional responses from the 'traveller' (pp. 2, 219). In *Marienbad,* the movements of the camera around the lifeless gardens, frozen statues, mirrored hallways and illusory spaces certainly appear to describe the emotional detachment and frozen state of the characters and their relationships (Pauly 2000. pp. 3, 325; Greene 1999, p. 33).

One of the paradoxes of the film is that, while the title makes direct reference to the world of the spas, this particular environment appears to be anything but therapeutic. Bruno, who is fascinated by seventeenth-century allegorical maps, writes about the way in which one in particular, Madeleine de Scudéry's *Carte du pays de Tendre* (1654) (published in conjunction with her romantic novel, *Clelie*), (Bruno 2002, plate IV) charts a psycho-geographical landscape traversed by the characters in the novel. Scattered across the terrain depicted by the map are towns, villages and monuments, each of which represents an emotional state, or stopping point along the routes followed by the individual characters, thereby mapping out the affective journeys (or emotional itineraries) generated by the shifting relationships between the members of the group (Scudéry 1973, p. 398). Scudéry's own map contains no spas but in his study of the subject J.S. Munro (1986) mentions that in one of the many imitations spawned by the novel (not specified) the lovers finally achieve their goal of *jouissance* only to find that the passionate emotions this generates give way to feelings of disgust manifesting themselves in physical symptoms of a kind best remedied by a spa cure, the function of which is to restore and rebalance bodily systems unbalanced by physical and psychological excess (p. 21). While this imaginary spa was defined by its position within a particular allegorical landscape, it was also grounded in the reality of life in the pre-modern French spa which, at that time, was exclusively medical in its function and with a reputation for dreariness. By contrast, the image evoked by the title and settings of *Marienbad* conjures up a rather more complex idea: that of a bounded space, infused with a 'spirit of place' which reveals itself in the cultural and moral values shaping spa life, in the configuration of the terrain and topographical and monumental features of the built environment and the sensory and emotional states driving the actions of the people moving around it.

Contrasting sharply with the image of the pre-modern French spa, other verbal and visual representations spa life usually emphasise the sensory and social dimensions of the pleasures on offer. In the modern period, when many spas instituted medicalized regimes and others developed into important pleasure resorts, the disjunction between the two organizing principles of spa life – pleasure and therapy – becomes acute. In literature the physical and cultural terrain of the spa becomes incorporated into an emotional geography that is metaphorical rather than allegorical in its function, and which is articulated through descriptions of active relationships with the environment, influenced by enlightened and romantic attitudes and values. In the nineteenth century the latter also determined the way people perceived health and illness (particularly consumption and depression) and expressed and performed their feelings (Lawlor 2006). Within spa medicine the assumption that minds and bodies were interlinked continued to influence the way the spa environment was conceived and organized, particularly in places practising forms of alternative medicine. Shifts in social sensibilities and cultural mores were manifested in changes to the built environment (Bothe 1984; Fuhs 1992; Grötz and Quecke 2006) as interior spaces as baths, pump rooms were remodelled and communal and mixed bathing facilities replaced with private ones. At the same time new leisure amenities catered for pleasure seekers and urban tastes. The impact of romantic *Naturphilosophie* was evident in the importance given to the creation of gardens à *l'anglais* and landscaped woodland walks where the gratitude of former guests was often inscribed on memorials along the way.

In our own time, the spa is situated uneasily within an emotional geography centred around sites of consumption for, while contemporary spas are modern commercial operations selling manufactured products and heavily designed experiences, they are also associated with forms of New Age philosophies centred on ideas of purification and naturalness, apparent in the careful design of new spas and the materials used. The visual and sensory impact of the styling, iconography and layout of the interior spaces reinforced by careful attention to the way that people experience movement from one area to another, and devices such as the use of scented candles and soothing music, are intended to induce pleasurable feelings of relaxation and mental spiritual well-being in their customers (Sinclair 2005; Murray, 2007).

Spa Memoirs

Despite the inherent difficulties of linguistic and cultural translation, some insights into the way that visitors interacted with the spa environment are offered by letters and journals from across the centuries which convey to present-day readers something of how people staying in the spas responded to their situation. For those who were ill, a major source of distress was not only the pain and anxiety caused by their health, but also the traumatic experience of the treatments they had to undergo. In 1676, for example, the aristocratic Madame de Sévigné travelled to Vichy (long before its nineteenth-century transformation into a leisure resort) where she took a cure for her rheumatism. Her letters give a vivid account of her experiences, including the drinking and bathing cure she was prescribed. The waters tasted vile: 'How nasty they are! One goes in at six o' clock in the morning to the springs. Everyone is there. One drinks, one makes a terrible face because – just imagine – the water is boiling hot and has a very strong, very disagreeable taste of saltpetre'[1] (Duchêne 1974, vol. 2, p. 296). But far worse was the hot douche which she describes as 'a fairly good rehearsal for purgatory' since she had to go completely naked into a small underground chamber where a woman controlled and directed a stream of boiling hot water all over her body at first, and then onto the affected joints. 'To go there without even a fig leaf is a rather humiliating experience' and when the water 'strikes at the nape of the neck it comes as a fiery shock such as you cannot imagine. And yet that is the vital centre.' She bore it stoically for: 'One must endure it all, and one does, and one is not

---

1   'Ah! Qu'elles sont méchantes... On va à six heures à la fontaine. Tout le monde s'y trouve. On boit, et l'on fait, mine fort vilaine mine, car imaginez – vous qu'elles sont bouillantes et d'un gout de saltpêtre fort. Désagréables! (Duchêne, R. 1974, vol, 2, p. 296).

scalded, and finally one lies down on a warm bed where one sweats profusely and that is what accomplishes the cure'[2] (vol. 2. p. 303). Two centuries later, in 1840, Mary Shelley, who was suffering from headaches and depression, visited the spa of Bad Kissingen in Bavaria. Her narrative of spa life was always intended for publication but still indicates something of her active relationship with her cure and surroundings. Fifteen days of drinking and bathing, induced a crisis: 'The body becomes inert and languid, with a sense of illness pervading the frame; the mind is haunted by apprehension of evil, and is disturbed by a nervous restlessness and irritability of the most distressing kind' (1844, vol. I. p. 196). Subsequently Shelley became convinced that her relationship with certain kinds of landscape was more therapeutic than her medical treatment (Kautz 2000, pp. 171–176).

Another frequent source of distress was food (Steward 2008). The British travellers who frequented German spas in the early nineteenth century particularly disliked the local way with boiled meat, a dish described by Sir Francis Head (1838) as something that 'a Grosvenor Square cat would not touch with its whiskers' (p. 70). People taking the waters in the spas, which were adopting medicalized regimes delivered by authoritarian doctors, were often subject to severe dietary restrictions as in Bad Kissingen, for example, where the authorities imposed fines on anyone selling forbidden items to the patients (Shelley 186). A steady source of income for the spa trade were patients suffering from the effects of dietary disorders. Problems of obesity or jaded appetites were often attributed to the psychological effects of excessive urban lifestyles and treated with 'reducing' or 'starvation' diets. A character in Schlomo Aleichem's epistolary novel of Jewish life, *Marienbad* (1911) plaintively expresses the sense of affliction these regimes could induce.

> The people who come here are those whom God has blessed with an abundance of money and an abundance of flesh. Perhaps it is really the very opposite – punished with an abundance of flesh. But alas, these people are the most miserable on earth. They crave food and aren't allowed to eat. They yearn to travel and can't. They desire nothing better than to lie down and aren't permitted. (pp. 49–50)

---

2   '[U]ne assez bonne répétition du purgatoire. On est toute nue dans un petit lieu sous terre, où l'on trouve un tuyau de cette eau chaude, qu'une femme vous fait aller où vous voulez. Cet état où l'on conserve à peine une feuille de figuier pour tout habillement est une chose assez humiliante... Représentez-vous un jet d'eau contre qu'une de vos pauvres parties, toute la plus bouillante que vous puissiez vous imaginer. On met d'abord l'alarme partout, pour mettre en mouvement tous les esprits, et puis on s'attache aux jointures qui on été affligées. Mais quand in vient a la nuque du cou: c'est une sorte de feu et surprise qui ne peut se comprendre cependant c'est lá le noeud de l'affaire... Il fait souffrir, et l'on souffre tout, et l'on n'est point brûlée, et on se met ensuite dans un lit chaud ou l'on sue abondamment, et voilà ce qui guerir' (Duchêne, 1974, vol. 2, p. 303).

People taking cures often did so in the belief that it was the healing powers of nature and self-discipline in the form of mineral waters, good air, early nights, exercise and restricted diets that would restore them to health, but many doctors seem to have regarded other features of the cure as equally important, such as the psychological effects of the orderliness and discipline of its daily routines on people who normally led chaotic or disorderly lives. These, together with the 'natural' surroundings, were believed to induce a sense of calmness and tranquillity in the inmates, distancing them from the pressures of the outside world (Jacobsson 2004). In places specializing in the 'nervous', spa doctors also did their best to discourage any kind of excitement. Shelley reports that the authorities, who controlled the heavily medicalized regime operating in Bad Kissingen, forbade parents to bring their children in case their presence would be too affecting (1844, vol. 1, pp. 198–199).

Guests often report on the irritation and distress created by fellow guests. In 1817 Shelley's step-brother Charles Clairmont, visited the French spa of Bagnères de Bigorre as a tourist. A true romantic, Clairmont passionately cared about the natural beauty of the 'divine scenery' and wrote to Shelley that the 'grand and solemn tranquillity of these mountains, chases every wild and low passion; it is impossible to live and breathe the serenity of this air, & not be virtuous' (Stocking 1995, vol. 1, p.106). However, he loathed the luxurious lifestyles of the elites who came there during the bathing season. 'The disgusting sight of the rich who annually come to loll away 3 months of the year in idleness, and to corrupt these otherwise simple people, is intolerable' (vol. 1. p. 107. Shelley herself was constantly depressed by the 'saddening sight of the sick' in Bad Kissingen and the 'regiment of sick people. It is odd enough to seek amusement by being surrounded by the rheumatic, the gouty, the afflicted of all sorts' (vol. 1, p. 184).

In many spas the pursuit of pleasure was as important as therapy. The early modern spas had a well-earned reputation as places of considerable sexual license and sensory pleasures, the legacy of which lived on in the mythology associated with spa life. And even in the modern period, as spa culture became more highly medicalized, the spas continued to attract pleasure seekers and in any case invalids needed distraction and were frequently accompanied by friends and family in robust health who needed entertainment. Frances Trollope (1834) wrote of Baden-Baden that it would be:

> almost impossible to find oneself in the midst of such an assembly surrounded
> on all sides with incitements to pleasure, and antidotes to melancholy, without
> feeling inspired with a strong inclination to enter into the spirit of the scene, and,
> in truth, I can conceive of no surer cure for an attack of the blue devils than the
> mere sight of it. (vol. 2, p. 14)

The leading spas functioned as modern pleasure resorts with cafes, theatres, ballrooms, shops and casinos, so that while the medical facilities embodied moral values of self-discipline, restraint and responsibility, a great deal of the

Figure 12.2   Postcard. Romantic emotions (the Kneipp cure). Collection of author

other side of spa life was associated with the kind of self-indulgence and excess which health manuals warned against (Steward 2002, 2006) and epitomized by the gaming rooms. Like many travellers, Trollope professed herself both shocked and fascinated by the sight of people at the tables, particularly the women. 'I used formerly to think that I could understand in what consisted the pleasure of gaming. I thought it arose from an animating vicissitude of hope and fear, which kept the spirits in a delightful flutter of excitement. But this was before I had watched its torturing effects and now I am utterly at a loss to conceive what the feeling is, which can bring men to endure so great an agony' (pp. 19–20).

Tales of Love and Death

The affective dimension of spa life is best studied by looking at the way it has been articulated and mapped out in imaginative literature where, as in the cinema, readers are invited 'to visit the ebb and flow of a personal and yet social psycho-geography' (Bruno 2002, p. 2) and the spa becomes a metaphor for wider social forces. At the same time however, there is plenty of historical evidence to show that the real, as opposed to the fictitious spas, were places in which love and romance flourished but where there was also a great deal of pain, despair, grief and death.

Notable examples of novelists, past and present, who have explored the potential of the spa as an invaluable form of *mise-en-scène* range from Jane Austen, whose novel *Northanger Abbey* (1817) draws on the author's observations of the marriage market of regency Bath to the contemporary writer Fay Weldon, whose *Spa Decameron* (2007) examines the lives of a group of women snowed up in a spa hotel in the process of going bankrupt.

There are many reasons why writers have found such a rich source of material in the spa, not least because so many were able to draw on considerable first-hand experience of spa life and were familiar with the general topography, daily routines and social tone, the details of which enabled the specificities of place to be convincingly rendered. A good example was the Edwardian novelist Ouida, whose romantic novel, *Moths* (1880) drew on her experience of the Austrian spa of Ischl, describing it as:

> [c]alm and sedate, and simple and decorous. Ischl has nothing of the *belle petite,* like her sister of Baden, nothing of the titled *cocotte* like her cousin of Monaco. Ischl does not gamble, or riot, or conduct herself madly in any way; she is a little old fashioned, still in a courtly way; she has a little rusticity still in her elegant manners; she is homely whilst she is so visibly of the *fine fleur* of the *vielle_ souche*. (vol. 2, pp. 252–253)

Novelists revel in the spatial ambiguity inherent in the idea of the spa for while the spas are enclosed and bounded physical spaces, they also constitute extensions of the cultural and social spaces of the world outside which shape and influence the social mores and psychological dispositions of their inmates. One of the great assets of the spa as a *mise-en-scène* is that makes credible the assembly of a cast of social types which, as the editor (1904) of Walter Scott's novel, *St Ronan's Well* set in the English borders, remarked, afforded:

> every variety of character, mixed together in a manner which cannot, without a breach of probability, be supposed to exist elsewhere' and for the sake of the plot it was possible to describe 'events extremely different from those in the quiet routine of ordinary life', some of which may in fact, and often do, take place. (p. xi)

Just as useful for narrative purposes was the transitory nature of spa life in that in post-Romantic literature a stay in a watering place often represents a temporary stopping point in the exterior and interior journeys of the protagonists. In fiction, as in reality, spa life is punctuated by arrivals and departures, by meetings and partings, and most of all by presence and absence. In the Bohemian spa of Carlsbad/Karlovy Vary it was once customary to greet new arrivals by the ringing of the bell, regular lists were issued to keep people abreast of comings and goings and departures were marked with bouquets. And in the spas frequented by invalids (such as Anne Bronte, who died in the seaside spa of Scarborough) the final departure of the terminally ill was memorialized in the local graveyard.

In fiction the spa is frequently a place associated with danger, chaos and immorality and sexual licentiousness. In the nineteenth century changing sensibilities and the desire to protect the reputation of their establishments led the authorities to discourage unseemly behaviour, but literary representations of spa life, such as Aleichem's *Marienbad* and Stefan Zweig's *The Burning Secret* (1913) (set in the Semmering outside Vienna) continue to represent spa life in terms of romantic and sexual entanglements. In any case the daily rituals structuring spa life focused attention on bodily sensations and awareness and people who are unhappy or separated from their family, with time on their hands and who find themselves in an environment where the conventions of everyday life are perhaps less rigidly observed than at home, tend to find ways of occupying themselves. In literature the claustrophobic atmosphere and ungrounded life of the spas represents a catalyst for the release of repressed desires and emotions so that it is unsurprising that in real life the social and psychological intimacies of spa life led to some famous love affairs, including Goethe's passion for a young girl at the age of 74 and Alma Mahler's passionate affair with the young architect Walter Gropius (Mahler, 1947, p. 144; Keegan, 1991, pp. 151–153) and that the troubled Franz Kafka enjoyed what was perhaps his only successful sexual relationship in a place dedicated to natural healing (Steward 2012).

Spa life, despite its *louche* aspects, frequently possessed a formality lacking in the majority of seaside resorts where the sea functioned as a visible symbol of the power of untrammelled nature (Corbin 1988). Ford Maddox Ford's *The Good Soldier: a Tale of Passion* (1926) revolves around the complicated relationship of two couples who regularly spend their summers in the medicalized German spa of Bad Nauheim. The narrator, who is revealed as a passionless man unable to read other people's emotions, declares himself unable to achieve any of the 'home feeling' and sense of 'anchorage' which he assumes the place has for the patients taking the baths, amongst whom is his wife who is being treated for a fictitious heart condition (which turns out to be the cover for a long-standing affair). He reflects that 'to be at Nauheim gave me a sense – what shall I say a sense almost of nakedness – the nakedness that one feels on the sea-shore or in any of the great open spaces.' At the same time the place seems repressively regimented and the orderliness artificial:

> one is too polished up. Heaven knows I was never an untidy man. But the feeling I had when … I stood upon carefully swept steps of the Englisher Hof, looking at the carefully arranged trees in tubs upon the carefully arranged gravel whilst carefully arranged people walked past in carefully calculated gaiety, at the carefully calculated hour, the tall trees of the public gardens, going up to the right; the reddish stone of the baths – or were they white half-timbered chalets? Upon my word, I have forgotten, I who was there so often. That will give you the measure of how much I was in the landscape. (p. 21)

As in Renais' *Marienbad*, the regulated and aesthetically arid environment obscures what gradually emerges as emotional turbulence and moral anarchy in the leading characters. As Graham Green (1965), who wrote an introduction to the book commented: 'A short enough book it is to contain two suicides, two ruined lives, a death, and a girl driven insane' (p. 8).

Although much of the action takes place outside the spa, *The Good Soldier* still exemplifies in an extreme form, the way that the affective dynamics of the spa environment are generated by its function as an arena for what some philosophers have regarded as the two basic forces in human life, the desire to avoid pain and death and the pursuit of pleasure although, as many others have pointed out, things are never quite that simple. In the nineteenth-century Russian novel the spa, far from inducing a sense of tranquillity in the protagonists, becomes a setting for fierce psychological conflicts in which human rationality and self-control are shown as powerless in the face of the darker forces of self-destruction. Dostoevsky who, like many of his compatriots, was tragically familiar with the gambling casinos of the German Rhineland spas – Wiesbaden, Baden-Baden and Homburg (Carter 2006), and in *The Gambler* (1866) it is in the casino in the fictitious spa of Roulettenberg in which the click of the roulette wheel and the fall of the dice fuel the elation and despair of the narrator as his addiction loses him everything, including the woman he loves. Turgenev, who spent much of his life in Baden-Baden, used it as the setting for his tragic novel, *Smoke* (1867) while in Mikhail Lermentov's *A Hero of Our Times* (1838–1840) the central character sets about destroying the life of a young woman he meets in a small Caucasian spa. The narrator's movements through its interior and exterior spaces – through the *Kurhaus,* ballroom, restaurant and promenade are accompanied by his reflections on his encounters with various people and the events to which they give rise. The '[P]assions', he muses, 'are merely ideas in their initial stage. They are the property of youth, and anyone who expects to feel their thrill throughout his life is a fool. Tranquil rivers often begin as roaring waterfalls, but no river leaps and foams all the way to the sea.' But, as he discovers to his cost, 'Tranquillity...is often a sign of great, if hidden power' (p. 128).

The contrast between the emotional conflicts created by the conflicting forces of Eros and Thanatos [love and death] and the apparent tranquillity of the spa environment is even more sharply drawn in *Venus in Furs* (1870) by the Austrian writer, Leopold von Sacher-Masoch who drew on an affair he once had with a woman he met at Baden in a narrative which begins with a meeting in a 'small Austrian spa' and evolves into a gruelling account of the emotional damage inflicted on the narrator by games of sexual and psychological dominance and subordination (Jacob 2007). Equally extreme in its own way was Arthur Schnitzler's short story '*Beatrice and her Son*' (1913), a portrayal of a lonely widow and her young son who spend the summer in villa at a lakeside spa resort where they both have affairs but finish up committing incest in the bottom of a boat which the mother then overturns.

In the 1890s the advent of the sanatorium novel, of which famous examples are Beatrice Harradan's *Ships that Pass in the Night* (1893) and, more recently, A.E. Ellis's *The Rack* (1968), was associated with the rapid growth in private clinics and sanatoria catering for people suffering from tuberculosis. The closed or semi-closed nature of these establishments allowed doctors enormous control and many elements of the treatments prescribed were intended to prevent and suppress any kind of disturbing feelings and emotions in their patients (Shorter, 1990: Barton, 2008). Within a literary setting the arousal and expression of any kind of strong feeling among sanatorium patients invariably has tragic consequences, as for example, in Thomas Mann's novella *Tristan* (1902) in which passionate music-making (the playing of Wagner's *Liebestod* on the piano) brings on a fatal attack and the defiant expression of love becomes a passport to imminent death. Inta Ezergailis (1975) has commented on the role of the spa resort in Mann's novel's and the tensions generated by various kinds of conceptual oppositions generated by the nature of the locale, such as the contrast between nature without and the man-made world within (p. 350), These are particularly acute in the *Magic Mountain* (1924) (the most famous example of the genre) in which the principal theme of the enmity and struggle between life and death is articulated through the narrator's journey of self-discovery. The physical features of the internal and external environment, such the snow, the large glass windows and divisions between the rows of balconies where patients were exposed to the winter sunshine, carry mythological and symbolic associations displaying the relationships between the characters (Ezergailis 1975, p. 356). The lighting in the spooky X-ray chamber and the way that the alpine snow fields are lit affect the narrator not only physically and aesthetically, but also emotionally, thereby playing a part in what becomes a near fatal encounter with disease and decadence (Evans, 2005, p. 160).

Conclusion

As these examples show the idea of the spa contains elements that are both constant and mutable. One of its unchanging features is the notion affectivity which lies at its core and informs the way that spas are experienced as places. For, however conceived, the rationale of the spa is to make a difference, to affect the emotional and physical state of its customers. As therapeutic landscapes and sites of pleasure therefore, the spas enjoy a place in the emotional topographies of the day and feelings and passions that are repressed or unleashed within them are representative of those that structure the lives of people in the world outside for, as with all travellers, those who visit spas bring their other lives with them. Contemporary spas have not yet achieved the literary success of their predecessors, perhaps because the kinds of experiences they provide are substantially different from those of the past. They are places where groups of women (and men), mothers and daughters, go to celebrate, bond or just 'chill out', forms of sociability that have an affective dimension. Spa life is no longer accompanied by the shadow of death or disaster which was always a potential companion in the past. Instead the contemporary health spa is an important part of modern consumer society in that it preys upon the fears and anxieties associated with aging and the loss of youthful vitality and attractiveness (Köstlin 2008). By enveloping its clients in a protective cocoon, it enables them to enjoy, without too much guilt, indulgence in forms of individualist narcissism and 'being good to themselves', in ways which take them, temporarily, out of the stresses and difficulties of their everyday lives. In this respect the attraction of the spa for many people still lies in the way that it bridges the gap between the physical, mental and emotional realities of their lives and how they would like them to be.

Bibliography

Alberti, F. (2006) 'Emotions in the early modern medical tradition', in Alberti, F. (ed.) *Medicine, Emotion and Disease, 1700–1950*, New York: Palgrave/ Macmillan, pp. 1–21.

Andrews, J. (2000) 'Letting madness range; travel and mental disorder, c. 1700–1900', in G. Revill and R. Wrigley (eds), *Pathologies of Travel*, Wellcome Series in the History of Medicine, *Clio Medica* 56, Amsterdam/Atlanta GA: Rodopi, pp. 25–88.

Anonymous (ed.) (1904) 'Introduction', in Sir Walter Scott, *St Ronan's Well* (Waverley Novels, 8, London/Edinburgh: Adam and Charles, pp. ix–xii.

Borsay, P. (2000) 'Health and leisure resorts, 1700–1840', in Clark, P. (ed.), *Cambridge Urban History of Britain, vol. 2 1540–1840*, Cambridge: Cambridge University Press, pp. 775–803.

Bothe, R. (ed.) (1984) Kurstädte in Deutschland zur Geschichte einer Baugattung, Berlin: Frölich und Kaufmann.

Brockliss, L.W.B. (1990) 'The development of the spa in seventeenth-century France', *Medical History*, Supplement No. 10, pp. 23–47.

Bruno, G. (2002) *The Atlas of the Emotions: Journeys in Art, Architecture and Film*, London: Verso.

Carter, E.J. (2006) 'Breaking the bank: gambling casinos, finance capitalism and Germany unification', *Central European History*, 39, pp. 185–213.

Chambers, T. (2002) 'Tourism and the market revolution', *Reviews in American History*, 30(4), pp. 555–563.

Corbin, A. (1994) *The Lure of the Sea: the Discovery of the Seaside 1750–1840*, London: Penguin.

Cossic, A. (2006) 'The female invalid and spa therapy in some well-known 18th century medical and literary texts', in A. Cossic and P. Galliou, *Spas in Britain and France in the 19th Century*, Newcastle: Cambridge Scholars, pp. 115–138.

Dixon, T. (2006) 'Patients and passions: languages of medicine and emotion, 1789–1850', in F. Alberti (ed.), *Medicine, Emotion and Disease, 1700–1950*, New York: Palgrave/Macmillan, pp. 22–52.

Duchêne, R (ed.) (1974) *Correspondance: Mme de Sévigné*, vol. 2, Paris: Gallimard.

Duncan, J. and Gregory, D. (1999) *Writes of Passage: Reading Travel Writing*, London: Routledge.

Durie, A. (2006) *Water is Best; the Hydro and Health Tourism in Scotland 1840–1940*, Edinburgh: John Donald.

Erfurt-Cooper, P. and Cooper, M. (2009) *Health and Wellness Tourism: Spas and Hot Springs*, Bristol: Channel View.

Evans, M. (2005) 'Madness, medicine and creativity in Thomas Mann's *The Magic Mountain*', in C. Saunders and J. Macnaughton (eds), *Madness and Creativity in Literature and Culture*, Basingstoke: Palgrave Macmillan, pp. 159–174.

Ezergailis, I. (1975) 'Thomas Mann's Resorts', *MLN*, 90(3), pp. 353–362.

Fermor, P.L. (1986) *Between the Woods and Waters: on Foot to Constantinople from the Hook of Holland; the Middle Danube to the Iron Gates*, London: Penguin.

Fuhs, B. (1992) *Mondäne Orte einer vornehmen Gesellschaft: Kultur und Geschichte der Kurstädte 1700–1900*, Hildesheim: George Olms.

Geslar, W. (2000) 'Hans Castorp's journey-to-knowledge of disease and health in Thomas Mann's *Magic Mountain*', *Health and Place*, 6, (2), pp. 125–134.

Gijswijt-Hofstra, M. and Porter, R. (eds) (2001) *Cultures of Neurasthenia*, Wellcome Series in the History of Medicine, *Clio Medica* 63, Amsterdam / New York: Rodopi.

Greene, N. (1999) *The National Past in Post-war French Cinema*, Princeton: Princeton University Press.

Grötz, S, and Quecke, S. (eds) *Balnea: Architekturalgeschichte des Bades*, Marburg: Jonas.

Guerini, A. (2000) *Obesity and Depression in the Enlightenment: The Life and Times of George Cheyne*, Norman: University of Oklahoma.

Head, F.B. (1838) *Bubbles from the Brunnen of Nassau, by an Old Man* (Originally published in 1824), London: Black.

Herbert, A.E. (2009) 'Gender and the spa: space, sociability and self at British health spas, 1640–1714', *Journal of Social History*, 43(Winter), pp. 361–383.

Ingram, A. and Sim, S. (2011) *Varieties of Melancholy Experience*, London: Palgrave.

Jacob, B. (2007). 'The "uncanny aura" of *Venus im Pelz*: masochism and Freud's uncanny', *The Germanic Review*, 82(3), pp. 269–285.

Jacobsson, A. (2004) 'Ruled by routine and ritual: spatial organization of the spa environment at Ronneby, south-east Sweden', *Garden History*, 22(2), pp. 213–228.

Jennings, E.T. (2006), *Curing the Colonizers: Hydrotherapy, Climatology, and French Colonial Spas.* London and Durham, NC: Duke University Press.

Kautz B.D. (2000) 'Spas and salutary landscapes: the geography of health in Mary Shelley's *Rambles in Germany and Italy*' in A. Gilroy (ed.), *Romantic Geographies: Discourses of Travel 1755–1844*, London: Macmillan, pp. 165–184.

Kearns, R. and Geslar, W. (eds) (1998) *Putting Health into Place, Landscape, Identity and Well-being*, Syracuse NY: Syracuse University.

Keegan, S. (1991) *The Bride of the Wind: the Life and Times of Alma Mahler-Werfel*, London: Secker and Warburg.

Kos, W. (1991) 'Zwischen Amusement und Therapie: der Kurort as soziales Ensemble', in H. Lachmeyer, S., Mattl-Wurm and C. Gargerle (eds), *Das Bad, eine Geschichte der Badekultur im 19. und 20. Jahrhundert*, Salzburg: Residenz, pp. 220–256.

Köstlin, K. (2006) 'Water, spa and the Western body: Paradigms, lifestyles and cultural practices', in P. Lysaght (ed.), *Sanitas per Acqua: Spa, Lifestyles and Foodways*, Innsbruck: Studium, pp. 37–55.

Křítzek, V. (1990) *Kulturgeschichte des Heilbades*, Stuttgart / Berlin/ Köln.

Lawlor, C. (2006) *Consumption and Literature: the Making of a Romantic Disease*, London: Macmillan.

Lempa, H. (2002) 'The spa: emotional economy and social classes in nineteenth-century Pyrmont', *Central European History*, 35(1), pp. 37–73.

Mackaman, D. (1998) *Leisure Settings: Bourgeois Culture and the Spa in Modern France*, Chicago: University of Chicago Press.

Mahler, A. (1947). *Gustav Mahler: Memories and Letters*, trans. B. Creighton, London: John Murray.

Mansén, E. (1998) 'An image of paradise: Swedish spas in the eighteenth century', *Eighteenth Century Studies*, 31(4), pp. 511–516.

Munro, J.S. (1986) *Mademoiselle de Scudéry and the Carte de Tendre*, Durham: University of Durham.

Murray, S. (2007) 'Material experience: Peter Zumthor's thermal baths at Vals', *Senses and Society*, 2(3), pp. 363–368.

Nolan, M. (1986) 'Pilgrimage traditions and the nature mystique in Western European culture', *Journal of Cultural Geography*, 7(1), pp. 4–20.

O'Dell, T. (2005) 'Meditation, magic and spiritual regeneration', in O. Löfgren and R. Willim (eds), *Magic,Culture and the New Economy*, Oxford: Berg, pp. 19–36.

Ouida (1880) *Moths*, London: Chatto and Windus, 2 vols.

Pauly, R.M. (2003) 'L'année derniere à Marienbad' [Last Year at Marienbad], in *eadem, The Transparent Illusion: Image and Ideology in French Text and Film*, New York: Peter Lang, pp. 323–327.

Scudèry, M. de (1973) *Clélie, histoire romaine*, Geneva: Slatkine (Reprint of 1660 edn: original work published in 1654).

Shelley, M. (1844) *Rambles in Germany and Italy in 1840, 1841 and 1843 by Mrs Shelley*, London: E. Moxon, 2 vols.

Sinclair, J.E. (2005) *Salons and Spas: the Architecture of Beauty*, Beverly, MA: Rockport.

Smyth, F. (2005) 'Medical geography: therapeutic places, spaces and networks', *Progress in Human Geography*, 29(4), pp. 488–495.

Steward, J, (2000) 'The spa towns of the Austrian-Hungarian empire and the growth of tourist culture: 1860–1914', in P. Borsay, G., Hirshfelder and R-E. Mohrmann (eds), *Aspects of European Urban Cultural Life in the Mirror of Art, Health and Tourism*, New York/Munich/Berlin: Waxmann, pp. 87–126.

Steward, J. (2002) 'The culture of the water cure in nineteenth-century Austria, 1800–1914', in S.B. Anderson and B. Taube (eds), *Water, Culture and Leisure. European Historical Perspectives*, Oxford: Berg, pp. 23–35.

Steward, J. (2008) 'The "social pathology" of tourism: food, diet and therapy in nineteenth and early twentieth century spa culture 1800–1914', in P. Lysaght (ed.), *Sanitas per Acqua: Spa, Lifestyles and Foodways*, Innsbruck: Studium, pp. 103–118.

Steward, J. (Forthcoming 2011) 'Travel to the spas: the growth of health tourism in Central Europe 1850–1914', in G. Blackshaw and S. Wieber (eds), *Journeys into Madness: Mapping Mental Illness in Vienna 1900*, Oxford: Berghahn.

Stocking, M. K. (1995) *The Clairmont Correspondence: lLetters of Claire Clairmont, Charles Clairmont, and Fanny Imlay Godwin*. Baltimore: Johns Hopkins University Press.

Todorov, T. (1996) 'The journey and its narratives', in C. Chard and H. Langdon (eds), *Transports: Travel, Pleasure and Imaginative Geography, 1600–1830*, New Haven and London, pp. 257–296.

Trollope, F. (1834), *Belgium and Western German in 1833, including visits to Baden-Baden, Wiesbaden, Cassel, Hanover and the Hartz Mountains*, London: John Murray, 2 vols.

Wallon, A. (1981) *La vie quotidienne dans les villes d'eaux 1850–1914*, Paris: Hachette.

Wechsberg, J. (1979) *The Lost World of the Great Spas*, London: Weidenfeld and Nicholson.

Weldon, F. (2007) *The Spa Decameron*, London: Quercus.

Wood, K. (2004) 'Spa Culture and the Social History of Medicine in Germany', PhD diss., University of Chicago.

PART III
Institutionalizing Emotions in Tourism

Chapter 13

'I'm sorry I got emotional': 'Real' Work and 'Real' Men at the Canadian Cottage

Julia Harrison

What makes grown men weep when they talk about their life at the Canadian cottage? What is it about some male second home tourists or cottagers as they are known locally respond so emotionally and passionately to this experience?[1] In the first decades of the 21st century, during the spring and summer months, the joys and rewards of the Ontario cottage experience are a recurrent theme in any one of the lifestyle, travel, magazine, business, real estate, and even news sections of at least one Canadian national newspaper (see for example Clark 2010; Ward 2010; Cheney 2002). *Cottage Life*, a magazine has been extolling the virtues of this experience since it began publication the late1980s. For many of those who have experienced, and remain committed to life at the cottage, there is little that could be more desirable than sitting on the dock, favourite beverage in hand, swathed in languid summer heat, surveying the calm and beauty of the lake as the sun slowly dips below the horizon. But it is more than this. In this chapter I discuss the cottage as a site of 'masculine domesticity' for a group of middle class Canadian men, a place where their labours are seen to constitute 'real work', and which carry with them intense emotional rewards. In the discourse about the 'the cottage' it is continually constructed as a bucolic place, a place of unending leisure and fulfilment; a place where family and friends gather, and treasured memories are forged. Cottagers with whom I had conversations in the Haliburton region of Ontario would in large measure agree with these representations. But for many of them such blissful moments emerge only from the background of labour and industry that owning a cottage demands. However, this latter reality, I quickly learned from the male cottagers I interviewed, encapsulates its own dimensions of enticing rewards, pleasures and enjoyment, which can be as satisfying as any moments of leisure stolen at the end of the summer's day.

1   I would like to acknowledge the financial support of the Social Science and Humanities Research Council of Canada and the Symons Trust Fund for their support of this research. I would like to thank all the cottagers who so openly shared their stories and their love of the cottage with me; Jessica Ellison for her editorial and research assistance; Svitlana Grouin for her excellent interviews and thoughtful reflections on them; and John Wadland for first taking me to the cottage and for all the great conversations we have shared there.

Ontario cottages by their very nature are largely seasonal properties on waterfronts subject to the vagaries of such environs. They are structures which at the very least must battened down in the fall to withstand the cold, the winds and the snows of winter, and then opened up again in the spring – activities which demand significant amounts of physical labour, can generate considerable sweat, even a few tears, if not colourful language. In addition to these seasonal labours, there is the ongoing maintenance of buildings, docks, septic systems, roadways, boats, and other 'cottage toys'. These tasks are separate and additional to any upgrades and improvements to the original structure that cottagers undertake. For example, it progressively became more desirable to have electric heat at the cottage, rather than to rely on a woodstove for warmth against the blustery winds of early summer and autumn. Such ongoing labours generate the seamless backdrop to the paradisiacal moments I alluded to above. These efforts, however, are not necessarily considered the burden that a non-cottager (such as myself) might presume them to be. Some, particularly the male cottagers I spoke with, provided a somewhat different assessment. They told me:

> A cottage is work. Many of these things require physical work of a scope and intensity that would not be acceptable in a city job. Oddly, many people relish this because of the deep satisfaction that comes with physical exertion and the ability to say, 'I built that with my own hands'.

> There's always something else to be fixed. You don't think about anything else, you're out in the fresh air. Cottaging is not for the weak.

In this chapter, with reference to a group of male cottagers in the Haliburton region of Ontario, Canada with whom I have conducted research, I attempt to situate historically some of the roots of the discourse of 'work' at the cottage in relation to ideas of the family, capitalist economy and 'masculine domesticity' in the immediate post WWII era (which is when many of the cottages in Haliburton were built). I begin, however, with a brief overview of my larger research project of which this chapter is but a small piece.

Finding Meaning in Cottage Life

My larger research project was intended to gain some understanding of what the cottage experience means to the middle class Ontario cottager. When I moved to Ontario over 15 years ago from western Canada, I was struck by the assumption communicated in the local media and in conversations with friends that everyone had, and continued to desire, the opportunity to spend time each summer at a waterfront property in Ontario's 'cottage country'. This experience was presented as the quintessential 'Canadian' experience, ignoring the fact that not all regions of Canada have a 'cottage culture', or even the thousands of lakes to provide the locations for such development; and secondly, that class, race, and cultural differences might not make this experience an accessible, or even a desirable one.[2]

Additionally, to a non-cottager the cottage could seem to have questionable 'virtues'. Tales of the regular weekend trips endured on clogged freeways; the annual labour required to install the dock, (and the strained back which resulted); the extermination of mice or other vermin which might have taken up residence over the winter; the requisite annual cleaning needed to simply rid the place of the dust, cobwebs and mildew that accumulated over the winter; and the complications of getting the septic pump running were just some of the things that seemed to occupy cottagers on the 'joyful' first weekend at the cottage in May – and this was only the beginning of the summer! These more immediate concerns join a coterie of others which range from worrying about the weight of the snow that accumulates on the cottage's ageing roof each winter; or the trees that may have fallen on the roof in the latest windstorm; the disappearing shorelines and deteriorating water quality of the lake; an ever-increasing tax bill; the rowdy renters who now seem to dominate the water with their high speed boats each weekend; and the appropriate inheritance strategies required to insure that family wars do not erupt over the property after its original owners are deceased. What makes this experience such a treasured one did not appear to be obvious to this outsider.

In fact less only about 8 per cent of Ontarians own cottages.[3] Many others have access to the experience through those owned by relatives and friends, or through an annual rental of a cottage for a week or two in the summer. Despite what a non-cottager might rationally perceive the experience to be, many cottagers have very strong emotional ties to their cottage. As one colleague told me early in my research, 'my cottage is everything to me'. I was later to be told by cottagers I interviewed that they would readily sell the family home, but the cottage was something that they would never part with. It held too much 'sentimental value'. It was where 'their heart was'. It was their 'true home'. I started my current research project to try to grasp more fully why the cottage experience generates such strong attachment and commitment.[4]

---

2   I do not mean to suggest that there is not a cottaging tradition in other parts of Canada. There certainly is, yet it does not appear to have been as ubiquitous as it is in Ontario. In fact to many residents of other parts of the country is a completely foreign experience—as it is for many working class, non-Caucasian Ontarians. The latter is a reality that seems to escape recognition in much of the discourse around cottaging in Ontario. For a discussion of the understanding of this latter experience as a 'Canadian' one, see Harrison 2010.

3   Statistics Canada data 1997 to 2008. See http://cansim2.statcan.gc.ca/cgi-win/ CNSMCGI.PGM?LANG=Eng&Dir-Rep=CII/&CNSM-Fi=CII/CII_1-eng.htm. (accessed on 8 November 2010).

4   My interest in this subject was prompted further as an outgrowth of my earlier work on the meaning of travel to a group of inveterate middle class Canada tourists (Harrison 2003), and as I mediated heated discussions among my undergraduate students, almost equally split between those who are cottagers and those who come from small towns who

It is important to note that there are several 'cottage countries' in Ontario, each with its own particular character and geography. I have focused my research in the largely middle class cottaging experience in the Haliburton area of Ontario. My comments below are based on lengthy interviews with 50 cottagers from a number of lakes in the Haliburton area of Ontario.[5]

Many, but certainly not all of the cottages in this area, were developed in the immediate post-World War II era. However, I did interview a few cottagers whose grandparents, often their grandfather, had had a very rustic hunting cabin in the area in the 1930s. A few others had spent their summers as children with their grandparents at cottages in the late 1930s and 1940s.[6] Such experiences were the exception, however.

The post-World War II expansion of cottaging in the Haliburton region was positioned as a much more affordable middle-class experience relative to the adjacent Muskoka region. The latter was one of the first areas in Ontario to be developed for cottaging and summer residence, beginning largely with an influx of wealthy Americans in the late 19th and early 20th centuries. Throughout the first fifty years of the 20th century Muskoka in very large measure became the purview of the wealthy, if not the very wealthy. It also achieved an iconic status for the cottaging experience in Ontario. Adjacent lake-filled areas like Haliburton offered a more affordable 'cottage country', although it certainly had been an area of tourist interest since the early decades of the 20th century (Baker 1930). Haliburton lacked the large lakes that are seen to be the jewels of the Muskoka experience, but the area includes many good-sized lakes that embody many of the aesthetic qualities – exposed Canadian Shield rock and tree lined shores – championed in Muskoka. Haliburton cottagers today would argue that 'their lakes' have many more virtues than anything that could be found in the overcrowded, elitist enclave of Muskoka. Haliburton developers in the 1950s and 1960s aimed their sales

---

receive the summer influx of cottagers, over whether they (the cottagers) should be classed as tourists (see Jaakson 1986).

5   A graduate student working on this research with me interviewed about 25 cottagers in Haliburton as part of her own research into their attitudes and ideas of nature at the cottage. Her interviews were structured by a protocol of questions she and I developed, intended to encompass my broader and her more specific research interests. Her transcripts have been added into my body of research materials. Both of us interviewed our cottagers once. A few have maintained ongoing email contact with me throughout the course of my research to date.

6   These cottages were located on lakes adjacent to Highway 35 a main access route through the region. This highway had been improved and upgraded in the 1930s as part of a government make-work project. A few of the cottagers who had spent time at these cottages in the pre-WWII era noted that their grandparents used these properties as subsistence plots. Their grandfathers would fish in the summer, freezing their catch for transport back to the city in the fall. Their grandmothers would plant large gardens at the lake and pick wild berries, canning, pickling or preserving all the produce to take back to the city for winter consumption.

campaigns at the newly emerging middle class southern Ontario residents, who had begun to experience a sufficient degree of prosperity that they could consider acquiring a summer cottage, no matter how modest. Acquiring such a property allowed them an opportunity to emulate the experience of the wealthier upper-class Muskoka cottagers, something particularly relevant to the upwardly mobile aspirations that can be seen to characterize this group.

It became obvious soon after would-be farmers/settlers arrived in the mid-19th century that the Haliburton area had very limited agricultural potential. Extensive tracts of land were soon sold to lumber companies, resulting in the heavy logging of the area by the end of the century. Rapacious extraction continued in the area until the 1930s (Reynolds 1973). But by the 1950s, a second growth forest had started to cover over the craggy landscape, masking its industrial scars, veiling it with the requisite aesthetic qualities to make it appealing to those who could imagine it as a recreational landscape.

Cottage lots were sold off on different lakes in the Haliburton area in the 1950s and 1960s in varying ways. Sometimes a local farmer, knowing his lakeshore land was of little value to his fragile enterprise, would sell off a few cottage lots. In other cases larger landowners in the area would subdivide a chunk of land for cottage development. In some cases, lumber companies started to sell off tracts of land to developers who would subdivide the property for cottage development. In my comments below I use as my central example a development that began on Haliburton Lake in 1952. The latter was a relatively large lake located in the northeast corner of the county. In many ways this expansion was typical of cottage development in the region during this period: two entrepreneurial individuals acquired a block of lakeshore land from a local timber baron who owned much of the waterfront property. They then subdivided the land into 100 foot lots with a small basic cottage to be erected on each. What was distinctive about the Haliburton Lake development was that there was limited recreational development on the lake prior to the 1952 development, possibly largely due to the relatively poor road access into the lake at this time. Secondly, it was a large development – 500 cottage lots – that were to be sold at one time. Some of the lots that were sold (particularly those in South Bay) might have been considered somewhat less than desirable as they were, as the advertisements said, 'high'. What this meant was that there was a steep, rocky, and tree covered embankment to be navigated to get down to the lake. A compensatory virtue was that the cottages were to be built near the top of these embankments, which did eventually provide relatively easy vehicular access. This topography required the construction by the cottagers of navigable paths or steps down the hill to get to the water. Additionally, as with many parts of the county, the Haliburton Lake area had been logged and many of the 'beach' and waterfront areas were generously littered with deadfall remnants of the activity. But because of the 'en masse' development on the lake, a strong sense of community developed as everyone was facing the same challenges in making their cottages habitable and their lakeshores accessible.

The cottages built as part of this development were basic constructions. All came with only partial internal partitions rather than full walls between the rooms; they lacked kitchen cupboards and counters; there was no indoor plumbing or water which meant it had to be ferried up the hill from the lake in pails; initially outhouses had to be dug and installed, to be followed often later with the installation of septic systems; some initially had few windows. In sum, little finishing had been done to the interiors of the cottages when they were turned over to their new owners. Many of the lots had only been cleared sufficiently to erect the cottage; parking and driveways had to be constructed, along with access routes to the water. And then there was the work to be done on the lakeshore to reduce the hazards for swimming and the use of boats. As one cottager told me his joyous childhood memories at the cottage are tempered by those of the never-ending list of jobs to be done each week.

Acquiring a Cottage on Haliburton Lake

Many of the Haliburton Lake cottagers I interviewed told me of the legendary mobs of would-be cottagers eager to put down a deposit on the cottage lots being offered for sale on Haliburton Lake in the fall of 1952. Various ads in Toronto newspapers had been placed by Ridout Real Estate for the 500 cottages lots offered for sale in the first major recreational development on this somewhat isolated, but very picturesque lake in Haliburton County. I heard stories of money literally being thrown at the salesmen who set up promotional booths in the fall of 1952 at venues such as the Toronto Sportsmen Show to market these properties. Cheques were being tossed at them faster than they could tally them. A $100 deposit would hold a lot, and the choice of one of four basic frame cottages. The full price of the package was $2500 (CAN), which could be paid off with monthly payments of $38.75 for five years. The development sold out quickly.

These Torontonians were buying their piece of paradise sight unseen, many without any real sense of where the lake was even located. They got their first chance to see their intended investment and to come up with the remainder of the $500 deposit on a rainy weekend in May, 1953. Ridout Realty chartered a train from Union Station in Toronto, and eventually several buses to take people up to Haliburton Lake, where these would-be cottagers, despite the inclement weather of the weekend began, as one newspaper reporter observed, 'envisioning swims, fishing trips and holiday fun' (Honeyford 1953, p. 25). People were taken out in small boats to see their proposed purchase. It must have taken a leap of faith to see these as cottage properties, for as I have said many could not even directly access their lots due to logging debris in the lake and the dense bush that covered some of them. However, few it seems were deterred. Some, the tales suggest, horse-traded lots among themselves while out on the water, but I heard no stories of the abandonment of purchases.

Information distributed to the prospective buyers outlined the construction details of the cottages, along with the 'extras' that could be included such as log siding and picture windows; the latter, of course, for additional costs. It also listed other amenities such as electrical wiring, plumbing and painting that would need to be done by the cottager himself, in his anticipated 'spare time' at the lake. It was clear from the very beginning that access to leisure time at the cottage on Haliburton Lake would cost these new cottage owners more than dollars. From its earliest days, it was expected that the experience would extract from them their physical labour. It also apparently presumed that the cottager, who was always of course referred to as male, would have a working knowledge of such things as wiring, plumbing and painting.[7]

Rebuilding the Family in the post-World War II Era

In the immediate post-World War II era, two related themes were widespread in Canadian public discourse. One was the rebuilding of the Canadian family; and other, the very nature of what was the ideal structure and nature of that family (Gölz 1993). The former was something seen by some to still be carrying the scars of Depression poverty, which had resulted in a declining birth rate, the conceptualization of children as a 'burden', and particularly relevant for my discussion here, what sociologist Gölz (1993, p. 12) described as 'the subversion of the unemployed male breadwinner's traditional familial authority'. Additionally, the topsy-turvy social realities of the World War II era had seen women temporarily enter the workforce in unprecedented large numbers. As the war effort ended and men arrived home in large numbers to take up new forms of employment, women were displaced to resume their more traditional, and assumedly preferred, roles of homemakers and mothers.[8] There was a sense that Canadian society in the immediate post-war era had to regain its stability in the face of the 'perceived relaxation of social morals and a concomitant rise in illegitimacy, and the increase in hasty and unstable marriages' (Gölz 1993, p. 13) that for some characterized the war years.

Initiatives like the 1944 Family Allowance Act in Canada were an attempt to re-stabilize and nurture the 'ideal' Canadian family, asserting what Gölz (1993, p. 17) calls the 'hegemony of familialism'. By default this Act reasserted quite

---

7   I am restricting my comments here to the experience of men at the cottage. With this focus I do not mean to suggest that the cottaging experience exempted women from physical labour. These early days at the cottage most certainly also increased the burden of performing basic domestic duties such as cooking, laundry (most of which was done in the lake or with a scrub board in a tub), and cleaning. Full treatment of this reality is the subject of another paper.

8   While women did leave the workforce, their departure was not as immediate or as permanent as it is often represented (Strong-Boag 1991, p. 479).

powerfully that the real place for women was in the home, raising children, while men resumed their appropriate role as the main breadwinner in the family (Gölz 1993, p. 28). The massive expansion of suburbs in Canada, both isolated women in the home, and in some measure established clear demarcations between work and non-work for men who now found themselves commuting further to their places of employment (Strong-Boag 1991; Rutherdale 1999).

The post-war Canadian revitalized 'modern family' was not the family of the Victorian era, particularly in reference to the role of the father. The 1950s family's key role and 'essence became almost exclusively interlinked with the provision of "close affectionate relationships, personal ties and happiness of belonging and being loved"' (as quoted in Gölz 1993, p. 27). Fathers were to play a new role here.

Marriages of the 1950s were understood to be companionate partnerships meaning, in theory, at the very least men played a more obvious role in the domestic lives and spaces of their families. Fatherhood was to be seen as part of family life (Rutherdale 1999, p. 353; Strong-Boag 1991, p. 475). Fathers were supposed 'to be warm and nurturing parents' as Gelber (1997, p. 94) has noted. This shift lead to the emergence of what Margaret Marsh called 'masculine domesticity', referring to 'the adoption of family- and-home-centred practices among fathers'. She includes three structural factors necessary for 'the emergence of masculine domesticity': sufficient family incomes for a middle-class standard of living; work schedules that allowed fathers to return home daily at consistent times; and sufficient family living space that permitted recreational spaces both within and out of the home (as quoted in Rutherdale 1999, p. 352). Such ideas determined that certain domestic tasks came to be labelled as male. Christopher Dummitt (1998) suggests that outdoor cooking, specifically barbecuing was one key example. He suggests that it 'linked outdoor cooking to symbols of virile masculinity and manly leisure' (Dummitt 1998, p. 212). The physical location of this cookery is a key point here.

Skilfully being able to cook hamburgers and hot dogs on the patio barbeque, however, was not the only example of masculine domesticity. Mothers continued to be responsible for the day-to-day lives of their children, but 1950s fathers were expected to take on a role as 'pals ... [as] hockey or baseball coaches' (Owram 1996, p. 86), unlike the more austere and distant patriarchal roles of their own early 20th century fathers. Regardless of these niche roles to be filled by father, the transition into the female domestic space of the suburban home was not always an easy one. Most comfort seemed to be found for the new domesticated father in spaces separate, or even completely removed, from the central domestic arena. Fathers could be found most contentedly located in spaces external to the main living spaces of the family home: basement workshops, patios, the lawn (an expanse which could always be guaranteed to need mowing!), the hockey arena, the baseball diamond, or even more distantly, organizing life in the campground, and most relevant here, at the cottage. Gelber (1997, p. 76) would argue that following the earlier 'disappearance of the library, men still seem to want a room of their own, [which lead to the] setting aside [of] some territory for themselves'.

Such masculine spaces 'permitted men to be both a part of the house and apart from it, sharing the home with their families while retaining spatial and functional autonomy' (Gelber 1997, p. 69).

To Gelber (1999, p. 5) one place men were busy carving out a masculine space in the feminine domestic domain of the suburban home in the post-World War II era was in their workshops. From here they took part in the 'great do-it-yourself boom of the 1950s'. In this context, household chores for them frequently became hobbies, and vice versa. At this point the bifurcation of work and leisure started to disintegrate, something with which the cottagers I spoke with would in large measure acknowledge (Gelber 1999, p. 6.). Through the 1950s, a man's workshop, located usually in the basement or garage of his suburban home, became 'command central' for husband/father, the hobbyist/do-it-yourselfer (Gelber 1997, p. 69).

In keeping with the externality of the domestic spaces most readily occupied by middle class fathers of the 1950s, and a measure of their commercial and financial success as breadwinners, were the vacations and holidays away from home they could afford and plan for their families (Rutherdale 1998, p. 316). Fred Bodsworth, a 1950s Maclean's columnist, posited that automobile camping was clearly a way that men could show their prowess in 'things domestic'. Such activities, he charged, put 'the male back in the role of provider and protector' (as quoted in Rutherdale 1999, p. 354). Planning and executing automobile camping trips, building cottages, and developing extensive knowledge of boats and motors for excursions away from home, are just some of examples of what I would call the physically externalized masculine domesticity in the 1950s.

The Cottage as a Do-It-Yourself Project

Of particular interest in any discussion of the cottage are those hobbyists who emerged as 'do-it-yourselfers', whose main interests were developing, building and repairing things and spaces in the domestic sphere. Being able to build, wire, plumb, or paint things oneself, rather than hiring a professional, to Gelber (1997, p. 68) gave these activities, 'an aura of masculine legitimacy', something which the proliferation of more effete office work failed to offer middle-class men. It re-connected these men with the experience of manual labour, guaranteed to produce a sweat, something which 50 years later, my cottagers affirmed constituted 'real work'. One of my cottagers corroborated such valences, as he suggested, 'nobody ever breaks a sweat sitting in front of a computer'.

By the 1950s 'being handy had, like sobriety and fidelity, become an expected quality in a good husband' (Gelber 1997, p. 98). It would seem that being able to successfully carry out home improvements, being able to do the myriad of manual labour projects needed to make cottages such as those being purchased on Haliburton Lake in the early1950s habitable, and as I would argue, family spaces, was simply expected if all those who bought them were 'typical suburban middle class men' of the era. And in large measure, from what I have been told, many of them were. Most lived their 'city lives' in some of the expansive suburban developments that sprang up around Toronto.[9]

But even if they possessed the handyman's basic skills, what prompted them to fully tax these by taking on a rather basic elemental cottage in the relative wilderness of Haliburton Lake? Why would they make the commitment to spend each weekend from May to September travelling over rough, often nearly impassable roads for up to six hours every Friday night, returning the same route every Sunday, to spend the intervening hours doing such things as digging outhouses, clearing land, or building steps down steep rocky embankments, swarmed by mosquitoes and black flies, often lacking the real tools and expertise needed to do the job?

Fathers and the Idea of the Family in the 1950s

The desire to acquire a cottage, even a pretty basic one, was spawned, at least in part, from the then contemporary middle class notions of what a 'good' Canadian (to be read here as middle class upwardly mobile Ontarian) father would do.[10] These men, if somewhat less overtly than those who had earlier crafted such things as the Family Allowance legislation, were engaged in their own project of affirming what the 'real' Canadian family was. Such initiatives were shaped by the ideological assumptions of the time that the modern Canadian family would be the place where 'close affectionate relationships, personal ties and happiness of belonging and being loved' would be fostered (as quoted in Golz 1993, p. 27). It is important to note here that the cottage experience was seen to play a key role in keeping families together and in building strong intergenerational kinship bonds. One cottager told me, 'if it were not for our cottage, we would not have a family'. She was referring to something far more than simply having produced her offspring – although I did hear more than one story of how many children were actually conceived at the cottage! She was referring to the strength of kinship relations that members of her family had been able to nurture due to the time they spent at the cottage. Many others I interviewed echoed her sentiments.

---

9   There are exceptions to this classification of those who owned cottages. On Haliburton Lake there is a small enclave of families who purchased cottages in 1952 who were line workers at General Motors in Oshawa, a smaller city about an hour drive east of Toronto. There were a few others who lived in other smaller urban centres, some of these had farming backgrounds dating back to the late 19th century. But none of these individuals continued to farm as their grandparents and in some cases their parents had done. None lived in rural settings in their lives 'away from the cottage'.

10   I make my comments here with specific and limited reference to middle class Ontario male cottagers. I am not implying that the latter is necessarily indicative or representative of other parts of the country. I am not in any way suggesting that what was done in Ontario should be taken as being symbolic of Canada, even if that was what many of my cottagers seemed to imply.

Cottages, I would argue, became arenas where many middle class fathers could further affirm their role and place in the domestic space. The more these structures became monuments to the 'do-it-yourself' ideal, the more firmly they were claimed as prime arenas of 'masculine domesticity'. As such many of the men I interviewed developed enormous emotional attachment to these places. In just talking to me, in many ways a stranger and certainly initially an outsider, about their attachment to their cottage, more than one male cottager began to quietly weep, leading one to apologize, as the title for this chapter suggests.

Throughout the 1950s and 1960s for many of these cottagers, the pattern of 'Mum and the kids at the cottage for the summer' and Dad commuting from the city for the weekends and taking up residence only for his annual two week vacation' emerged. Ironically, women often spent far more time than their husbands did at the cottage. Regardless, I had more than one female cottager tell me that she committed herself to life at the cottage as it was a place so rich with meaning for her husband, even if for many years, had she been honest, she would have admitted a significant degree of ambivalence about being resident at the cottage alone with her children all summer.[11] In addition, many of these men spent the vast majority of their time when they finally arrived at the cottage fully engaged in a wide array of manual labour projects – which many insisted were fun in their own right – not experiencing the 'swims' and 'fishing trips' and 'holiday fun' it was once imagined that they would. Clearly there is a link between these labours and the meaningfulness of this place for these men, and its influence on their families.

The Canadian Family at the Cottage in the 1950s

Veronica Strong-Boag (1991, pp. 486–487, 491–492) argues that in the ubiquitous and uniform enclaves of standard plan three bedroom bungalows that came to constitute the Canadian suburbs in the 1950s, 'women were [left] to forge the moral basis for post-war Canada'. It was women who worked to change these capitalist real estate developments into humane spaces, fighting for improved public transport, schools, libraries, playgrounds, shopping facilities, sidewalks, garbage collection, and sewers, and founding along the way parent-teacher groups and other community organizations and advocacy groups while their husbands were away at the office (Strong-Boag 1991, pp. 495–496). So if their hard work and diligence began to transform the suburbs from corporate investments to more suitable, even something initially approaching humane places to raise a family, what drove families to leave them for the summer? Why re-locate to spend as much time as possible with one's children at a place which lacked many amenities, often including such basic things as running water, indoor toilets, laundry facilities,

---

11   These women would also acknowledge that they came to see the cottage as a most valuable experience for their children.

access to commercial shops and services, and where a black bear, rather than your neighbour was just as likely to greet you when you stepped out your door?

No matter to what extent of the landscaped lawn and garden that surrounded your three bedroom suburban bungalow, or the expanse of the adjacent playgrounds or schoolyards that were developed, suburbs would always remain urban spaces. They would lack that something that being close to the lake, surrounded by rocky shores and trees offered. As such were they the best locations for the nurturance of the 'real' Canadian family? Could they provide the appropriate leisure spaces for the family?

Roberts and Sutton-Smith convincingly argue that 'class or national character influences the choice of leisure activity, and in that activity … "the ideological heritage of a social system" is maintained or reinforced' (as quoted in Gelber 1999, p. 14). Particular leisure activities are embraced when they engage a group's basic values and beliefs, their ideology according to Gelber (1999, p. 15). Thus what was it about the 1950s suburb that for some challenged basic ideological beliefs about the best place to nurture a Canadian family? And how were these values more aptly affirmed at the cottage?

The authors of the 1947 Canadian Youth Commission report sentimentally claimed that Canada moulded 'her families in ways which were her own, wielding the power for climate and space … in the hard struggle with nature' (Gölz 1993, p. 17). They continued that it was the 'the snows, the winds, the spaces, the woods and the rocks of Canada … *made* the Canadian family' (emphasis added; as quoted in Gölz 1993, p. 11). Such influences, even if somewhat romanticized, would perfunctorily dismiss the suburb as the best location to raise a family.

While suburbs may provide the necessary amenities for a modern family – comfortable houses, schools, libraries, shops, and community groups along with viable employment for the family breadwinner – some would argue that they separated the Canadian family from the primary influences that shaped the desired national character. Tropes such as the mythic pioneer carving out a life from the beautiful but all-too-often unforgiving – and unproductive – landscape, as I have argued elsewhere are frequently imagined to instil economic, emotional, social, aesthetic, nationalistic, moral value, and ultimately what it means to be Canadian (Harrison 2010; Wolfe 1977; Luka 2006, p. 279). If such experiences were understood to be the fundamental ones that shaped basic tenets of the Canadian character and ideology, then a periodic return to them in pursuit of a leisure experience would be something that could hold a comfortable resonance. Additionally, if the suburbs of the 1950s were primarily the domain of women, and despite the territorial claim of men to the patio, basement workshop, hockey arena and baseball diamond, then the cottage, like the campground, could also be claimed as space of masculine domesticity. Somehow it seems that such masculine spaces retained an aura of greater veracity as 'Canadian' spaces than the female space of the suburb.

Such spaces were more obviously directly linked to the rocks, woods and waters of the Canadian landscape which some claimed shaped the national psyche of the era. Potentially these were additional male spaces in which a 'real' Canadian family could be nurtured. These spaces required that men reclaim or re-learn in significant ways how to carve a domestic space from a more primal landscape, for as many were to learn, excavating slabs of the Canadian Shield to install a septic system, or hauling enormous deadfall logs from the beach could prove to be far more challenging than anything encountered in the building of the rumpus room in a suburban bungalow. Life in what must have seemed for some the 'harsh conditions of the backwoods' was not the life of the suburb, even if one takes into account that the development at Haliburton Lake was a pretty tame version of the 'backwoods'. It was still a long way in many aspects from the female domain of the suburb. As Strong-Boag (1991, pp. 489–490) suggests, 'wives were tethered to their [suburban] communities in ways that few husbands could match ... the suburban house remained first of all a workplace for female residents'. And in the end that is what possibly made the emerging 1950s cottage appealing. It can be seen as a quintessential example of the 'reassertion of traditional male control of the physical environment ... in a way that evoked pre-industrial manual competence' (Gelber 1997, p. 68). The cottage was so brilliantly exemplary of this as it demanded such a wide array of 'masculine skills' – engineering, plumbing, electrical, mechanical, large scale painting, lumbering, excavation, carpentry, and design – be undertaken. All required a multiplicity of knowledge, planning, skills, and use of tools. Such masculine domestic skills were attributed to men, as women were largely 'limited ... to helping their ... husbands and acting as an appreciative audience to their triumphs' (Gelber 1997, p. 68). Such were the benefits of the truly externalized domain of masculine domesticity, the cottage.

Conclusion

One might not expect a middle class Canadian man who owned a cottage on a piece of waterfront property to quietly weep in mid-conversation with a researcher they had only just met. The embarrassed apologies that followed flagged the unexpected nature of such occurrences. What was it about the experience of these Haliburton second home male tourists or cottagers that prompted such emotional eruptions? In this chapter I have argued that one source of the men's deep attachment to their cottages can be seen to be linked to a particular masculine identity grounded in notions of what it means to be 'Canadian'. The latter connects these men to a profound sense of home and belonging that is tethered to notions of the strength and physical competencies required to carve a comfortable life from the vast and unforgiving Canadian northern landscape. Such efforts afford these men the opportunity to work like 'real men'. These second homes demand that they perform 'real work' that incorporate a vast array of physical labours. The latter are something that stand in contrast to those that are sedentary, such as office work, activities that fail to make one, 'break a sweat'.

The cottage in sum provides an externalized space within the domestic sphere for men to claim. Their willing and almost unrelenting investment of physical labour in this domain fuels their emotional investment in it. By extension such activities symbolized a commitment to, and pleasure in, their family. As such these spaces have direct links to the re-definition of the identities and roles of men that emerged in the immediate post-World War II era in middle class suburban expansion in Canada. Affordable postwar cottage development in Haliburton County in Ontario, Canada became a place 'thick with meaning' for middle class men (Williams and Kaltenborn 1999). The cottage was far more than piece of waterfront property with a modest dwelling on it to these individuals. It was a profound symbol of what they saw themselves to be. It made sense that they might express intense emotion when talking about their connection to such places.

References

Baker, R.H. (1930) *A Brief History of Names in the County of Haliburton*, Haliburton: Provisional County of Haliburton.

Cheney, P. (2002) 'Cottage wars', *Globe and Mail*, May 18, pp. F1, F8.

Clark, A. (2010) 'That crazy cottage commute', *Globe and Mail*, 23 July, http://www.theglobeandmail.com/site-search/?q=clark+crazy (accessed January 1, 2011) [newspaper article]

Dummitt, C. (1998) 'Finding a pace for father: Selling the barbeque in postwar America', *Journal of the Canadian Historical Association*, 9(1), pp. 209–223.

Gelber, S. (1997) 'Do-It-Yourself: Constructing, repairing and maintaining domestic masculinity', *American Quarterly*, 49(1), pp. 66–112.

Gelber, S. (1999) *Hobbies: Leisure and the Culture of Work in America*, New York: Columbia University Press.

Golz, A. (1993) 'Family matters: The Canadian family and the state in the postwar period', *Left History*, 1(2), pp. 9–49.

Harrison, J. (2003) *Being a Tourist: Finding Meaning in Pleasure Travel*, Vancouver: University of British Columbia Press.

Harrison, J. (2010) 'Belonging at the Cottage', in J. Scott and T. Selwyn (eds), *Thinking Through Tourism*, New York: Berg, pp. 71–92.

Honeyford, H. (1953) 'Villagers welcome summer residents', *The Telegram*, 4 May, p. 25.

Jaakson, R. (1986) 'Second-Home Domestic Tourism', *Annals of Tourism Research*, 13(3), pp. 367–391.

Luka, N. (2006) *Placing the 'Natural' Edges of a Metropolitan Region through Multiple Residency: Landscape and Urban Form in Toronto's 'Cottage Country'*, University of Toronto.

Owram, D. (1996) *Born at the Right Time: A History of the Baby-Boom Generation*, Toronto: University of Toronto Press.

Reynolds, M. (1973) *In Quest of Yesterday: Haliburton County*, Lindsay: John Deyell Company.

Rutherdale, R. (1998) 'Fatherhood and masculine domesticity during the Baby Boom: Consumption and leisure in advertising and life stories', in L. Chambers and E. Montigny (eds), *Family Matters: Papers on Post-Confederation Canadian Family History*, Toronto: Canadian Scholars Press, pp. 309–333.

Rutherdale, R. (1999) 'Fatherhood, masculinity, and the good life during Canada's Baby Boom, 1945–1965', *Journal of Family History*, 24(3), pp. 351–373.

Strong-Boag, V. (1991) 'Home dreams: Women and the suburban experiment in Canada, 1945–1960', *Canadian Historical Review*, 72(4), pp. 471–504.

Ward, B. (2010) 'The cottage-country grim reaper', *Globe and Mail*, 6 July, http://www.theglobeandmail.com/life/facts-and-arguments/the-cottage-country-grim-reaper/article1630094/print (accessed January 1, 2011)

Williams, D. and Kaltenborn, B. (1999) 'Leisure places and modernity: The use and meaning of recreational properties in Norway and the USA', in D. Crouch (ed.), *Leisure/tourism Geographies: Practices and Geographical Knowledge*, London: Routledge, pp. 214–230.

Wolfe, R. (1977) 'Summer cottages in Ontario: Purpose-built for an inessential purpose', in J. Coppock (ed.), *Second Homes: Curse or Blessing?*, Oxford: Pergamon Press, pp. 17–33.

Chapter 14

Romancing the Colonial on Ilha de Mozambique

Pamila Gupta

Introduction

The image of Pedro repeatedly saying 'Obama, Obama' with his big wide eyes, infectious smile and tattered clothes as he followed me through the labyrinth of narrow alleyways that make up Ilha de Mozambique stays with me. It is a refrain that I both smile at and feel saddened by for it is the conditions of history that allow this little boy to understand that my being American equals the promise or 'audacity of hope' of someone like U.S. President Obama with his Muslim name and mixed African/American parentage, and what he could potentially bring to this somewhat forgotten place. Ilha is at the same time a tourist's dream of azure beaches and white sand, a former capital of Portuguese East Africa and centre for a longstanding African slave trade, and a crumbling UNESCO world heritage site (since 1991) that has seen the last of its international funds largely dry up and is now in a state of disrepair and ruins, its thin veil of charm still holding sway however over the few tourists or anthropologists like myself who decide to venture to this desolate island located off the Eastern coast of Northern Mozambique. What follows in this chapter are a series of vignettes or thick description Geertzian stories of fieldwork that I encountered on my visit to Ilha during the month of April 2009. These stories, in turn, have the potential to shed light on what I would like to evoke as 'romancing the colonial' – very much a starting point for thinking analytically about the larger cultural and material spaces of colonial nostalgia that tourist industries endorse and which tourists are drawn to, inhabit and experience when they go elsewhere in search of the past. Perhaps some tourists come away feeling a sense of aesthetic and architectural wonderment, and/or a reconciled sense of self in relation to more complex historical contexts than initially imagined. Or perhaps it is simpler than that and the lure of colonial nostalgia makes them leave feeling relaxed after a few days of rest and relaxation, with a bit of colonial history thrown in; a brief respite from a complicated present. There is no one singular response. However, I do want to argue that there is a politics to this indulgence in the colonial past,[1] an emotive and sensory power that suggests both the forgetting (and the remembering in unexpected ways)

---

1   I want to explore this indulgence in the colonial past even as I recognize and support the initiative to protect these invaluable sites of history and heritage on Ilha de Mozambique.

Figure 14.1   Statues, Ilha de Mozambique © Pamela Gupta

of the layered conditions of history (and history-making) that make tourism on Ilha a possibility here and now. It is little Pedro following me around, with echoes of 'Obama, Obama' ringing in my ears that keep me attuned to how these inflections of colonial nostalgia constantly reverberate and jar with the postcolonial present.

Mise en scène

'Haunting', 'magical', 'time-warped' are all adjectives frequently used to describe Ilha de Mozambique.[2] The *Lonely Planet* guidebook's entry on Ilha introduces us to this hard-to-get-to, out of the way, intriguing place:

> Tiny, crescent-shaped Ilha de Moçambique (Mozambique Island) measures only 3 km in length and barely 500m in width at its widest section. Yet it has played a larger-than-life role in East African coastal life over the centuries, and today is one of the region's most fascinating destinations. Close your eyes for a minute and imagine the now-quiet streets echoing with the footsteps of Arab traders, ushered in on the monsoon winds. Or hear the crisp voice of the Portuguese governor-general barking orders from his plush quarters in the Palácio de São Paulo. Or try to imagine the sweat, anger and despair of the Africans herded into the closed cells of the Fortaleza de São Sebastião before being sold into slavery. Today, Ilha de Moçambique is an intriguing anomaly – part ghost town and part lively fishing community. It's also a picturesque and exceptionally pleasant place to wander around, with graceful praças rimmed by once-grand churches, colonnaded archways and stately colonial-era buildings lining the quiet, cobbled streets of the Stone Town. In Makuti Town, with its thatched-roof huts and crush of people, narrow alleyways echo with the sounds of playing children and squawking chickens, while fisherman sit on the sand repairing their long, brightly coloured nets. Since 1991, this cultural melting pot has been a Unesco World Heritage site and – while there are still many crumbling ruins – there's fresh paint and restoration work aplenty. (Fitzpatrick 2007, pp. 137–138)[3]

The romance of the colonial could hardly be more evocative than this. I have often heard tourists describe Ilha as what Zanzibar was ten years ago,[4] suggesting that while Zanzibar is now a tourist ridden island full of fancy boutiques and restaurants as well as meticulously cleaned streets – that which satisfies every tourist whim available at every turn of the corner – Ilha hasn't quite lost (or at

---

2   http://www.lonelyplanet.com/mozambique/northern-mozambique/ilha-de-mocambique (accessed on 27 June 2009).

3   Interestingly, Mary Fitzpatrick, the author of the *Lonely Planet* guidebook (2007), gets many of the basic facts of Mozambique wrong, provides misinformation and incorrect maps. She clearly visited when there was a boom in UNESCO funding for now most of these sites lay in a state of disrepair. As part of my anthropology of tourism study I looked for these inconsistencies between text and context. How much are our tourist experiences shaped by the guidebooks we read?

4   Comparison is a key analytic central to the discourse of tourism---comparisons between tourist places, sites, and experiences are so often used to make sense of a place and people as well as function as part of the engagement with other tourists while travelling. The fact that Zanzibar becomes a key comparison point for Ilha is not only interesting but analytically significant for showing how Ilha operates in historical and cultural time and space.

Figure 14.2   Street lamp, Ilha de Mozambique © Pamela Gupta

least not yet) its disarming charm of what once was and what is now co-mingling to create elements of surprise, or the unexpected in the midst of colonial decay and ruination on the one hand, and renovation and heritage on the other, these same interstitial traits together assuring us of its modernity (as a place worth seeing)

even as it maintains its conjuncture of different sensibilities, sensations, and smells
– European, Portuguese, Arab, Indian, African, and Mozambican. Herein lays its
value.[5] That there exists a larger sense of urgency for visiting and experiencing the
peculiar charm of Ilha before it is lost to history (like Zanzibar before it) only adds
to its appeal, its allure for tourists and anthropologists alike.[6]

Engaging Colonial Nostalgia, Excavating Ruins

> Thus nostalgia [*nostalghía*] is the desire or longing with burning pain to journey.
> It also evokes the sensory dimension of memory in exile and estrangement; it
> mixes bodily and emotional pain and ties painful experiences of spiritual and
> somatic exile to the notion of maturation and ripening. In this sense, *nostalghía*
> is linked to the personal consequences of historicizing sensory experience which
> is conceived as a painful bodily and emotional journey. (Serematakis 1996, p. 4)

It must be remembered that nostalgia more generally is a longing for something
that cannot be restored, something that is dead, gone, irretrievable, lost. It is also
a response to loss. What follows in this next section is a brief engagement with
colonial nostalgia as a subject and object for anthropological enquiry. As William
Bissell (2005) persuasively argues, we need to take it seriously as we encounter
it during fieldwork, rather than view it from the sidelines as something slightly
uncomfortable to avoid, as simply 'poor or fictitious history', or as something to
be dismissed as 'false consciousness' by those who indulge in and endorse it in its
present tenses. That anthropology itself was constituted as a nostalgic discipline
doesn't help – this makes it both that much more difficult to come to terms with as
well as its study that much more critical and timely (Bissell 2005, pp. 215–216).
Colonial nostalgia is in fact 'deeply unsettling' (Bissell 2005, p. 216). Neither
can we simply label it a 'legacy' or 'vestige' of colonialism nor can we leave
it as just that as Ann Stoler (2008, p. 196) has forcefully argued.[7] Instead, we

---

5   See Gupta (2010a), 'Islandness in the Indian Ocean'. I discuss how islands are
unique spaces of interstitiality, where the layering of complex histories (of multiple
religions, colonialisms, etc.) adds to the unique charm and potential tourism on these
spaces, and which makes the case for comparison between Zanzibar and Ilha an apt one,
only the former is rapidly losing those layers through renovation while Ilha has not quite
yet, but will someday, perhaps inevitably when it has recovered from its war torn past.

6   When I visited Ilha it was low tourist season April, May and June, with about
15–20 tourists on Ilha on average per day. According to Gabriel during the height of the
tourist season from July to August, there are about 100 tourists on Ilha on average per day.
Interview with Gabriel Melazzi, Ilha de Mozambique, 19 April, 2009.

7   Ann Stoler (2008, p. 196) writes: 'A legacy makes no distinctions between what
holds and what lies dormant, between residue and re-composition, between a weak and a
tenacious trace. Such rubrics instil overconfidence in the knowledge that colonial history
matters, far more than it animates an analytic vocabulary for deciphering how it does so.'

require a deeper understanding and more sophisticated language for thinking of its *effects* and *affects*. In other words, that which continues to be negated is both its widespread practice as well as its attraction, its ongoing appeal. Particularly in light of the fact that we are experiencing as Richard Werbner (1998, p. 1) has suggested, an expansive growth or 'striking boom' in colonial nostalgia the world over, there is real sense of urgency for engaging with it as anthropologists, particularly those studying tourism and tourists, since it is often the edifice upon which heritage tourism develops, as well as that which tourism actively recoups or recovers in some sense.

I also want to argue that it is the very material architectural ruins of colonialism that have the power to evoke such nostalgia (in all of us, anthropologists, tourists, and locals alike) for the romance of the colonial in all its past, present, and future tenses. As Nicholas Dirks (1998, p. 10) reminds us,

> The [colonial] ruin is the document of civilization par excellence; it signifies the most onerous toil of the slaves and subalterns who executed the political and architectural ambitions of great civilizations, and the history of its contemplation generates nostalgia, which is the forgetting rather than the remembering of history, the forgetting of the conditions of possibility of history, not to mention its later course ... the ruin puts us in awe of the mystifications that made civilization magnificent in the first place. The ruin is culture, both its reality and its representation.

It is the power of the colonial ruin to function simultaneously as materiality and metaphor that gives it its resilience over time (Stoler 2008, p. 203). And finally, if in fact nostalgia is the 'incurable modern condition' as Svetlana Boym (2001, p. xiv) argues, it is not going away anytime soon, particularly as we move further away from the demise of colonialism, and as we (fast) approach the long-ness of the 21st century ahead of us.[8]

Thus, when we decide to make colonial nostalgia the subject of serious anthropological enquiry, we must first keep in mind that it is anything but a singular discourse (Bissell 2005, p. 216). Rather as Kathleen Stewart (1988, p. 227) reminds us, it is a cultural practice operating in historical time, as dependant on whom the speaker is as 'where the speaker stands in the landscape of the present'.[9] Second, as Bissell (2005, p. 221) argues, we must take into account that the density and intensity of emotion tied to particular colonial nostalgias is very much tied to rapid shifts or transitions that take place within a given society.

---

8   And as we move further and further away from the demise of colonialism, or as the past-ness of colonialism is even more past.

9   Here it is interesting to think about Portuguese colonial nostalgia comparatively with respect to Goa and Mozambique in order to discuss their divergent postcolonial paths. In the latter context, I was taken on an historic tour in Inhambane only to find that the city's one commemorative statue of Vasco de Gama was located next to an abandoned car garage.

Specifically, it is often the dramatic turn of these ruptures (and the subsequent inability to cope with them) that only adds to the sense of loss and that creates a sense of history to that loss that can best be retrieved nostalgically. In the case of Mozambique, its experience of the *long durée* of history includes two centuries of Arab trade and African slavery along the coast, four centuries of Portuguese colonialism, including two of which it was ruled from Portuguese India,[10] a protracted war of independence (1961–1974), colonial independence (1975), and then a drawn out civil war (1977–1992) that overlapped with a brief period of Socialism (1977–1989).[11] These are all historical processes that have yet to be fully reckoned with in postcolonial Mozambique, a fledgling nation-state that is only recently experiencing a slow political and economic recovery, with vast quantities of funding coming into the country via international NGOs in the face of a high incidence of AIDS, floods, and poverty.[12] Ilha's recognition as a UNESCO world heritage site was signalled towards the end of Mozambique's civil war due to its abundance of rich Indo and Afro-Portuguese architectural heritage from the 16th and 17th centuries.[13] However, as Barbara Kirshenblatt-Gimblett (2004, p. 57) has suggested, we need to inject a notion of caution in realizing what changes such a status effects:

> World Heritage is first and foremost a list. Everything on the list, whatever its previous context, is now placed in a relationship with other masterpieces.

---

10   Mozambique, considered part of Portuguese East Africa was ruled by the Viceroy stationed in Portuguese India from 1640 until 1752. See Manfred Prinz (1997). It is for this reason that there are such fine examples of Indo-Portuguese artefacts still intact on the island. These traces or links are particularly visible in the Governor's Palace and was the main impetus for the UNESCO funding focused on Ilha. See http://whc.unesco.org/en/list/599 (accessed on 11 June, 2009).

11   See Ndege (2007) for a basic chronology of major 'events' in Mozambican history.

12   I argue that Mozambique is a fledgling but *not* a failed state, an important distinction. As Mahmood Mamdani has suggested for Africa more generally, many budgets of humanitarian aid organizations exceed those of fledgling nation-states like Mozambique. This is why their full impact must be assessed, particularly since they often assume a 'moralizing and depoliticized' discourse wherein individuals are viewed as wardens of the state rather than as citizens active in a process of state-building. M. Mamdani public lecture, Boekehuis Bookstore in Johannesburg, SA, 20 June, 2009. Many of these NGO workers based in Mozambique and its neighbouring African countries become the tourists who visit Ilha. I met one such British NGO worker from Botswana who was staying in my same guesthouse on Ilha. I myself was struck by the number of NGO and charity workers, trucks, staff buildings in Mozambique more generally. A study needs to be done on NGO workers as tourists.

13   'The fortified city of Mozambique is located on this island, a former Portuguese trading-post on the route to India. Its remarkable architectural unity is due to the consistent use, since the 16th century, of the same building techniques, building materials (stone or macuti) and decorative principles'. http://whc.unesco.org/en/list/599 accessed 11 June 2009.

The list is the context for everything on it. The list is also the most visible, least costly, and most conventional way to 'do something' something symbolic – about neglected communities and traditions. Symbolic gestures like the list to confer value on what is listed, consistent with the principle that you cannot protect what you do not value. UNESCO places considerable faith – too much faith, according to some participants in the process – in the power of valorization to effect revitalization.

Third, colonial nostalgia is very much, following Bissell who interestingly makes a case for studying it in Zanzibar, 'a social practice that mobilizes various signs of the past (colonial and otherwise) in the context of contemporary struggles' (2005, p. 218). In other words, it constantly disrupts the binary between the past and the present, suggesting that it is neither linear, nor simple, nor easy to interpret (Bissell 2005, p. 236).[14] Particular to my case study, what does indulging in colonial nostalgia on Ilha today tell us about contemporary politics on the island itself, in Mozambique more generally, and in relation to its African neighbours as well as its former colonizer, Portugal? And what specific signs of Ilha's past – its history of Arab trade, colonialism and Catholic missionaries, African slavery, its suzerainty by Portuguese India, and its experience of Third world socialism – how are they mobilized or actively remembered for present day purposes and contestations? It must be recognized that Ilha's Portuguese Catholic past is being represented in the context of a 95 per cent Muslim presence.

Lastly, we must explore colonial nostalgia not only for the kinds of forgetting, or 'silencings of the past' that are evoked as Michel-Rolph Trouillot (1995) has suggested for Haiti but also for its powerfully sensorial ability to conjure up and remember the past through the smells, tastes, and textures of the present as Nadia Serematakis (1996) has suggested for Greece.[15] Is it an individual or a collective (national) amnesia, or both that is taking place? How much does indulging in colonial nostalgia by tourists on Ilha function as a space and time for forgetting (even if it is temporary) Mozambique's violent history, the awkward space between its colonial past and war torn present? Or in fact does the romance of the colonial seduce us to return instead to the original Greek meaning of nostalgia as a longing, an ache for (what once was) despite its burning pain, its difficulties to journey (Serematakis, p. 4)? Are there in fact daily constant reminders, like little Pedro following me around, or the faint waft of shit coming in from the ocean in my early morning walks on the island, or the proud flag of the *Renamo*

---

14   It is not linear, just as colonial nostalgia is often a circular discourse, operating 'sideways' as Svetlana Boym (2001, p. xiv) has suggested.

15   Nadia Serematakis (1996) very evocatively returns to the Greek understanding of *nostalgia* as less a yearning for or sense of loss with regard to the past, but rather that every engagement with the past through the sensory and bodily experiences in the present re-activates that past, bringing it into the present. In some ways, she is suggesting a form of nostalgia that is a more politicized engagement with the past.

Figure 14.3 Hospital de Mozambique, Ilha de Mozambique © Pamela Gupta

[*Resistência Nacional Moçambicana*] Party flirting in the window of a newly polished government building, or a colonial heritage site in a state of disrepair, its UNESCO completion date way past expiration. Do in fact stories 'congeal' around colonial ruins, as do their critiques as Ann Stoler (2008, p. 201) has suggested on one occasion? Thus, I want to use this ethnographic case study to open up a critical space for rumination and reflection on colonial nostalgia in all its complicated and convoluted neo-colonial tenses,[16] and how it allows us access to multiple different strands of remembrance, multiple implied pasts as seen from particular landscapes of the postcolonial present (Bissell 2005, p. 216).

Black – Waiting for Da Gama

I arrive on Ilha late at night. After a two hour flight from Beira, a five hour bus ride, and an hour-long *chapa* [mini taxi] that finally crosses the Indian ocean over a

---

16   Stoler (2008, p. 199) writes: 'As Renato Rosaldo reminds us, imperialist nostalgia is not a postcolonial pleasure but a concerted colonial one, a mourning contingent on what colonialism has destroyed.'

3.5 km long narrow bridge, I reach a dimly lit spot on the southern tip of the island
to await my last form of transportation to get to my final destination, a small bed
and breakfast enchantingly named Patio de Quintalinhos, located on the western
side of the island. I am greeted by João who explains that he does the regular am
and pm runs on the island, ferrying anyone and everyone around on the island at
regular intervals. Only he forgets to drop me off, so as we circle the tiny island
for the second time, I peer out the window just in time to see the hulking figure of
Vasco da Gama that dominates the north Western end of the island. It is da Gama
at his best – a statue at least ten metres in height, arms outstretched towards the
ocean, made of tarnished black marble, the stark illumination lending itself to his
ghostly apparitional quality. I cannot wait to see him in the morning light.

Green – Restoring the Door of Camões

My very charming bed and breakfast is run by Gabrielle Melazzi and his very
charming family. It has a beautiful balcony-cum-terrace on the rooftop that
overlooks the oldest mosque on the island, a bustling place with its green hued
peeling painted walls and Muslim morning call to prayer or *azan* that wakes me
every day without fail and where I inevitably end each evening with a *Laurentina*
(Mozambican-produced) beer in my hand perched on the precipice of the building,
watching the comings and goings of people entering the mosque, which is used
today by the majority Muslim population that inhabits this island. Italian by birth,
Gabrielle trained as an architect before setting off the travel the world. He arrived
on Ilha nine years ago as a backpacker and fell in love with the place, deciding in
that moment to make it his future home.

He currently is an odd man about town – stylizing any of the new fashionable
and hip restaurants that have cropped up on the island in the last five years,
renovating and running his boutique hotel which was once the home of a wealthy
Muslim trader before the civil war that plunged Mozambique into a ten year period
of chaos and violence,[17] and raising his three very young sons. When he bought the
abandoned property from the state seven years ago, it was for a mere US$5,000,
he tells me. He wasn't alone in seeing the island's allure for many other young
European backpackers like himself also decided to buy up these houses scattered
throughout the island, banking on their future potential. Worst case scenario would
be that he would lose his initial meagre investment, is what was going through
his mind at the time. He was young, in love and travelling the world he says.
The house would realistically fetch US$50,000 (not including the renovations he
has added to the property's value) if he were to decide to sell it and move back
to Milan with his young family. In a moment of reflection, he tells me that it is

---

17 The house was more than likely abandoned shortly after Mozambican
independence, when nationalization of property by the state took place. It was during this
time that many people lost their property rights.

something he does think about for the near distant future. However, he has too many restoration projects that he is involved with to leave just now.

I ask Gabrielle about what happened to the UNESCO initiative that was projected onto the island in 1991 to help preserve its Portuguese heritage.[18] He immediately corrects me when I assume out loud that it is largely government corruption that has prevented the completion of so many of the now abandoned UNESCO initiated heritage projects that I see on my daily strolls on the island. I cannot help but notice that Ilha is littered with signs with a completion date long gone in front of a half restored Portuguese fort, church, or house. Instead, it is largely state bureaucracy he says, the trickling down of money through multiple governmental organizations that leaves hardly any left over for the costly restoration work that needs to be done on the ground.[19] What exactly is the difference between corruption and inefficient government bureaucracy, I think silently to myself. However, Gabrielle is quick to note that only recently the higher ups at UNESCO realized what was happening, and have now sought to rectify the problem by basing two architects on the island to promote a second phase of restoration. And there is Portuguese and Japanese money coming to the island as well he adds, the former because of Ilha's rich architectural heritage, and the latter because the corpse of a Japanese Catholic missionary was recently found in a shallow grave behind the much decorated Governor's Palace.[20]

Despite all these problems, Gabrielle is hopeful. He himself has recently taken on a project with an Italy based partner to renovate the house that Luís de Camões, Portugal's national hero and famed writer, lived in during his two short term residences on Ilha, between the years 1567–1569. It was here that the blind man supposedly first conceived of the idea for *Os Lusíadas* before returning to Lisbon a few years later to write his epic poem immortalizing Vasco da Gama's journey to India, which was then published in 1572. It is Camões door that I get to see one lazy hot afternoon, as Gabrielle had to remove its hinges from the physical structure of the now abandoned courtyard house. He keeps the precious door protected inside a storage space as it was being eroded away by monsoon rains that regularly visit the island each year from November to April. It is rather unremarkable I think to myself as I finally get to touch it. Instead, it is the statue of Camões that stands on the eastern side of the island I am more interested in. He too is looking and gesturing toward the Indian Ocean – only his delicate feminine

---

18   One is reminded of Barbara Kirshenblatt-Gimblett's (2004) argument that valorisation by UNESCO does not translate so easily into revitalization. While UNESCO may initiate heritage preservation, it is up to other donors to continue the fundraising and renovations.

19   Gabriel gave me the example that if a granting foundation has given US$100,000 for a heritage renovation project, realistically only 20,000 actually goes to cover restoration costs by the time it goes through the government bureaucracy. Interviews with Gabrielle Melazzi, Ilha de Mozambique 19–22 April, 2009.

20   Interviews with Gabrielle Melazzi, Ilha de Mozambique 19–22 April, 2009.

frame in green oxidized slightly rusted metal stands in clear juxtaposition to the statue of Vasco da Gama that I first encountered on my nocturnal arrival on Ilha.[21]

Pink – Touring the Portuguese Governor's Palace

Sunday morning, I am greeted warmly by Abdul, the tour guide who will take me and the other visitors on a walking tour of the Palácio de São Paolo, an imposing pink façade of a building from the seventeenth century for which every detail inside and out has been tended to. I pay the entrance fee of 135 *Meticais* (about US$5) and pick up a map and wait for the next guided tour. I soon find out that my fellow tourists are an American family from Ohio. They are visiting Ilha for the first time, the older grey haired woman dressed in comfortable *Reebox* tennis shoes informs me as we all wait in a huddle to start the tour of the island's 'historical showpiece' as my *Lonely Planet* guidebook (Fitzpatrick 2007, p. 139) describes it, or as I conceive it in that moment – the jewel in the Portuguese crown on Ilha. I soon get caught up in understanding the building's complicated, layered, and interstitial past as Abdul narrates it to us in his almost perfectly American accented English.[22] It was during the 19th century that Ilha experienced its golden age for it first served as the grand capital city of Portuguese East Africa, and housed a series of acting Governors and their visitors. I cannot help get caught up in its atmosphere of colonial nostalgia par excellence as we wander through the palace's many rooms – its perfectly intact Baroque architecture, Venetian chandeliers, Indo-Portuguese latticed wooden chairs and beds that I immediately recognize from my own travels in Goa, its Chinese and Indian stylized kitchens, and finally its mosaic inlaid rickshaws imported from India for express use by the royal family, Abdul tells us.

However, Ilha slowly lost its prestigious position, just as the Portugal's East African empire began its own descent into crumbling disrepair and decline. Its former position as the centre of a far flung and bustling trade in African ivory and slaves, spices from China, Venetian glass, Indo-Portuguese furniture, and Catholic religious iconography was lost when the capital was moved further south, to Lourenço Marques (present day Maputo). The political territorial divisions of

---

21 Da Gama stands guard on the Western side of the island, and Camões is positioned on the eastern side of the island. I suggest that they metaphorically stand in as protectors of Ilha, past, present and future. The symbolism of this and the fact that their bodies lie in state together in Belém, Lisbon (Portugal) in the *Monasterio de Jerónimos* also makes their intertwined histories that much more crucial for understanding the effect and affect of their statues in Ilha.

22 The palace was first a Jesuit college from 1610 until the expulsion of all members of this religious order from the Portuguese territories, including Ilha in 1759. Next it held the position of Governor's residence for acting Portuguese Governors between 1763 and 1898. Historical dates provided by Abdul, the Mansion's official tour guide. Conversation 20 April, 2009.

Portuguese East Africa also shifted during this time, and the Palace was minimally maintained as a residence for Provincial governors of this district, before nearby Nampula became the capital of the province.[23] During the civil war it remained closed, Abdul informs us, its treasures quietly safeguarded by its unpaid caretakers. I notice that our guide doesn't have much more to say on this topic as my feeble attempt to probe deeper into this part of the palace's history fails. We visit the small light filled chapel that is attached to the palace, a perfectly preserved and beautiful example of 17th century Indo-Portuguese religious art. Abdul ends our historical tour of the church cum residence cum guest house by proudly informing us that Samora Machel, independent Mozambique's first African leader, but whose presidency was short-lived before he died under mysterious circumstances in 1986 in an airplane crash, was the first and the last African man to sleep in the palace. I rather like the way Abdul's story-telling ends, I think to myself. I then make my way to the next marker on the Portuguese heritage tour, the infamous 16th century *Fortaleza de São Sebastião* only to discover that it has been closed for several years due to ongoing renovations, unbeknownst to me as well as Mary Fitzpatrick, the author of my *Lonely Planet* guidebook, whom I cannot help but get irritated with for I keep noticing that she gets minor facts and directions wrong. Gabriel tells me later that it is a real shame to have missed the fort as the views from its walls are breathtaking. However, he says not to expect its opening any time soon.

Later that afternoon, as the sticky heat of the day finally gets to me, I decide to go to the Hotel *Escondinho* ['little hidden'] to use the one available pool on the island. I am swimming laps when I recognize the voices of the same American family that had earlier been on the tour of the palace with me. We all exchange greetings before I go back to reading my book at the poolside. I quietly listen in on their conversation as the kids splash about in the pool and learn that they are Christian missionaries stationed in nearby Nampula[24] – it is the grandparents who are the first time visitors from a farm in Ohio whereas the immediate family comes often, bringing all their foreign visitors to Ilha each time for its inescapable charm and assurance of a good holiday.[25] It was his parents the previous year, I overhear. Changing out of my wet bathing suit in the bathroom, I also meet a friendly Indian looking woman struggling to change her 6-year-old daughter's

---

23   Between the years 1956 and 1971 the palace served as a guest house for visiting Portuguese dignitaries. From 1971 onwards, in the undefined space between colony and independent nation, it functioned as a Museum of Colonial History. Historical dates provided by Abdul, the Mansion's official tour guide. Conversation 20 April, 2009.

24   Before that they were missionaries stationed in South Africa and Namibia. I overheard the father saying that the kids now attend the American school in Nampula, 20 April, 2009.

25   Here it would be interesting to look more closely at missionaries as tourists as they are a larger than life presence (like the NGO workers in some sense) in places like Mozambique. Once flying out of Maputo, I met a husband/wife missionary team from Utah, they were Mormons and they gave me the astounding figure of some 1,000 Mormons alone stationed in Mozambique. Conversation at Maputo airport, Mozambique, 2 December, 2008.

swimsuit. We exchange pleasantries and I ask where she is from. They are on holiday, visiting from Malawi – the men and children appropriately dressed in swimming suits whereas she and the other young mothers all took quick dips in the pool in their full clothing, jeans, t-shirts and all.[26] It is when the Portuguese owner of the restaurant starts yelling at the local staff for their incompetence that I decide it is time to leave.

Rust – Visiting the Hospital de Mozambique

I first walk past the Hospital de Mozambique on my first disoriented evening on Ilha. Gabriel has assured me that there is one restaurant open very late, and as I am starving I follow his directions very carefully to look for the hospital (I won't miss it he assures me) on my left where I will then turn to see the lights of the restaurant. It is exactly as he says only the hospital is far more imposing than I would have ever imagined. Its green ornate gate is wide open, the remnants of a fancy fountain appears dried up and rusted, freshly hung laundry is blowing in the faint breeze, but its flowery signpost in Portuguese (*Hospital de Mozambique*) remains intact.[27] I cannot help but stare at it as eat my dinner of Portuguese *caldo verde* soup and cheese toast sitting on the terrace of a chic restaurant, surrounded by mostly Italian and French tourists drinking wine and eating fancy risottos and pastas, seemingly enjoying themselves.[28] I find out later that Gabriel designed the rooftop bar. It takes three days for me to muster up my courage to enter the building that is half horror house, half homeless shelter, and unbeknownst to me at the time, also a fully functioning hospital. As I walk up the steps, the many children playing, chatting and lingering on the steps tell me that I cannot go in. As I politely ask why (not), I hastily peer in hoping to catch a quick glimpse, for something to catch my eye. As my eyes adjust to the immediate darkness from the blinding sunlight, I realize that I am about to enter compartmentalized residences where sheets have been hastily put up in an attempt at privacy. The children point instead to a side entrance. I

---

26   Here it is interesting to think about the interstitiality of an island space (Gupta 2010a) like Ilha as well as its relation to neighbouring African countries for the different kinds of ties it has to different communities and its appeal for different kinds of tourists; here Muslim Indians who can have a holiday in a predominately Muslim context.

27   That these signs are still very much in practical use is relevant and significant. I would like to develop further the fact that these old signs are used in present day contexts in another paper.

28   Gabriel told me that it is mostly Italian, Spanish and French tourists who come to Ilha, and more recently Swedish and Swiss tourists. Not many South Africans visit Northern Mozambique, surprisingly. However, according to Gabriel, many South Africans think Northern Mozambique is 'too old, too crappy, and too black' to come. They prefer Southern Mozambique which historically has been a tourist playground for South Africans, particularly sex tourism during the height of apartheid. Interviews with Gabrielle Melazzi, Ilha de Mozambique, 19–22 April, 2009.

enter accordingly and wander through the hospital's labyrinth like structure. I get lost at one point before I stumble into what I quickly realize is a renovated room filled with seemingly functioning hospital beds, threadbare but spanking clean cotton sheets placed on each of them. I turn the corner to see an ambulance and three nurses wearing crisp white uniforms, and brand new stethoscopes swinging from their chests as they hurriedly walk past me. I find a waiting room full of sick patients patiently awaiting their turn to be seen, by whom I cannot fathom exactly. My gaze turns towards a temporary structure that looks like it has the makings of a half filled pharmacy. I wander in disbelief until I find the same side entrance/exit that does not disturb the families living in the makeshift temporary quarters filling the front part of the hospital.

I am checking my email at the one internet café on the island that seems to be working when I strike up a conversation with a friendly woman from Ilha who has recently returned after 20 years of living in Sao Paolo, Brazil. She now works in the tourist industry on Ilha. We agree to meet for a coffee later that evening, which we do at a charming café, a larger than life poster from an exhibit in Italy of one of Mozambique's most famous photographers, Ricardo Rangel looming over us as we chat.[29] Since it is late, Sandra offers me a ride back to my guesthouse. As we speed past the hospital, she shakes her head and points to it and tells me that she was born there, back in the day when it was a famous hospital. 'I know' she says, 'It is hard to believe.'[30]

Whitewash – Stumbling across the Lar of São Francisco de Xavier

I am walking in the renovated section of Ilha near the Palace, surrounded by the pink, green, and yellow hues being reflected off the painted but peeling walls when I stumble across a nondescript doorway that is quietly labelled 'Lar of São Francisco Xavier'. I am more than curious given my longstanding interest in the history of this Spanish missionary-turned-saint who travelled widely in the Portuguese colonies in the mid-16th century. I tentatively step inside this *lar* ['home'] to find a group of young men loitering about, smoking and chatting in the inside corridor. I politely ask what this place is exactly, and am told to go next door to find the resident priest who will perhaps talk to me. The priest seems friendly enough when I knock on his door – we make a proper appointment to meet the next afternoon. It turns out that the Lar is a sort of Catholic youth hostel, a place for wayward boys to get an

---

29   Ricardo Rangel is Mozambique's premier photographer who died recently on 11 June, 2009. I had the wonderful opportunity to meet him and see many of his unpublished photographs in November, 2008. I dedicate this chapter to him.

30   Sandra returned to Ilha in 1997, after 20 years of living in Brazil. In our very candid conversation, she reflected on the openness of Brazilian society as compared to Ilha's social ills – poverty, homelessness, schooling, a sad and closed people in comparison to Brazil. Interview, 20 April, 2009.

education and hopefully find a space for themselves. Later that day back at the guesthouse I ask Gabriel about the Lar and relate my interest in Xavier. He tells me to go see the Chapel of St. Francis Xavier which is located near the bridge that connects the southern tip of Ilha to mainland Mozambique, the one I crossed in the dark upon my arrival on Ilha. I wander through these dirty streets, walkways I have not traversed as of yet as I have tended to always move north towards the renovated part of town where most of the colonial attractions and concerted attempts at heritage tourism are located. I pause to see and smell the fresh fish that is being sold in the daily outdoor market, alongside the mostly empty stalls sometimes with a pathetic single orange or tomato being sold. I stumble across an impromptu market of used clothing – mostly t-shirts branded with all familiar American names like *Nike, Puma, Reebok*,[31] being sold on the grounds of an ancient Catholic church in a complete state of disrepair and abandonment – its scratched barely legible date on the facade looking like it says 1622 but I cannot be sure.[32]

I find the whitewashed chapel of St. Francis Xavier quite easily, asking a woman selling sodas and chips in a small shop located across the street just to make sure. She smiles and says yes, that is it, but that it is probably closed. Sure enough, the white picket fenced gate surrounding the property is open but there is a brand new padlock on the main door. I turn to go back the way I came. Three hours later I arrive back in front of the chapel, only this time in the SUV of Father Attanasio who has kindly agreed to open it for me to take a quick look around.[33] It is simple and austere inside. I immediately gravitate towards the small statue of Xavier that dominates the poorly lit room. Next to it is a large rock that the missionary supposedly sat on when he was preaching the Catholic faith during his two month residence on Ilha in the year 1548.[34] As Father Attanasio locks up the chapel, he apologizes for its sparseness, explaining that at one time the

---

31   These are most likely charity donations that are being sold for profit. How the clothing got to Ilha would be an interesting journey of political economy to trace.

32   According to my Lonely Planet guidebook (Fitzpatrick 2007, p. 138), it is the church of Santo António. Unfortunately, the author does not provide any additional information on its history.

33   Father Attanasio opens it for special visitors, he told me later. Last year a visiting Spanish dignitary and Catholic Church leader came to Ilha with a group of students, and wanted to see the chapel. In 2007, Father Attanasio opened the chapel for an Indian-born Cardinal from Rome who had a deep interest in Xavier, given his ties to Goa and India. The community even held a special mass on this occasion inside the chapel. According to Attanasio, most people on Ilha don't know full story of Xavier, even as he visited the island. Interview 21 April, 2009.

34   The presence of this rock fits with the standard hagiography of Xavier and the power of contagion, that is, the things in his life are seen as valuable evidence or proof of his being there. See Gupta (2010b). Xavier visited Ilha, maybe more than once between 1542 and 1552. Apparently the rock itself had been only returned to Ilha in 1883, before that it had remained on the mainland. Father Attanasio didn't know anything more than this fact about the history of the rock or Xavier's visit to Ilha.

chapel housed valuable Moorish influenced *azulejo* tiles and mosaics imported from Portugal. They had been stolen at some point and sold for money, probably during the war he quietly adds.

Dusk – Contemplating the Jardim de Memorias

It is my last evening on the island as I walk the now familiar streets of Ilha. I decide to cut across one of the side streets for what I think looks like a good viewing spot for seeing the sunset over the Indian Ocean. I pause in front of the *Renamo* office building with its proud flag flying at fully mast and its impeccable front garden,[35] and a lone man selling a few freshly caught fish on an upturned bright red coloured plastic bucket. I can see that he doesn't really expect me to buy the fish but I pause just the same. As I wander down an unfamiliar street, no longer nervous about getting lost on the tiny island, I notice a gate and placard labelled with 'Jardim de Memorias' in front of what looks like a small museum built into the shoreline. I hastily go inside for a quick look around for it appears that it is about to close and I am leaving tomorrow early morning – I have a long bus ride ahead of me the next day. Inside I find a beautiful pristine garden space filled with benches, trellises, and monuments to the history of slavery on the island. There is a circle of disturbing statues that I gather to be artistically rendered beheaded slaves on stakes. It sends shivers up my spine. Next to it is a deep well, with a small commemorative placard next to it. The *jardim* ['garden'] has been set up as a space for contemplation, almost a Zen garden located in the midst of a history of brutal violence. I can see that it would be worth a second visit even as I tour it rather quickly, feeling bad for I can see that the gatekeeper and his wife are waiting for me to leave so that they can close up and go home to their family for

---

35 The independence and post-civil war politics of *Frelimo* [Frente de Libertação de Moçambique] vs. *Renamo* [Resistência Nacional Moçambicana] are complicated both in Mozambique more generally and on Ilha de Mozambique. More generally, *Frelimo* was a broad based Marxist based guerilla movement formed in 1962 under the leadership of Eduardo Mondlane and with a stronghold in Northern Mozambique; after his assassination in 1969, the group eventually negotiated Mozambique's colonial independence from Portugal with Samora Machel as its elected President in 1975. The new government then became engaged in a protracted civil war (1975–1992) with *Renamo*, an anti-Community political party that was sponsored by the white minority governments of Rhodesia (now Zimbabwe) and apartheid South Africa. Both political parties still maintain pockets of support throughout the country. For additional information, see Norrie MacQueen (1997). Later on during my tour of the island, I spotted a *Frelimo* building elsewhere on a side street in a less prominent location. Interesting that *Renamo* makes more of a display of itself on Ilha, but perhaps this makes sense given the historical context wherein Northern Mozambique was really more of a stronghold for *Frelimo* in the past. Perhaps it is precisely because *Renamo* has less of a hold on Ilha, that its offices are so prominent in the hopes of recruiting members.

Figure 14.4   Municipal office, Ilha de Mozambique © Pamela Gupta

dinner. I leave just as the sun quietly slips behind the building, noticing on the way out that that the museum was only completed in 2007, which explains why it is not listed in my increasingly outdated *Lonely Planet* guidebook. According to the inauguration date, its UNESCO funds were complemented by generous funding from the French government and the French overseas department (DOM) of La Réunion, an island in the Indian ocean with its own deep history of slavery that was connected to Ilha via their disturbing trade in bodies, and which ensured that this monument and museum would be completed and not left in a state of disrepair as compared to the fate of so many other colonial ruins and memories on Ilha.

Effect and Affect

> We would do well to bring the ruins up close and work our way through the rubble in order to rescue the utopian hopes that modernity engendered, because we cannot afford to let them disappear. (Buck-Morss 2002, p. 68)

I leave Ilha early the next morning, less with my initial feeling of despair that the deeply layered histories of this faraway place are in a process of complete forgetting by romancing the colonial. Rather, I realize that forgetting *and remembering* are both taking place side by side, in complicated ways, in everyday moments of affect (Stewart 2007), infused by colours, textures, smells, bodies and voices, and by different individuals, not just by anthropologists like myself, standing in this postcolonial heritage tourism landscape. Maybe it is my own utopian desire to see hope in the colonial ruins that surround me, but I cannot help but leave thinking of all those glimpses I gathered on my grand tour of Ilha, my reveries inside its colonial past constantly being punctured by its many present (and future) colliding tenses, and which no doubt are sensorially and somatically felt by other audiences as well, including the many diverse tourists who visit this interstitial island space for a day, a week, a month or a lifetime. It is the bulk of da Gama contrasted with the grace of Camões; it is Abdul ending his tour of the *Palácio de São Paolo* with the fact that Mozambique's first independence President Samora Machel was its last visitor; it is those sculptural renditions of beheaded slaves on stakes located in the *Jardim de Memorias*; it is Gabriel's three little boys running around the guesthouse, speaking Portuguese, Italian, and Makhuwa simultaneously.[36] It is Pedro's smile.

References:

Bissell, W. (2005) 'Engaging colonial nostalgia', *Cultural Anthropology*, 20(2), pp. 215–248.
Boym, S. (2001) *The Future of Nostalgia*. New York: Basic Books.

---

36 I am trying to explore if the widespread practice of indulging in colonial nostalgia can potentially be a liberating exercise rather than simply confining it to a politics of conservatism, and thus ignoring its interrogation.

Buck-Morss, S. (2002) 'On time', in *eadem, Dreamworld and Catastrophe-The Passing of Mass Utopia in East and West*, Boston: MIT Press, pp. 42–95.

Dirks, N. (1998) 'In near ruins: Cultural theory at the end of the century', in N. Dirks (ed.), *In Near Ruins: Cultural Theory at the end of the Century*, Minneapolis: University of Minnesota Press, pp. 1–18.

Fitzpatrick, M. (2007) *Lonely Planet: Mozambique*, London: Lonely Planet Publications.

Gupta, P. (2010a) 'Islandness in the Indian Ocean', in P. Gupta, I. Hofmeyr and M. Pearson (eds), *Eyes Across the Water: Navigating the Indian Ocean*, Pretoria: Unisa Press, pp. 275–285.

Gupta, P. (2010b) '"Signs of Wonder": The Postmortem travels of Francis Xavier in the Indian Ocean World', in A. Jamal and S. Moorthy (eds), *Indian Ocean Studies: Cultural, Social and Political Perspectives*, London: Routledge, pp. 197–228.

http://whc.unesco.org/en/list/599 (accessed on 11 June, 2009).

http://www.lonelyplanet.com/mozambique/northern-mozambique/ilha-de-mocambique (accessed on 27 June 2009).

Kirshenblatt-Gimblett, B. (2004) 'Intangible heritage as metacultural production', *Museum*, 56(1–2), pp. 52–64.

MacQueen, N. (1997) *The Decolonization of Portuguese Africa*, New York: Longman.

Ndege, G. (2007) *Culture and Customs of Mozambique*, Westport, CT: Greenwood Press.

Prinz, M. (1997) 'Intercultural links between Goa and Mozambique in their colonial and contemporary history: Literary Mozambiquean traces', in C. Borges and H. Feldmann (eds), *Goa and Portugal: Their Cultural Links*, New Delhi: Concept Publishing Company, pp. 111–127.

Serematakis, N. (1996) *The Senses Still: Perception and Memory as Material Culture in Modernity*, Chicago: University of Chicago Press.

Stewart, K. (1988) 'Nostalgia – A Polemic', *Cultural Anthropology*, 3(3), pp. 227–241.

Stewart, K. (2007) *Ordinary Affects*, Durham, NC: Duke University Press.

Stoler, A. (2008) 'Imperial debris: Reflections on ruins and ruination', *Cultural Anthropology*, 23(2), pp. 191–219.

Trouillot, M. (1995) *Silencing the Past: Power and the Production of History*, Boston: Beacon Press.

Werbner, R. (ed.) (1998) *Memory and the Postcolony: African Anthropology and the Critique of Power*, London: Zed Books.

Chapter 15

Dancing Tourists: Tourism, Party and Seduction in Cuba[1]

Valerio Simoni

In the last two decades social science research on tourism started paying increased attention to bodies, affects, and emotions, examining key aspects of the tourist experience that cannot be reduced to the interpretive (Veijola and Jokinen 1994; Franklin and Crang 2001; Fullagar 2001; Selänniemi 2003; Little 2005). To contribute to such growing scholarship, this chapter focuses on the ambivalent relations between partying and seducing in touristic Cuba. Drawing on ethnographic material gathered in this Caribbean island between 2005 and 2007, the aim is to unpack the generative frictions that stemmed from a variety of partying/seducing situations, and to consider how pleasurable states of being were brought about, what they afforded, as well as the tensions they produced.

Partying is a realm in which experiential states – what may be referred as party 'feelings' and 'vibes' – are brought to the fore, encouraging those sensibilities in which 'the experience itself is more important than the hermeneutics' (Bruner 2001, p. 902). To illuminate such party 'feelings' and 'vibes', I consider the case of dancing, which was a key and constitutive ingredient of festive scenarios in touristic Cuba. The examination of how dancing was enacted and reflected upon by tourists and Cuban people provides fruitful insights into the interplay between partying and seducing, and enables us to shed light on emerging tensions between playfulness and seriousness, pleasure and control, emotions and reason – tensions that were at the core of touristic encounters and relationships in this Caribbean country. By drawing attention to relational idioms that brought into play notions

1 Earlier versions of this chapter were presented at the *Research Training Programme* for PhD candidates at Leeds Metropolitan University in May 2009, and at the International Conference *Emotion in Motion: The Passions of Tourism, Travel and Movement*, organised by the Centre for Tourism and Cultural Change, Leeds Metropolitan University, in July 2009. I am indebted to the participants that contributed to these two events for their insightful comments and remarks, and to David Picard also for his suggestions on the first draft this chapter. The collaboration of tourists and Cuban people I encountered during fieldwork enabled me to gather the empirical data on which this text is grounded, and I am grateful for their time and willingness to discuss with me. Any mistakes and shortcomings are on my behalf. Finally, I would like to thank the Fundação para a Ciência e Tecnologia for supporting my research via a post-doctoral grant (SFRH/BPD/66483/2009).

of partying, festivity, pleasure, and sensual/sexual seduction, the examination of dancing in touristic Cuba shows how these idioms could alternatively converge and constitute a continuum, or split up and differentiate, as contentious boundaries between and among them were (re)drawn.

On the one hand, partying appears to act as a privileged platform to encourage people to 'let go' and 'open up' to the other. It generated shifts in peoples' mode of engagement: from a realm of rational thinking and interpretation, to one of pleasurable feelings and 'flows' where affects and intimate desires took over calculations. This is how partying opened up possibilities in the relationships that tourists and Cubans could achieve, becoming a privileged arena for seduction, and paving the way to the development of sexual relationships and romance.

On the other hand, the examination of dancing practices also shows how the partying-seducing continuum was continuously unsettled and put to test by the emergence of controversial expressions of difference. This generated tensions that threatened to breach festive atmospheres and disrupt pleasurable feelings and flows. Once interpretive thinking, rationalizations, and doubts (re)gained salience, asymmetry and distrust – the two key issues challenging the establishment of touristic encounters in Cuba – were brought to the fore.

By tracking how shifts and bifurcations between these two contrasting scenarios operated, the chapter reveals how dancing practices could alternatively lead to subsume or to materialize elusive boundaries between partying and seducing, drawing attention to the profound implications of such processes and their tactic manipulation by the protagonists involved. In turn, this sheds light on how tourists and Cuban people responded to the main promises and challenges of their encounters and relationships.

Empirically, the research is grounded in seven months of ethnographic fieldwork carried out in Cuba between February 2005 and March 2007. During this time, I observed and participated in interactions between foreign tourists and members of the Cuban population in the city of Havana, the beach resort of Playas del Este, and the rural town of Viñales. The issue of my access and my relationships with tourist and Cuban research participants has been thoroughly addressed elsewhere together with the challenges and opportunities that arise when doing research, as a foreigner, in a tourism context in Cuba (see Simoni and McCabe 2008; Simoni 2009). What needs to be specified in regards to investigating festive situations and dancing experiences, is that methodological challenges increase since we are not dealing exclusively with practices, discourses and rationalizations, which may be easier to follow and pinpoint, but also with states of being, feelings, and 'vibes' which often refract and stand in opposition to reasoning, logic, meaningful conceptualizations and interpretive thinking. To account for these feelings and 'vibes', my ethnography cannot solely rely on straightforward descriptions and reports of conversations, and will also consist of more tentative evocations, intuitive feelings, and first-hand impressions.

Regarding the structure of the chapter, it is organized in four sections followed by a conclusion in which the main arguments developed throughout the text are reviewed and further elaborated. The first section starts by addressing some key features of tourism in present day Cuba that contribute to explain both the promises and challenges of touristic encounters in this Caribbean island. This leads to a better appreciation of the potential of partying and seducing to generate connections in the tourism realm. It also opens the way to the second section of the chapter, which underlines the importance of materializing festive atmospheres and party 'vibes' in order to kick-start and project forward relationships between tourists and Cuban people. Music and dance emerge as quintessential features of partying in touristic Cuba, and the third section delves deeper into these elements showing how dancing relationships become privileged vehicles for the development of ludic sociabilities and intense pleasurable feelings. Addressing more closely the corporeality of dancing practices, and drawing attention to its enabling and limiting qualities, the fourth section follows how (dis)continuities between partying and seducing are brought about and manipulated, becoming a source of controversies. This finally leads to consider the possibilities afforded by highly ambiguous situations of interaction, which find expression in peoples' creative uses of 'cultural differences' and 'misunderstandings'.

Tourism and Touristic Encounters in Cuba: Promises and Challenges

When I undertook my first fieldwork trip to Cuba, in February 2005, international tourism to this Caribbean island had been growing exponentially for almost two decades, generating unprecedented societal changes. During that period, the number of international tourists had seen a tenfold increase, surpassing 2 million. The dramatic economic crisis affecting the country from the end of the 1980s had prompted the Cuban authorities to renew their efforts in developing the tourism industry, seen as a key source of hard currency. Alongside the new impetus given to tourism, other major reforms took place with the beginning of the Special Period in Time of Peace (*Período especial en tiempo de paz*) in 1990 – a time of austerity and economic hardship that followed the collapse of the Soviet Union, which since the 1960s had entertained privileged relationships with Cuba. The government efforts to expand the tourism capacity of the island and attract international visitors materialized in 'mass-oriented' tourism infrastructure built in selected coastal locations, promoting Cuba's 'sun, sand and sea'.

If cheap packages to beach resorts at a very competitive price in the Caribbean market lured tourists to the island in the early 1990s, other tourism promises also contribute to explain the growing interest of foreign visitors for Cuba. Amongst them, the possibility of experiencing traces of the island's peculiar history: from stunning examples of colonial architecture; to the relics of pre-revolutionary times; to the ever-present signs of the Revolution and its ongoing epic. The cigars, the rum, and the increasingly successful Cuban music and dances were other crucial ingredients projected on the international stage as unique qualities of this island, and evoking the possibility of exciting parties and hedonistic consumption.

Last but not least, the 'character of Cuban people', their hospitality, kindness, and joyfulness being among the quintessential features highlighted in tourism promotion material in the mid 1990s (Michel 1998). Cuban people were thus described as 'amiable and warm', as 'living out of smiles, dances, and music', displaying 'a lascivious and languorous joy' and a 'passion for life' (Michel 1998, pp. 276–277). Prolonging the semantic register of these praising remarks was the emphasis on the 'exuberant', 'passionate' and 'sensual' character of Cuban people, which is still a recurrent way of describing the island's inhabitants in tourism guides and publications. Thus, Cuba becomes 'probably the most sensual country on hearth, not to say sexual' (Gloaguen ed. 2007, p. 36). These images, echoed in several mainstream tourism publications, willingly interlock Cubans' inclination for partying, their exuberance, and the diffuse sexual permissiveness that supposedly characterizes them. In the *Time Out* guide, Havana is therefore portrayed as:

> a city for music-making an spontaneous parties; a bottle of rum and a boom
> box is all you need and the legendary Cuban exuberance does the rest. Bodies
> are a free source of fun; sexual activity starts young and goes on to a full and
> interesting (often promiscuous) adult sex life. (2004, p. 27)

Partying and dancing, exuberance and passion, sensuality and sexuality: these are among the key tropes and semantic continuities that still project Cuba on the international tourism stage, and which are addressed more thoroughly in this presentation.

However, an assessment of the predominant tourism narratives that characterized Cuba at the time of my fieldwork (2005–2007) also reveals another side to the glittering mirror of images outlined above, pointing towards a less idyllic and morally controversial face of tourism development on the island. An additional scenario, characterized by 'tourism hustling' and 'prostitution', had emerged and progressively taken salience on the tourism scene. Such scenario was encapsulated by the notion of *jineterismo*, a neologism derived from the Spanish for 'rider', 'horseman' (*jinete*), which in the context of tourism in Cuba evoked the 'riding of foreigners' for instrumental purposes. It was with the beginning of the Special Period and the worsening economic crisis that informal practices and *jineterismo*, already burgeoning on the island (Palmié 2004; Kummels 2005), acquired new dimensions and an increased visibility. More and more widespread and routinized, they became part of a culture of the 'struggle' (*lucha*) – a common expression to indicate Cubans' day-to-day struggle to get by (Palmié 2004, p. 241), to look for dollars 'in the street' (*en la calle*) (Berg 2004, p. 84), whether legally or not (Argyriadis 2005, p. 47). In this new context, Palmié remarks that any 'unregulated association with foreigners … was encouraged' (Palmié 2004, p. 241).

More and more Cubans, particularly among the younger generations, saw in the increasing number of tourists that visited the island a possibility to access hard currency and fulfil other aspirations. However, serious challenges and limitations restrained their possibilities to develop fruitful relationships with foreigners. Key among these challenges: the Cuban authorities' selective efforts to control tourism and police Cubans' interactions with tourists. In this respect, scholars have emphasized how *jineterismo* is a highly contentious phenomenon, whose characterization and repression by the authorities is often informed by discriminatory fault lines that bring issues of morality, nation, race, class and gender into play (Fernandez 1999; Berg 2004; Simoni 2008, 2009). Another major obstacle for the establishment of touristic encounters has to do with the worldwide, unsavoury reputation acquired in the last decade by *jineterismo*, notably via tourist guidebooks and world of mouth suggestions circulating among tourists. Such narratives inform tourists' expectations and predispositions towards the prospect of meeting Cuban people, raising serious doubts about the compatibility of each other's desires and agendas.

Jineterismo speaks the language of inequalities, confronting tourists with their advantageous economic position, reiterating their status of privileged outsiders, and emphasizing differences between them and the Cuban population. It also highlights their lack of knowledge of local conditions, and the possibility of being duped and deceived by *jineteros* and *jineteras*. Magnifying the divide between visitors and residents, *jineterismo* makes of the Cuban/tourist 'grammar of distinction' (Comaroff and Comaroff 1997) an overarching frame of identification that haunts a wide range of touristic encounters in Cuba and threatens the viability of relationships. While tourists are often puzzled by the suspicion of 'hidden interests' and 'contrived emotions', Cubans also wonder about the nature of the tourists' engagement. This infuses their interactions with a high degree of ambiguity, generating controversies, and calling for ways of settling 'what relationships are (really) about'.

For Cuban people who strived to establish bonds with foreigners, the development of personal relationships held the promise of ameliorating economic conditions and being able to travel abroad via the tourist connection. As other researchers have shown, what is important to consider here is that 'relationships that create long term obligations and commitments' (Cabezas 2006, p. 516) could be judged far more beneficial and gratifying than any short term economic transaction. To achieve such long term commitments, however, the radical notions of difference evoked by *jineterismo*, and the paralyzing threat of deception they generated among tourists, had to be overcome. How did tourists and Cubans deal with, and eventually move beyond, the threats of deception and reciprocal exploitation? How did they negotiate their potentially conflicting agendas? How did they deal with issues of (dis)trust and asymmetry, and eventually managed to achieve various types of personal relations?

These are among the key question that motivated my investigations, and which my research in Cuba tried to answer. What emerged (Simoni 2009) is that to re-qualify limiting notions of difference, asymmetry, and distrust, and to project their connections forward, tourists and Cuban people enacted relationships that brought into play notions of 'friendliness' and 'friendship', 'festivity' and 'seduction', 'intimacy' and 'sexuality'. In the remaining sections of this chapter the relational idioms of festivity and seduction, and their controversial entanglements, constitute the main focus of attention.

Evoking and Materializing Party, Opening Up Possibilities

Several of my Cuban research participants explicitly told me about the importance of getting tourists into a 'party mood'. For ex-*jinetero* Fernando, who was among my key informants on *jineterismo*, the possibility of *irse de fiesta* ('go party') with tourists invariably marked a favourable turning point. Once partying was on the way 'that's it (*ya*)!' he told me, implying that relationships were likely to get smooth and successful from then on: tourists would become affable and easy to deal with, and were likely to leave any potential worry behind. Therefore, a range of opportunities could open up, enabling Cuban people to have both fun and capitalize in fruitful relationships (expanding and reinforcing them, gaining easier access to cash and other coveted goods, etc.). But what did partying mean to Fernando and other Cuban people who engaged with tourists? When would they consider that a *fiesta* had materialized? Even though there was hardly any clear threshold marking a party's beginning, there were nevertheless certain conditions that people tended to equate with a festive state, with having fun and pleasure. In this respect, music, dance, and indulgent consumption (particularly of alcoholic beverages) seemed to be amongst the key ingredients required to materialize a party atmosphere.

Explicit evocations and prescriptive remarks on what the 'party mood' ought to be about could also be formulated, notably when Cuban people considered that their tourist companions were reluctant to engage in the festive atmosphere and 'go with the flow'. Enticements to 'let go', to enjoy and indulge in pleasure could be supported by the rather unquestionable assumption that tourists were in Cuba to enjoy themselves. 'One should enjoy!' (*Hay que disfrutar!*) – was the widespread encouragement, activating ideals of tourism as the pursuit of pleasure. Such incitements also relied on implicit assumptions of what having fun and pleasure were all about. Partying as dance, as indulging in pleasures, as intoxication and immoderate consumption of food, drinks, sex, etc. – such were the images of party that were brought to the fore.

A culturalist blend could also be added to these exhortations, evoking for instance how Cuba was the perfect place to enjoy and indulge: in Cuba 'everything is possible' (*todo es possible*) – especially if you had the means for it. Cuba as 'paradise island' (Schwartz 1999), as the land of endless opportunities for pleasure, where the limits could be pushed forward, where music was everywhere, where everyone loved to dance, where people were hot and where eroticism, sensuality, and sexual fulfilment – at their best – were always accessible and around the corner. As considered above, these were among the key promises of tourism in Cuba, and my research participants tended to be acutely aware of them. 'Party and enjoy since you are on holiday! Since you are in Cuba and this is what Cuba is about!' Such instigations were legion among Cuban people who wished tourist to 'let go'. They were geared at arousing and swelling the visitors' party mood, to bring about euphoria, happiness, and open up possibilities.

Besides these exhortations to party, to have fun and enjoy pleasure, fieldwork also led me to observe and participate in the sort of 'whirls' of hedonistic consumption and playfulness that took off from touristic encounters. Such were the afternoons among groups of tourists and their Cuban partners at the beach of Santa Maria, the prime tourism spot on the Playas del Este, about half-an-hour drive east of Havana. These occasions generated highly euphoric and electrifying moments, in the course of which people displayed a happy and cheerful mood, where ludic sociabilities took shape via the telling of jokes, singing, dancing, clapping hands, hands shaking, hugging, embracing, raising glasses, drinking a toast, etc. The euphoric character of these moments was given continuity, extended, and amplified by ordering new drinks, buying new bottles and making sure everyone's glass was never left empty. People would plan ahead how the party could possibly follow, which bar or club to choose for the night, which drugs to get, etc.

Sensuality and sexual arousal certainly played a crucial role in the materialization of these party atmospheres. In Santa Maria for instance – and I am prevalently referring here to interactions involving male tourists – planning ahead and enticing a climaxing feel could for instance consist of passionate conversations about the 'girls' to meet. When tourists where already accompanied by a Cuban partner, then excitement, playful seduction, and sensual pleasures could be brought forward and publicly displayed by caressing, touching, and kissing each other. The verbal and the corporeal, touch and feel, sound and movement, ingestion of food, drinks, drugs – all these elements could concur and intertwine to bring about an euphoric party 'vibe', to generate excitement, and what may be referred as quintessential 'liminoid' states of being (see Turner 1977; Graburn 1983; Selänniemi 2003).

Dancing Relations: Getting Into the Flow?

On the beach in Santa Maria, live music and dancing became pivotal aspects in bringing about a festive atmosphere. In this privileged tourism location, the performances of itinerant musicians constituted a sort of 'happening', drawing people from the immediate surroundings and encouraging participation in the event. Mingling together, tourists and Cuban people would sing along and clap their hands to the rhythm, contributing to create a contagious festive mood. On such occasions Cuban women eager to make the acquaintance of foreigners, would display their scantily clad bodies, and engage in sensual dance movements that could entice the tourists' attention - charming, seducing, and tantalizing them with cheerful smiles and piercing glances. These moments were generally rather short lived, but from them could generate connections that led to other festive developments.

Besides the beach in Santa Maria, invitations to join the dance and party were even more widespread and compelling at nigh time in the clubs and discos of Havana – places where dancing was almost prescribed as the main form of engagement. Invitations to dance, or 'the dancing of the tourists' (*bailarselo*) – whereby tourists explicitly became the object of the dance – were among the privileged tactics to get in touch with foreigners – a classic *entrada* (opening, entry point). Gender differences as to how invitations proceeded certainly deserve attention. They often intersected with the type of music and dance involved. In the case of salsa for instance, and in conformity with the prevalent 'dance floor etiquette' (Fairley 2006, p. 478), men usually took the first step. Men were also supposed to be leading, guiding and orienting the female partners' moves throughout the dance, and I soon realized that whereas Cuban men approached tourist women to dance salsa, the contrary was less common. Rare too was having male tourists who took the 'responsibility' of being the leader and invited Cuban women.

But occasionally there were visitors who willingly took such initiative, particularly people who were experienced salsa dancers and felt confident in this dancing style. Some tourists I met told me that they had come to Cuba especially with the idea of improving their skills, and to get a chance to dance with the locals. These were the tourists who had the resources, and seemed particularly predisposed to reach 'peak experiences' while dancing, giving way to states of 'flow' akin to those theorized by Csikszentmihalyi (1975), discussed by Turner (1977) in relation to *communitas*, and further elaborated by Graburn (1983) in connection with tourism. Graburn (1983) summarizes the concept of flow the following way:

> the non-reflective state that is characteristic of a person who is totally and excitedly engaged in some important activity, in which action and awareness merge, self-awareness gives way to attention focused on a limited field which the participant is engaged in mastering, a feeling which is a reward in itself, not a means to an external end. (p. 14)

If experienced tourist dancers were getting relatively easy into flow when dancing, this exciting state could also take hold of less experienced visitors, particularly once people were determined to leave aside their inhibitions and 'let it go'. I this respect, the remarks of anthropologist Yvonne Daniel, who examined rumba dance performances in a tourism context in Cuba, seem particularly evocative. Writing about tourists' involvement on these occasions, Daniel (1996) considers how people 'explore their rhythmic, harmonic, and physical potential and arrive at sensations of well-being, pleasure, joy, or fun, and at times, frustration as well' (p. 789). Thus:

> tourists access the magical world of liminality which offers spiritual and aesthetic nourishment (Daniel 1990; Turner and Bruner 1986; Turner and Turner 1978). Tourism, in moments of dance performance, opens the door to a liminal world

that gives relief from day-to-day, ordinary tensions, and, for Cubans dancers and dancing tourists particularly, permits indulgence in near-ecstatic experiences (Graburn 1989). (Daniel 1996, p. 789).

In Havana, I also participated in events akin to those described by Daniel, in which improvisation and spontaneity played a very important part, and which saw a contagious festive atmosphere leading tourists and Cubans to reach peak-like experiences by dancing together. From then on, people could stick to their newly found partners and move on together to other places and events that could help them to keep 'high', get on with the dance, and prolong the party.

As these considerations suggest, dancing and partying tended to be close allies in the realm of touristic encounters in Cuba. They called for and constituted each other, generating fun, pleasure, and euphoria, and giving way to ludic sociabilities and a sense of festive *communitas*. Nevertheless, there were also occasions in which the close connections between dancing, festivity, and enjoyment could be breached. This brings me to address more closely the corporeality of dance itself: a crucial aspect that opened up possibilities, while simultaneously leading people to delineate different types of engagement and relational idioms. My concern is here with the ways in which physical proximity could facilitate touch, sensuality, and titillation, and with their more or less reflexive manipulations – which some people saw as moving beyond the fun and playfulness of dancing proper. As contentious boundaries materialized, notions of what dancing was (or was not) about and which were its limits emerged.

From Dance to Seduction

As several of my Cuban research participants made clear, dancing was a privileged path to seduce and tantalize tourists, to try and build a relationship that could go beyond the dancing itself, opening up further possibilities. Besides salsa music – which was the favoured vehicle for Cuban men to lead and seduce tourist women into the dance floor – in recent years another type of music and dance has gained increasing popularity in Cuba – one in which the female body acquires centre-stage, and which has become an essential seduction tool in the hands of Cuban female dancers. It is the case of *regeton*, which I would like to consider more in detail here. *Regeton* is considered a quintessential 'Latino' musical genre that emerged in the 1990s, and which blends Jamaican reggae and dancehall styles with Latin American musical influences. Ethnomusicologist Jan Fairley has recently brought attention to the emergence, in late 1990s Cuba, of '"new" dance/moves involving "solo" female body' (2006, p. 472), and has considered these changes in style as they intersect with the recent popularity of *regeton*. New dancing styles include 'the *despelote* (all-over-the-place) and *tembleque* (shake shudder) and the *subasta de la cintura* (waist auction)' (Fairley 2006, p. 472). Always according to Fairley (2006), these moves:

define a solo female dance style which involves fast undulating and turning / swirling of the area from below shoulders and chest to pelvis (as if one is hula hoop-ing or belly dancing). Often accompanied by hand and body gestures mimicking self-pleasuring, in the 1990s it constituted a noticeable change in dance style, of women dancing to be 'looked at' both by their partners, by their prospective partners, and by other spectators, using their body as a/their major asset. This was in striking contrast to the more normative couple dancing. (p. 472)

In her article, Fairley elaborates on the relationships between these new moves, *regeton*, 'back-to-front' dancing – a dancing style 'which sensualizes the bottom and pelvis in fetishistic fashion' (2006, p. 477) and 'where the woman seems to lead' (2006, p. 482) – and the world of *jineteras*. According to her, these changes in dancing:

developed in the climate of modern sexual flirtation and potential liaisons between Cubans and Cubans, and Cubans and non-Cubans in the heady atmosphere of Havana clubs in the 1990s when *jinetera* (service culture) and sexuality as 'convertible currency' was prime ... The difference with *regeton* per se post 2000 is that it is notably danced out between Cubans. On occasions it is also danced out between Cuban women and foreigners, although publicly few foreigners are very good at it. (Fairley 2006, p. 483)

In the course of my fieldwork I realized that whether foreigners were 'good' or 'bad' at dancing *regeton* did not seem to diminish its importance in captivating, titillating, and sexually arousing them. Tourist men were confronted with Cuban women dancing *regeton* 'on their own', displaying their bodies and engaging in sensual and more overtly sexual moves. This could be a very efficient tactic to capture the tourists' attention and produce a first connection, reinforced perhaps by sustained staring of each other, a wink, or a kiss from distance.

Essential in this case was also the physical contact afforded by the dance, whereby tourists' bodies could be physically aroused through the contact and friction of the women's bottom on their crotch. As pertinently emphasized by Fairley, in *regeton* the women seem to lead the dance. Therefore – and independently of foreign men being able to dance *regeton* 'properly' – by simply allowing the Cuban partner to undulate and swirl their bottoms against them tourists were in a sense already part of the dance. Normative scripts of dancing etiquette, which relied for instance on formalized invitation (as in salsa) seemed not that relevant in these cases. Instead, a couple could be created in rather surreptitious and improvised ways, with solo dancers suddenly getting together and start moving and 'rubbing' their bodies.

As I repeatedly noticed in clubs and bars, couples were being created through *regeton*/back-to-front dancing, with Cuban women regularly 'stirring up' their partners' 'fire' through the physical friction of their bodies. These often appeared to be part of reflexive tactics to help 'keep the tourists high', to move from playful 'as if' to serious engagement, to avoid the emergence of 'reason', of potential second thoughts and changes of mind, whereby decreasing arousal could lead to take other aspects into consideration (e.g. 'Who is this women?', 'Does she really likes me?' 'What's her agenda?', 'Am I really interested in pursuing the relationship with her?'). When successful, the skilful bodily moves of Cuban women could give dancing relationships a decisive twist towards the realms of seduction, sexuality, and romance. However, these seduction processes were far from being always effective, and there were also instance in which people drew boundaries as to how far, and in which direction, their relational engagement would go.

For one, the sexually explicit references of *regeton* embarrassed several of my tourist informants, especially those who were not familiar to this dancing style. Others were on the contrary drawn quite easily into sensually/sexually evocative dancing enactments, especially those who already positive predispositions and expectations on the matter, cherished the dancing-seducing continuum, and were eager to move relationships further. Others still were willing to get involved in a playful mode, just for the fun of it and to get a feel of such experience of physicality and close contact. Here was when relationships could get more 'serious' and take an unexpected turn, as visitors got 'hooked' and 'succumbed' to the overwhelming sensuality and sexuality of the dance, ending up 'conquered' by the Cuban woman involved. As excitement grew, other considerations and moral commitments could be put aside, and a shift from playful detachment to full-blown engagement could occur. Intentions and agendas, rational planning and reasoning could be taken over, bypassed or reformulated following overwhelming intensities of affect, physical sensations and sexual arousal.

The possibility of this serendipitous scenario – which saw people surrender the driving force of their actions to bodily sensations and sexual arousal – was also one that unsettled some of tourists I spoke to, who were reluctant to the idea of 'losing control'; of letting their physical urges dictate the course of events. Evoking his own struggle between two major drives and modes of engagements, this is how a young Spanish man putted it: "on one side you have *reason* which tells you something, on the other you have the *desire*" (my emphasis). Himself, he was following 'reason', and thus refrained from getting involved with Cuban women – particularly when going out in clubs and discos as he predicted that such a relationship would draw him into the sort of exchange of sex for money that he much despised.

A further scenario I became familiar with saw tourists getting on the dance-floor, but then retracting once they perceived that a dancing relationship was metamorphosing into 'something else', bringing about other relational idioms. Breaking an engagement that they considered had gone 'too far'; they would therefore establish boundaries between, for instance, playful dancing and appropriate partying on the one hand, and more overtly sexual relational idioms on the other. Issues of agency, of free-will and consent could also arise, as people considered that they had not given their dancing partners a green light to shift towards overt sexual seduction. 'He always tried to kiss me!' was the outraged reaction of a Swiss woman, as she told me about her unpleasant dancing experience with a Cuban man. This raises questions about sensuality/sexuality: their modalities, and their inclusion or exclusion from notions of partying.

Tourists who anticipated and wished to circumvent any potential misunderstanding on their type of engagement, reached the conclusion that it was best for them to avoid dancing with Cubans altogether. Besides the unsettling prospect of losing control of oneself, was thus also the concern of being misinterpreted, of giving the impression that one was up for an 'unbounded' party, open to endless possibilities – particularly in terms of sexual inhibition and availability. Consequently, this reduced people's ability to let go, to get into the flow and into those festive states that made of dancing a paramount activity.

However, Cuban people were particularly skilled at reiterating their encouragements and exhortations. Understandably, they were also reluctant to assume the role of 'abusive dancers', of people who had 'improperly instrumentalized' dancing practices to seduce tourists. In order to settle controversies and overcome their tourist partners' reluctance, or at least answer their criticism, Cubans could rely on the productive potential of ambiguity itself, highlighting misunderstandings and mobilizing them in their favour. This is a crucial process that informs more generally touristic encounters and relationships in Cuba, one that saw ambiguity being metaphorically 'ridden', and misunderstandings tactically played out. In the specific case of dance, what happened was that the boundaries outlined by tourists between dancing engagements on the one hand, and the idioms of seductive and sexual relationships on the other, were blurred and redrawn by their Cuban companions.

In this scenario, when confronted with tourists' reluctance to engage in sensual/sexually evocative dancing performances, Cubans would argue that this was precisely the way such dances should be performed, and that their partners had simply misunderstood what the entire situation was about. 'This is how we dance in Cuba!' could claim the Cubans involved, relying on their legitimacy, as insiders and experts in the field, to prescribe what pertained to Cuban dance, what was right or wrong, what was part of a dancing style and what went beyond it. Seduction and sexual advances were thus normalized as integral to the realms of dancing, partying, and playful festive engagements. Therefore, what tourists had experienced as an abuse, as taking advantage of physical proximity, was reformulated as a normal and desirable cultural experience, as an experience of Cuban-ness itself. Partying/seducing/abusing: the overlaps and boundaries between these different interpretations of dancing were shifted and redrawn via the riding of ambiguity and the enactment of misunderstandings.

Conclusion

In tourism research, (a)symmetry and (dis)trust have been two of the key features highlighted by scholars to characterize the basic traits of tourist-local relationships, pointing to issues of instrumentality, social distance, and stereotyping (Cohen 1984; Crick 1989; van den Berghe 1994; Nash 1996). In the Cuban case, asymmetries were arguably the driving force of *jineterismo* – a relational idiom that emphasized economic inequalities between tourists and Cubans, and which justified instrumental and manipulative behaviours geared at extracting resources from privileged foreigners. However, any hint of such behaviours posed serious challenges to the development of touristic encounters, given the tourists' reluctance to engage in potentially deceptive and exploitative interactions. Instead, relationships tended to develop along other lines, according to other relational idioms. The aim here was to consider the relational idioms of partying in their entanglements with processes of seduction.

I have shown that a key feature of festive relationships, of relationships informed by a party atmosphere, was to encourage people to 'go with the flow', to follow feelings and desires and set aside rationalizations, 'questioning gazes' (Bruner 2001) worries, and doubts. In the realm of touristic encounters in Cuba, partying was precisely constructed in ways that could minimize pragmatic concerns, most notably the concern of dealing with instrumentally and economically motivated behaviours (i.e. *jineterismo*). Partying tended to downplay differences and inequalities, infusing a sense of mutuality between the protagonists involved. Setting asymmetries aside, the idea brought forward was rather that people were all equal members of a same partying community/*communitas*. As for the related issue of distrust – the other major threat hampering the development of relationships between tourists and Cuban people – we may argue that successful enactments of partying in Cuba had the potential of obliterating such mind-absorbing issue altogether. The question of trusting each other was ideally bypassed by encouraging people to 'leave worries behind' and 'let it go'. The move from 'reason' to 'embodied feelings and emotions' helped put trust on hold, releasing people from such preoccupation.

But these ideal scenarios, that Cubans' exhortations to party often evoked, did not always thrive unchallenged. The example of dancing has enabled me to unpack the oscillation between 'letting oneself go', 'going with the flow' on the one hand, and making rationally sense of relationships on the other. Particular attention has been devoted to the question of what dance could afford – the possibilities it opened up, notably through physical contact between visitors and Cubans – as well as its limits. Thus, I have considered processes of seduction as they emerged from dance, trying to account for embodied practices, feelings, 'vibes', and states of flow, and to show how these could bring about shifts between different relational idioms. I also examined how doubts and ambiguities were often on the brink of emerging, ready to breach flows, to disrupt liminalities whose enabling potential was easily taken for granted but not always shared. As ambiguities and doubts erupted and became hard to sustain, the imperatives of rationalization and justification moved back in.

Once we pay attention to these tensions, the problematic character of taken-for-granted assumptions emerges, pinpointing controversies, and revealing potential lines of rupture and disagreement. In return, the examination of these tensions, and of the processes of explicitation, differentiation, and boundary creation they gave rise to, grants us access to people's own reflections on their (otherwise implicit) modes of engagement (Boltanski 1990). Ambiguities and doubts bring the protagonist of touristic encounters to specify the nature of their involvement and – in this specific case – to formulate their assumptions on what partying and seducing ought to be about.

To conclude, I hope I have been able to show in this chapter how an ethnography of dancing (the) tourists in Cuba can give us access both to embodied enactments of partying and seducing and to peoples' reflexive interpretations on them. As tensions and ambiguities emerge, connections between partying and seducing are being cut and remade, highlighting frictions and shifting divides between playfulness and seriousness, pleasure and control, emotions and reason, equality and asymmetry.

References

Argyriadis, K. (2005) 'El desarrollo del turismo religioso en La Habana y la acusación de mercantilismo', *Desacatos*, 18, pp. 29–52.

Berg, M.L. (2004) 'Tourism and the revolutionary new man: The specter of *Jineterismo* in late 'Special Period' Cuba', *Focaal – European Journal of Anthropology*, 43, pp. 46–56.

Boltanksi, L. (1990) *L'amour et la Justice comme compétences: Trois essais de sociologie de l'action*, Paris: Editions Métailié.

Bruner, E.M. (2001) 'The Maasai and the Lion King: Authenticity, nationalism, and globalization in African tourism', *American Ethnologist*, 28(4), pp. 881–908.

Cabezas, A.L. (2006) 'The eroticization of labor in Cuba's all-inclusive resorts: Performing race, class, and gender in the new tourist economy', *Social Identities*, 12(5), pp. 507–521.

Cohen, E. (1984) 'The sociology of tourism: Approaches, issues, and findings', *Annual Review of Sociology*, 10, pp. 373–392.

Comaroff, J.L. and Comaroff, J. (1997) *Of Revelation and Revolution Vol. 2: The Dialectics of Modernity on a South-African Frontier*, Chicago and London: University of Chicago Press.

Crick, M. (1989) 'Representations of tourism in the social sciences: Sun, sex, sights, savings, and servility', *Annual Review of Anthropology*, 18, pp. 307–344.

Csikszentmihalyi, M. (1975) *Beyond Boredom and Anxiety*, San Francisco: Jossey-Bass Publishers.

Daniel, Y.P. (1996) 'Tourism dance performances: Authenticity and creativity', *Annals of Tourism Research*, 23(4), pp. 780–797.

Fairley, J. (2006) 'Dancing back to front: *Regeton*, sexuality, gender, and transnationalism in Cuba', *Popular Music*, 25(3), pp. 471–488.

Fernandez, N. (1999) 'Back to the future? Women, race, and tourism in Cuba', in K. Kempadoo (ed.), *Sun, Sex, and Gold: Tourism and Sex Work in the Caribbean*, Lanham: Rowman & Littlefield Publishers, pp. 81–89.

Franklin, A. and Crang M. (2001) 'The trouble with tourism and travel theory?' *Tourist Studies*, 1(1), pp. 5–22.

Gloaguen, P. (ed.) (2007) *Le Guide du Routard: Cuba*, Paris: Hachette.

Graburn, N.H.H. (1983) 'The anthropology of tourism', *Annals of Tourism Research*, 10(1), pp. 9–33.

Kummels, I. (2005) 'Love in the time of diaspora. Global markets and local meaning in prostitution, marriage and womanhood in Cuba', *Iberoamericana*, 5(20), pp. 7–26.

Little, K. (2005) '"Paradise from the other side of nowhere": Troubling a troubled scene of tourist encounter in Belize', in D. Picard and M. Robinson (eds), Proceedings of the International Conference *Tourism and Performance: Scripts, Stages and Stories*, 14–18 July, 2005, Centre for Tourism and Cultural Change, Sheffield Hallam University, Sheffield, (CD Rom).

Michel, F. (1998) 'Le tourisme international: une bouée de sauvetage pour Cuba?', in F. Michel (ed.), *Tourismes, Touristes, Sociétés*, Paris: L'Harmattan, pp. 251–287.

Nash, D. (1996) *Anthropology of Tourism*, Oxford: Pergamon.

Palmié, S. (2004) '*Fascinans* or *Tremendum*? Permutations of the State, the Body, and the Divine in late-twentieth-century Havana', *New West Indian Guide*, 78(3/4), pp. 229–268.

Schwartz, R. (1997) *Pleasure Island: Tourism and Temptation in Cuba*, Lincoln and London: University of Nebraska Press.

Selänniemi, T. (2003) 'On holiday in the liminoid playground: Place, time, and self in tourism', in: T.G. Bauer and B. McKercher (eds), *Sex and Tourism: Journeys of Romance, Love, and Lust*, New York: The Haworth Hospitality Press, pp. 19–31.

Simoni, V. (2008) 'Shifting powers: The (de)stabilization of asymmetries in the realm of tourism in Cuba', *Tsantsa: Review of the Swiss Anthropological Society*, 13, pp. 89–97.

Simoni, V. (2009) 'Touristic Encounters in Cuba: Informality, Ambiguity, and Emerging Relationships', PhD Thesis, Leeds Metropolitan University.

Simoni, V. and McCabe, S. (2008) 'From ethnographers to tourists and back again: On positioning issues in the anthropology of tourism', *Civilisations*, 57(1–2), pp. 173–189.

Time Out: Havana and the Best of Cuba (2004) London: Penguin.

Turner, V. (1977) 'Variations on a theme of liminality', in S. Moore and B. Myerhoff (eds), *Secular Ritual*, Amsterdam: Van Gorcum, pp. 36–52.

van den Berghe, P. (1994) *The Quest for the Other: Ethnic Tourism in San Cristóbal, Mexico*, Seattle and London: University of Washington Press.

Veijola, S. and Jokinen, E. (1994) 'The body in tourism', *Theory, Culture and Society*, 11(3), pp. 125–151.

Chapter 16

On Edge in an Impossible Paradise

Kenneth Little

Impossibly Beautiful

There is a particular quality of light, sound, and touch as you approach the beach in Placencia, a rapidly growing seaside fishing village in southern Belize that has 'gone crazy' for tourism. It lends itself to a feel for the place, the impact of which, as Jim and Cindy said the first moment they laid eyes on it, 'takes your breath away'. It's some combination of sun, sea, sand and sky that intensifies an array of sensations as it dampens others. Much of this intensification and dampening is already encoded as advertising cliché, a carefully calculated indexing of pleasure in paradise 'to die for'. In such cases these sensations stabilize momentarily into the commercial and cultural tropes of escape, paradise, and natural beauty that Belize has progressively activated commercially over the past ten years.

And yet the place still conjures a sensory impact that is almost more than a body can take. Your body builds its substance out of layers of sensory impacts drifting in the beach side surf, skin impossibly wet, warm and salty, eyes trained on the light clouds and the passing coconut tree tops or on watching colourful tropical fish dart about the live corals, ears submerged in the gentle pulse of wave action that surrounds, buoys, and carries you gently drifting along. On the beach your body surges with the rush and flow, the push and pull of sensations, gets with the picture, takes a tour to the ruins, goes diving, celebrates, gets side tracked, falls down, crawls on hand and knees, hits the wall, reorganizes, spends a day on the beach laying in a hammock, gets sunburned and then does it all again. It knows itself as states of vitality, exhaustion, and renewal.

It's like your body can't help itself. This deserves to be mentioned because it shapes so much of the immediate tourist sensations of this tropical place as 'impossibly beautiful'. Tourists are quick to pick up on these sensations and go with their flows. It's all more than something seen or revealed, and much more than a representation can offer. Rather, it is something felt as almost overwhelming and it has an impact: it packs a punch. When you feel it, your skin dimples and tingles and your body is filled with an excitement you can't quite put into words, yet you sense it all the same in that breathtaking moment: a virtual to real move, an incorporeal folding into the corporeal, the body in movement, coincident yet disjunctive (Massumi 2002).

The beach sand feels warm, powder soft, the water crystal clear, and the sky is a profoundly deep blue seduction. These feelings are never separate or exacting points of excitation. Each is fuzzy at the edges, open-ended intensifications, incipiencies, affects unlocking sensations' potentials as mischievous interactions, radiance spreading uncontained. The beauty and power of this paradise dream world is felt in the play of sensations intensifying into something, as feelings suffuse each other and into the slow drift that builds these breathtaking moments into intensifying impacts: a body event as viral contagion, you pass it along with each excited touch, look, intake of breath, or smile. These are feelings in a state of emergence, feelings on the verge of their naming, still unfolding, fugitive, chaotic, and shifting. The body's give and take in relaxation, its impulses, its waves of giddy sensation and tension, are like the waves lapping the Placencia beach, each the same but different in their making and breaking, and in this movement, in the suffusion, there is immanent possibility, a potential, a force gathering itself to a point of impact to instantiate something. It is a sensation that scampers along the edges of a feeling 'suggesting where a feeling might lead if it is left unchecked' (Stewart 2003, p. 2).

This is the body as disjunctive encompassment, a kind of continuity but unlike one that follows a narrative line exhausting its signifying possibilities in meanings or as a type or illustration of some socio-political process. Here, the body becomes a continuous displacement of the subject, the object, and their general relation, creating and created through a folding and an unfolding of sensations freed of the terms that name them (Massumi 2002, p. 51). On a beach in Belize, they are actual sensations, felt forces gathering to become something impossible to describe. These tropical sensations are the forces of feeling that add to what one brochure helpfully calls 'the impossible beauty of a Caribbean paradise' (Destinations Belize, brochure, nd). That's the tourist Placencia. It generates a 'body without image', an additive movement from the incorporeal to the corporeal that registers as an included disjunction, or what Massumi calls incorporeal materialism (2002, p. 60). It's like recognizing some feeling in your body that you have no name for yet or recognizing the feeling that grows in you when you have some name on the tip of your tongue but you can't quite get it out: wonderment and frustration, tension, movement, change.

A Case of Topical Nerves

I begin with impacts and the intensification of sensations in the space of a beach front tourist paradise but only to disrupt the vibe with the burdens of that same paradise, conjured out of the unnerving re-appearance on Placencia Bay Beach of a tourist locally named 'Peter Pete'. Re-appearance because a few locals with long memories remember when he first appeared in Placencia to perform a crazy, daily raking ritual and when he mysteriously disappeared, not to be seen again, leaving only a nervous tension in the air, an agitated buzz throughout the village. That was in 2001, a few months before Hurricane Iris, and that was when Harry lost his money and made friends with a tree, and that's when a couple of big

Figure 16.1 'Peter Pete at work' © Kenneth Little 2009

drug dealers seemed to make Placencia their new headquarters, and that was when rumours of the Rapture seemed to take a forceful grip on local sociality. It was like one impossibly crazy thing followed by another but with no connecting logic, just a pile up of confusing and confused random crazy events that conjured a serious edginess that spun life out of control: life becoming impossible for almost everyone living in Placencia at the time.

Peter Pete simply re-appeared on the beach one day in March of 2009 and then a couple of weeks later he did his disappearing act again. Peter Pete, the redundancy of his name seems to mimic the sounds and rhythm of soft waves gently licking the shore-line against the relaxed, repetitive scratching of Peter Pete's red plastic rake. Because that is what Peter Pete did: he raked the beach daily, through the morning and over long, hot, breezy afternoons. No one really knew where he came from, only that he appeared from the 'who knows where' to spend his time compulsively raking the same few square meters of beach front sand before he disappeared as quietly and mysteriously as he had appeared. Why he raked, Peter Pete wouldn't say, for he hardly ever said anything to anyone, and that, along with the public performance of his odd and empty ritual, once again generated a nervous intensification of dread mixed with humour that conjured a discordant shiver that ran through the nervous system of a village that no longer seems able to keep up or on track with 'everything' going on these days.

This time Peter Pete's presence coincided with a new rash of violent physical attacks on resident expats and tourists. No one that I talked to blamed Peter Pete for the attacks, but his sudden re-appearance and then disappearance and his odd behaviour served to focus everyone's attention on tourist encounters in this 'paradise by the Carib Sea'. These encounters bred an excessive exchange of stories about drug dealers, brutal local violence, other strange tourists, pirates, crazy locals, infidelities, theft, mysterious land deals, government corruption, tropical environmental collapse, and strange weather: flows and lines of narrative force that rubbed up against each other and the arresting tourist image of paradise producing a friction that generated a menacing and nervous alarm that has seriously 'roughed up' life in Placencia.

Peter Pete seemed benign, but no one could walk past him and his incessant almost manic raking without a comment or without taking the opportunity to watch his mute performance and to speculate, to look for signs of some crazy move or encounter. Everyone on the beach had something to say about him. It made Miss Gloria worry. 'He da make wi crazy, 'she muttered one day. 'Watch out for he. Da man no right.' If Peter Pete stopped his manic raking at all it was to talk to local marginals: the crack heads, a prostitute that seemed to be charmed by him, and a couple of strange expats whose everyday eccentric behaviour (as ersatz pirates, drunken prophets, nervous loafers, for example) could be compared closely with Peter Pete's. Witness to all of this, Miss Gloria worries about her kids and her property and she is not alone. If only Peter Pete would say something, give up his intentions, explain the crazy raking, hour after sweaty hour, day after day, but he proffers nothing. So villagers watch him and watch for him while tourists usually give him a wide birth. 'Just another crazy tourist Ken.' Mr. Harry says to me one day. 'Do you know him?' Harry's question comes with a tense laugh that belies his family's disturbing worries about everyday life these days with a village so full of strangers, projects, deals and 'odd stuff just happening' that they hardly recognize it anymore.

Few could figure out where Peter Pete slept or where he ate when he wasn't raking. Miss Gloria and several of her neighbours reported him to the police, but the police said that they had more important things to do than deal with a crazy tourist raking the beach. So most locals simply felt uneasy and puzzled by the performer and the performance. This meant that everyone kept an eye out for him, just in case. Someone said that he was this rich guy from California who lives in Honduras now, but likes to make side trips to Belize when he gets bored. But why Placencia? And that's when concerned locals tried to put two and two together as they started scanning the village for signs of bigger trouble: the drugs, the money, odd looking strangers, strange looking land deals, the new stores, the big boats suddenly at anchor in the bay, the new cars, the new foreign clothes, locals disappearing without explanation.

Meanwhile, Peter Pete sang to himself to the tunes on his IPod, smiled at passers-by, raked and then seemed to dissolve into the beach along with the sun late in the afternoon, only to show up in the morning at the same spot and at the same time the hotel and resort workers started their daily jobs of raking the garbage and sea grass off the beach. Peter Pete copies their moves: rakes, takes a break, rakes some more, places the garbage in piled up heavy-duty black plastic bags ready for daily beach garbage pick-up. Peter Pete even used his own garbage bags, filled them and neatly piled them up. It all means more work for Rick and Vernon, the village beach garbage guys, and they don't like it. 'We got lots to do. Enough! No Man, we no pick up after dis tourist', Vernon said in a gruff tone that belied a feeling he has about the place, the tourists, and a disquieting everyday life that seems all the more unmanageable as it becomes less recognizable: as it becomes impossible.

Peter Pete is like one big pressure point conjuring a bundle of ambiguous images, stories, and 'rogue vitalities' (Stewart 2003, p. 2), a strange and crazy tourist creating make work projects for locals (not a happy predicament), but doing a pretty good job, in the opinions of others, of keeping the place clean and setting a nice example, but putting still other locals, who aren't as conscientious about their own garbage details, to shame and so making them angry and jumpy. But Peter Pete made everyone jumpy, and that jumpiness added to the twitchy intensity of the jumpiness locals now feel around the place anyway. And that's just one line of flight, one potential in the act of unfolding, territorializing onto some plateau of jumpy nervous public feelings that rubs up harshly against tourist-induced images of the place as a pleasure world.

As such, Peter Pete is a mixed force of affective excess, mysterious as he is nonsensical. As such he is an example, 'a singularity, a disjunctive self-inclusion, a belonging to itself that is simultaneously an extendibility to everything else with which [he] might be connected' (Massumi 2002, pp. 17–18). This assemblage of mystery and nonsense, dread and giddiness fashioned out of an ambiguous and odd assortment of practices, tools, and feelings, shocks locals into nervously taking positions, re-thinking priorities, and more generally making decisions about tourists and other things for which there is no motivation or reason to do so more than an urgent, edgy network of demanding and troubling feelings that are making life impossible.

Locals like Miss Gloria and Mr. Harry and their neighbours in Placencia made sense of Peter Pete through their stories, not by constructing an explanation for his appearance and disappearance or his odd behaviour, but by offering accounts of his mysterious traces and effects and the nervous impacts conjured out of contact with him. And as the stories piled up like shipwrecks on a reef, rocked by waves of telling and re-telling, the talk formed a tidal rush of dramatic and excessive images and forces that overwhelmed the merely referential and meaningful. Peter Pete as a body without an image flashed up uncontained by meaning onto the Placencia shore line. Story subjects, objects, and events became performers in a spectacle that exceeded linear reason and the discipline of cause and effect, truth and lie. As such Peter Pete is what Sian Ngai calls a 'bad example' (Stewart 2003, p. 2). He doesn't stand or work as a solid representation of some ideology or structure at work in Belize; rather, he becomes a site of tendencies, where forces gather to a point of impact to instantiate something. A bad example is a singularity: first, an affective intensity, a force that suggests where a trajectory might lead if left unchecked, which then becomes an event that literally 'makes sense' of that force at the point of its affective and material emergence (Stewart 2003). The power of the story telling that focused on a strange man on the beach was that it drew listeners and watchers into a space of tense and lingering forces, some seen, others unseen, an affecting presence, a cultural poetics in the act of making something of itself. Peter Pete became an act of creative contagion (Massumi 2005, p. 19), a troubling state of suspense and suspension that haunted the place and its people, pulling them up short, and that lingered as a troubled impulse struggling to 'make sense' and make something of things more generally.

It was the impulse to make something sensible of circumstances and events by fashioning stories about Peter Pete that turned the sight of him and his sudden disappearance one day into a tactile force. Placencia is a place of impacts, rapidly transforming into a spectacle of some homogenized, global, dream world, adventure pirate paradise, as if by some horrid and seductive mimetic Disney magic, before everyone's very eyes, connecting locals up with the spasmodic effects and currents of global flows of capital, information, people, and culture. This arresting presence of Peter Pete entered local senses, lodging there, growing in intensity, forming into a state of nervous suspense filled with resonance. His presence and disappearance figures the immanent intensity or force of what Gilles Deleuze calls affect, the double sidedness of things where, as Brian Massumi explains, the virtual meets the actual, and where what 'matters', as a materialization of local life in the making, is the permeable edge of potentiality itself (2002, pp. 12–18; cf. Zournazi, pp. 1–3, 11–12).

Looking for something positive, some sign or something meaningful about everyday life in Placencia with Peter Pete in it, locals start to realize that the only thing that might be possible is some lingering, awful disclosure that acts as some anxious, unspeakable incomposability, an undecidable, crazy force of becoming, an emergent vitality that quite literally charges up the place by the sheer presence of Peter Pete, making life impossible. Far from anything forming as named 'feelings' or 'emotions' fashioned out of some representational discourse or some known subject position, such emergent vitalities take shape in the surge of intensity itself as an emotion before it is actually named as such and thus placed as part of an established discourse, a moral narrative, or an ideology. Vitalities intensify at random in fleeting gestures of affect, if only for a moment, before they become folded into a normative system. The point is to evoke the vitality of things in their movement, at the moment of their becoming. More compelling than a linear narrative and more restive, multiple, edgy and unpredictable than a representation, these fractious vitalities are constitutive events or acts that animate and literally compose cultural forces at the point of their affective and material emergence (Stewart 2007, pp. 2–3).[1]

---

1 I am addressing questions concerning the historical specificities of affects and their possible relationship to specific tropical contexts and conditions, like the regional

Rapture and the Raelians

And if Peter Pete were not enough to conjure a state of nervous disjunction, an unregistered difference in the act of emergence, a charged up flow that makes Placencia feel jumpy, aggressive, and unsteady, as if life were becoming impossible, there are other tourist impacts that have equally taken the place by surprise, caught it up short, stressed it out, and made it edgy. Public culture, and the incipient structure of feelings out of which it is being fashioned in Placencia, ricochets from one crazy moment of impact to another as if time were a network of punctuated moments of rupture that hold a charge in the act of articulating something. But what?

Take Bob, a retired evangelical minister from a small coal camp in West Virginia, who, along with his wife Diane, owned and operated The Beachfront Inn and Chapel until it went broke early in 2008 and they sold out to 'some big developer'. Just who, he wouldn't say. Bob and Diane are gone now, while their resort sits rotting. It's a haunting ruin that most people stay clear of. 'It gives everyone the creeps', Mr. Harry says. He heard that some tourist was murdered there late last year, while squatting on the land. But while others have heard the same story no one is really sure and there is no public record of a body or official news of the event. Such an obvious absence conjures another anxious presence that grows alarming as it touches onto Bob's intimate history with the place.

Bob and Diane moved to Maya Beach in 1998. Bob felt commanded by powerful spiritual signs that came to him in the form of the Lord's voice after a series of intense 'prayer appeals' that hit him hard. But there were other signs too like the time he saw the face of Jesus in the clouds gathering above Maya Beach

---

contemporary Caribbean political economy in which Belize operates as a weakly defined nation/narco state on the edge of global empire, but I do so not in a didactic manner or through an explanatory framework (see Massumi 2002). Mine is the story of a Belize caught in the grips of social, political and economic forces, the potentials of which are always unpredictable, shifting, unsteady, and immanent. I am trying to track ordinary life in the clutches of this unpredictability as that life seems to become more and more impossible to live. This is the equivalent, however, of capturing air with your hands. Certainly, some assemblage of power and money flows, bodily impacts and states, institutions, ways of experiencing space and time, dreamworld and catastrophe technologies begin to assemble and disassemble through and out of what gets called the postmodern capitalism of neoliberalism. Working within definitions and distinguishing features of specific historical, economic and political processes does not get at this unfolding, nor does it allow us to track forces felt but still unrecognized and ungathered by concepts: the active generativity of forces in a state of emergence (Stewart 2003), This guides my use of affect as an emergent force of sensation's move into bodily matter and not primarily as a structure of feeling. Affect as an emergent force is an act of making a history, not describing one or one about getting it right: history, power, society, economy without an object.

To know more about the debates concerning how affect is used as a concept see Clough (2008), Hemmings (2005), Puar (2008) and Thrift (2004).

Figure 16.2   'Bob's tourist dream world in ruins' © Ken Little, 2009

while swimming there during a holiday. That was a sign to buy the property. That's when he knew he was 'taking the Lord's path'. He successfully sold 'rapture tourism' for several years and made a 'small fortune', enough to think about expanding. But while he weathered Iris, the hurricane that hit the peninsula with such a devastating force in 2001 that it left nothing but heartache and ruins behind, his resort didn't, and he spent much of his nest egg on repairs. But the guests returned, 'praise the Lord', to spend a week or two with Bob and Diane praying and scanning.

Bob's guests spent their time watching for special wave patterns and scanning Fox News 24/7 and praying. There is an art to all of this that Bob shares with his guests. He got the idea about wave patterns while reading from the Book of Revelations. Bob said Revelations is really the blueprint, the book of signs that in 1998 he could no longer afford to ignore. Bob figures that the signal for the Rapture will be found in strange weather that will be preceded by unique wave patterns, as the sea prepares itself. The rapture, he calculates, is very close at hand, so it is important to be vigilant. It's a matter of logic. Fox News stories, he figured out on his own with no help from the Bible, would cluster into a pattern of signs too. News and the waves were parallel signal systems that he and his guests turned into a 'detection machinery'.

These tourists were not distracted by the beautiful surroundings. They came to scan and pray. The locals and the nay-saying 'hard drinking' expat 'philistines' that lived around them started to compare Bob and his visitors to that other crazy tropical experiment in Caribbean evangelical work and worship in Jonestown, Guyana. The Jimmy Jones cult effect, the commanding voice of the Lord, the dreams of a final paradise, a return to Eden, martyrdom, Cool-aid and the glorious ending of the world in the rapture: all a Belizian tourist made line of flight pushing up against and pulling away from a growing yet diffused structure of village feelings, a tension so palpable that it also served to make life increasingly impossible: public sensibilities in chaos, a place and its people and guests growing oddly amused, aggressive, unstable and strange. That's when Harry asked one day: 'Why do we get all the crazies?'

Before anyone could give Harry a good answer, an answer of sorts presented itself. The Raelians are coming, and they are serious about establishing an embassy in Belize, a welcome centre for human beings from another planet, the uber-tourists, the ones who created life on Earth in the first place, and who now wish to return to visit and take a tour of their experiment in cloning (Amandela, Friday March 27, 2009). What better place than Belize? 'It now can live up to its name. Belize is an ancient and sacred place.' Bernard Lamarche explains on Channel 7 TV news, on April Fool's Day no less, while standing next to nervous looking government officials. The Raelians want to give Belize tourism a whole new look and purpose, and spin it way into another dimension. 'To boldly go where no one has gone before?' Harry asks. And the suggestion takes him up short, and sadly he begins to wonder what's happening to the little nation he loves so much. But Harry is good at laughing such things off, as if the laughter might make this event disappear, before he does his own disappearing act and sells out and moves away.

The Raelian offer morphs the state of a collapsing sovereign Empire under chaotic contemporary conditions as international capital mysteriously disappears and reappears from the centre of power through the efforts of schemers and dreamers whose ruthless cunning has shaken Belize's economy into panic mode so that a solution like the Raelian offer begins to sound like its own salvation. It's how a mysterious, cloning culture of Raelian enterprise suddenly appears on the margins of Empire and of the possible, to 'save the day' in Belize. It's a new take and tale on the Imperial magic trick that conjures as much giddiness as it does uneasy, impossible expectation.

They say that the money to be generated from the multi-million dollar Raelian embassy/tourist centre would be in the hundreds of millions of dollars and attract over fifty thousand tourists a year. 'That's better than the cruise ships to which Belize has attached itself ball and chain', the Minister of Tourism, Civil Aviation, and Culture says on the *Love FM Morning Show*, his voice a strange mixture of authority, confusion, excitement and hopelessness. With that kind of foreign currency in the assets column of its national development plan Belize may stand to win big time. But Belizians have heard it all before: the impossible promises, the unfulfilled expectations. 'Who knows, a welcome centre for aliens might catch on. It can't hurt. We'll have spacemen for you to study Ken,' Harry quips, 'We'll call it super-natural Belize.'

Empire eclipsed by the Universe, tourism in the grandest of styles conjuring another odd and nervous tourist moment in paradise. Here the productive forces of global capital are at work on a new presence, a new now, a fore-history of tourism construction sites for outer space guests along with whole new tourism infrastructures of resorts, casinos, spas, golf-courses, and eco-tourism technologies, all sovereign enterprises that rub up against the ruins of the rapture, a new after-history of future decay and world destruction. And in the gap, in the present, in the now, the impossible job of keeping fore-history and after-history from collapsing in on each other.

Money Grows on Trees

Take another bad example, a late afternoon in paradise that no one will ever forget when Placencia was showered with US dollars. 'Lord, the money was blown' in like manna from heaven', Miss Julia exclaimed. This was another mysterious arrival, unrivalled in its impact as an arresting force, at once vastly familiar and seductive and entirely uncharted, even shocking. Familiar and seductive, because this has always been the promise of the state and the tourism entrepreneurs, that money would flow 'like the air we breathe' with more tourism and everyone would benefit; uncharted and shocking, because, among other things, no one expected money to flow quite in this way. More mystery and intrigue. More giddiness mixed with dread.

This is really the story about Mr. Harry who, while fishing one day in early January, 2001, is said to have found a bale of cocaine floating in the water off Little Water Caye. It was said to be tied to a stash of hundreds of thousands of dollars. It was said that Harry pulled it from the water and, once back on shore, hid the treasure up a tree. His nephew Bobby recounted the story of which many locals now have versions, even if they won't go out of the way to tell them:

> Harry finds this serious fuckin' stuff. He hides it, like pirate treasure. Soon he looks like he won the lottery. He's not fishin' or workin' tourists. I know what he's doin. He's into the money and the coke. So life is a party. He starts hanging out with tourists all day, buying drinks all over the place. Relaxin' and talkin'; maybe too much. He buys a new boat and motor, top o' the line shit. He's lookin' good and wants to start a tourist dive shop business with me. Now everyone starts askin' how he can do that. Maybe the big drug dealers get suspicious. Harry doesn't care. He's gettin' high all the time. He's not payin' attention. So one afternoon it's really windy. Harry is drunk but he seriously needs some cash so he heads for his secret bank in the tree, 'cause for Harry, money grows on trees. That's what he tellin' everybody. So that's got everybody lookin' in the trees for his money. People followin' him around all the time but no one

finds his money tree. Harry, he's too smart. But he fucks up. He left the bag of
money open or something and the strong wind … All of a sudden all this money,
hundred dollar bills, fiftys, twentys, tens, it start blowin' all over the place, down
the street, onto the beach, in the water, in the air, on the road. It's rainin' money
and it's landin' everywhere. No one can believe it, but they're pickin' up bills.
Harry figures its gotta be his money. Not happy. By the time he gets back to his
bank in the tree, almost nothin' left, all blown away.

It was just after Harry's money blew into town that locals like Bobby remember
their first-ever sighting of Peter Pete. Bobby guessed he was the drug dealer who
must have heard about the money and came after it and the coke. That's when
Harry 'got lost' for a couple of months leaving villagers and who knows who else
wildly searching Placencia for any connections between otherwise disparate and
unusual things, scanning for signs of wealth and euphoria, of criminal threat, and
suspicious behaviour in an increasingly unsocial, uncertain, and chaotic world and
a life turned impossible that started to get on everyone's nerves. It is impossible to
tell the drug dealers from the tourists, or either from the international resort/condo
speculators whose side deal scams have created a state of emergency as they buy
up what's left of the titled land in Placencia for a song and a dance. They sell
spectacles of local culture in the image of an escape to a pristine paradise with laid-
back, friendly natives who have been, as Ellis once said, 'pretty much voted off
the island'. Peter Pete as a troubling local presence was just one impulse-machine
pumping a contact sensuousity into the Placencia nervous system, seducing and
shocking locals and expat-tourists alike.

Today Harry has cultivated another relationship with trees. A couple of
years ago he named a tree 'The Tree of Wisdom' and put a sign on it. Everyone
thinks it was the tree he used to hide the money he found, but Harry isn't saying
anything much about the tree. That means everyone has a theory and it keeps
local interests up and everyone in the loop. Harry says that he uses the tree
for 'teaching purposes'. That means he sits under the Tree of Wisdom and gets
drunk with unsuspecting tourists who are seduced by his antics and wicked sense
of humour. They buy the beer while Harry tells the stories. They end up very
drunk and short on cash. But that's how tourists find 'local wisdom', Harry says.
The tourists wake up feeling 'enlightened' and a lot worse for wear wondering
what happened and feel a sense of anxiety mixed with relief that they are still in
one piece but happy that they got to share an intimate moment with the locals.
Shared wisdom all around, that's the way Harry likes it (Little 2010). It's a world
of shared banalities masking as local flavour that can be a basis of sociality or
an exhausting enervation, or simply just something else to do. Little moments
of contact are felt as pleasures and warning signs, as exotic intoxications and
repetitious daily routine. It's an odd ordinary that throws itself together out of
seductions, intoxicating encounters, local need for distractions, shape-shifting
solutions of a sort that help shake the drudgery of the everyday with something,
anything, else in a place that is transforming into a monstrous tourist pleasure

Figure 16.3   'The Tree of Wisdom' © Ken Little, 2009

space unlike anything any local could ever have imagined. It's a Placencia where disparate events and sensations come together to form an odd ordinary, the repetition of which leaves a residue like a habit – a living cliché and another moment in which life becomes impossible.

Apocalyptic Dreamworlds

Here we have a set of intersecting moments that collectively fold and unfold into a sense of strange goings on in Placencia and that make life there seem impossible. The uncanny sensation of half-understood invisible apocalyptic or unexpected and contingent forces, spectres and spectacles, powerfully populate the place and possess it with strange new spirits. Private lives and public worlds getting their wires crossed and snagged up on each other. Dreamworld and catastrophe, success and failure, prosperity and collapse, the Universe and the local, exist alongside of each other, inextricably tied as immanent to each other's details and making. Here, an incipient structure of public feelings begins to form along the lines of apocalyptic discourses that take the shape of the rapture and the Raelians or in the form of mysterious flows of money; it throws itself together as affective forces, energetic incitements as much as material signifiers. This set of forces of public feelings is life becoming impossible. It is an affective becoming that resonates as an included disjunction, vibrating with tension that lodges in the body, histories executed through the body in lines of tension and relaxation as happenings, as things happening. Whether these affects are feared, seductive, romanticized, subdued or unleashed, they always point to a generative immanence lodged in things as they take shape in the surge of intensifications as moments of vital impact.

The Rub

There is not a day that goes by that someone in Placencia, doesn't say something about how life is becoming impossible. Impossibly cruel and corrupt, impossibly strange, impossibly transformed socially and ecologically, impossibly out of control and violent: impossible to live. I am trying to track impacts and vitalities, the formations of bodily sensations that open onto the affective intensities of life becoming impossible, as a scene of immanent forces folding into an assemblage of public feelings, public culture in the act of its becoming (after Agamben 1993). I am trying to track the troubling state of suspense and suspension that haunts the place and its people and that lingers like a jumpy, chaotic and creepy impulse trying to 'make sense' of things that come into view as habit, shock, intensity, resonance, or resistance (after Stewart 2007, pp. 1–7). Lives in the gaps, or the interstices of this contact zone throw themselves together as event (movement) and as sensation (affect), something becoming, some incorporeal materialism, a disjunctive encompassment, dreamily inhabitable but exhausting, a tropical dream world and an uncanny ordinary. Examining moments of encounter and lingering on the impacts of life becoming impossible means tracking sensations – free-floating, affective agitations and sites of collective feelings – as the movement of emergent and potential emotional forces coming into play in this new state of emergency, taking shape as neo-liberal exception, on the nervous edge of an impossible tropics in Belize.

But it is here on this uneven terrain between what can be imagined as possible and what may be beyond the scope of the possible altogether, the impossible, that forces of sensation begin to instantiate. Impossibility, or the potential of rupture between the chaos of a world of the possible and what acts beyond it, a moment without end, an unspeakable, unrealizable, that which escapes the grid of intelligibility, has no horizon, it's a passage not a presence, a becoming, a becoming impossible, that which I cannot conceive yet nevertheless reach toward (Manning 2007), an expressive fragility in the making of some condition, good or bad on a beach in Belize.

References

Agamben, G. (1993) *The Coming Community*, trans. Michael Hardt, Minneapolis: University of Minnesota Press.

Amandela (2009) 'Raelians want an embassy in Belize', 27 March, front page.

Clough, P. (2008) 'The affective turn: Political economy, biomedia and bodies', *Theory, Culture and Society*, 25(1), pp. 1–22.

Hemming, C. (2005) 'Invoking affect: Cultural theory and the ontological turn', *Cultural Studies*, 19(5), pp. 548–567.

Little, K. (2010) 'The tourists are just wild about Harry, or not: Becoming insensible on a beach in Belize', Tourism and the Seductions of Difference. A Conference of the Tourism Contact, Culture Research Network (TOCOCU), Lisbon, Portugal, 9–12 September.

Manning, E. (2007) *Politics of Touch: Sense, Movement, Sovereignty*, Minneapolis: University of Minnesota Press.

Massumi, B. (2002) *Parables for the Virtual: Movement, Affect, Sensation*, Durham, NC: Duke University Press.

Puar, J. (2007) *Terrorist Assemblages: Homonationalism in Queer Times*, Durham, NC: Duke University Press.

Stewart, K. (2003) 'The perfectly ordinary life', *S&F-Online* Issue 2.1 *www.barnard.edu/sfonline/ps/stewart.htm*.

Stewart, K. (2007) *Ordinary Affects*, Durham, NC: Duke University Press.

Thrift, Nigel (2004) 'Intensities of feeling: toward a spatial politics of affect', *Geografiska Annaler*, Series B, 86, pp. 57–78.

Index

Adler, J. 28, 31
affection 11–12
Africa 90, 93, 95, 249, 253, 258
aggression 102, 111
anger 2, 8, 32–34, 36, 38, 41, 129, 249
Aristotle 14, 24
awe 3–9, 11–16, 28–30, 57, 74, 79, 82,
    153, 200, 252

Bausinger, H. 179–180
Belize 16, 283–296
Bruner, E. 3, 11, 14, 30, 37, 95, 267, 274,
    279
Buddhism 49, 57

Camus, A. 21
Certeau, M. de 164
Clifford, J. 5
Cohen, E. 59, 126, 278
Coleman, S. 122
colonial nostalgia 247–248, 251–252,
    254–255, 258, 265
communitas 58, 118, 124–133, 156,
    274–275, 279
Crick, M. 278
Csíkszentmihályi, M. 77, 274
culture shock 6, 28, 29, 57, 87, 90, 100,
    102, 103

Di Giovine, M. 27, 117, 118, 121, 126,
    128, 129
Durkheim, E. 117

Edensor, T. 40
Eliade, M. 105, 117
emotion(s) 1–8, 21–30, 85–87
    and body 283–284
    and culture 8–9, 23–25
    and dance 268–75
    and history 214-216

and language 13–14
and nature 4–5
and space 100–101, 118–123, 161–176,
    199, 211–221
as social performance 9, 30
emotional knowledge 3
existentialism 21, 129, 131

Freud, S. 4, 32, 58, 78, 100, 101
Frey, N. 3, 5, 50, 51

Geertz, C. 25
Gell, A. 140, 150–151
Goffman, E. 10
Goody, J. 8
Graburn, N. 29, 51, 52, 57, 66, 126, 273,
    274, 275
Greenblatt, S. 4

Harrison, J. 16, 35, 81, 233, 242
Heidegger M. 26
Hochschild, A. 9
Holocaust 12, 37, 161–162, 165, 168, 170,
    180, 192, 207
Honeymoon psychosis 100

image 151–152

Japan 38, 50–68
Jerusalem syndrome 6, 26, 76, 99, 105,
    110, 114

Kant, I. 8, 24, 153, 154
Kenya 16, 87–95
Kierkegaard, S. 131, 132

Lanfant, M. 3
La Réunion 1, 8, 12, 13, 15, 265
Levi-Strauss, C. 25, 118
Little, K. 16, 35, 267, 283, 293

Lonely Planet 249, 258–259, 262, 264

MacCannell, D. 3, 10, 11, 13, 28, 34, 126, 164, 204
Maslow, A. 22, 74, 76, 77, 82
McCabe, S. 181–182, 268
modernity 25, 250, 265

Nash, D. 278
Nazi 16, 34, 161, 163, 165–167, 169, 171–173, 175
Nietzsche F. 25, 26, 78
nostalgia 8, 35, 57, 61, 251–252, 254, 258; *see also* colonial nostalgia

Paris syndrome 6, 26, 57, 76, 102, 104
Parkin, D. 140
passion 2, 24, 25, 29, 31, 35, 82, 117, 129, 132, 133, 139, 179, 185, 194, 214, 215, 118, 221, 223, 231, 270, 273
peak experience 74, 76–82
phenomenology 11
Picard, D. 1, 7, 15, 76, 267
pilgrimage 5, 10, 16, 37, 52, 57, 99, 105, 107, 114, 117, 133, 139, 145, 156, 172, 186, 190, 212, 214
Pina-Cabral, J. 140
Pratt, M.L. 14

Ricoeur, P. 30
Robinson, M. 15, 16, 179
Rojek, C. 22, 203
Romanticism 2, 9, 79, 80, 165, 172

Sahlins, M. 118
Sartre, J.-P. 26, 42, 189
semiosphere 10

Semprun, J. 170–175, 177
sex, sexuality 5, 35, 66, 76, 212, 218, 221–222, 260, 268, 270, 272, 273, 276–278
Simoni, V. 14, 35, 49, 52, 267–268, 271
Smith, V. 40
social norms 3
spa 211–224
Stendhal 6, 27, 29, 31, 76, 101
Stendhal syndrome 7, 26, 29, 38, 101
stimulus 4
suicide 199–208
symbolism 104, 122, 167, 188, 203, 258

tourist emotions 2, 3, 23–24, 74
tourist experience 1, 12, 38, 76, 100, 161, 203, 267
tourist gaze 28, 181, 203, 208, 193–194, 234, 237, 239, 244
travel forms 55–58
travel syndromes 6, 100
Turner, V. 58, 105, 117, 118, 124–128, 139, 273–274
Tylor, E. 50

UNESCO 28, 247, 249, 253–255, 257, 264
Urry, J. 22, 28, 52, 164, 179, 203

Van Gennep 50, 117
Veblen 10,

Weber, M. 25
White House syndrome 103–104
world heritage 7, 28, 247, 249, 253
World War II 3, 16, 37, 53, 59, 168, 179–185, 189, 192–194, 234, 237, 239, 244